Explori

The Exploring Corporate Strategy Series

Series editors

Gerry Johnson
Lancaster University Management School

and

Kevan Scholes
Sheffield Hallam University

Exploring Corporate Strategy (Text and Cases)
Gerry Johnson, Kevan Scholes and Richard Whittington

Exploring Corporate Strategy (Text only)
Gerry Johnson, Kevan Scholes and Richard Whittington

Exploring Public Sector Strategy
Gerry Johnson and Kevan Scholes

Exploring Strategic Change
Julia Balogun and Veronica Hope Hailey

Exploring Techniques of Analysis and Evaluation in Strategic Management
Véronique Ambrosini (editor)

Exploring Strategic Financial Management
Tony Grundy

Exploring Strategic Change

Third Edition

Julia Balogun
Cass Business School, City University

Veronica Hope Hailey
Cass Business School, City University

Series editors

Gerry Johnson
Lancaster University Management School

Kevan Scholes
Sheffield Hallam University

FT Prentice Hall
FINANCIAL TIMES

An imprint of **Pearson Education**

Harlow, England • London • New York • Boston • San Francisco • Toronto
Sydney • Tokyo • Singapore • Hong Kong • Seoul • Taipei • New Delhi
Cape Town • Madrid • Mexico City • Amsterdam • Munich • Paris • Milan

Pearson Education Limited
Edinburgh Gate
Harlow
Essex CM20 2JE
England

and Associated Companies throughout the world

Visit us on the World Wide Web at:
www.pearsoned.co.uk

First published under the Prentice Hall imprint in 1999
Second edition published 2004
Third edition published 2008

ISBN 978-0-273-70802-5

British Library Cataloguing-in-Publication Data
A catalogue record for this book is available from the British Library

Library of Congress Cataloging-in-Publication Data
Balogun, Julia.
    Exploring strategic change/Julia Balogun, Veronica Hope Hailey.—3rd ed.
        p. cm. — (The exploring corporate strategy series)
    Includes bibliographical references and index.
    ISBN 978–0–273–70802–5 (pbk. : alk. paper) 1. Organizational change.   2. Strategic planning.
    I. Hope Hailey, Veronica.   II. Title.
    HD30.28.B344 2008
    658.4'012—dc22
                                                                2008013990

10 9 8 7 6 5 4 3 2
12 11 10 09

Typeset in 10/13 Garamond by 74
Printed by Asnford Colour Press Ltd, Gosport, UK

The publisher's policy is to use paper manufactured from sustainable forests.

Brief contents

Contents

List of figures and tables

Figures

Tables

List of illustrations

Preface

Exploring Corporate Strategy by Gerry Johnson, Kevan Scholes and Richard Whittington is well established as the leading text in its field in Europe and beyond, with worldwide sales exceeding 800,000. It is a text provided for students and practising managers which aims to develop their conceptual understanding of why and how organisations of many different types develop and change their strategies. It does so within a practical context whilst drawing on best strategic management practice as researchers, writers and practitioners understand it.

Exploring Corporate Strategy has always placed great emphasis on the processes of strategic management and the problems and importance of managing strategic change. *Exploring Strategic Change* has been written to extend this focus on managing change. Like *Exploring Corporate Strategy*, it is written in a practical and applied way whilst drawing on best practice from researchers, writers and practitioners. This third edition of *Exploring Strategic Change* uses examples from both private and public sector organisations to pursue four main themes:

- that the task of managing change is context-specific and therefore an understanding of the organisation's change context is essential;
- that analysing the change context allows change agents to make design choices on the basis of 'best fit' for the organisation;
- that once the change process has been designed, the next task is to both design and manage the transition;
- that there are established levers and mechanisms for managing transition.

The first half of the book focuses on the design of the change process and the analysis of the change context within an organisation. Chapter 2 addresses the subject of design choices by providing a menu of design options which are discussed within six overall groupings: change paths, change styles, change start-points, change targets, change levers, and change roles. These are discussed at this point in the book in order that the reader is aware of the range of choices that are available to a change agent. Chapters 3 and 4 then examine the importance of determining contextual fit when selecting appropriate design choices. Presented in Chapter 3 is a diagnostic framework, the change kaleidoscope, which helps identify the key contextual features in an organisation. The kaleidoscope features are: time scope, preservation, diversity, capability, capacity, readiness and power. Not only does analysis of these features allow the reader to make appropriate design choices, it also prevents these features from becoming barriers to change during the transition process itself. Both Chapters 3 and 4 illustrate how different features impact on different design choices. Chapter 4 demonstrates this through the use of three case studies of companies experiencing change and transition.

The second half of the book examines the transition process in depth. Chapter 5 explains the role of visioning in change and also introduces the idea of different stages of transition: mobilise, move and sustain. Both Chapters 5 and 6 examine the various mechanisms that can be used for each stage of transition. These include both symbolic levers and human resource management processes. Chapter 7 explores the actual management of the transition process. In addition to considering how the nature of the transition state should affect the way change agents conceive of transition management, this chapter considers the skills required of change agents, with a focus on political aspects, the central role of middle managers in change and the role of recipients, including issues to do with resistance, employee engagement and fairness and justice. The first and final chapters use a change flow chart to pull together the various stages of the change process that are detailed within all the other chapters. Chapters 1 and 8 also put forward thoughts about the centrality of change capability as a competence for managers in the twenty-first century and the personal skills and attributes required of effective change agents. Chapter 8 revisits a theme emphasised throughout the text: namely the need for those leading change to be skilled at both reading the organisational context they are operating in, and being able to reconfigure this context to enable the change processes they wish to put in place.

The website at **www.pearsoned.co.uk/balogun** provides resource material to aid in lecture and seminar presentation.

Julia Balogun and Veronica Hope Hailey

Acknowledgements

Many people have contributed to the process of writing this third edition of *Exploring Strategic Change*. We would like to thank Aniello Genovese and Tara Rees-Jones, for helping us to construct a manuscript fit for the publishers. We would like to thank Professor Derrick Neal, Professor Rees Ward, Mandy Bennett, Professor Mark Saunders and Dr Caroline Clarke for helping to provide case studies for this book. Thanks as always also go to the many MBA students and Executives who offered important comments on the ideas presented in this book. In addition, some of the case material presented in this third edition was collected through the Change Management Research Consortium (CMC). We would like to thank the companies who are members of the CMC and other academics involved in the research, specifically: Dr Clare Kelliher, Dr Elaine Farndale and Dr Sue Abbotson. Finally, we must thank our patient and long-suffering families, who put up with the long hours we spend at our computers. This book is dedicated to all of them.

To Paul, Guy and Annys
and John, Helen, Mary, Frances, Joanna and Sarah Jane

Publisher's acknowledgements

We are grateful to the following for permission to reproduce copyright material:

Figure 2.6 and Table 2.1: Adapted from Johnson, G. (1998) 'Mapping and re-mapping organisational culture', in V. Ambrosini, G. Johnson and K. Scholes, *Exploring Techniques of Analysis and Evaluation in Strategic Management*. Hemel Hempstead: Prentice Hall. Copyright © 1998 Pearson Education Ltd. Reproduced with permission; Illustration 2.2: Copyright © Mandy Bennett VP Organisation and Development, GSK Pharma Europe and Julia Balogun; Illustration 2.8a,b: Adapted from McCann, A. (2005) 'The Forestry Commission: cultural change to deliver a new strategy', in G. Johnson, K. Scholes and R. Whittington, *Exploring Corporate Strategy,* 7th edn. Prentice Hall. Copyright © 2005 The Forestry Commission and Pearson Education Ltd. Reproduced with permission; Illustration 3.5: Adapted from Evans, R. (2007) 'Telly vision', *People Management,* 22: 24–2 (March). Reproduced with permission; Illustration 4.3: Copyright © Paul Arnold, 2002. We acknowledge with thanks the help of Peter Morgan of Bayer DS EU in the preparation of this case; Figure 5.6: Adapted from Beckhard, R. and Harris, R.T. (1987) *Organizational Transitions: Managing Complex Change,* 2nd edn. Upper Saddle River, New Jersey: Pearson Education, Inc. Reproduced with permission; Illustration 5.10 Copyright © Mandy Bennett VP Organisation and Development, GSK Pharma Europe and Julia Balogun; Figure 6.8: Adapted from Gratton, L., et al. (1999) *Strategic Human Resource Management.* Oxford: Oxford University Press, Figure 9.1, p. 185. Copyright © 1999 Oxford University Press. Reproduced with permission; Illustration 6.3: Prepared by Sara Stanton, Team Talk Team, Kraft UK 2006, 2007; Illustration 6.6: Extracted from the Change Management Consortium report for Ernst and Young, January 2007, by Veronica Hope Hailey, Sue Abbotson and Elaine Farndale; Figure 7.3: Adapted from Balogun, J. (2006). 'Managing change: steering a course between intended strategies and unanticipated outcomes', *Long Range Planning,* 39(1): 29–49. Copyright © 2006 Elsevier. Reproduced with permission; Figure 7.7: Reprinted from Grundy, T. (1998) 'Strategy implementation and project management', *Journal of Project Management,* 16(1): 34–50. Copyright © 1998 Elsevier. Reproduced with permission; Figure 7.8: Adapted from Balogun, J. and Hope Hailey, V. (1999). *Exploring Strategic Change,* Harlow, England: Prentice-Hall. Copyright © 1999 Pearson Education Ltd. Reproduced with permission; Figure 7.9: Reprinted from Grundy, T. (1998) 'Strategy implementation and project management', *Journal of Project Management,* 16(1): 34–50. Copyright © 1998 Elsevier. Reproduced with permission; Illustration 7.2 : Extracted from Doherty, N. (1997) 'Downsizing in Tysons Ltd', in S. Tyson (ed.) *The Practice of Human Resource Management,* London: Pitman Publishing. Copyright © 1997 Pearson Education Ltd. Reproduced with permission; Illustration 7.3: Written by Mark NK Saunders from: Saunders, M.N.K., Thornhill, A. and

Lewis, P. (2002) 'Understanding employees' reactions to the management of change: an exploration through an organisational justice framework', *Irish Journal of Management,* 23.1:85–108 and Thornhill, A. and Saunders, M.N.K. (2003) 'Exploring employees' reactions to strategic change over time: The utilisation of an organisational justice perspective', *Irish Journal of Management,* 24.1: 66–86; Case study 1: Ward, R. Neal, D., Hope Hailey, V. and Balogun, J. (2007) DCSA: transforming a public sector communications agency (case study). Copyright © 2007 Rees Ward. Reproduced with permission; Case Study 2: Balogun, J., Clarke, C. and Hope Hailey, V. (2008) BCP Aerospace (case study). Copyright © 2008 Julia Balogun, Cynthia Clarke and Veronica Hope Hailey. Reproduced with permission.

In some instances we have been unable to trace the owners of copyright material, and we would appreciate any information that would enable us to do so.

Exploring strategic change: an introduction

1.1 INTRODUCTION

For many years now it has been said that the pace of change experienced by organisations and those who work in them is increasing. Change has become a way of life, in part because organisations are experiencing many different types of change. As industries consolidate, there are increasing numbers of mergers and acquisitions. The pressures on organisations to compete in a more global arena are leading to different competitive pressures and more strategic alliances. Rapid technological change is forcing organisations to adopt new technologies and change the way they both work and interface with their suppliers and customers. There has also been a series of management fads over the last two decades such as culture change programmes, total quality management, and business process re-engineering. In addition, many organisations need to change their strategy just to remain competitive. Yet the sad fact is that the success rate for most of the change programmes launched within organisations is poor. Figures quoted vary, but many commentators put the failure rate at around 70 per cent.[1]

As a result, change management is becoming a highly sought-after managerial competence. It is increasingly recognised that implementation skills are required throughout the organisation, not just within the senior management ranks. Large organisations, in particular, need to rely on their middle managers to push through, and in many cases lead, change initiatives. Change management is part of the generic managerial toolkit. This book aims to help managers and students alike to understand more about change management and to extend their competence in this area, by building on the concepts presented in its sister text, *Exploring Corporate Strategy* by Gerry Johnson and Kevan Scholes. It starts where most other strategic texts end – with frameworks that can help managers put their strategic plans into practice.

Exploring Corporate Strategy and *Exploring Strategic Change* share compatible perspectives on change. *Exploring Corporate Strategy* presents four views of the process of strategic management. One view is that strategy can, and indeed should, be designed. As such, strategy is the outcome of careful, objective analysis by top management, with the associated implementation of new strategies occurring down through the organisation via detailed planning. The second view is that strategic management is not so much about formal planning, but is more of a negotiated process, subject to both managerial and cultural influences. Organisations can, and some would argue inevitably do, become captives of their own cultural heritage. Often the collective experience of the individuals within an organisation, and their taken-for-granted assumptions about their organisation and their competitors, customers and marketplace, lead to strategies which are adaptations of the past. From this perspective change is about breaking out of the strategic inertia that has accumulated from previous years of success and is embedded within the organisation's culture. The third view emphasises how new ideas can originate from within organisations due to the diversity of the individuals within, and how these new ideas can lead to the emergence of new strategies. The fourth view explores strategy as discourse, emphasising how the language of strategy and strategists can facilitate, yet also constrain, the strategy development process. Language may shape the strategy agenda in terms of what is discussed and how. This suggests that the potential for organisational change and renewal is a struggle between the diversity of ideas and cultural and political inertia, which may also be captured in the language of the organisation. The role of the proactive manager is to find ways of ensuring that the outcome from strategic debate is positive change rather than damaging inertia.

Exploring Strategic Change, at one level, views change management as a task that requires the explicit development of clear plans. However, organisational culture is also of central importance. A cultural perspective on organisations provides insight into barriers to change, and how these barriers can be overcome. *Exploring Strategic Change* therefore draws on this perspective to help managers understand the complexity of the change task they are undertaking, and the range of interventions that need to be deployed to help effect change. *Exploring Strategic Change* also emphasises that change is about people – changing people and the way they behave – which requires more than a plan and some changes to organisational structures and systems. Thus change often requires significant investment in terms of managerial time and energy, as well as financial investment. Finally, *Exploring Strategic Change* emphasises that due to the complexity of the change task, successful change requires the development of a context-sensitive approach. There are no formulae or ready-made prescriptions that can be rolled out. This is the key message of this book – the need for context sensitivity. *Exploring Strategic Change* presents a framework, the change kaleidoscope, which can be used to help achieve successful change.

The book is aimed at both business students and practising managers. However, throughout the book, reference is made to the *change agent*. This term refers to the person responsible for 'making the change happen' in any organisation. Many different people can fulfil this role. In some organisations it may be the Chief Executive, in others the Human Resources Director, or even a selected team of people who have responsibility for managing the change process.

There are two main sections to the book: the first section, Chapters 2 to 4, explores the role of context in developing appropriate approaches to change; the second section, Chapters 5 to 7, examines how to turn the chosen change approach into a reality and make change actually happen. However, this introduction starts by explaining some of the assumptions underpinning this text. Consideration is given to:

- The nature of organisational change and the philosophy behind this text.
- The need to develop a change approach which is suitable for the organisation's specific context.
- The managerial and personal skills required by successful change agents.
- The difference between the design of recipe-driven or formulaic approaches to implementation and more context-specific approaches.

The chapter concludes with a flow chart that explains the structure and content of the book.

1.2 THE NATURE OF ORGANISATIONAL CHANGE

There are two schools of thought about how change occurs in organisations. The first sees change as continuous, with organisations transforming on an on-going basis to keep pace with their changing environment. The second sees change as a process of punctuated equilibrium. (See Figure 1.1.)

Figure 1.1   A punctuated equilibrium model of change

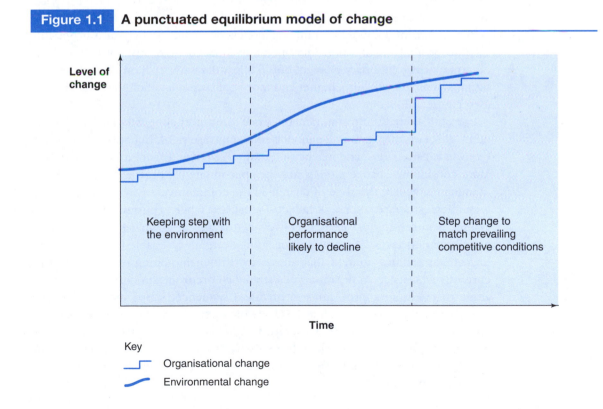

Key
- Organisational change
- Environmental change

From this latter perspective, periods of adaptative and convergent change are interspersed by shorter periods of revolutionary change.[2] Convergent change is adaptation within the existing way of doing things – it leads to extension and continuity of the past, whereas revolutionary change is a simultaneous change in the strategy, structure, systems and culture of an organisation leading to a radically different way of operating. Convergent adaptation through time leads to considerable inertia and resistance to new ways of doing things, which means that revolutionary change is likely to be reactive and forced by an impending crisis. An organisation becomes a victim of its own success as past ways of competing become embedded and taken for granted. A good example of this pattern of change has been seen at the British retailer Marks and Spencer over recent years. M&S had a particular way of doing things. It offered customers a selective range of quality merchandise at reasonable prices under the St Michael brand, focusing on classic wearable basics and essentials rather than fashions. It worked with British suppliers to ensure quality control. Specialist buyers operated (on the assumption that they knew what M&S customers wanted) from a central buying office which then allocated goods to stores. Central policies on store layout and management were followed to ensure consistency of image and standards. Since the stores had no changing rooms, M&S provided a no-quibble refund on all items purchased. Credit cards were not accepted – only the M&S store card. This formula worked for years, until changes in the retail industry in the 1990s rendered it uncompetitive, forcing change upon M&S from 1998 onwards.[3] It was only in 2006 that M&S appeared to have turned the corner.

Proponents of the more continuous models of change argue that it is possible to transform an organisation incrementally through time, leading to the same outcome as revolutionary change, but in a less dramatic fashion. Models of continuous change argue for a higher and more consistent level of on-going change. (See Figure 1.2.)

In reality, there is little empirical evidence to support either view more than the other. It seems that both these models of change are right, but apply to different types of organisations, and maybe different stages of an organisation's life-cycle.[4] More continuous change models may be appropriate for organisations operating in industries where the pace of change in the competitive environment and new technologies is rapid, such as hi-tech industries, where constant organisational change is necessary for survival. However, it is not clear what form continuous transformation takes. Some argue for strategic renewal enabled through a strategic organisational context that allows for the championing of initiatives that currently sit outside an organisation's strategic core from the bottom up. Others argue that semi-structures, links in time and sequenced steps within particular organisational processes, such as NPD, enable incremental and on-going continuous change by providing the structure for the planning of change, yet not the rigidity to prevent that change from then happening. Others argue for the creation of ambidextrous organisations that are capable of simultaneous exploitation and exploration.[5]

| Figure 1.2 | A continuous model of change |

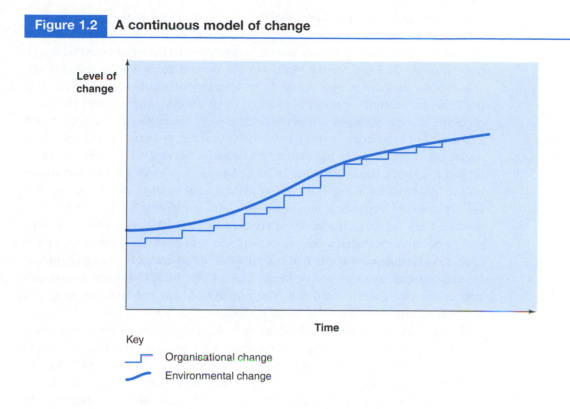

Time

Key

⌐ Organisational change

∿ Environmental change

Punctuated equilibrium models are more likely to apply to industries where changes to the competitive conditions occur less frequently and where it is possible to remain competitive for a period of time without making any significant changes to the way an organisation operates. There is ample evidence that successful organisations breed their own downfall through building inertia and rigidity into their systems, processes and people as they configure themselves to deliver using only a recipe that has delivered success in the past,[6] leaving themselves unable to respond to changing competitive conditions. Some famous organisations, such as ITT, a vast diversified conglomerate which was celebrated in its heyday for much managerial innovation, never recovered and have disappeared from the landscape, whereas others, such as IBM and the British retailer Marks and Spencer, have managed to effect some level of change and have survived to tell the tale. However, this pattern can also occur in hi-tech industries. Intel Corporation, the microprocessor manufacturer, was in the position at the end of the 1990s where it had been configured to ensure exploitation of its opportunities in the PC market to such an extent that the internal corporate venturing that had enabled more continuous strategic renewal over the previous 20 years had been driven out.[7]

This book is most concerned with organisations undertaking a step change, either in a proactive manner in recognition of the need for pre-emptive change given potential threats that may arise in the future, or in a reactive manner in response to an immediate need, such as a direct competitive threat. The focus is on intentional, planned change: change circumstances in which the leaders of an organisation (or maybe even a division or a department) have examined their strategic position and deliberately formulated a new strategy which requires the organisation, and the people within it, to operate differently in some way. This could be, for example, a decision to enter a new market with existing products, requiring minimal changes within the organisation. Alternatively, it could involve a radical shift in strategy, and therefore the structures, systems and culture of the organisation. So, for example, when Lou Gerstner became CEO of IBM in 1993, he had to effect a turnaround and build a platform for future growth that would rescue IBM from its malaise. He put in place a new strategy of putting the customers first and expanding into services whilst attempting to fix, close or sell product lines. He also introduced the concept of 'One IBM' to overcome the silos and hierarchy, introduced a crisis-driven culture, and downsized and delayered as part of cost reductions. Today IBM is a provider of integrated hardware, networking and software solutions and no longer a mainframe maker.[8] However, an organisation like IBM cannot stand still. The turnaround was only the first step in a longer-term transformation that is still on-going.

Our position as the authors of this book is that despite the rhetoric frequently heard today about the need for organisations to be more flexible, and to be capable of reinventing themselves through on-going continuous and emergent change, there are still many organisations who, for a variety of reasons such as new forms of competition, find themselves in the situation where they need to undertake a step change in their strategy, like IBM. Both authors frequently encounter such organisations in the course of their work. However, such step change does not have to occur in a revolutionary manner. It can take many different forms. This is discussed in Chapter 2. Furthermore, this does not mean that more continuous models of change are not viable. Indeed, the incremental change processes advocated by some continuous models of change can occur on a planned basis. The end goal of a planned change process may also be to create a more flexible 'learning organisation' capable of on-going adaptation and self-reinvention.

In addition, change is an on-going process. In today's more dynamic competitive environment, no organisation can stand still. As this introduction has already stressed, change cannot be reduced to prescriptive recipes and neat linear processes. The content of change (what is actually changed), and the process or the way change is implemented, need to be determined by the context of change – both the internal organisational context, which includes the culture, capabilities, resources and politics of an organisation, and the broader external competitive context.[9] The changes made will in turn alter the context, leading to a different set of change needs (see Figure 1.3).

Finally, as stressed at the beginning of this introduction, it isn't 'organisations', but people, that change. For an organisation to change, the people within it must change. Of course, buildings, technology and products can all be changed, but if

Figure 1.3   **Change as a process through time**

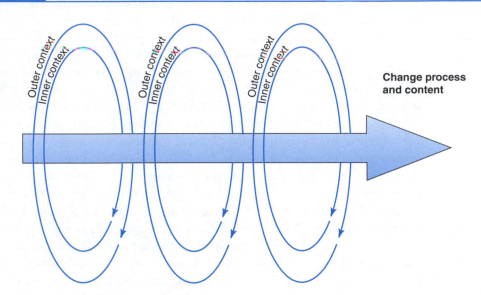

Outer context
Inner context

Outer context
Inner context

Outer context
Inner context

**Change process
and content**

an organisation is to really change, then the people within that organisation also need to change the way they behave. This makes managing and achieving change a challenging undertaking for any manager. One extension of this line of argument is that the nature of organisations and organisational change is so complex that it is virtually impossible to manage change. Whilst this book acknowledges that people are unpredictable and can react to change in many different ways, it also argues that the process of change can be facilitated, if not controlled. The management of change is a competence that can be developed by practitioners, as well as being an exciting area for research. *Exploring Strategic Change* aims to give practitioners practical advice they can implement within their workplace, and at the same time, adds some new concepts to the broad range of academic literature on the management of change.

1.3 CONTEXT-SPECIFIC CHANGE

This book, unlike other texts, does not advocate 'one best way to change'. Change needs to be *context-specific*. In other words, the design and management of any change process should be dependent on the specific situation or context of each organisation. It is dangerous to apply change formulae that worked in one context directly into another.[10] Description should not be turned into prescription. All too often the lessons obtained by researchers, consultants or practitioners from a few case studies of organisational change are turned into best practice. Cases can be very important for illustrating what is possible. However, a limited number of cases, particularly when repeatedly cited, may imply that the formula that works for these organisations is generally applicable[11] when this is not the case. This is particularly true when the cases represent certain contexts, such as companies starting afresh at greenfield sites, or high-technology companies.

An alternative is to develop a contingency approach in which different contextual configurations are associated with a particular set of change design choices. Again, this is something this book avoids. To be feasible, such an approach typically requires a focus on a limited set of implementation options and a restricted range of contextual features.[12] For change agents this means that instead of identifying 'best practice' solutions or 'recipes', they need to start looking for 'best questions'. Even exhortations from 'best practice' models that sound like common sense, for example, 'you must get senior management support before attempting to manage change', may not be generally applicable. If the senior management are themselves major blocks to the implementation of change, the change agent may need to start with some other intervention and hope to gain senior support later on in the change process. Yet how can this be determined without analysing the context of each organisation? This book argues, therefore, that the internal and external context of the organisation should be examined as the starting point to determine the appropriate change process. Change agents should not automatically refer to best practice solutions or contingency approaches without understanding the applicability of these models to their context and what is feasible and what isn't. However, understanding an organisation's change context requires the change agent to develop certain managerial and personal skills. These are discussed next.

1.4 MANAGERIAL SKILLS FOR THE CHANGE AGENT – ANALYSIS, JUDGEMENT AND ACTION

Change agents need to develop their *analytical judgmental* and *implementation* skills. All three of these are important. Without analysis, the temptation is to draw upon ready-made change recipes; without judgement after contextual analysis, change agents can miss the most critical aspect of the change context; and without action, the process can remain a planning exercise which never tackles the reality of change within the organisation.

Therefore, change agents need to possess *analytical* abilities, rather than to know the '10 best ways to run a change programme'. They need to be able to dig deep into an organisation, to understand its culture and the motivations of its staff, in order to develop a full and holistic picture of the change context of the organisation concerned. This is discussed in Chapter 3. However, the practitioner equally needs to be wary of 'paralysis by analysis'. It is easy to become overwhelmed by a detailed analysis.

An additional skill is being able to *judge* which are the most critical features of the change context. To give a medical analogy, a doctor giving a patient an examination following an accident might discover that the patient has cracked ribs, but also lymphatic cancer. The ribs can be treated immediately, but clearly the most critical condition, requiring longer-term and more intensive care, is the cancer. Similarly, the change agent has to prioritise or weight the organisational features she or he uncovers in terms of how critical they are to the change process. The key skill for a change agent is to be able to recognise what is critical in the particular change context, and then to design a change process that addresses the critical area. This idea is examined further in Chapter 4 through a series of change case studies and is referred to as *change judgement*.

Finally, a change agent needs to develop the ability to manage the *implementation* of change. Management is practice, not just analysis – it is about making things happen. Two key aspects of implementation that have to be addressed are which interventions to make in a change situation, and in what order to apply them. The change agent may recognise that a reward system must be changed within an organisation along with changes to production systems and job roles and responsibilities. Yet to avoid confusing the employees with too many simultaneous change initiatives, the agent has to decide which initiative should be carried out first and which one can wait until later. Choosing and sequencing change interventions are discussed in Chapters 5 and 6 of this book.

1.5 PERSONAL COMPETENCIES FOR THE CHANGE AGENT – SELF-AWARENESS

In addition to the managerial skills of judgement, analysis and action, change agents also need to possess *self-awareness*. This is not the only necessary competence – others, such as the ability to deal with complexity, and to be good at influencing those around them to sell change, are widely recognised change agent competencies. Yet *self-awareness*, the capacity to understand one's own prejudices, preferences and experience, is equally important. Individuals view organisations in fundamentally different ways. Without realising it, change agents often allow their personal philosophy to influence the change approach and interventions they choose. As a result, they may give limited consideration, if any, to the actual change context and its needs. Change agents should be driven by the needs of the organisation, rather than by their own perceptions or prejudices of what has constituted 'good' change management in the past. It may also be easier for change agents to understand, and if necessary argue against, other people's prejudices or biases if they are armed with a certain degree of self-awareness.

A simple way to illustrate this point is to look at an individual's subjective/objective orientation. The following distinctions are often made between subjective and objective:

- *Objective*: rational, logical, analytical, facts, data, hard, quantitative.
- *Subjective*: intuitive, experience, moral, feelings, emotions, soft, qualitative.

Illustration 1.1

change in action

An objective versus a subjective world view

An objective perspective

'Organisations are physical and tangible. Things are done according to rules and regulations which are written down . . . there is something tangible and measurable about organisations . . . I'm very tool oriented . . . my inclination is to state very clearly what the objective is, to chart the process and assume that others working with me have sufficient rationality to see it similarly to myself.'

A subjective perspective

'Organisations should not be thought of as physical entities which can be controlled and modelled . . . An organisation is a social entity, something that is socially constructed by the people within it. I see an organisation in terms of its meaning systems rather than its physical aspects . . . This concept of organisation does have implications for the way I view change. For a start we have to be careful not to impose an objective mindset on what we see as an organisation and assume it is something we can control . . . An organisation includes peoples' attitudes and views, and for change to occur these have to change too. This is not to say that if you force people to change their behaviour by imposing new control systems and ways of behaving on them, they will not also change their attitudes. But you have no guarantee that they will change their attitudes in the way you want or anticipated, you cannot control the type of meaning change that occurs . . . If you take my view of organisations to an extreme, it in fact suggests you cannot control or manage change at all. As such all you can do is to facilitate change.'

Objective assessments are seen as hard and measurable. Decisions are made on the basis of tangible facts and figures. Subjective assessments are seen to be based on something less tangible, more intuitive than data driven.

Managers with a preference for either objectivity or subjectivity might describe organisations and their approach to change in a similar way to the respondents in Illustration 1.1. A manager taking an objective view of organisations may conceive of change in terms of reconstruction, not necessarily perceiving a need to tackle underlying beliefs and assumptions. This sort of change agent may feel more comfortable with a directive change approach which involves little participation: they may not see a need to understand a wide variety of views at different levels of the organisation, instead seeing the organisation in mechanistic terms.

In contrast, managers with a more subjective orientation are more likely to assume that any change approach will need to allow for the existence of differing perspectives within the organisation, and will therefore want to work hard at fostering consensus. Such managers may rely on a more participative approach, which allows for greater involvement from all levels of the organisation. There is likely to be a greater emphasis on softer interventions such as communication.

Whilst subjective and objective perspectives are not opposite ends of a spectrum, for any change agent, an awareness of which perspective predominates within their own mind will make them aware of how they will view change. Their perspective must not become a prejudice or a formula. If an organisation is not in crisis and there is little readiness for change, a more objective manager should not automatically dismiss the option of extensive communication to generate some degree of readiness, even if it is not her or his preferred way of working. Likewise, if an organisation is in real crisis, a more subjective manager may have to accept that there is insufficient time for extensive consultation with all staff members, however much it goes against their personal philosophy.

1.6 THE TRANSITION STATE: DESIGNING CONTEXT-SENSITIVE APPROACHES TO CHANGE

There are many different ways of conceiving of the overall change process. However, it is commonly accepted that during change, it is necessary to consider three states – the current, the future and the transition.[13] (See Figure 1.4.)

Essential inputs to the diagnosis of the current organisational state are an understanding of the organisation's competitive position and the need for change, and an understanding of the internal organisational context. It is also necessary to develop some sort of vision of the desired future organisational state. The transition state, the process of changing the organisation from what it is now into the desired future organisation, can only be designed once the current organisational state is understood and the desired future organisational state has been specified, at least in outline. Since this book assumes that readers already have an understanding of how to diagnose the current organisational state, and how to develop an outline of the desired future state from, for example, *Exploring Corporate Strategy*, the main concern here is the transition state.

The transition state, the process of actually making the desired changes happen, often receives less attention than it merits. Implementation is conceived of in terms of the up-front planning for change, with scant attention given to managing the transition process itself. Yet the transition state is not like either the current or future states. It is not possible to move from the current to the future state overnight. It might be possible to redeploy and relocate people in terms of named

Figure 1.4 Change as three states

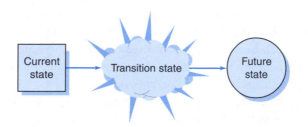

Figure 1.5	A formulaic approach to change design

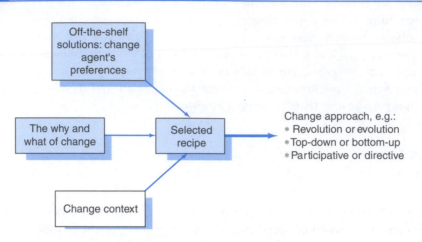

job roles and locations over a weekend, but to change the behaviour of those people, and particularly to change the organisation's shared beliefs, will take much longer. Specific attention is required to both the design and management of the transition state.

Typically, lengthy consideration is given to the why and what of strategy development. The internal and external *context* of the organisation is analysed in order to gain an understanding of the current state and *why* change is necessary. In addition, the strategists decide on the *content* of change – *what* actually has to change and the nature of the future state. However, what many change agents do at this stage (see Figure 1.5) is to turn to a number of existing change solutions. They then derive the design of the change process from these predetermined change formulae, often, unfortunately, selecting a solution that is not appropriate to the current organisation's change context, although it might suit their personal preferences. This is not to denigrate the value of past experience or previous learning. However, the past must also be analysed with reference to the current context. Change agents need to ask themselves questions such as 'Why did that work well for that organisation at that point in time?', 'What are the differences between that organisation's context then, and this organisation now?' and 'How might that affect the approach to change?'

A context-sensitive approach to change sees the stages in the design process as shown in Figure 1.6. As above, the *why* and *what* of change is analysed. The change agent then carries out an *analysis* of the *change context,* which examines the organisational features pertinent to the change situation. These include aspects such as the scope of change required, the time frame, the power of the change agent to effect change, the diversity within the workforce and the capability for change within the organisation.

Using the contextual analysis, the change agent *judges* which are the most *critical* features of the current change situation. For example, in some organisations the

Figure 1.6   **A context-sensitive approach to change design**

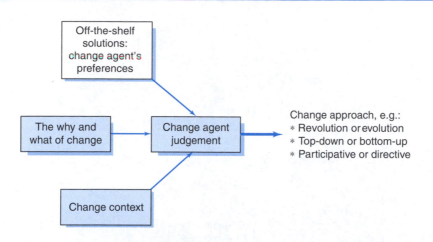

existence of strong professional groups may create diversity among the workforce. Professionals such as hospital consultants will often identify more readily with the values and aims of their professional association rather than with their employing organisation. It would be difficult to design a successful change process within a hospital without taking this into account. In organisations which employ few professionals, this feature may not be so critical. Finally, the change agent considers the appropriate *design choices*. Information derived from the contextual analysis will start to make some design options seem unworkable and others either possible or essential. For instance, if the organisation has only a small amount of money to invest in change, some of the more expensive, educative styles of change that use expensive management development options may not be feasible.

This text uses a diagnostic framework, the *change kaleidoscope* shown in Figure 1.7, to help with this process. The kaleidoscope contains an outer ring concerned with the organisational strategic context, a middle ring concerned with the features of the change context, and an inner ring which contains the menu of design choices open to change agents:

- The *organisational strategic change context* refers to the broader strategic analysis conducted to determine why the organisation should change and what it should change to. This analysis is the focus of *Exploring Corporate Strategy*.

- The *change contextual features* are aspects of the organisation to do with its culture, competences and current situation, which change agents should consider before selecting the change approach. These features can be extracted from the broader organisational strategic context, and can be used by change agents to help determine the appropriateness of any change approach for a particular context. It is these features that are examined as part of the contextual analysis, and they are explored in depth in Chapter 3.

Figure 1.7   **The change kaleidoscope**

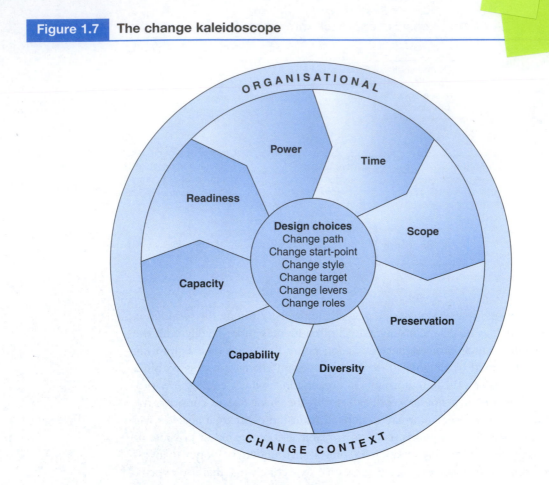

- The *design choices* are the range of options a change agent needs to choose from when selecting an appropriate change approach. For example, what type of change path is best here? Is it necessary to do something radical and fast? Or would it be more effective in the long term if it were a staged change process, planned over time? Where should the change start-point be? Should the change be organised so that it cascades down from the senior management, or would it be better if it was piloted on the edges of the organisation first? This range of choices is explored in detail in Chapter 2.

As explained above, the contextual features in the change kaleidoscope do not carry equal weight in all organisations – some will be more important than others in different organisational change contexts. This is why the diagnostic framework is called a kaleidoscope as its configurations of features will constantly shift according to the organisation being analysed. The kaleidoscope for an organisation will also change through time in response to earlier change interventions put in place. It is not static. The aspect of judging the relative criticality of organisational features is examined in more depth in Chapter 4.

1.7 THE TRANSITION STATE: DESIGN AND MANAGEMENT

Once the change agent has selected a change approach, this is not the end of the story. One of the key managerial skills is *action*. The change agent now has to design the change interventions or levers that will deliver the selected approach, and also manage the process of implementation.

The issues that need to be considered in *designing the transition* fall out of the design choices made. For instance, as a result of the design choice phase, it may have been decided to focus on changing employee behaviours as a means of achieving change. In order to achieve that behavioural change, the change agent will need to deploy a series of levers and mechanisms, such as new reward systems and training. However, the identification of the primary levers and mechanisms is only the beginning. If the new reward system is to be effective, other things may also need to be changed, such as the appraisal mechanism. Existing practices that could obstruct the new required behaviours also need to be identified and removed. As pointed out above, there are also issues about timing. Are new rewards and training to be introduced simultaneously, or will new rewards be introduced to reinforce the training? There are also likely to be many other changes which have to be scheduled. All these different interventions need to be sequenced during the transition along with other change interventions such as communication of the need for change, and the form of the changes. Effecting transitions is therefore a complex business.

Chapter 5 addresses this issue. It introduces the idea that transitions have three phases, *mobilise, move* and *sustain*, and considers the various activities that are necessary to take an organisation through all three phases. It also explains how any organisational change process is underpinned by the personal transitions of individuals within that organisation. Chapters 6 and 7 discuss transition management techniques such as communication and resistance management that can make transition through the change process more effective for the organisation and more acceptable to employees.

1.8 PUTTING THE JIGSAW TOGETHER – A CHANGE FLOW CHART

For change to be successful, managers charged with the responsibility of managing this activity need to address the complexities of both context and process. However, the very complexity can be off-putting. Figure 1.8 presents a flow chart of the steps this text is advocating to inject some clarity into the process. It shows which questions have to be addressed at different stages of the change process.

Stages 1 and 2 are addressed within strategy texts such as *Exploring Corporate Strategy*, although this text will revisit the development of the desired current and future states in more detail in Chapter 5. Stage 3, analysing the change context and identifying the critical change features, is presented via

| Figure 1.8 | The change flow chart |

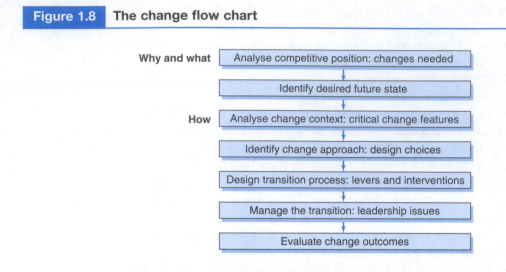

a fuller account of the *change kaleidoscope* in Chapters 3 and 4. Stage 4, determining the design choices, follows on from stage 3, but this text discusses the design choices in Chapter 2, before the contextual features are described, since it is easier to appreciate how the contextual features impact on the design choices once the range of design choices is understood. Chapters 5 and 6 consider stage 5, the design of the transition, by exploring the different stages of transition, the use of different change levers and mechanisms and the overriding importance of appropriate communication at all stages. Chapter 7 discusses how to manage the transition and considers issues such as how to monitor the success of the change process, how to resource the transition given the competencies required of change agents, and topical issues such as the role of justice and fairness in change processes.

1.9 SUMMARY

This opening chapter has established the links that exist between this book and its sister text, *Exploring Corporate Strategy*. It has also introduced the role of the *change agent*. In particular, the chapter has introduced several central concepts that underpin the philosophy of the whole book:

- The view that change can be facilitated, if not controlled.
- That all change design must be context-specific, which requires change agents to possess managerial skills of analysis, judgement and implementation, and personal competencies such as self-awareness.
- The difference between formulaic and context-specific approaches to change implementation.

- Transition as a stage in change which demands that attention is given to both its design and management
- A general change flow chart, which identifies different decision-making points in the strategic change process and sets out the overall way this text recommends a change agent approach the management of strategic change.

These central concepts underpin the rest of the chapters of the book. *Exploring Strategic Change* aims to provide an intelligent guide to managing change in today's complex organisational environments. It is hoped that readers will gain worthwhile insight into the challenging subject of change.

REFERENCES

1. See Beer, M. and Nohria, N. (2000) 'Cracking the code of change', *Harvard Business Review,* (May–June), pp. 133–41.
2. This model of change is explained in more detail in several articles and books. See Romanelli, E. and Tushman, M.L. (1994) 'Organizational transformation as punctuated equilibrium: an empirical test', *Academy of Management Journal,* 37 (5), pp. 1141–66; Tushman, M.L. and Romanelli, E. (1985) 'Organizational evolution: a metamorphosis model of convergence and reorientation' in *Research in Organizational Behavior* 7, Cummings, L. and Staw B. (eds) Greenwich, CT: JAI Press; Miller, D. and Friesen, P.H. (1984) *Organizations: a Quantum View,* Englewood Cliffs, NJ: Prentice Hall.
3. Collier, N. (2002) 'Marks and Spencer' in *Exploring Corporate Strategy*, 6th edn, Johnson, G. and Scholes, K. (eds.) Harlow: Pearson Education.
4. A good review of the competing perspectives can be found in Burnes, B. (2000) *Managing Change: A Strategic Approach to Organisational Dynamics*, 3rd edn, Edinburgh: Pearson Education.
5. See Brown, S.L. and Eisenhardt, K.M. (1997) 'The art of continuous change: linking complexity theory and time paced evolution in relentlessly shifting organizations', *Administrative Science Quarterly,* 42, pp. 1–34. See Burgelman, R.A. (1983) 'A process model of internal corporate venturing in the diversified major firm', *Administrative Science Quarterly,* 28, pp. 233–44. Also see O'Reilly, C.A. and Tushman, M. (2004) 'The ambidextrous organization', (April), pp. 74–81.
6. See Miller, D. (1992) 'The Icarus paradox: how exceptional companies bring about their own downfall', *Business Horizons*, (Jan–Feb), pp. 24–35.
7. See Burgelman, R.A. (2002) 'Strategy as vector and the inertia of coevolutionary lock-in', *Administrative Science Quarterly*, 47, pp. 325–57.
8. See Applegate, L., Austin, R. and Collins, E. (2006) 'IBM's decade of transformation (A): the turnaround', Harvard Business School Case, 9-805-130. Also Hemp, P. and Stewart, T.A. (2004) 'Leading change when business is good', *Harvard Business Review,* (Dec), pp. 60–70.
9. For a fuller discussion of a processual view of change, see Pettigrew, A. and Whipp, R. (1991) *Managing Change for Competitive Success,* Oxford: Blackwell Publishers.
10. Many authors make this point. See, for example, Pettigrew, A. and Whipp, R. (reference 9 above); Jick, T. (1993) *Managing Change: Cases and Concepts*, Homewood, IL: Richard D. Irwin; Nadler, D.A. and Tushman, M.L. (1989) 'Organizational frame bending: principles for managing reorientation', *The Academy of Management Executive,* 3, pp. 194–204.
11. This is discussed by Guest, D. (1990) 'Human resource management and the American dream', *Journal of Management Studies,* 27 (2), pp. 377–97. Also see Storey, J. (ed) (1989) *New Perspectives on Human Resource Management,* London: Routledge, and Blyton, P. and Turnbull, P. (eds) (1992) *Reassessing Human Resource Management*, London: Sage.

12. For a fuller review of change contingency models and the dangers of applying learning from these models prescriptively, see Hope Hailey, V. and Balogun, J. (2002) 'Devising context sensitive approaches to change: the example of Glaxo Wellcome', *Long Range Planning* 35 (2), pp. 153–79.
13. The concept of change as three states, the current, the future and the transition, is advanced by Beckhard, R. and Harris, R.T. (1987) *Organizational Transitions: Managing Complex Change,* 2nd edn, Reading, MA: Addison Wesley.

WORK ASSIGNMENTS

1.1. There are a number of books by renowned senior executives who have managed change in their organisations. Why should these texts be read with caution?

1.2. Suggest why different approaches to change management might be appropriate in different organisations, such as a university, a high street bank, or a multinational enterprise.

1.3. Explore your personal perspectives on organisations (drawing on Illustration 1.1) and how this might limit the way you approach change.

1.4. What are the factors that can cause change initiatives to fail in organisations?

Understanding implementation choices: the options to consider

2.1 INTRODUCTION

Chapter 1 introduces the concept of the change kaleidoscope (see Figure 2.1). It shows that a change agent faces a bewildering array of implementation decisions – the *design choices* – that need to be made about how change should be implemented within his or her particular context. This chapter

---

Figure 2.1 **The change kaleidoscope**

explains these different design choices, and the options within each choice. Although in practice a change agent would consider issues of content first, in this chapter, the design choices from the change kaleidoscope are explained in detail before the contextual features, because it is simpler to explain the contextual features and how they link to the choices that need to be made once the choices are understood.

The change kaleidoscope separates the array of choices that need to be made on any implementation approach into six categories, within which there are a range of alternatives. The six categories are:

- *Change path*: the type of change to be undertaken in terms of the nature of the change and the desired end result. This category is referred to as *change path* as distinct from *change type*, as in some circumstances it is necessary to under-take an enabling phase of change before it is possible to undertake the actual changes required.

- *Change start-point*: where the change is initiated and developed, which could be summarised simplistically as top-down or bottom-up, but there are other choices.

- *Change style*: the management style of the implementation, such as highly collaborative or more directive.

- *Change target*: the target of the change interventions, in terms of people's attitudes and values, behaviours or outputs.

- *Change levers*: the range of levers and interventions to be deployed across four subsystems – technical, political, cultural and interpersonal.

- *Change roles*: who is to take responsibility for leading and implementing the changes.

This chapter discusses each one of these choices in more detail.

2.2 CHANGE PATH

There are four types of change – adaptation, reconstruction, evolution and revolution. See Figure 2.2. The change path focuses on the choices in terms of these types of change, but also the way these different change types can be combined to deliver a more phased approach to change.

2.2.1 Types of change

The four main types of change illustrated in Figure 2.2 are defined in terms of two dimensions – the *end result of change*, and the *nature of change*. The *end result* is about the extent of change desired. Change can involve a *transformation* of the organisation or a *realignment*. *Transformation is 'change which cannot be handled within the existing paradigm and*

Figure 2.2   Types of change

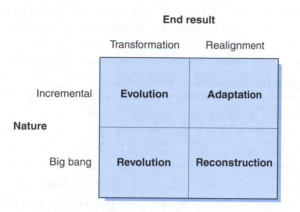

organisational routines; it entails a change in the taken-for-granted assumptions and "the way of doing things around here".[1] It is a fundamental change within the organisation requiring a shift in strategy, structures, systems, processes and culture.

Many European multinationals are attempting transformational change as they move from an operating model in which the business units based in individual countries act as autonomous baronies and fiefdoms, with their primary focus on doing what is best for their local market irrespective of the impact of other business units across Europe, to a pan-European way of operating. In this new operating model, country heads, marketing teams, NPD, and manufacturing all have to work more collaboratively across country boundaries to exploit growing similarities and develop strategies and plans that are about maximizing performance across Europe, rather than competitively with a 'not invented here' mind-set and much reinvention of the wheel designed to exploit (declining) local differences. The new structures put in place to deliver this shift hide what in reality is a change to the shared assumptions and beliefs. This is true of Unilever, the personal care and household products company. Traditionally, Unilever has operated as a portfolio of self-contained, independent country-based companies. Since 2005 the new CEO, Cescau, has changed the structure to a more integrated, globally coordinated business model, with global category organisations (marketing, R&D) focused on end consumer needs and regional go-to-market (i.e., sales) organisations to meet the needs of shoppers and the retail customers (primarily supermarkets). This in turn requires country managers to move from being independent entrepreneurial general managers to 'chief customer officers', and requires all country-based and globally based staff to start working together.[2]

Realignment is a change to the way of doing things that does not involve a fundamental reappraisal of the central assumptions and beliefs within the organisation, although it may still involve substantial change like a major restructuring. Piaggio, the Italian manufacturer of the iconic Vespa scooter, has recently been through a realignment. In 2003 the company's losses reached £94 million, and 46,000 hours of work were lost to strikes in that year alone. The company was hampered by outdated working practices. Between October 2003 and 2006 the immediate steps taken included solving the debt crisis, boosting quality, improving worker relations and introducing new models. Worker demands for factory air conditioning to improve the working environment were met and used along with guarantees of no job cuts to persuade the unions agree to flexible working and improved productivity. Investment in machinery to reduce faults and refurbished buildings to improve workflow helped to cut errors. The quality of outsourced components was increased whilst the costs were reduced by switching sourcing to China and India. The product range was rationalised to focus on the more profitable bigger models of scooters. By mid-2006 the focus had switched from recovery to growth and the company was preparing to float.[3]

In reality, of course, there is no clear dividing line between a realignment and a transformation. The end result of change is more like a continuum. However, broadly speaking, the more any planned change challenges the guiding assumptions and beliefs of an organisation, the more the change approaches a transformation.

The *nature of change* is the way change is implemented, either in an all-at-once, big-bang fashion over a period of, say, a year to 18 months, or in a more step-by-step, stage-by-stage incremental fashion. These two dimensions, the *end result of change* and the *nature of change,* provide the explanation for the four different types of change.

2.2.2 Adaptation and reconstruction

Adaptation is non-paradigmatic change implemented gradually through staged initiatives. *Reconstruction* is also non-paradigmatic change undertaken to realign the way the organisation operates, **but** in a much faster and dramatic fashion. A large number of change attempts fit within these two categories, including many turnarounds such as the one described at Piaggio above. See Illustration 2.1 for more examples. Many such change programmes are clearly significant and important to the longer-term survival of an organisation. However, adaptations and reconstructions can also be carried out for other reasons, such as a merger. In 2005 in the UK, a new organisation was developed to deal with organised crime. The organisation, called SOCA (the Serious Organised Crime Agency), was a result of pulling together teams currently working for the National Crime Squad, the National Criminal Intelligence Service and customs (those dealing with drug trafficking and immigration crime). The sheer logistics of just welding these previously disparate groups into one organisation working from one head office, with a unified structure, ways of working and performance management systems, took 18 months.

Illustration 2.1   *change in action*

Delivering adaptations and reconstructions

Adaptation at JC Penney

JC Penney, the US retailer, started to undergo an adaptation in 2000 to get the business back on its feet. Between 2000 and 2004 the then chief executive sold the non-core drug store and financial business, pulled out of Latin America, centralised buying and HR and put further store growth on hold. Shops were also remodelled to suit the modern retail market, combining the easy-access patterns now familiar to customers from mass discounters with the service expected of the traditional department store. His successor has continued the change process by pursuing a growth strategy.[4]

Reconstruction at Hewlett-Packard

In April 2005 Mark Hurd was appointed chief executive of the once famous, but now struggling, computer and printer maker. Four months later he announced that HP would lay off 15,300 workers in the next year, 10 per cent of its workforce worldwide, as part of an attempted turnaround. In addition, the printer and personal computer division was split into two, and the central sales group reorganised. Cutbacks were made in some areas of R&D and pension benefits were frozen. New executives were brought in from outside. However, investments are being made to drive growth, and not just in R&D. The 85 data centres spread across the world are being replaced with just 6. Employees in the old data centres will be made redundant and the property sold off. Savings are also being pumped into the engineers and salespeople. Almost 1,000 sales reps have been brought in to improve service to major accounts.[5]

Adaptation at Marks and Spencer

Stuart Rose took over as Chief Executive at M&S in 2004. After 30 months of restructuring at the beginning of 2007 and close to the end of his three-year plan, he finally declared M&S to be in recovery. Rose has focused on rejuvenating the management team, cutting costs and improving product. On his arrival he took personal charge of clothing, the core business, and dismissed the previous incumbent. He also brought colleagues with him to head up operations and logistics. Directors uncomfortable with the new regime left. Rose has improved supplier terms, reduced stock commitments, shifted sourcing to Turkey and southeast Asia, cut markdowns and focused on successful subbrands such as Per Una for women, closing down other initiatives such as Lifestores and Per Una Due. Rose also focused on stopping waste and unnecessary administration costs, closed underperforming stores and put in place redundancies. On the investment side, he moved stores into out-of-town retail centres, upgraded stores and introduced high-profile advertising, 'Your M&S', using the likes of Twiggy and Brian Ferry. Now as the core business responds, he is stretching the brand into, for example, electricals and jewellery.[6]

Reconstructions and adaptations such as the ones discussed above do sometimes lead to more fundamental transformational change (see section 2.2.5). Thus the adaptation at JC Penney is moving into a transformational phase as the current chief executive attempts to consolidate the turnaround with a culture change which creates greater staff engagement. Consolidation at Marks and Spencer also requires deeper and more fundamental change. Rose is also seeking to make cultural change by, for example, improving decision-making accountability and putting in place a training initiative aimed at creating a 'can-do' attitude in store staff. However, not all such initiatives lead to longer-term change. Some organisations become trapped in a downwards spiral of reconstruction. This appears to be true of Ford, the US car maker. Bill Ford, who took over as Chief Executive in 2001, first outlined a revitalisation plan that would save $7bn in pre-tax profits within five years. As targets slipped, a new turnaround programme, the way forward, was announced in January 2006. Current attempts by Alan Mulally to reinvigorate the company will represent the third attempt in the last five years to do this.

2.2.3 Evolution

Evolution is transformational change implemented gradually through different stages and interrelated initiatives. It is likely to be planned, proactive transformation, in which change is undertaken by managers in response to their anticipation of the need for future change. As part of the peace settlement in Northern Ireland, the Royal Ulster Constabulary of Northern Ireland needed to be moved from a military organisation to one that provides policing in the community. The organisation's name change to the Police Service of Northern Ireland in 2001 was the first step on a long path of transformation started by the Chief Constable, Sir Ronnie Flanagan, and completed by his successor, Huw Orde. Some of the actions included new recruits to be drawn from a 50–50 pool of Protestants and Catholics; the force to be reduced from 13,500 to about 7,500; the force's crown-and-harp cap badge to be scrapped; all RUC officers to receive human rights training and accept a new police oath; and a new policing board to replace the existing police authority. However, there was also a significant culture change that had to occur: the RUC was militaristic and hierarchical compared to other police forces, with methods of policing that separated its officers from the community to safeguard them from attack. Police operated from fortified stations in armoured vehicles and did not dare tell their children what they did for a living for fear of attack from extremists from both sides.[7]

However, the RUC example is an unusual transformation. To describe in more detail how evolutions unfold, Illustration 2.2 describes the evolution undertaken by GSK Pharma UK following the merger in the UK between Glaxo Wellcome and SmithKline Beecham in 2000. It shows how a series of integrated and phased initiatives and investments have created a new culture and organisational identity that is not reminiscent of either GW or SKB.

2.2.4 Revolution

Revolution is fundamental, transformational change, such as that at GSK, but it occurs via simultaneous initiatives on many fronts, and often in a relatively short space of time, such as 18 months. It is more likely to be a forced, reactive transformation,

Illustration 2.2

change in action

Evolution at GSK UK

Building GSK Pharma UK in 2001

Glaxo SmithKline (GSK) was formed from the merger in December 2000 of Glaxo Wellcome and SmithKline Beecham, two large, international pharmaceutical companies. This created an organisation with a combined turnover of £20.5bn, operating in 70 countries and employing over 100,000 people. However, the focus of this illustration is the post-merger integration of GW and SB in the UK Pharma, the UK Sales and Marketing division.

On merger, the two organisations were seen as culturally different. Whereas GW's culture was characterised as being democratic and open, SB was deemed to be both more directive and faster-moving. Furthermore, in UK Pharma, although the newly appointed General Manager was ex-SB, his senior management team and the rest of the organisation was 50–50 ex-SB and ex-GW. Therefore there needed to be a new culture. It was hard for one or the other of the legacy cultures to predominate.

Destination workshops were held with employees from both companies prior to the official completion of the merger. Employees were asked to pretend they were already in the new organisation, and were sending 'wish you were here' postcards to their colleagues describing the three key elements that embodied the new organisation. The outputs from the workshops were collated to create a list of 20 key factors that each organisation wanted. In comparing the results of GW and SB, it was found that they were almost identical. HR fed the key factors from the destination workshops to the senior team at a subsequent workshop, and through the cultural web framework (see section 2.6), they used these factors to develop a paradigm for the new UK Pharma. The developed paradigm had the acronym PASSION: Pride, Authentic, Stimulating and supportive,

Simple, 'I make a difference', Outward looking and Nimble. Cultural web workshops were then run for employees. The senior team invited all employees over a number of lunchtime seminars to complete the other elements of the cultural web to support the central paradigm of PASSION. In total 60 lunchtime workshops were held, which generated thousands of flip charts for each element of the paradigm. The flip charts were then collated and used to build a cultural web that related to the new organisation.

The next phase for HR and the senior team was to map what GSK were already trying to do, for example, redesigning the layout of the head office, to see if it actually matched with what people wanted from the organisation. The office was an old GW office with '*GW stamped over it and the offices were real offices with hard walls and small windows and it was traditional*'. The office was completely redesigned to be open, in GSK colours, with glass-walled offices where they did exist, and senior managers sitting with their teams.

A number of mechanisms were put in place to support the new culture. These included:

- *PASSION awards*. These awards ranged across different levels to indicate different levels of achievement, and were offered to employees that made a contribution to the organisation in a manner that related to the PASSION paradigm. There were also a series of pins; bronze, silver and gold, corresponding to the relative magnitude of staff contribution.
- *Communication*. Regular quarterly meetings, atrium briefings, kept everyone up to date on the latest news, strategies and performance. The company intranet displayed the PASSION paradigm, its meaning and its relevance. Internal communication went through e-mail and voice mail.

change in acti

- *Measurement*. HR and the senior team used a bi-annual Internet survey, the 'temperature check', aligned around the different elements of PASSION to measure what they were trying to do and how the employees were responding to it.
- *Objective-setting scheme*. Objectives were set for individuals each year, cascaded down from the top of their business area. The achievement of objectives was linked to pay – a big shift for GW people.
- *People development*. This included readily available training programs, individual development plans, and 360-degree performance feedback.
- *Organisation 'feel'*. As part of being authentic, people were allowed to wear what they wanted to work.

Building on PASSION in 2002: PASSION is not a spectator sport

Whilst at head office there had been a complete merger of the two legacy organisations, the sales force continued to operate as they had always done, with some slight adjustment to territorial boundaries. The cultural change exemplified by PASSION had yet to fully grip the sales force. The main aim for 2002, therefore, was to engage the sales force as well as sustaining PASSION. There were four main challenges:

- To build on the work already done (not start something new).
- To help leaders, teams and individuals understand that PASSION isn't something done to them, they make it happen themselves.
- To build an 'adult: adult' organisation to replace the legacy 'parent: child' organisations.
- To provide everyone with the support they need to live PASSION for themselves and others.

The theme for 2002 was to help everyone understand that PASSION was something they had to make happen to themselves. Using the phrase 'PASSION is not a spectator sport', GSK Pharma embarked on a communication campaign which likened the new culture to the World Cup and Commonwealth games. Employees were either 'on the pitch with GSK' or 'off the pitch and on the terraces'. The tough message was that if you didn't want to get on the pitch and play, you should leave.

To keep PASSION alive, a series of postcards were distributed to the employees, which followed up on the sporting theme. There was one card for each element of PASSION, and each card was sponsored by one member of the senior management team, with a sporting picture on the front and a message on the back from that manager saying what that particular element of PASSION meant for him or her. A PASSION progress report was also compiled. Employees were asked to write reports as to how they were living with PASSION. Once compiled, the report was distributed throughout the organisation.

The challenge for 2003: PASSION – raising your game

Come 2003, GSK faced some tough commercial challenges with not much new in the pipeline in the short term, although longer term there were some good things. Thus the immediate cultural challenges for 2003 were to revisit the cultural web to assess progress, to develop leadership excellence through role-modelling of PASSION and the development of individual, peer and team leadership, and to generally raise the level of performance against PASSION. Using the 2003 theme of 'Raising your game', the aim was to get individuals to see what they could do to maximise their contribution to the business, and to link this to the focus of GSK – helping more sick people to live longer, feel better and do more. 'Raising your game' wasn't about doing more or working harder, but rather considering what could be done differently that would make a difference and add value. Some practical and fun activities were planned to help individuals with this. Whilst consultants had not been used in the process so far, a small consultancy organisation was brought in to help with this theme.

PASSION into 2004, 2005 & 2006

The Temperature Check in November 2003 showed that there was still more work to be done on 'I make a difference', 'Outward looking', and 'Nimble'. Therefore the challenge in 2004 was to adjust the 'Raising our game' programme to address these issues for individuals, teams and leaders. By 2005 and 2006, with a new integrated way of doing business across Europe for GSK, the challenge moved to ensuring that PASSION was still relevant.

due to the changing competitive conditions the organisation is facing. If an organisation's strategy is still rooted in the ways of behaving that used to lead to success, then the mismatch between the strategy being pursued and the new strategies required may be great enough to force fundamental change in a short space of time if the organisation is to survive. An organisation may also need to implement planned transformation rapidly, because, for example, the organisation sees the need to pre-empt fast competitor response, or realises that rapid change is necessary to meet changing customer needs.

A point this book returns to later, however, is that it takes people time to change their behaviours, and even longer to change their attitudes and the way they think about their work. Furthermore, not all individuals within an organisation are willing or able to undertake the changes asked of them. Change is therefore facilitated by a process of natural attrition as those less able or willing to change leave the organisation and are replaced by individuals more suited to the new ways of working required. So, for example, when the Royal Ulster Constabulary became the Northern Ireland Police Force, those who didn't want to change were allowed to go with good service records. Change can, of course, take some time. Therefore, one way to achieve a revolution may be to literally (physically) change the people. United Business Media, the trade publisher, has done just this. In two years, David Levin has transformed the business portfolio of UBM from a display print advertising business with a mixture of print and TV interests into a focused business-to-business publisher making the majority of its profits from events and exhibitions by buying and selling a number of businesses.[8] For most businesses, however, such a radical approach is simply not feasible. Therefore, in reality, revolutions are few and far between. Most transformational change – whether effected at the corporate level by selling off old businesses and acquiring new ones to transform the corporate portfolio, or effected within the businesses through strategic, structural and cultural change – occurs through a more evolutionary path. Furthermore, whilst it may be possible to transform a corporate portfolio in terms of the range of businesses within a short space of time, as shown by the example of GSK above, longer-term change is often needed to weld the new corporate entities into a cohesive whole. Like any newly formed organisation, UBM now has to deliver against its portfolio of acquisitions and divestments.

2.2.5 Paths of change

The last point of the above paragraph is important as it emphasises why this book talks about *paths of change* as opposed to *types of change*. The eventual aim of an organisation may be to achieve transformation, possibly as part of a turn-around, but the organisation may lack the resources, skills, or finance to achieve transformation. Alternatively, the organisation may be in a crisis, and losing a lot of money, and therefore need to stop the rot before any longer-term change can be undertaken.

The most popular change path is that of reconstruction followed by evolution (see Figure 2.3). In fact, it has almost become a change formula in its own right. To give a well-known and popular example first, British Airways in the 1980s effected a much-cited cultural transformation. However, this followed a financial turnaround of the airline. Between 1981 and 1982 the workforce was downsized dramatically; unprofitable routes were closed; cargo-only services halted; offices, administration and staff clubs cut; and a pay freeze imposed. Only then, in autumn 1982, was attention turned to changing the airline's image and culture from an organisation more about transportation to one focused on customer service.[9] The

| Figure 2.3 | Paths of change |

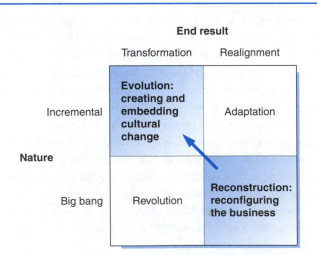

reconstruction resolved the financial crisis at the airline, and provided both money and time for the culture change. It also shook staff out of their complacency and into a recognition of the need for change through some of the drastic measures taken to restore profitability.

Similarly, change was initiated at GE, the international corporation with businesses as diverse as financial services, aircraft engines and lighting, by Jack Welch in the early 1980s, following his appointment as CEO. However, up until 1988, the changes had arguably been mainly to do with a series of reconstructions, such as altering the GE infrastructure, working practices and political make-up.[10] Come 1988, Welch realised that if a genuine transformation was to be achieved, culture change was also needed, and this couldn't be delivered through restructuring. Therefore, the initial change effort was extended into the 1990s by a 10-year programme called 'Work-Out'. However, it would not have been possible to put Work-Out in place had GE not already been through a change which left it in a financially sound position and created a desire and commitment for change. GSK Pharma UK (see Illustration 2.2) is also an example of reconstruction (the creation of a single merged entity legally and structurally from two previous stand-alone entities) followed by an evolution (the development of a new integrated culture). More recently, this has been the change path taken at Fiat Auto. See Illustration 2.3. Marchionne, the CEO, has implemented a rapid reconstruction focusing on the cost base of the business whilst simultaneously paving the way for a more fundamental and longer-term cultural transformation of the business.

Existing examples of change therefore suggest that, dependent on the context of the organisation, it may be necessary to undertake an enabling realignment phase, either in the form of an adaptation or a reconstruction, before embarking on a longer-term transformation. Indeed, when organisations are underperforming badly, a rapid reconstruction focused on restoring profitability will be essential to the longer-term survival of the organisation and a necessary first step on the path to transformation. More will be said about this in Chapters 3 and 4. It may also be necessary, following a transformational change, to move to adaptation, to ensure that the changes are embedded throughout the organisation,[11] to sustain competitiveness. Subsequent reconstructions may also be needed. British Airways, for example, has been through a series of reconstructions in the 1990s and the early 2000s as it fights to remain a key player in the fiercely competitive airline industry. Similarly, earlier reconstruction might not be enough and may need to continue during attempts at transformation. At Unilever the shift to a more global integrated structure since 2005 (described in section 2.2.1) requires a transformation, but there has also been an on-going programme of cost reduction and product portfolio change since 1999. Staff numbers were reduced by 47,000 between 2004 and 2007. Half the senior leaders left the business between 2005 and 2006 because they did not fit the new mind-set. This process has recently been augmented with an announcement that Unilever is to axe another 20,000 staff, close up to a fifth of its factories and dispose of various businesses it no longer deems core or competitive. The aim is to reinvest in growth businesses.[12]

Illustration 2.3

Change paths: transforming Fiat

Sergio Marchionne took over as Fiat's Chief Executive in June 2004 (the fifth chief executive in three years). The Fiat Group had underperformed the industry since 1997, and come 2003, Fiat was losing the equivalent of £1 million a day.

Marchionne put in place a turnaround that involved selling non-core assets (such as the finance operations and the insurer, Toro Assicurazioni), cutting costs, paying off debt, and finding partners (such as Tata Motors) to help invest in products. The turnaround also involved the resolution of a dispute with former partner General Motors that netted Fiat £2 billion in February 2005.

As part of the cost cutting, factories were closed and senior managers were made redundant. A total of 210 managers lost their jobs, 30 per cent of the executive core. This move saved £86 million and the 300-person team overseeing cars, agricultural equipment and trucks was demolished. In all, by 2006, more than 12,000 jobs, mainly at Fiat Auto, had gone. Marchionne also fired the head of Fiat's auto unit in February 2005, taking the job himself and subsequently taking out most of the managers below him. Stopping the rot in the auto business was Marchionne's biggest challenge, since it had lost money for three years in a row by 2005. To complete the turnaround, many new and redesigned car models have been introduced. Future plans place the success of the turnaround on the new and redesigned Bravo and Punto.

The turnaround was also based on a culture change at Fiat. At the beginning of 2005 Marchionne said 'a profound cultural transformation is underway following a management reorganisation that has delivered a more agile & efficient structure'. Poorly performing executives used to be sent to work in more remote places rather than being sacked, and heavy central control from the HQ in Turin limited local initiative. There was a traditional command-and-control structure. Marchionne has brought in a tougher Anglo-American approach. The company now has leaner and flatter structures. Most top executives have been replaced and younger managers have been promoted. By 2006 the auto business had just 27 leaders, many below the age of 40. Marchionne has also brought in outsiders. He has aimed to introduce more freedom but also more responsibility.

By the end of 2006, not only had the steeply vertical management approach gone, so had other aspects of the culture. Executives no longer booked meetings via secretaries rather than walking to a fellow manager's office close by. Tie wearing is now optional. Marchionne himself wears pullovers instead of suits and has introduced his own touches such as playing Bach as a background track in lengthy brainstorming sessions. He holds management meetings on Saturdays and Sundays.

However, there is still more to be done. Marchionne intends to make Fiat one of the top-performing mass-market automakers by 2010. Fiat needs to close the gap against Toyota in terms of production quality and efficiency and match Toyota's world-class manufacturing standards. Marchionne said, 'We need to swallow hard, swallow our pride, and learn from others who do it better than we do. Speed, simplicity and self-confidence are key.'

Adapted from Sylevers, E. (2 March 2005) 'Losses narrow at Fiat as chief pursues turnaround', *The New York Times*. Mackintosh, J. (19 May 2006) 'Sergio Marchionne: moving into a higher gear', *F T.com*. Marchionne, S. (2006) 'The re-making of Fiat: remodelling the last chance saloon', *Speech to the Automotive News Europe Conference,* 20–22 June, Vienna, Austria. Hunston, H. (2006) 'Bravo Fiat!', *Institute of the Motor Industry Magazine,* December 2005. 'Fiat chief takes the steering wheel'. (18 February 2006) BBC News, Business. 'Fiat's turnaround takes root' (10 November 2006) *BusinessWeek.com*.

2.3 CHANGE START-POINT

Change start-point refers to where the change is initiated and developed, or rather the locus of control and influence. There are two main approaches – top-down or bottom-up. A more recent approach is through 'pockets of good practice'. In addition, whatever the start-point selected, change can also be implemented organisation-wide simultaneously, or more gradually via pilot sites.

2.3.1 Top-down change

Much of the prescriptive change literature has emphasised a top-down approach, in which the direction, control, and initiation of the changes come from the strategic apex of the organisation. It usually involves a programme of change determined and implemented by the top management or their representatives.

However, although top-down change is clearly driven by the top executives, this does not mean that a top-down change approach is never collaborative or participative. In top-down change initiatives, the plans developed can be via collaboration with senior managers, and a wider group of individuals within the organisation. IBM has recently used Internet discussion forums, known as 'Jams', to get input to top management strategic reviews from the wider IBM workforce. When conducting a review of the business in 2003, the senior managers used a 'ValuesJam' to get input from all employees on what they thought about the IBM values – as many as 50,000 logged on and joined the discussion over a three-day period. The jam discussions were then analysed by company analysts to distil the main themes and used to finalise a new set of IBM values.[13] Similarly, part of the selling of the plans can be to use employee participation in workshops to work out some of the details of implementation. The programme might also include a comprehensive programme of staff involvement through road shows or workshops.

Top-down change may have to be imposed in a directive or coercive manner, particularly in a crisis or turnaround situation where there may be no alternative but to deliver a short, sharp reconstruction. For example, when taking over as Chief Executive of the AA, the British motoring organisation, in September 2004, Tim Parker found an inefficient organisation with low levels of productivity and a declining membership. By 2006 he had laid off about 2,000 people (a quarter of the workforce) including middle managers, call centre staff and patrolmen. Operations that were not making money, such as the vehicle-inspection arm, had been sold off or closed down. New working-hour arrangements and pay deals were negotiated to encourage patrolmen to do the job rather than just work set hours. However, cost savings have also being used to invest in areas such as marketing to build membership and a new fleet of vehicles for patrolmen.[14] This directive form of top-down change design has the advantage of being speedy to implement. Staff can also feel that there is a clarity in the nature of the change, which can be an advantage at a time of uncertainty.

2.3.2 Bottom-up change

Emergent or bottom-up change has a very different starting point and logic compared to top-down change. Responsibility is passed downwards into the organisation to encourage ownership of the change process by employees, and to make change self-generating. This is partly because the assumption here is that responsibility for change should not just lie with the senior managers, but also because in certain change contexts, a top-down approach may not encourage the needed ownership and commitment to the required changes. Since bottom-up change is an emergent process, it can be much slower to mature than top-down change initiatives. Bottom-up change is also more unpredictable in its consequences as it is subject to interpretation and negotiation by the very staff who put the changes in place. Senior management have far less control over the process.

It is possible to combine a top-down approach with a bottom-up approach.[15] Advocates of this sort of approach argue that certain activities, such as mobilising support for change, may need to be done in a top-down way, whereas others, such as creating a vision for change, can be more participative. The leader of a change effort may be directive about the fact that the departments within a business unit must change to meet the aspirations of the vision. However, the leader then allows each department or section to choose the way in which they want to implement that vision, to ensure ownership and commitment. The changes that emerge within each department, and the new behaviours these changes engender, then need to be institutionalised and supported in the organisation through top-down actions, such as changes to organisation-wide systems and structures.

2.3.3 Pockets of good practice

The third approach, *pockets of good practice,* is less well known. Change is initiated in one part of an organisation by an individual or individuals within that department or division to, for example, take advantage of a new business opportunity, or to implement new best practice in terms of processes and systems. The department then becomes a pocket of good practice and provides a role model to the rest of the organisation.[16] Jewson, a timber and builder's merchant in the UK, have instituted pockets of good practice in their branch network, led by their managing director of operations. The BM2000 initiative was designed to achieve sharing of best practice across branches. The top 30 managers were brought together monthly for two days to enable sharing of experiences and ideas. Both in-house and external speakers would attend these events to discuss developments in other areas of the business and particular topics. Many changes have been implemented through the group, such as improved transport efficiency and flexible working.[17] This example illustrates how individuals can create best practice in their part of the organisation that will encourage other parts of the organisation to do something similar, due to improved performance and the corporate reputation this then earns them.

There are certain situations where this type of change approach can work well. This would not be a style to use to initiate rapid organisation-wide change. However, when an organisation is in a phase of incremental change, allowing managers to use their judgement to develop on-going change initiatives may be a useful way of delivering self-sustaining continuous improvement in organisational practices. It may also be a useful approach in organisations where change management expertise is patchy, or it is hard to gain buy-in to organisation-wide change. A danger is that this type of change will only lead to further organisational change if the practices established by the individuals concerned are then copied by others.

2.3.4 Pilot sites

Whichever approach is selected, this can be combined with an organisation-wide approach to change, or change based on *pilot sites* as the start-point. This may initially involve implementing change in just one department or division, or it may involve using a new start-up site. The advantages of pilot sites are many:

- It is possible to test out the impact of new systems and procedures, and iron out any unforeseen faults or problems before the changes are made throughout the organisation. It is also possible to identify and rectify potential and actual problems and weaknesses with the accompanying change management interventions, such as training and communication.

- A successful pilot can be used to mobilise awareness of the need for change and support for the changes in an environment where change awareness is low.

- Pilot sites followed by a gradual roll-out programme reduce the amount of change management expertise and resources needed at any one time. A change team can move from site to site.

For these reasons, there are certain contexts that lend themselves to pilot sites. Organisations that are geographically dispersed, with many similar operations in different locations, such as retailers, are an obvious candidate for change implemented on a site-by-site basis. A pilot at one or a few site(s) can be improved and replicated for subsequent sites. Jobcentre Plus, for example, was created by the Department of Work and Pensions in the UK in 2002 by merging the Benefits Agency with the Employment Service to improve and integrate benefits payment and job seeking. This required not just the integration in many towns of two offices and sets of staff, but also a rebrand and a refurbishment of integrated centres and a culture change process to create integrated teams and changes to ways of interacting with job/benefit seekers. It was a £750 million programme involving 1,000 offices that started with an initial group of 'pathfinder' offices and was then rolled out on an office-by-office basis between 2002 and 2006.[18] Large, global organisations may have many different manufacturing sites, for example, or many local country sales and marketing divisions which are best dealt with individually as part of an on-going change programme. Both large public and private sector organisations may also have multiple call centres or processing units where, again, change can be introduced at one site to try a new approach before a more general roll-out.

Pilot schemes can also be used in other ways. They can be used to implement a rolling series of change initiatives in one site or to introduce new ways of working on a department-by-department basis. Another option is to use a pilot project, as opposed to a pilot site, to develop new ways of working that can be adopted on a more general basis. Illustration 2.4 describes the way Clerical Medical Investment Group used a pilot approach to develop a new sales model. Here the

---

Illustration 2.4   *change in action*

Implementing change through a pilot at CMIG

Clerical Medical Investment Group (CMIG) is part of the HBOS Group (Halifax Bank of Scotland), and competes in the life insurance sector. Following its acquisition by HBOS in 1997, a business transformation was initiated in 1998 to position CMIG as a top-five IFA (independent financial adviser) provider. The main objectives of the transformation were to change the nature of relationships with IFAs through shifting the sales model from product push to relationship building; to improve customer service standards to be in line with a top-five IFA provider; and also to introduce efficiency to reduce unit costs by 2003 in real terms.

Customer Relationship Management (CRM) was the key business transformation programme for the core business. It emerged out of discussion within the sales and marketing planning group in May 1997. CMIG was a 'product pusher' like everyone else in the market at that time. *'We went out to IFAs and said "use our widget because it's better than someone else's widget because it's got three yellow dots on it." Looking forward then, with government intervention in our business, we saw reduced margins, then products were starting to become simpler, so the ability to differentiate around*

products would become more and more difficult' (Senior Managers). They were convinced that CMIG had to 'differentiate in a way that was difficult to copy' rather than merely grow based on price. The intent was to build long-term, mutually beneficial relationships with targeted IFAs (those identified as having the most potential for a profitable relationship), so that CMIG could grow its business by helping the IFAs to grow theirs. The aim was to achieve this by shifting to the provision of value-added services to IFAs rather than just pushing products. This required a shift in emphasis of the sales force and the creation of linked sales/administration teams providing support to particular IFAs.

The sales and marketing director with senior and middle management colleagues designed a vision of how to do business in terms of value-added services. They then set up a pilot project team as a first step to implementation. The team was divided into work streams whose job it was to flesh out the vision in terms of the sales process, the customer service, the training needs, and the behavioural change needed. Four sales managers and four sales consultants from four different parts of the country were involved in the pilot, along with five selected IFA organisations in each of the four areas. Team members were chosen because they were influential within the business – they were either very cynical or very enthusiastic about the idea, but all were 'opinion formers in the sales force'. The pilot tried and tested various initiatives with these IFAs over a period of about 9–12 months. A pilot team was also put into the customer service division to support the aim of creating linked sales/administration teams as part of CRM.

The pilot was very successful. Therefore, the CRM programme developed from it was rolled out across the whole sales force through a training programme designed by the pilot project team. Other changes were needed to support the new ways of working and the new behaviours across the whole organisation. For instance, the bonus scheme needed to be aligned, the performance management system upgraded, and the contact systems redesigned. In addition, senior managers supported the delivery of CRM. There wasn't a newsletter, or a meeting with managers, where CRM wasn't talked about and given priority.

Adapted from Balogun, J., Camm, G., Collier, N. and Hope Hailey, V. (2002) *Clerical Medical Investment Group: A Case of Business Transformation*.

pilot approach was partially politically motivated: the aim was to get key opinion leaders on side.

There are also disadvantages to pilot sites:

● Each site and department involved in an implementation may be different. Changes made to the implementation approach to mitigate against the problems identified in one site may not be suitable for another site.

● The time it takes to run a pilot may give opponents of change more time to build their resistance, particularly if there is not a strong and powerful backer of the changes. The approach used at Clerical Medical was designed to avoid this by engaging key influencers in the pilot project.

● The use of pilot sites creates a prolonged period of change, and therefore uncertainty for staff, and the need for the use of parallel systems and processes for the organisation.

● Organisations have found it difficult to transfer changes made at new Greenfield sites to existing sites and departments.

2.4 CHANGE STYLE

The style of change is to do with issues about how the process of change is managed. There are many classifications of management styles during change, but broadly speaking, change styles can be seen as sitting on a continuum from coercion, in which change is forced on people, to education and delegation, in which change is delegated. (See Figure 2.4.)

Figure 2.4	Styles of managing change

STYLE	DESCRIPTION	ADVANTAGES	DISADVANTAGES
Education and delegation	Use small group briefings to discuss things with people and explain things to them. The aim is to gain support for change by generating understanding and commitment.	Spreads support for change. Also ensures a wide base of understanding.	Takes a long time. If radical change is needed, fact-based argument and logic may not be enough to convince others of need for change. Easy to voice support, then walk away and do nothing.
Collaboration	Widespread involvement of the employees on decisions about what and how to change.	Spreads not only support but ownership of change by increasing levels of involvement.	Time consuming. Little control over decisions made. May lead to change within paradigm.
Participation	Involvement of employees in how to deliver the desired changes. May also include limited collaboration over aspects of the 'how' to change as opposed to the 'what' of change.	Again, spreads ownership and support for change, but within a more controlled framework. Easier to shape decisions.	Can be perceived as manipulation.
Direction	Change leaders make the majority of decisions about what to change and how. Use of authority to direct change.	Less time consuming. Provides a clear change direction and focus.	Potentially less support and commitment, and therefore proposed changes may be resisted.
Coercion	Use of power to impose change.	Allows for prompt action.	Unlikely to achieve buy-in without a crisis.

2.4.1 Education and delegation

Education and delegation involves convincing employees of the need for change through means such as training, gaining their commitment and support for change, and then delegating change to them. This may involve more than just talking to employees. It could involve, for example, sending managers on benchmarking visits to other organisations to learn how things could be done better and then expecting the managers to implement the ideas and opportunities they identify. The change process at Lufthansa (see Illustration 2.9 below) describes this style of delivering change through the 'Explorer 21' network and the 'Climb 99' initiative. The 'Samurai of Change' group was also developed from an education and delegation intervention in the form of a four-week change management training course.

This change style is easily confused with collaboration and participation. However, education and delegation is more to do with equipping employees with an understanding, and then encouraging them to use their learning to propose and implement change projects supportive of the organisational change goals. However, there are problems with this style of leading change:

- It can be difficult to generate commitment to action from it. Workshops and seminars can be seen as an interesting exercise, and fun to do, but change will only occur if a series of explicit actions are identified and carried out.

- It can be necessary to inject some energy, emotion and direction into the process. Otherwise, an awareness of the need for change may be developed, but this awareness will not translate into a commitment to doing something about it, especially if there is no onus on senior managers to take note of ideas that arise and act on them.

- It can be very time consuming and costly if there are large numbers of employees to be convinced. A multinational company operating in many different countries with maybe thousands of employees could find such an approach difficult to undertake.

2.4.2 Collaboration

In collaboration, there is widespread involvement of employees in both what to change, and how to deliver the needed changes. Employees are asked to contribute to both the goals set for change and the means of achieving those goals. This may be through participative face-to-face meetings, such as workshops or focus groups in which, for example, consultants introduce participants to analytical tools and frameworks that can provide new insights on the participants' business and lead to identification of the critical change issues and an explicit consideration of actions to be taken, and by whom. The principle behind collaboration is that the more employees are involved, the more likely they are to support and be committed to the changes that they have helped design, and the more likely they also are to sell those changes to others in the organisation. In other words, collaboration can be used to bypass resistance. Furthermore, collaboration can be used not only to determine what to change and how, but also to create an awareness of the need for change by challenging complacency within the organisation.

However, collaboration does not have to involve face-to-face situations, as the example of IBM and their 'ValuesJam' shows (see section 2.3.1 above). In organisations where employees are widespread, face-to-face collaboration is difficult. Faced with this problem, and a change-resistant group of middle to senior managers, UNHCR, the international aid organisation, used a collaborative technique called Project Delphi to reach beyond these managers and get involvement from a broad group of staff in a review of the UNHCR operations. To deal with rapid growth in the 1990s and be seen as well managed in order to maintain a flow of funds to cover the work of UNHCR, the head office needed to become less bureaucratic, and more responsive to the needs of the field. Staff everywhere were asked to hold a Delphi Day to brainstorm in small groups about how their work could be changed to improve the way UNHCR worked. A total of 2,200 ideas were collected from 100 Delphi groups in over 118 country offices and distilled into a change plan.[19]

Collaboration can be a good management style to use when dealing with professionals, such as hospital clinicians, or even academics, who value the freedom and autonomy they normally have in their work. Such groups of people are likely to rebel against more directive interventions, which they perceive to limit their autonomy and their right to have a say in their future. In addition, well-educated, highly professional workforces are increasingly less likely to respond to top-down direction and imposition without an obvious change crisis, which is why IBM used the ValuesJam approach. However:

- Collaboration can be time consuming, and is therefore not a technique to use in a crisis situation.

- Employees may not come up with the suggestions or ideas wanted by senior managers, so there is a loss of control.

- If employees are consulted and then ignored, this will do more harm than good, as it can raise expectations about what it is possible to achieve. The employees will feel devalued, and perceive the senior managers to be practising tokenism in respect of collaboration.

- The ideas offered by existing employees could be within the existing way of thinking, or the existing organisational paradigm, and the existing way of working within the organisation. This could stifle creativity and transformational change. Some organisations use external facilitators and consultants to challenge ideas and thinking in order to overcome this problem.

Illustration 2.5 shows what can happen to a change initiative that is collaborative/participative in intent, but it becomes time consuming, and creates tensions between different parts of the organisation whose interests are compromised during the process. Good intent is then overtaken by the need for rapid change.

Illustration 2.5

From collaboration to direction

The ViZieR project was started in 2002 following the merger of seven previous organisations into one administrative organisation for the Dutch employee benefit regulations. It was a project intended to deliver provisions purchasing reintegration. The aim was to create a new organisation unit by September 2003. What was needed was a redesign of the work processes and administrative systems since the seven legacy organisations all did things differently. Since management were keen to engage people in the design and implementation process, they adopted a collaborative change model. This model had a '*project strand*' to deliver the hard deliverables such as systems, and a simultaneous '*change strand*' to feed the project strand with the information and ideas to develop the new work processes and systems.

First there was to be a diagnostic phase with conferences in the change strand to develop the design outline and the subprojects required in a collaborative manner. The project strand would then staff and run these projects. During the design phase there were to be mini-conferences in the change strand to examine the work of the subprojects and finalise the design. In the pilot phase the change and project strands were to work more closely together with workshops to assess the effectiveness of the pilots and finalise implementation plans. Then in the implementation phase, there were to be joint evaluation and information meetings.

As planned, three large conferences took place at the beginning of January 2003 to gain widespread participation. However, at these events senior managers set some parameters, specifying parts of the design. Furthermore, one of the two departments involved became concerned that too much of their work would be transferred to the other department. This problem slowed down the work in the change strand, and top management intervened to keep the project moving forwards. A consultant was appointed to take things forwards.

The consultant introduced a project methodology and put the emphasis on the project strand, kicking off the subprojects required. The outcomes of this work were still presented at mini-conferences to the wider staff group as originally planned, but the purpose of the mini-conferences was changed. The emphasis was not on dialogue and collaboration. Instead, the mini-conferences were used more as a means of consultation, with staff asked to comment on the plans. Senior managers also said they wanted results quickly. Gradually, therefore, the change strand and the planned collaboration disappeared as the senior managers took more decisions to keep the project on track. Staff were still given the chance to comment on two pilot schemes, but come June 2003, it was announced that the ViZieR project was at an end. The new work processes were to be implemented in a top-down and directive manner. Surveys revealed that the early collaborative approach built trust and confidence that then evaporated once top management intervened and adopted a directive approach. However, the senior management interventions did mean that the goals of the project strand were achieved and that new systems and procedures were introduced as planned.

Adapted from Sminia, H. and Van Nistelrooij, A. (2006) 'Strategic management and organization development: planned change in a public sector organization', *Journal of Change Management,* 6 (1), pp. 99–113.

2.4.3 Participation

Participation is limited collaboration. The principle that involvement will equal greater commitment still justifies this approach to change. However, employees are allowed only limited involvement in certain areas of change, such as *how* the desired changes can be achieved. For example, employees may be told of the overall vision and change goals for a firm, such as to achieve greater efficiency, greater productivity, and to eliminate waste. They can then be asked to think about what they need to do differently if they are going to help to deliver that vision. GSK UK used participation to get involvement in the development of the future culture post-merger through both the employee postcards exercise and the employee lunchtime seminars. (See Illustration 2.2 above.)

Participation can also be a particularly good approach to use when there is a group of high-energy or more enthusiastic change adopters who can be brought into the change process. Kraft Foods UK used participation to good effect when putting in place a change programme in 2006. One of the change initiatives was to make the organisation a more fun place to work again. The recent intake of graduates were involved in this initiative and charged with developing a rolling programme of events for 2006 which would get all employees involved. (See Illustration 6.3, Chapter 6.)

Alternatively, employees may be asked to contribute to the design and delivery of specific tasks which will assist the overall change process. A series of working parties may be set up to address issues, from new working practices to communications. In some change initiatives, the participation is literally limited to consultation. Members of the change design team may hold workshops to tell staff of the change ideas being proposed and ask their opinion as a form of input to the process, but this is more a process of keeping staff informed and asking for their approval, than actively seeking input.

Obviously, the participation management style enables the change leaders to retain greater control over the outcome of the change process, as they are setting the overall goals if not the means of achieving the goals. Unfortunately, it may be seen by employees as a type of manipulation, an attempt to pay lip-service to employee involvement, particularly if participation is limited, or employees are told what outcome is expected from a workshop, or whatever type of forum is used to achieve their participation. Participation can also be a time-consuming way of delivering change, although less so than collaboration.

2.4.4 Direction

When those leading change make the majority of decisions about what to change and how, and use their authority to *direct* the achievement of change, this is a management style of direction. This approach effectively separates the thinkers from the doers. The thinkers come up with the change ideas and 'sell' them to the doers, who are then supposed to implement these plans and the ideas. There may still be an attempt to sell the changes to the employees, to encourage them to buy into the changes and support them. There can still be an extensive communication effort in which employees are involved in workshops to debate the implications of change for themselves. However, employees are not invited to contribute to the goals or means of change, except in a limited way. Many turnarounds, for example, involve this style of change. Marchionne used direction to effect turn-around at Fiat (see Illustration 2.3), as did Rose at M&S (see Illustration 2.1), and Tim Parker at the AA (see section 2.3.1).

The advantages of this approach are that it is easier to retain control over the direction and content of change, and decision making is faster than it would be under a style which involves consultation. Thus many organisations requiring a rapid change use this style. However, even when rapid change is required, it may not be possible for those leading change to impose it. For example, partners leading change in a partnership organisation have no power to impose change on other partners. They may have no choice but to rely on a collaborative approach that triggers questioning and challenging of the status quo, such as workshops and feedback, to encourage others to recognise and agree to the need for change. Once the partnership generally have agreed on the need for change, it may be possible to be directive with others in the organisation. This illustrates that the context determines the type of style that is likely to be effec-tive, and that the approach may be different for different groups of staff. Other features of the organisational context may also lead organisations to use this style (see Chapters 3 and 4). The disadvantages of direction are that:

- The lack of employee consultation and involvement might create more resist-ance to the proposed changes. As a change style, it is more likely to be suitable in an organisation which is either in crisis, or in which there is a widespread awareness of the need for change.

- An imposed change process may result in impressive rhetoric within an organi-sation, with little change in actual behaviour or job and ultimately organisational performance. Staff may find it easy to repeat the language of the change process without really embracing the change at an emotional or behavioural level.[20]

2.4.5 Coercion

Coercion is an extension of direction. Here change is imposed on staff, rather than staff having the idea of change sold to them. It is a way of achieving rapid change, but as with direction, it may lead to greater resistance. Given the lack of effort devoted to explaining the need for change to staff, or to encouraging buy-in for the changes, this approach is unlikely to work unless there is a very *real* crisis that is felt by most staff within the organisation. However, unless the coercion is such that all aspects of behavioural change can be enforced in some way, the result may still be lip-service to the changes rather than actual change.

2.5 CHANGE TARGET

An important design choice requiring consideration is the different organisational levels at which to intervene. Some change processes concentrate on attempting to change the values of employees, others emphasise behavioural change, whilst others may only seek to change the performance objectives or outputs of employees.

2.5.1 Outputs

Change can focus on changing the nature of outputs or performance objectives to in turn trigger a change in behaviours. The target is the *outcome* of what people do in terms of managerially determined outputs or objectives, for example, profit margins, hourly sales levels, levels of customer response. This usually involves the redesign of performance measures, such as rewards and control systems.

A focus on outputs is useful when high levels of autonomy are required. Individual, national or functional business divisions may require a degree of independence from the parent corporation in order to manage the change in a way that is appropriate to their specific country's context or the nature of their staff. Alternatively, autonomy may be required by individual staff themselves as in the case of doctors or consultants or city traders. For example, an investment bank will employ many traders to make their financial deals for them. These traders are usually highly self-motivated and skilled, valuing the independence and autonomy in their jobs. Their primary motivation, and performance measure, is the achievement of their commercial targets and the high financial bonuses this earns them. Therefore, in any change situation, changing these measures and rewards is likely to be a more suitable target and effective intervention, than any attempt to prescribe their behaviours. The traders would not feel their autonomy was under threat.

A focus on outputs is also appropriate when rapid performance improvements are needed, such as at M&S under Rose. If an organisation is in *crisis* and needs to effect a rapid reconstruction, then there will have to be financial outcome measures such as profitability, levels of debt or stock levels. The desired outcomes might also include hard measures to do with internal efficiency, such as cost reduction, which in turn may be associated with targets such as staff reductions, levels of waste, and cycle times. Furthermore, there is evidence that results-driven programmes, which focus on achieving specific, measurable, operational improvements within a short time frame in order to help achieve specific organisational goals, can yield considerable benefits.[21] The achievement of such goals will also provide visible early wins in the change process.

However, care needs to be taken when targeting outputs. In one organisation, call centre staff were told to keep potential customers talking for two minutes once they reached them by phone, as the call centre staff were then more likely to make a sale. There were soon many complaints from customers about the two-minute messages left on their answering machines. Such stories are common-place: staff change their behaviours to meet the new performance metrics, potentially in ways other than intended. This has been a particular debate in the UK as part of public sector service reform where use of league tables and per-formance targets has become common. For example, Accident and Emergency units have recently had their government waiting targets moved from seeing 90 per cent of patients within four hours to seeing 98 per cent of patients within four hours. A recent British Medical Association survey of medical staff found that a third of doctors believed A&E data was being manipulated to ensure government targets were met, while 66 per cent of medical staff stated that patients may be moved to inappropriate areas of the hospital to meet waiting targets.[22] In other words, activities elsewhere were being distorted to deliver against the targets.

This doesn't mean that measures shouldn't be set as part of a change process. The warning is that hard output performance targets alone are often inadequate to achieve desired change outcomes. Furthermore, simplistic measures such as levels of absence may be measuring levels of fear rather than levels of motivation, and may be masking problems. Other, more qualitative measures are often still needed to support and reinforce other interventions. Change outputs can, for example, be used to describe the behaviours required of people, how the behav-iours of staff need to change on a day-to-day basis, and the types of outputs they are expected to produce in the future. Such more qualitative measures are impor-tant because they enable the change agent to devise ways to communicate to staff what is required of them, to develop suitable training interventions and to assess whether the desired change outcomes are occurring.

2.5.2 Behaviours

An alternative approach is to focus primarily on enforcing new behaviours. Those that support this view argue that the individual can only change if the organisational system in which the individual operates is changed. Figure 2.5 summarises this argument.

Programmatic change targets individual attitude change to effect behaviour change.[23] The underlying principle of this approach is that ways of behaving are underpinned by individual attitudes and beliefs. So change should be aimed at individuals and their attitudes. Yet individual behaviour is constrained by the organisational system in which individuals work. Roles and responsibilities, and existing ways of working, force particular behaviours onto individuals if they are to function effectively in an organisation. If individuals learn new attitudes, but are then returned to the old organisational system, they will not be able to

Figure 2.5   **Attitudes versus behaviours**

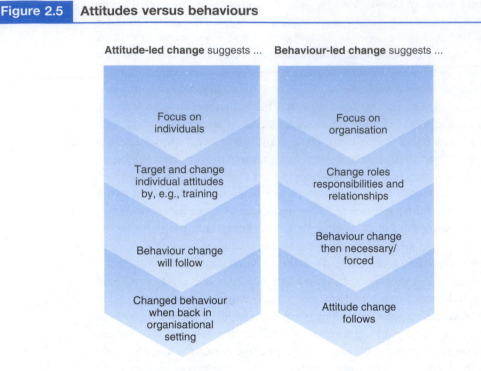

practice the new ways of behaving that accompany their new attitudes. If instead the organisational system is changed (task alignment), and individuals are placed in job roles with different responsibilities and different relationships to their peers, subordinates and superiors, this will force them to behave differently, and ultimately to think differently, leading to a change in attitudes.

A focus on work-based behaviours can therefore be used to effect behavioural and accompanying attitude change and maybe, ultimately, value change.[24] Illustration 2.6 describes how training programmes focusing on behaviours were used as the target at the Forestry Commission in the UK with the intent of ultimately affecting the central values, assumptions and beliefs of the organisation.

Behaviours may also be targeted for other reasons:

- Behaviours are an appropriate target in changes involving reconstruction or realignment, which require some degree of behavioural adjustment without a fundamental change in the shared organisational values or beliefs.

- The prescription of behaviours may be useful in service outlets such as McDonald's where routinised procedures ensure quality of delivery or product.

- In a crisis situation where there is little time, the enforcement of behavioural change may be an appropriate initial intervention, since value change can take a long while to develop.

Illustration 2.6

Implementing change at the Forestry Commission of Great Britain

David Bills was appointed Director General of the Forestry Commission (FC) at the end of 1995. He found an organisation low in morale after years of bruising change. The FC was created in 1919 following the first world war to combat deforestation by rebuilding and maintaining future timber reserves. It was renowned for its expertise in forestry. The staff were forestry experts whose business was timber production, organised in a hierarchical and military fashion with 'District Officers' who wore uniforms and issued orders through a 'chain of command'.

Things changed in the second half of the twentieth century. Mechanisation increased productivity and there was a growing awareness of conservation issues. Also, come the 1990s, there was government pressure for public sector reform including greater efficiency. In 1994 the FC embarked on an efficiency drive leading to redundancies in field staff, and therefore increased pressure on the remaining staff, as forest districts were combined, working processes were simplified, new labour-saving machinery was introduced and other work was outsourced. However, more fundamental change was needed. The FC needed to become an organisation that could balance commercial enterprise with social responsibilities such as public access to forests for health and recreation. It had to move from an organisation that thought about the trees in a forest to one that thought about the spaces between the trees to make a forest work socially and environmentally.

Bills knew he had to start by slimming down the organisation, but as part of this he was able to change the executive team, creating a coalition more able and willing to lead change. Yet Bills also knew he needed to improve the leadership capabilities of 250 senior and middle managers. He appointed a steering group to develop a brief and select an external partner for what was in reality a culture change process. The steering group and the consultants jointly designed a three-day leadership event to make managers more aware of why change was needed and to explore the organisation culture and how their own behaviour impacted this culture and needed to change. The workshops ran throughout 2001 and using the cultural web (see Illustration 2.8), developed specific implementation recommendations. David Bills and his team went through the workshop themselves and regularly attended many of the other workshops. In addition, 'Connect' workshops were developed for all staff to improve two-way communication and initiate local actions to support the required changes. Groups were encouraged to work on a plan of action they could take back to their local managers for implementation. These workshops were voluntary, but 40 workshops were held and 1,600 people of all grades attended during 2001.

A review of the feedback from the leadership events and workshops revealed the need for more to be done to sustain and deepen the momentum of change. New values were developed for the FC: teamwork, professionalism, respect, communication, learning and creativity. To support the implementation of these values, a new programme was developed to target behaviours. Again, the programme was designed by the consultants with the aid of a steering group. Case studies of fictitious but archetypal FC characters were developed. Actors were brought into the three-day programme to help people put the characters into real-life scenarios as described by the new desired culture, and then work through the scenarios and the outcomes the characters brought on themselves through their behaviours. The delegates were able to reflect on and discuss the situations the characters found themselves in due to their habitual attitudes and behaviours and how these behaviours (and, by inference, the delegates' own behaviours) needed to change. These workshops were attended by 400 senior and middle managers and supervisors by March 2004. Through these events the delegates were able to move from talking about culture to talking about real behaviours. Interviews within the districts revealed that real behavioural change had occurred.

Adapted from McCann, A. (2005) 'The Forestry Commission: cultural change to deliver a new strategy', in *Exploring Corporate Strategy*, 7th edn, Johnson, G., Scholes, K. and Whittington, R. (eds) Prentice Hall.

2.5.3 Values

Interest in values as a lever for change was particularly strong in the 1980s, associated as it was with developments in human resource management and the increasing popularity of culture change programmes.[25] In the 1980s, the belief was that if employees could be made to adhere to a predetermined set of corporate values, they could then be given licence to innovate freely. In other words, by prescribing shared values, appropriate employee behaviour would emerge in such a way that there would be less need for bureaucratic rules and regulations. Appropriate values would drive appropriate behaviour, thus reducing the need for other types of managerial controls on employees.

However, the evidence shows that this approach can be fraught with difficulty in certain organisational contexts:

- Many espoused value statements are devalued in employee eyes if these are not reflected in changed behaviours, particularly from senior managers. So values such as 'individuality' or 'people are our greatest asset' quickly became relegated to meaningless slogans in many companies.[26]

- An emphasis on managing values may lead to staff feeling manipulated or brainwashed, which can result in cynicism about the values themselves.

- The acknowledgement of all kinds of diversity within organisations may undermine the attainment of a common set of values. In hospitals, for example, there are consultants, nurses and managers, each with their own professional allegiances, and different professional values, identities and motivations. Can common values be achieved across such diverse professional and occupational groups, or for that matter, different national cultures or business divisions?

In addition, some organisations feel that the dividing line between organisational values and individual values is hard to define. They therefore feel uncomfortable with this level of intervention, and question the legitimacy of trying to alter something as personal to an individual as their set of values. Yet if an organisation needs to achieve fundamental, transformational change, this by its very nature requires a change in the assumptions and beliefs shared by the organisation's employees. This was why IBM kicked off their ValuesJam in 2003 (see section 2.3.1 above). The CEO, Sam Palmisano, did not see a new organisation structure as the solution to creating a more integrated workforce that matched the reintegration of the industry. What was needed was a common set of simple guidelines that were meaningful across a large, global organisation and that could then drive appropriate behaviours. Therefore, there are circumstances where targeting values, or if not values, the shared assumptions and beliefs, is appropriate.

Yet value change is a difficult thing to achieve, and targeting values is not the same as putting up value statement posters or issuing pocket-sized cards with the values printed on them. Unfortunately, however, many organisations do believe that to get values change, the development of a communication package around a set of new values is sufficient. See Illustration 2.7, which describes a fairly typical approach to values change. This organisation not only did not follow through on

---

Illustration 2.7

change in action

When targeting values doesn't lead to change

Technocom (TC), a Scandinavian company, was created as a stand-alone entity from its parent organisation in 2001. TC produced sophisticated systems and applications for its parent company and had the potential to market its applications to other companies. Given its origins, TC was research-oriented with an engineering-led project culture that placed importance on technological advancement rather than delivering a quality product on time, to budget. It was decided to launch a culture change to address the perceived lack of market/customer orientation.

TC hired consultants to help with the culture change project. One of these ran a series of culture workshops with 80 senior managers to form an agenda for the culture change programme. The workshops engaged in activities such as SWOT analyses and looked at leadership behaviours as well as other aspects of the organisation. A target culture was developed at the end of the workshops by the consultant and the Chief Technical Officer (CTO). However, the consultants were not retained and responsibility for the programme was passed to HR. They refined the target culture to consist of a 'winning culture' with three business drivers (excellent customer relationships, magnificent technology, powerful teamwork) and five shared values: our way of working: commitment; leadership: trust and inspiration; communications: openness; decision making and rewards: empowerment; organisation structure and teamwork: clarity. Each value had attached to it a number of winning behaviours. A communications package, or 'culture kit', was developed with a brochure, individual and group exercises, and a video of the CTO explaining the new vision.

The culture change was launched at a management meeting in February 2002. The next step of the process was a series of workshops for all employees in February and March, run by junior managers using the cultural kit and based on the knowledge they had gained from the launch meeting. The purpose of the workshops was to encourage employees to consider how their behaviour needed to change if the new culture was to be incorporated. Feedback was to be collected from the workshops and passed on to the senior managers so that the organisation could identify the behaviours that it should stop, keep and change. The feedback was to be presented at a follow-up event.

However, there was never any certainty about how many of the junior managers ran the workshops they were supposed to run. There were no sanctions against those that didn't. Furthermore, action plans that resulted from the workshops that were run were not followed up by the senior managers. In addition, the programme involved no changes supporting performance management systems, work practices and environment, or leadership behaviours. As a result, the culture change programme had very little impact on the organisation. The CTO subsequently claimed that the purpose of the culture change programme was more to do with creating an inspiration for rethinking than to achieve anything concrete.

Adapted from Alvesson, M. and Sveningsson, S. (2007) *Changing Organizational Culture: Cultural Change Work in Practice*, Routledge.

their planned programme, but as is so often the case, the managers didn't put in place any changes supporting performance management systems, work practices and environment, or leadership behaviours. Change through a focus on employee values requires an intensive focus on personal development programmes supported by organisation-wide change. This is discussed next in section 2.6.

2.6 CHANGE LEVERS

One of the issues facing any change agent is the range of levers and interventions to use. Organisations are composed of a number of interconnected and interdependent parts or subsystems, and are most effective when the major components are in alignment with each other, just like a car engine. Given the interdependency of these subsystems, it is difficult to change one part in isolation. Either other parts of the organisation with which the changed part interconnects will counteract the effect of the change, or the change made will force domino change effects, maybe unforeseen, in the other parts of the organisation. Readers who have read *Exploring Corporate Strategy* will be familiar with one tool based on these principles – the cultural web shown in Figure 2.6.[27] The web models organisations through six interlinked and interdependent subsystems all interconnected with the paradigm.

The cultural web provides organisations with a way of auditing their organisation's culture, and the barriers to change it presents. It is also possible to use the web to build an outline vision for a desired new organisation. A comparison of the

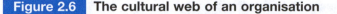

Figure 2.6   The cultural web of an organisation

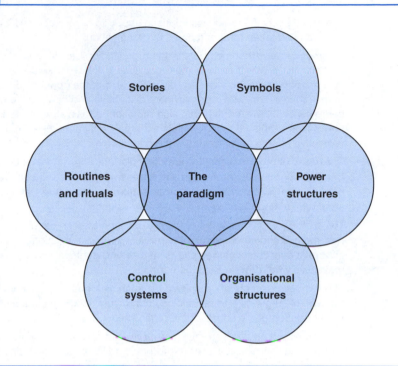

Source: Adapted from Johnson, G. (1998) 'Mapping and re-mapping organisational culture', in *Exploring Techniques of Analysis and Evaluation in Strategic Management*, Ambrosini, V., Johnson, G. and Scholes, K. (eds) Hemel Hempstead: Prentice Hall. Reproduced with permission.

new and old webs gives managers a feel for the extent of change to be under-taken. For those not familiar with the web, Table 2.1 provides an explanation of the different elements.[28] As with other such frameworks, it is suggested that to achieve effective change, it is necessary to use interventions in all parts of the web. Transformational change initiatives, requiring a change in the shared assumptions and beliefs, in particular, are more likely to fail if change prac-titioners apply a change recipe which concentrates on the use of a range of levers and mechanisms from just one or two of the subsystems that make up the whole. This will be particularly true if these changes are introduced in isolation without considering how they link together to form a coherent change strategy. Consideration should be given to both hard aspects, such as structures and sys-tems, and the softer aspects, such as symbolism and communication.[29]

Illustration 2.8 shows completed present and future webs for the Forestry Commission of Great Britain. The juxtaposition of the current and future webs next to each other shows the extent of change that was required at the Forestry Commission if the strategic changes discussed in Illustration 2.6 were to be delivered. Their new paradigm shows that there was a need to transform the organisation from a top-down, hierarchical, task-driven and conservative bureaucracy, into a more outwards-looking, innovative and influential orga-nisation. In order to support this transformation, the organisation structure

Table 2.1	Elements of the cultural web

- The *paradigm* is the set of assumptions about an organisation which are held in common and taken for granted in that organisation.

- The *routine* ways that members of the organisation behave towards each other, and that link different parts of the organisation. These make up 'the way we do things around here' on a day-to-day basis, and at their best lubricate the working of the organisation, and may provide a distinctive and beneficial organisational competency. However, they can also represent a taken-for-grantedness about how things should happen, which is extremely difficult to change and highly protective of core assumptions in the paradigm.

- The *rituals* of organisational life are particular activities and events, such as training programmes, promotion and assessment, and sales conferences, which point to what is important in the organisation, reinforce 'the way we do things around here' and signal what is especially valued.

- The *stories* told by members of the organisation to each other, to outsiders, to new recruits and so on, embed the present in its organisational history and flag important events (successes and disasters) and personalities (heroes and mavericks who 'deviate from the norm').

- The *symbolic* aspects of organisations, such as logos, offices, cars and titles, or the type of language and terminology commonly used, become a short-hand representation of the nature of the organisation.

- The formalized *control systems*, measurements and reward systems that monitor and therefore emphasise what is important in the organisation, and focus attention and activity.

- The *power structures* are also likely to be associated with the key assumptions of the paradigm. The most powerful managerial groupings in the organisation are likely to be the ones most associated with core assumptions and beliefs about what is important.

- The *organisational structure* is likely to reflect power structures and delineate important roles and relationships, again emphasising what is important in the organisation.

Source: Adapted from Johnson, G. (1998) 'Mapping and re-mapping organizational culture', in *Exploring Techniques of Analysis and Evaluation in Strategic Management*, Ambrosini, V., Johnson, G. and Scholes, K. (eds) Hemel Hempstead: Prentice Hall. Reproduced with permission.

and control systems would have to change, but new ways of working and managing would also have to be introduced (rituals and routines), and new symbols and stories would have to replace the old ones reminiscent of the organisation's history.

For simplicity's sake, this book reduces the six subsystems in the web to three: a *technical* subsystem to do with organisation structures and control systems; a *political* subsystem to do with both formal and informal power structures; and a *cultural* subsystem to do with symbols, stories, and routines and rituals. However, Illustrations 2.6 and 2.8 show that there is a fourth subsystem of change levers to consider: the *interpersonal* to do with communication, training, education and personal development. This fourth subsystem is necessary as all forms of change typically require some level of communication and training, which cannot be captured in the technical, political and cultural subsystems.

Not all changes require a fundamental realignment of all subsystems. A change that only involves adaptation, or maybe even reconstruction, will not necessitate a fundamental shift in the paradigm. It is also likely that earlier decisions about design choices will determine what range of levers should be used. There is a link between the range of levers and mechanisms to use and the change target, as illustrated in Figure 2.7:

- If the target is *change outcomes* then it is likely that this can be achieved by changing rewards and performance measures and targets, particularly since this is only likely to be an appropriate intervention target if existing values remain appropriate.

- If the target is *change behaviours* then this is about putting in place interventions to do with organisation structure (particularly roles and responsibilities), performance management, control systems to support and measure the behavioural changes occurring, and supportive training.

- If the target is *change values or assumptions and beliefs,* then the range of interventions to use has to include intensive communication, education, training, and personal development, to help employees understand exactly what is expected of them in the new culture.

However, the more the target is on *values,* or on *behaviours* with the ultimate intent of driving in new *assumptions and beliefs,* the more there will need to be a simultaneous focus on both the personal development and communication initiatives, and mutually supportive and consistent changes in all organisational subsystems, including symbols and routines, to ensure there are no contradictory messages sent to staff about the end goals of change. Many organisations underwent change through a mixture of restructuring, downsizing and business process re-engineering initiatives throughout the 1990s in a response to increasing competition. A common complaint is that employees receive mixed messages about the intent of change, because supportive symbolic changes have not been made. Managers talk of innovation, quality, teamwork and empowerment, but continue to use old, routine ways of behaving to punish mistakes, cut costs and reward individual performance. Illustrations 2.6 and 2.8 on change in the Forestry Commission illustrate this need for consistency across all subsystems with a target on behaviours to get at values, whereas Illustration 2.7 illustrates a failed attempt at change through a target on values and a misconception that change can be achieved through communication alone. However, which change levers to use and when is a complicated topic that will be revisited in Chapters 5 and 6.

Illustration 2.8   *change in action*

Mapping the extent of change at the Forestry Commission of Great Britain

Present web

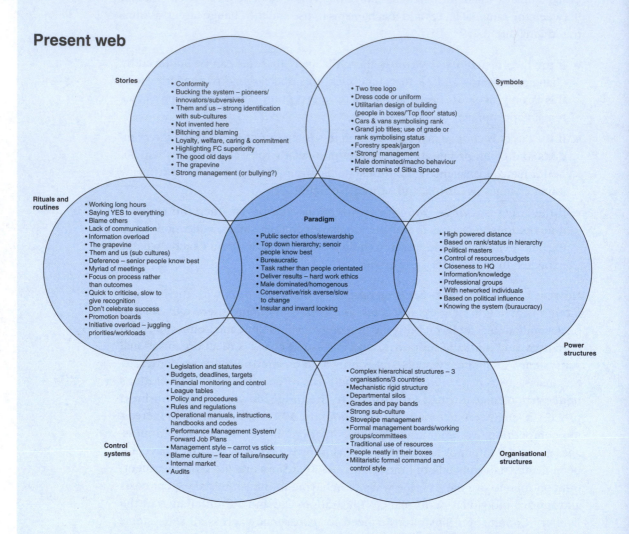

Stories
- Conformity
- Bucking the system – pioneers/innovators/subversives
- Them and us – strong identification with sub-cultures
- Not invented here
- Bitching and blaming
- Loyalty, welfare, caring & commitment
- Highlighting FC superiority
- The good old days
- The grapevine
- Strong management (or bullying?)

Symbols
- Two tree logo
- Dress code or uniform
- Utilitarian design of building (people in boxes/'Top floor' status)
- Cars & vans symbolising rank
- Grand job titles; use of grade or rank symbolising status
- Forestry speak/jargon
- 'Strong' management
- Male dominated/macho behaviour
- Forest ranks of Sitka Spruce

Rituals and routines
- Working long hours
- Saying YES to everything
- Blame others
- Lack of communication
- Information overload
- The grapevine
- Them and us (sub cultures)
- Deference – senior people know best
- Myriad of meetings
- Focus on process rather than outcomes
- Quick to criticise, slow to give recognition
- Don't celebrate success
- Promotion boards
- Initiative overload – juggling priorities/workloads

Paradigm
- Public sector ethos/stewardship
- Top down hierarchy; senoir people know best
- Bureaucratic
- Task rather than people orientated
- Deliver results – hard work ethics
- Male dominated/homogenous
- Conservative/risk averse/slow to change
- Insular and inward looking

Power structures
- High powered distance
- Based on rank/status in hierarchy
- Political masters
- Control of resources/budgets
- Closeness to HQ
- Information/knowledge
- Professional groups
- With networked individuals
- Based on political influence
- Knowing the system (buraucracy)

Control systems
- Legislation and statutes
- Budgets, deadlines, targets
- Financial monitoring and control
- League tables
- Policy and procedures
- Rules and regulations
- Operational manuals, instructions, handbooks and codes
- Performance Management System/Forward Job Plans
- Management style – carrot vs stick
- Blame culture – fear of failure/insecurity
- Internal market
- Audits

Organisational structures
- Complex hierarchical structures – 3 organisations/3 countries
- Mechanistic rigid structure
- Departmental silos
- Grades and pay bands
- Strong sub-culture
- Stovepipe management
- Formal management boards/working groups/committees
- Traditional use of resources
- People neatly in their boxes
- Militaristic formal command and control style

Future web

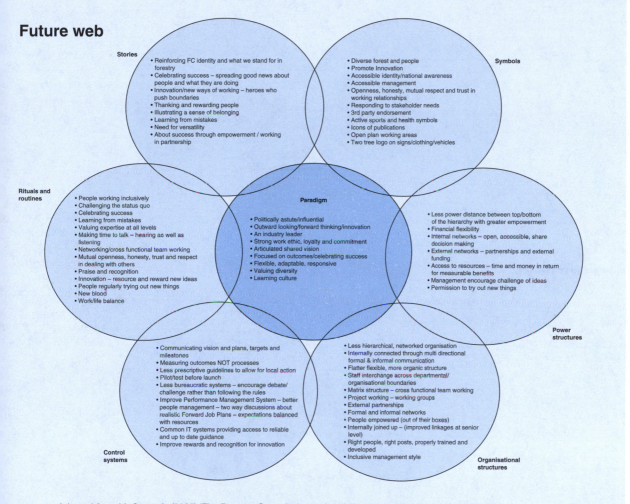

Stories
- Reinforcing FC identity and what we stand for in forestry
- Celebrating success – spreading good news about people and what they are doing
- Innovation/new ways of working – heroes who push boundaries
- Thanking and rewarding people
- Illustrating a sense of belonging
- Learning from mistakes
- Need for versatility
- About success through empowerment / working in partnership

Symbols
- Diverse forest and people
- Promote Innovation
- Accessible identity/national awareness
- Accessible management
- Openness, honesty, mutual respect and trust in working relationships
- Responding to stakeholder needs
- 3rd party endorsement
- Active sports and health symbols
- Icons of publications
- Open plan working areas
- Two tree logo on signs/clothing/vehicles

Rituals and routines
- People working inclusively
- Challenging the status quo
- Celebrating success
- Learning from mistakes
- Valuing expertise at all levels
- Making time to talk – hearing as well as listening
- Networking/cross functional team working
- Mutual openness, honesty, trust and respect in dealing with others
- Praise and recognition
- Innovation – resource and reward new ideas
- People regularly trying out new things
- New blood
- Work/life balance

Paradigm
- Politically astute/influential
- Outward looking/forward thinking/innovation
- An industry leader
- Strong work ethic, loyalty and commitment
- Articulated shared vision
- Focused on outcomes/celebrating success
- Flexible, adaptable, responsive
- Valuing diversity
- Learning culture

Power structures
- Less power distance between top/bottom of the hierarchy with greater empowerment
- Financial flexibility
- Internal networks – open, accessible, share decision making
- External networks – partnerships and external funding
- Access to resources – time and money in return for measurable benefits
- Management encourage challenge of ideas
- Permission to try out new things

Control systems
- Communicating vision and plans, targets and milestones
- Measuring outcomes NOT processes
- Less prescriptive guidelines to allow for local action
- Pilot/test before launch
- Less bureaucratic systems – encourage debate/ challenge rather than following the rules
- Improve Performance Management System – better people management – two way discussions about realistic Forward Job Plans – expectations balanced with resources
- Common IT systems providing access to reliable and up to date guidance
- Improve rewards and recognition for innovation

Organisational structures
- Less hierarchical, networked organisation
- Internally connected through multi directional formal & informal communication
- Flatter flexible, more organic structure
- Staff interchange across departmental/ organisational boundaries
- Matrix structure – cross functional team working
- Project working – working groups
- External partnerships
- Formal and informal networks
- People empowered (out of their boxes)
- Internally joined up – (improved linkages at senior level)
- Right people, right posts, properly trained and developed
- Inclusive management style

Adapted from McCann, A. (2005) 'The Forestry Commission: cultural change to deliver a new strategy', in *Exploring Corporate Strategy*, 7th edn, Johnson, G., Scholes, K. and Whittington, R. (eds) Prentice Hall. Copyright © 2005. The Forestry Commission and Pearson Education Ltd.

Figure 2.7   Linking change target and change levers

a. Targeting outputs

b. Targeting behaviours

Figure 2.7   *continued*

c. Targeting values

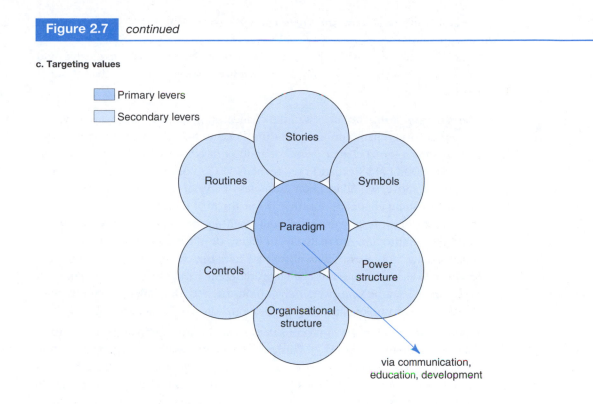

2.7 CHANGE ROLES

Change is only likely to succeed if someone is responsible for leading that change, although it is also accepted that this responsibility may not reside with just one person. A change agent needs to be supported by additional change agents. There is less faith placed in the one charismatic and heroic figure,[30] particularly since it is now recognised that change is complex and requires consideration and management of many different tasks. One individual could not hope to manage a major change effort entirely on his or her own. This is not to say that the role of leadership has been trivialised in any way. Major change efforts in particular are likely to require a champion who shows tremendous commitment to, and enthusiasm for, the vision he or she wants to see implemented in the organisation.

However, within change roles there are two choices. It is first necessary to choose the way change is to be managed and the *nature of the change agent role(s)*. It is then necessary to consider *who should fill* the chosen roles. Change always involves leadership in one form or another. However, leadership is a *quality* or a *competence*, rather than a role. Someone can be in a leadership role with formal position power, yet lack the credibility to win the support of those around him/her. Thus all the change roles described here require individuals who can act as leaders, and will be ineffective if the incumbents who take the roles can't do so. Chapter 7 says more about these capabilities.

None of the different ways change can be managed are mutually exclusive, and there are pros and cons for each role. (See Figure 2.8.) The primary change agent roles are:

- *Change champion*. The success of the change programme is based on a key, pivotal figure. The 'champion' may be the CEO, the MD, another senior manager acting as the internal change agent, or another director such as the HR Director. The new CEO of M&S, Stuart Rose, or the new CEO of the AA, Tim Parker, both mentioned above, would be good examples of change champions. If the individual championing change is not the CEO or the MD, then they may need to gain the support of more powerful individuals within the organisation if they are to push change through. Alternatively, in bigger or more geographically dispersed organisations, a number of individuals may fulfil the championship role, with different individuals leading the change in different parts of the business. In such cases, there may be one overall champion, such as the Chief Executive, with local change champions in each organisational division or department.

- *External facilitation*. External consultants may be appointed and play a pivotal role in the change process.[31] This may be in the form of advice, providing change management training, or more active participation. Illustration 2.7 of the Forestry Commission shows how consultants can provide extensive facilitation of change through workshops and management development. Others, such as GSK (see Illustration 2.2), have a great deal of change capability in-house and only employ consultants for specialised expertise.

- *Change action team*. A team of people within the organisation may be appointed to lead the changes, which may be in the form of a steering committee. If this team does not consist of senior and influential people, the team is likely to need the support of a more powerful individual or group of individuals in major change efforts. Illustration 2.9 discusses the change process at Lufthansa in the 1990s. It illustrates many uses of change action teams, but the change effort also involved *championship* from the CEO, Jurgen Weber, and extensive *functional support* from HR in the design of communication, performance management systems, and management development.

- *Functional delegation*. Change responsibility may be assigned to a particular function such as HR, or operations management. In major change efforts, unless the function head is endowed with a large amount of authority, or is acting in a supporting role as at Lufthansa, the individual is likely to need the backing of a more powerful figure such as the CEO.

Transition management is a time-consuming activity, and there may be a trade-off to be made between the amount of time managers need to devote to keeping the business going, and the amount of time they have to act as a change resource. For example, an organisation's MD may decide to lead the change, supported by

Figure 2.8	The pros and cons of different change roles

	PROS	CONS
Leadership	● Can create drive, determination, and strong focus on the change project.	● Leader may not be credible/believed. ● Leader may not have track record of delivering on promises. ● Leader may lack time given other operational duties. ● Leader may lack change management skills/expertise. ● Leader may be part of problem (e.g. not acknowledging need for change). ● Multiple leaders in different parts of the organisation may pull change programme in different directions/lack coordination.
External consultants	● Have experience. ● Can be objective – carry no organisational baggage. ● Can be used as a soapegoat for bad news. ● Can facilitate, to open up conversations about the need for change. ● Can overcome organisational barriers/politics. ● Dedicated resource.	● Cost a lot. ● Cannot lead change as not seen as having any stake in the organisation's future. ● No accountability. ● May not know the business well. ● No ownership and need to deliver.
Change action team	● Good ownership for change initiatives. ● Knowledge of organisation and issues. ● Potentially influential with their peer groups. ● Sustainability and follow-through. ● Can involve individuals with change expertise (e.g. organisation development specialists).	● Can make design long winded due to multiple inputs/perspectives. ● Can be time consuming. ● Can lead to compromises in design. ● May lack power.
Functional delegation	● Use of expertise (human resources, organisation development). ● Knowledge of area. ● Individuals may identify more strongly with their immediate manager.	● Individual(s) may lack power required to intervene in other parts of organisation. ● May be biased in favour of their part of the organisation. ● May focus only on their area at expense of others. ● May lack expertise.

Illustration 2.9

change in action

Using change teams at Lufthansa

The transformation process at Lufthansa started in 1991, when the company was almost bankrupt. The transformation process involved three phases – an operational turnaround (1992–1994), structural change and privatisation (1994–1996) and finally strategic development (cost leadership, the STAR ALLIANCE, and moving to an aviation group). By 1998, the CEO was able to announce the company's best results ever. The change reversed a record loss of DM 730 million in 1992 to a record pre-tax profit of DM 2.5 billion in 1998.

The record losses in 1991 created some awareness of a crisis, but Lufthansa was a state-owned company – longevity was assumed. The first step of the change process was a change management programme in 1992 that led to the birth of a group called 'Samurai of Change'. This group convinced the CEO of the need for fundamental change. To take change forward and create a group of managers prepared to lead change, the CEO invited 20 selected senior managers to attend a workshop in June 1992 at the training centre in Seeheim. This meeting led to 'Program 93': 131 projects including staff reductions of 8,000, downsizing the fleet (stationing aircraft in the desert), and increasing revenues. The Seeheim workshop was repeated three times with groups of 50 people, to encourage a wider ownership of change and to build commitment to the ambitious goals. Teams were appointed to head the projects, mostly led by members of the 'Sumarai of Change'. An Operations Team was put in overall charge. Communication was achieved through the use of town meetings. The CEO held these meetings himself when visiting the various Lufthansa

units. About 70 per cent of the projects were delivered during the turnaround. The remaining longer-term strategic projects were launched later. Networks of change agents were developed through the establishment of the teams during the turnaround, which led to formal and informal groups implementing new ideas.

Corporate restructuring followed. Lufthansa was changed from a functional organisation into autonomous subsidiaries including cargo, technical maintenance, and systems that could support the core business of the passenger airline. Problems with the pension fund had also been resolved so that privatisation, first discussed with the German government at the start of the turnaround, could now proceed and by 1997 the privatisation was complete. Attention was then focused on some of the outstanding strategic goals. First, Program 15 was launched to deliver cost leadership in the fiercely competitive airline business. It aimed to reduce costs by 20 per cent within five years and was led by a task force. This program was integrated into line managers' objectives and performance evaluations. The task force emphasised the importance of the programme symbolically. It positioned its office next to the CEOs, talked about progress regularly in the town meetings and the staff journal, and publicised success stories. Second, the STAR ALLIANCE was initiated. Third, further moves were made to develop Lufthansa into an aviation group rather than an airline, by building on the subsidiary structure already in place.

To help sustain change, Lufthansa now has an 'Explorers 21' network (young professionals) and the 'Climb 99' initiative (an action learning network of experienced managers). Both programmes start with a leadership self-assessment. Participants then visit excellent companies worldwide to develop recommendations for Lufthansa. There are also congresses at which members discuss their ideas with senior management to agree on concrete action plans. Participants are encouraged and supported to follow through on the change initiatives they propose.

Source: Adapted from Bruch, H. and Sattelberger, T. (2001) 'Lufthansa's transformation marathon: the process of liberating and focusing change energy', *Human Resource Management, Fall 21*, 40 (3), pp. 249–59; (2001) 'The turnaround at Lufthansa: learning from the change process', *Journal of Change Management*, 1 (4), 344–63; (2001) Lufthansa 2000: Maintaining the Change Momentum, London Business School Case, reference LBS–CS01–001.

a change team of other senior managers, but also appoint external consultants to provide advice and assistance, and additional resources when needed.

2.8 SUMMARY

A key issue when planning an appropriate change implementation approach is to decide which design choices to take. This chapter has explained that there are six main design choices a change agent needs to examine – the change path, the change style, the change start-point, the change target, the range of change levers, and the key change roles. All of these choices need consideration in relation to the context of change, to avoid the application of simplistic change recipes.

However, choosing which options to take is not straightforward. Within each of the choices there are a number of options, which creates a wide variety of possible permutations:

- The *change path* may involve more than one type of change, for example, an enabling phase of adaptation or reconstruction, followed by evolution or revolution.

- The *change start-point* options include not just top-down or bottom-up change, but also some combination of the two or pockets of good practice. These choices can be exercised organisation-wide, or within pilot sites.

- The *change style* may vary from highly collaborative to coercive, and is not necessarily dictated by the change start-point. Top-down change, for example, can still be collaborative. The change style may also vary by staff level or occupational groupings.

- The *target of change interventions* may be attitudes and values, behaviours or outputs. However, outputs are normally used to indirectly achieve behaviour change, and behaviour change may be used to effect value change.

- The *range of change levers* is affected by the choice of change target, but may be other choices such as change style. The range of levers and interventions that can be used includes not just harder technical and political interventions such as structures and systems, but also softer cultural interventions such as symbols and routines, and interpersonal interventions to do with communication, education and training.

- The *change roles* are often some combination of change championship, functional delegation, the use of external consultants, and change action teams. It is also necessary to consider separately the suitability of individuals appointed to the chosen change roles.

The first and most important choice is the change path. The other choices, such as change start-point, style, target and so on, then need to be made for each phase of the change path. None of these choices can be made without reference to the change context. Chapters 3 and 4 elaborate on this chapter to explain how to create linkages between the context and the design choices.

REFERENCES

1. This definition is taken from *Exploring Corporate Strategy*. The concept of the paradigm is also discussed extensively in *Exploring Corporate Strategy,* Chapters 5 and 14. An organisation's paradigm is the shared, although often taken-for-granted, assumptions and beliefs of the organisation that shape the way things are done in the organisation.
2. See 'Patrick Cescau, Group Chief Executive, Unilever' (15 August 2007) *CEO Today,* www.sovereign-publications.com/ceo-art-leadership.htm, and Hall, J. (6 August 2007) 'Can Unilever wash whiter than white?', www.telegarph.co.uk.
3. See Mackintosh, M. (14 June 2007) 'Out of an inferno and into profit', *Financial Times,* p. 11.
4. See Birchall, J. (19 March 2007) 'Lessons in motivating staff', *Financial Times, FT Special Report Business Turnarounds,* p. 4.
5. Lashinsky, L. (3 April 2006) 'Can HP win doing it the Hurd way?', *CNNMoney.com,* Darlin, D. (25 September 2004) 'At Hewlett-Packard, a chief wounded by divided attention', *The New York Times,* www.nytimes.com, accessed 13 July 2007, and Burrows, P. (9 October 2006) 'Controlling the damage at HP', *Business Week,* www.businessweek.com, accessed 13 July 2007.
6. See Rigby, E. (19 March 2007) 'M&S comes out of intensive care – but is not yet fighting fit', *Financial Times, FT Special Report Business Turnarounds,* p. 4. Also Rose, M. (2007) 'Back in fashion: how we're reviving a British icon', *Harvard Business Review,* (May), pp. 51–58. Also Collier, N. (2008) 'Marks & Spencer (B)', in *Exploring Corporate Strategy,* 8th edn, Johnson, G., Scholes, K. and Whittington, R. (eds) Prentice Hall.
7. *CNN.com* (5 February 2007) Specials 2000: Conflict & Hope in Northern Ireland: Identity Crisis for Police.
8. Davidson, A. (4 March 2007) 'Media chief exhibits alluring model', *The Sunday Times, Business Section,* p. 6.
9. There are many sources of information for the change process undertaken at British Airways in the 1980s. Two good sources are Goodstein, L.D. and Burke, W.W. (1991) 'Creating successful organization change', *Organizational Dynamics,* 19 (4) pp. 5–17, and Leahey, J. and Kotter, J.P. (1990) 'Changing the culture at British Airways' Harvard Business School, case number 9–491–009.

10. The story of the transformation at General Electric led by Jack Welch is told in Tichy, N.M. and Sherman, S. (1993) *Control Your Destiny, or Someone Else Will*, New York: Doubleday. Also by same authors, a summary of the Work-Out programme, (1993) 'Walking the talk at GE', *Training and Development*, (June), pp. 26–35.

11. For a discussion of change paths and other examples of matching change style to context, see, for example, Stace, D.A. (1996) 'Dominant ideologies, strategic change, and sustained performance', *Human Relations*, 49 (5) pp. 553–70. See also Beer, M. and Nohria, N. (2000) 'Cracking the code of change', *HBR*, (May–June), pp. 133–41.

12. See reference 2 above.

13. See 'The HBR interview: Samuel J. Palmisano' (2004) *Harvard Business Review*, (December), pp. 60–70.

14. Goodman, M. (4 June 2006) 'AA moves up a gear on the road to recovery', *Sunday Times Business Section*, p. 6.

15. For a fuller description of how to combine a top-down approach to change with a more bottom-up approach, see Beer, M., Eisenstat, R.A. and Spector, B. (1990) *The Critical Path to Corporate Renewal*, Boston: Harvard Business School Press.

16. For more on pockets of good practice, see Clarke, M. and Meldrum, M. (1998) 'Creating change from below: early lessons for agents of change' *Leadership and Organizational Development Journal*, 20 (2), pp. 70–80.

17. For examples of pockets of good practice, see Butcher, D. and Atkinson, S. (2000) 'The bottom-up principle', *Management Review*, 89 (1), pp. 48–53, and Butcher, D. and Atkinson, S. (14 January 1999) 'Upwardly mobilised: against the grain: catalysing change at Jewson', in *People Management*, Butcher, D. and Atkinson, S., pp. 28–33.

18. See Department for Work & Pensions, OGC Case Study, DWP Jobcentre Plus Rollout: Integrated Supply Chain.

19. Sayers, I. and Johnson, G. (1998) 'The UNHCR case – achieving the impossible', in *Exploring Corporate Strategy*, 5th edn. Hemel Hempstead: Prentice Hall.

20. For a discussion of imposed change, see Willmott, H. (1993) 'Strength is ignorance: slavery is freedom: managing culture in modern organisations', *Journal of Management Studies*, 30 (4), pp. 515–52.

21. See Schaffer, R.H. and Thomson, H.A. (1992) 'Successful change programs begin with results', *Harvard Business Review*, 70 (1), pp. 80–9. For an example of the use of performance measures in change, see Hwee, C., Demeester, L. and Pich, M. (2002) *AlliedSignal Aerospace Repair and Overhaul (Singapore) (A)*, INSEAD, Case number 602–034–1.

22. Professor Mayhew challenges Government A&E waiting times, *www.cass.city.ac.uk*, 5 February 2007.

23. For a fuller discussion of the merits of attitude- versus behaviour-led change, see Beer, M., Eisenstat, R.A. and Spector, B. (1990) 'Why change programs don't produce change', *Harvard Business Review*, 68 (6), pp. 158–66.

24. Whilst we know that behavioural change will lead to a shift in accompanying attitudes, as yet there is no evidence that a change in behaviours will lead to value change.

25. For a discussion of the role of values in change, see Hope, V. and Hendry, J. (1995) 'Corporate cultural change – is it relevant for the organisations of the 1990s', *Human Resource Management Journal*, 5 (4), pp. 61–73.

26. See Lencioni, P.M. (2002) 'Make your values mean something', *Harvard Business Review*, 80 (7), pp. 113–17.

27. This book uses the cultural web (see *Exploring Corporate Strategy*) as a way of analysing organisations and designing levers and mechanisms to achieve the desired future organisation. For an alternative means of analysing organisations and designing levers and mechanisms to achieve the desired future organisation in terms of three subsystems (technical, political and cultural), see Tichy, N.M. (1983) 'The essentials of strategic change management', *The Journal of Business Strategy*, 3 (4), pp. 55–67.

28. For more information on how to complete a cultural web, see Johnson, G. (1997) 'Mapping and re-mapping organisational culture', in *Exploring Techniques of Analysis and Evaluation in Strategic Management*, Ambrosini, V., Johnson, G. and Scholes, K. (eds) Harlow: Prentice Hall.

29. Tichy in reference 27 above, and also see Orgland, M. and Von Krugh, G. (1998) 'Initiating, managing and sustaining corporate transformation', *European Management Journal,* 16 (1), pp. 31–8.

30. For a discussion of leadership during change, see Pettigrew A.M. and Whipp, R. (1991) *Managing Change for Competitive Success,* Oxford: Blackwell Publishers. Also Nadler, D.A. and Tushman, M.L. (1989) 'Organizational frame bending: principles for managing reorientation', *The Academy of Management Executive,* 3 (3), pp. 194–204.

31. For a comparison of internal and external change agency roles, see Ginsberg, A. and Abrahamson, E. (1991) 'Champions of change and strategic shifts: the role of internal and external change advocates', *Journal of Management Studies,* 28 (2). pp. 173–99.

WORK ASSIGNMENTS

2.1. Identify different organisations undergoing change from newspaper articles or another source. What types of change (transformation versus realignment) do these organisations need to implement and why?

2.2. Using Illustration 2.1, and the other examples given of Vespa and SOCA, consider what these examples suggest about the key characteristics of reconstructions and adaptations.

2.3. Using Illustration 2.2, Evolution at GSK, consider how evolutions differ from reconstructions and adaptations.

2.4. Consider why examples of bottom-up change are rare.

2.5. Consider an organisation with a wide number of different stakeholder groups, like a hospital or a university. Identify the different stakeholder groups and how this might affect your choice of change styles.

2.6. For the organisations you identified in question 2.1, what change targets would you select and why?

2.7. What are the advantages and disadvantages of choosing to target either outputs, behaviours or values in managing change?

2.8. Using Illustration 2.8 of the before and after webs for the Forestry Commission of Great Britain, consider what technical, political and cultural interventions are needed to deliver the desired change. As part of this, consider the old things that need to change/be removed and the new things that need to be out in place. Also, using Illustration 2.6, consider what interpersonal interventions were used at the Forestry Commission to supplement the technical, political and cultural interventions.

Analysing the change context: how context affects choice

3.1 INTRODUCTION

Chapters 1 and 2 have introduced the concept of context-sensitive approaches to change, and the change kaleidoscope (see Figure 3.1) as a diagnostic framework that can aid the incorporation of context-sensitivity into change design by

Figure 3.1   **The change kaleidoscope**

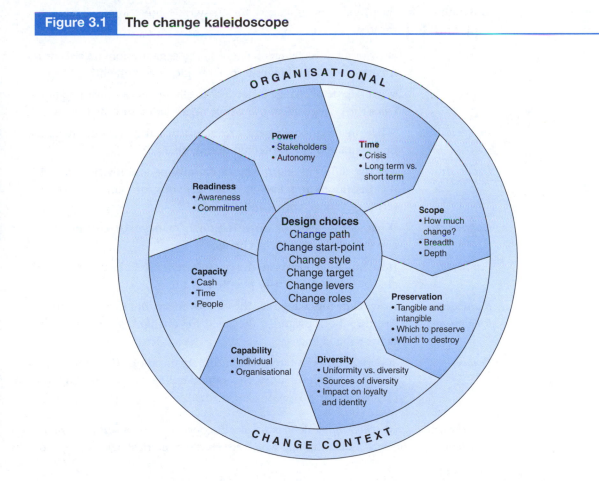

enabling change agents to pinpoint the key contextual features of their change context. Chapter 1 has stressed that successful change, by its very nature, depends heavily on context and circumstance. It is dangerous to apply change formulae that worked in one context directly into another. Longitudinal research examining best practice change management in successful companies has established that these companies do not follow trends or change recipes, but instead customise their change approach to meet the needs of their organisation at any one point in time.[1] It has to be appreciated that even organisations that seem very similar are, in reality, very different. Yet unfortunately the complexity and daunting nature of the change task can make existing models look attractive, and this tempts managers to reach for existing 'off-the-shelf' solutions. Chapter 2 has explained the different design choices from the kaleidoscope and the options within each choice.

Chapters 3 builds on Chapters 1 and 2 by providing the reader with an understanding of how to analyse the contextual features in the middle ring of the kaleidoscope, and use an understanding of these contextual features to make context-sensitive design choices. The chapter does this through an in-depth analysis of each contextual feature and the provision of examples to illustrate the implications of each feature for change design choices. The eight contextual features are:

Time:	How quickly is change needed? Is the organisation in crisis or is it concerned with longer-term strategic development?
Scope:	What degree of change is needed? Realignment or transformation? Does the change affect the whole organisation or only part of it?
Preservation:	What organisational assets, characteristics and practices need to be maintained and protected during change?
Diversity:	Are the different staff/professional groups and divisions within the organisation relatively homogeneous or more diverse in terms of values, norms and attitudes?
Capability:	What is the level of organisational, managerial and personal capability to implement change?
Capacity:	How much resource can the organisation invest in the proposed change in terms of cash, people and time?
Readiness for change:	How ready for change are the employees within the organisation? Are they both aware of the need for change and motivated to deliver the changes?
Power:	Where is power vested within the organisation? How much latitude of discretion does the unit needing to change and the change leader possess?

The *Oxford English Dictionary* defines a kaleidoscope as '*a constantly changing group* of bright objects; a tube through which are seen symmetrical figures produced by reflections of pieces of coloured glass and *varied by rotation of the tube*'. The kaleidoscope does not give predictable configurations that lead to more formulaic change recipes. Instead the pieces of coloured glass, the eight contextual features, remain the same but are *constantly reconfigured* to produce different pictures for each organisational change situation they are used to assess. Therefore the change designs will also vary. Certain features infer certain design choices, but the potential permutations are endless. This chapter can only give a few examples for each feature.

3.2 TIME

Time is to do with how long an organisation has to achieve change (Figure 3.2). Is the organisation in crisis or is it concerned with longer-term strategic development? Time can also be affected by stakeholder attitudes. Is the stock market, for example, expecting short- or long-term results from change? What constitutes a crisis or a long period of time will vary according to the industry sector. Some industries are very fast-moving by nature and so their timescales may be more condensed than others. For instance, the telecom sector is used to rapid and

Figure 3.2   **Contextual feature: time**

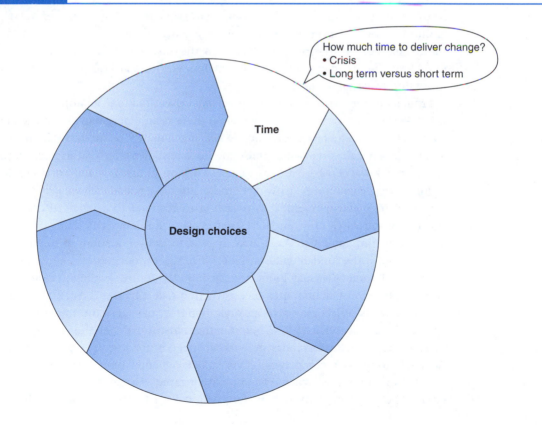

frequent change – so what constitutes a short timescale for one of the telecom companies may look very different to an organisation operating in the aerospace engineering industry.

3.2.1 Assessing time

How much time an organisation has to deliver change should have been determined by the strategic analysis. It may be that an organisation is in a crisis situation, with rapidly declining market share and profitability, and therefore in need of a reactive, rapid turnaround and recovery change process. This may be due to a change in the competitive conditions the organisation is facing, such as the arrival of new competitors and/or the development by competitors of different products and services. Alternatively it could be that an organisation has become complacent and failed to keep up with the trends in its marketplace, continuing instead to pursue strategies still rooted in the ways of behaving that used to lead to success, placing the organisation in an uncompetitive position. The now-famous case of the UK's high street retailer Marks and Spencer in the mid-1990s is an illustration of an organisation reaching crisis point after years of senior management denying the need to change (see Chapter 1, section 1.2).

An organisation may also need to implement proactive change rapidly, either to pre-empt fast competitor imitation, or to meet changing customer needs. In addition, stock market and shareholder pressures may lead to the need for rapid change. Illustration 3.1. describes the fast action implemented at the family-owned toy manufacturer Lego in Denmark to ward off predatory activity following huge losses in 2003.

From a change management perspective a crisis situation can appear attractive. It is easier to start or trigger change when there is an emergency. People seem to overcome their reluctance to change when it is a matter of survival. The needs of an emergency can serve to legitimise methods and measures that in normal times would not be accepted, such as longer working hours, pay cuts or freezes, or redundancy programmes. However, there are also real disadvantages to crisis-driven change management. It is tempting to respond to a financial crisis with short-term measures only, such as strict cost-cutting strategies that may include downsizing programmes. These may appear to deliver a solution to the shareholders, but if the fundamental problems leading to poor performance over time are ignored, then crisis may loom large again in the future, leading to a downward spiral with reconstruction after reconstruction (see Chapter 2, section 2.2.2). In addition, whilst crisis may give an organisation's managers the impetus to start change, there may be no cash to invest in the transformation at the very time when it is most needed. Research has shown that speed is not always conducive to introducing innovation to companies – it very much depends upon the industry sector.[2]

Some organisations struggle to implement rapid change even when there is a crisis. This is particularly true of international civil service bodies such as the

Illustration 3.1

Rebuilding with speed: delivering turnaround at Lego

The toy manufacturer Lego is well known for its brightly coloured construction bricks which young children love across the world: Lego is sold in over 130 countries. It was started in 1932 by a Danish carpenter named Ole Kirk Christiansen, and the family are still active in the firm today. The philosophy of the firm is that 'Play is good for the soul'. Lego's name is taken from the Danish phrase for play well: *leg godt*.

However, the company started to 'play' badly during the late 1990s, culminating in an operating loss of 1.6 billion Danish Kroner on sales of 6.8 billion Kroner in 2003. Commentators saw it as ripe for takeover, but the Christiansen family decided to save the business. They invested 800 million Kroner of their own money back into the business. They also appointed a former McKinsey consultant – Knudstorp – to the top job to manage the turnaround for them.

Knudstorp moved swiftly. In March 2004, 3,500 of the firm's 8,000 employees were made redundant and the jobs of another 2,400 workers were put at risk within the firm's hometown of Billund. Factories were to be closed in high-cost economies such as the USA and Switzerland with others to be opened up in Eastern Europe and Mexico. A simplified management structure was also introduced.

This swift but painful action appeared to be delivering the results the Christiansen family wanted to see. Sales were up by 19 per cent for the first half of 2006, and for the same period the company recorded profits of 238 million Kroner rather than the losses experienced in previous years.

Adapted from 'Picking up the pieces', (17 August and 26 October 2006) *The Economist*.

United Nations. The European Commission, mainly based in Brussels and Luxembourg, is one of the three main decision-making bodies in the European Union. It has 118 offices across the world and 27 commissioners, each holding responsibility for a particular policy area. There are 30,000 staff from a multicultural background, all concerned with initiating and implementing policy for the European Union. In 1999 an independent report attacked the commissioners for not being aware of malpractice within the institution, and the chaos that ensued resulted in the resignation of all 27 individual commissioners – a political crisis. Nevertheless, the strategic change plan that was implemented in response to this crisis has been described as difficult by its own senior management: 'You cannot turn a great big ship like the commission around overnight. It's a slow process.' The need to deal with the political sensitivities of the member countries and the diversity of the staff inhibits the pace of change at the Commission even after a crisis.[3]

Alternatively, some organisations may have the luxury of time on their side and be able to implement change in a pre-emptive manner, before the organisation is showing many visible signs of decline in competitiveness. In such circumstances there is more time and resource available to invest in a transformation. However, the problem in such non-crisis-driven change situations is how to generate readiness for change. There is no 'burning platform' for change.[4] Why engage in something as risky and painful as change when there is no obvious need? These issues have an impact on the design choices made, and explain why some texts on change advocate the exploitation, or the creation, of a crisis to trigger change. The pharmaceutical firm Glaxo Wellcome in the UK faced a similar situation in the early 1990s. They knew that their blockbuster drug, Zantac, was due to come off patent in the mid-1990s and that their major customer, the National Health Service, was undergoing significant change. The senior team recognized that the organisation needed to change in order to be able to respond to these developments. However, one of the challenges for management was to persuade the sales force of the need for change when the company was recording very good business results and the individual sales representatives were very happy with their work, the organisation and the bonuses they were making. A great deal of effort was put into change initiatives that pulled the workforce out of their complacency.[5]

3.2.2 Time and design choices

If there is *limited time* available to the change agent, particularly if the organisation is in a crisis for whatever reason, then some design choices become automatic. Initial change initiatives are likely to involve some type of *realignment,* probably via *big-bang reconstruction* as at Lego, as opposed to a more *incremental* approach, since the immediate need is to stem the decline in the organisation's competitive position. This then places an organisation in a position where it can embark on longer-term and more fundamental transformation if this is needed. Chapter 2 describes how this path is taken by many organisations. If there is money available, maybe from a parent group or other stakeholders such as national governments who are prepared to invest in the turnaround process, it may be possible to go for a more revolutionary approach from the start, but this is unusual.

Such *big-bang* approaches, whether reconstruction or revolution, are also likely to be more *top-down* and *directive* in approach, and supported by a *change champion role.* This is partly because there is not the time for more participative approaches, but also because the crisis legitimises the action and there is likely to be a greater willingness among staff to follow top management edicts. However, if an organisation needs to change rapidly, but there is not a felt need for change, then again the change agent may need to force change in order to trigger the realisation of the inevitability of action among employees. It should not be assumed that a crisis will create a felt need for change at all organisational levels. The attitude of more junior employees may be that it is the responsibility of the senior managers to resolve the problems. The *change target,* particularly with reconstruction where the aim is not an immediate shift in values, will be *behaviours,* or even *outputs* to effect rapid change. Change will therefore be delivered via harder interventions to do with structures and control systems, which may include new rewards to incentivise different behaviours.

If organisations have the luxury of *time,* then this enlarges the design choices available to the change agent. For instance, they can choose to map a particular change *path* whereby the organisation starts with one form of change, which over time develops into another type of change. Organisations can start with adaptation aimed at increasing the organisational and individual capability for change, and then move into more fundamental and transformational evolution. Similarly, when time is not an issue, it is possible to consider change processes which are educative, participative or collaborative in *style*. Highly participative or collaborative change processes take time to cascade through an organisation. Furthermore, if there is no obvious need for change, such participative approaches may be needed to gain a recognition of the need for, and a buy-in to, change. Many of the change initiatives implemented by Glaxo in the early 1990s were as much about raising awareness of the need to change as they were about change itself.[6]

Decisions about the change *start-point* can work either way. If awareness of the need for change is low, then getting the change process started may still require a *top-down* approach. Other contextual features also affect the choice. If there is a low capability for change among staff, then the approach may have to be *directive* in style as well. On the other hand, there may be parts of the organisation that are more ready for change, or have senior managers more willing to embrace change than some other managers, enabling change to be initiated via *pilot sites*. Alternatively, the time for change and the capability for change among staff may allow for the creation of awareness of the need for change, and the development of what should be changed, via a more *bottom-up* approach. Staff diversity also has an impact here. Even in circumstances where there is a low readiness for change, staff groups that value their autonomy may need to be involved through a more participative approach if they are to buy in to change.

In terms of change *targets,* when there is more time available and some sort of transformation is required, then it may be possible to target *values,* although of course a change agent could still choose to target *behaviours* to drive in *value change* as would need to be done in circumstances where there was less time. This in turn impacts on the change *levers*. Longer-term change interventions, particularly those where the intention is to aid value change, include communication, management development programmes and personal development initiatives such as coaching or mentoring.

Time also affects the choice of change roles. Change agents need to ask whether there is sufficient time to establish and develop a change action team. Also, the potential champions of the change – be it the Chief Executive, the HR Director, or another change agent – need to be screened for competence and capability. If they require a great deal of coaching in change leadership, yet there is no time to develop this, then support may be needed from external consultants or champions. If time is available, then teams can be established to spread the vision and required changes throughout the organisation.

3.3 SCOPE

Scope is the required outcome of the change, varying from realignment through to more radical change aimed at transformation of an organisation (Figure 3.3). Whether the whole organisation needs to change, or just one division or department, also affects scope.

3.3.1 Assessing scope

The scope of the change determines just how much change is necessary. There are two aspects to scope – the depth of the change required in an organisation and the physical spread of change across the organisation. One of the most critical pieces of analysis to be undertaken is to carefully scope the extent of the change planned. Many of the problems that emerge in the process of change do so because insufficient time was spent on thinking about the depth and breadth of the intended change. Senior managers often underestimate the depth of the change and therefore fail to invest sufficiently or manage it with sufficient care. For instance, to some senior managers in an IS department, the new information system that they are proposing to implement may appear to be a non-controversial piece of change.

Figure 3.3   **Contextual feature: scope**

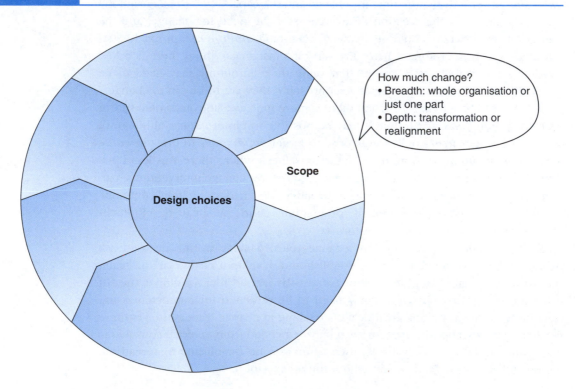

However, if the end result of that system results in a change in people's behaviour or attitudes because the new system forces them to do their jobs differently, then an unintended consequence may be a cultural change at lower levels, which was neither anticipated nor managed. For instance, in one university a new information system was introduced for centrally storing student evaluations of their lecturers' performance. However, it also allowed open access to students and all university teaching faculty for the first time: members of the teaching faculty could view the performance results of their peers. The result was a changed dynamic between the students and their teachers, and between members of faculty.

The *depth of change* required is equivalent to the extent of change discussed in Chapter 2 when considering the types of change to be undertaken and the change path to be followed. As such, it is one of the key determinants of the type of change, although by no means the only one. It also impacts on design choices other than the type and path of change. When considering the depth of change, it is therefore necessary to consider whether the desired changes involve *transformation,* a change which cannot be handled within the existing paradigm and organisational routines and entails a change in the taken-for-granted assumptions and 'the way of doing things around here'; or a *realignment,* a change to the way of doing things that does not involve a fundamental reappraisal of the central assumptions and beliefs within the organisation. We can illustrate the difference between the two with reference to the retail banking industry in the UK. The banking industry underwent many changes in the 1990s, all of which were, fundamentally, forms of realignment since the changes never altered the fundamental purpose of the banks-banking – and did little to shift the internally focused, conservative, risk-averse nature of the banks. However, new entrants throughout the 1990s, in the form of direct telephone banking and the supermarkets, coupled with growing customer sophistication and demand, required the banks to respond in a more fundamental fashion. The banks had to switch from being bankers to being retailers of financial services. This necessitated a shift in the fundamental beliefs and assumptions: the banks needed to become responsive, customer-focused organisations.

A useful framework that can be used to help assess the scope of change is the cultural web. This framework has already been introduced in Chapter 2 as a way of considering the range of levers and interventions that need to be used to effect change (see Chapter 2, section 2.6), and the extent of change required. By drawing up a current cultural web for an organisation, and then an outline web of the sort of organisation needed if the desired changes are to become a reality, the extent of required change can be determined. The two webs provide a picture of how different the future organisation needs to be from the current one. If the changes impact what sits in the paradigm, then the change is likely to be transformational in nature (see Illustration 2.8 on the Forestry Commission).

The questions about the *physical spread* of the change process concern formal structures rather than informal cultures. Is change limited to a small department, or a particular national division, or a particular layer of management? Or, alternatively, is it a change process that should affect the whole organisation?

If the change is to be both broad and deep, then difficult questions must some-times be asked about the level of investment an organisation is willing to provide to make the change actually happen. The merger of the Inland Revenue and the Customs and Excise into Her Majesty's Revenues and Customs (HMRC) in 2005, which formed part of the UK government's public sector transformation pro-gramme, was such a change. It is the largest public sector merger in UK history. The merger was to deliver greater efficiencies through the introduction of a new structure, new technology, lean processing within the administrative processing units and a cultural transformation. Given the scale of the changes but also the size of the organisation (100,000 people), the scope was huge and the change challenge for senior managers was extremely demanding.[7]

3.3.2 Scope and design choices

The depth or extent of change obviously impacts on the *type* of change required in terms of *adaptation, reconstruction, evolution* or *revolution,* and therefore the choice of *change path*. However, other contextual features, such as time, capacity and capability, also affect the change path. If the *scope* of change sug-gests a need for *realignment* rather than transformation, the other main factor is likely to be time. A short timescale points to reconstruction, with the associated design choices described in section 3.2.2. A longer timescale suggests adaptation, which brings with it a wider range of design choices – again see section 3.2.2.

If the *scope* of change points to *transformation,* then the choice of change path is more complex. The discussion above on the impact of time on design choices explains how, in a crisis, an organisation has little time to effect change, and probably a low capacity in terms of cash to invest in the change process, and therefore may need to initially undertake reconstruction, even if the ultimate aim of the change process is transformation rather than realignment. Very few organisations achieve transformation in a revolutionary way.

If the organisation has more *time* to effect a *transformation,* or has carried out a reconstruction that has in turn gained the organisation more time, then there is a wider range of design choices from which to choose. Illustration 3.2. shows the extent of the change that was necessary within Prime Focus and the length of time it took in order to rebuild the business. As well as management and cultural change, job redesign and ICT development were targeted as critical areas for transformation, alongside cost-cutting measures. Prime Focus took several years to accomplish this transformation, splitting the change process clearly into a period of reconstruction which focused on restructuring followed by a period of evolution.

However, when needing to carry out a transformation, with or without time on its side, an organisation can still be constrained from revolution or evolution by aspects such as a lack of readiness for change or a lack of capability for change. This may point to the need for some sort of realignment first, either with personal

Illustration 3.2

change in action

Transformational change at Prime Focus

In 2002 Prime Focus Regeneration Group, a community regeneration and social housing organisation, launched a change programme called 'Quantum Leap' in order to 'reshape the way the business functioned from top to bottom'. The scope was so deep and so broad that it took several years and several phases to implement all the necessary change. The drivers for this programme were not only a need for greater efficiency and cost reductions. Some years earlier, the organisation had suffered the fallout from a fraud scandal, and transformational change was seen as a way of shaking off that sour legacy.

The change programme had two distinct phases. The first phase focused around restructuring and bringing in new management control systems and IT systems. Four regional offices were merged into one new building and a new ICT system was introduced. The second stage, launched in 2004, was described as a period of organisational development. Senior managers mapped out the current state of the organisation and remodelled the organisation into a 'future state'.

A total of 300 people had to be transferred from the old structure into the future structure, and 65 roles were identified as superfluous to needs. But major staff losses were avoided through a recruitment freeze and a termination of temporary contracts. The categorising system 'STAN', which stood for 'Stay as you are; Transfer to a different location; Assimilate to a new role or New Post', was used. Approximately 200 staff needed to be reassigned without any possibility for claims for constructive dismissal. The HR team had to assess matches between old and new roles. A firm of external consultants were used to develop a range of assessment and development exercises to develop and measure for new competencies. Staff were interviewed individually and then invited to apply for three of the new roles. They then went through Assessment and Development exercises for each role.

By 2005 all staff were installed in a new head office and the new ICT system was helping to deliver an improved customer service. Overheads had been reduced by £1.6 million and staff turnover had been reduced. In 2007 the association merged with a Coventry-based Housing Group, and together they became 'Midland Heart'. The new organisation manages more than 31,000 properties and is one of the country's largest social housing and regeneration projects.

Adapted from Cottee, P. (10 August 2006) 'Change of heart', *People Management*, pp. 42–44.

development interventions to build a capability for change, and/or the use of maybe more participative change approaches to build a readiness for change. See section 3.6 on capability and section 3.8 on readiness. Alternatively, the power of the change agent to deliver transformation may be limited, in which case early interventions may be to do with the use of political levers aimed at building support and a stronger power base for the change agent.

The scope of change also has implications for the change *target*. Ultimately, if an organisation is to deliver transformation, it needs to drive in change to the central assumptions and beliefs in the paradigm, which means that at some stage it may need to *target values,* or at least *behaviours,* with the intention of driving in *value* change. This also has implications for the range of *levers and interventions,* as explained in Chapter 2, as at some point it will be necessary to invest in education, training and personal development interventions. If the organisation is not cash-rich, this may limit its ability to invest in such change levers. In such circumstances it may be necessary to first target behaviours via a full range of levers and interventions, such as structures, systems, routines and symbols, and then to support these changes through time with appropriate education and training.

The power of an integrated set of levers and mechanisms to deliver change in a relatively short period of time is illustrated by the changes wrought at St George's, a senior school in London, by Lady Marie Stubbs, who was brought out of retirement to take over the headship of the school, which was notorious for the murder of one of its head teachers, Philip Lawrence, outside the school gates in 1995. In 2000 the school was temporarily closed after another violent incident and the departure of the head teacher. School attendance was down to only 70 per cent, and on most days only just over 50 per cent of the staff were in school. Students were noisy, uncooperative and verbally abusive. Daily fights broke out. There was a strong divide between staff and pupils. Yet 17 months after the arrival of Lady Stubbs, the school was being praised as a model of good practice by school inspectors. She used a range of change levers – technical, political, cultural and interpersonal – to achieve this turnaround. The school was repainted and recarpeted and the playground was improved. Political changes included the selection of new staff who were of a similar attitude to herself. Many symbolic changes also occurred. Students were no longer locked out of the school at break time – a central internal atrium was created instead; a breakfast and after-school club were introduced; a tannoy system was put in which pumped any music requested including garage music; a nearby private school lent St George's pupils the use of its sports facilities; role models such as Kevin Keegan, the footballer; Ralph Fiennes, the actor; and comedian Lenny Henry all visited the school. The pupils were also treated differently – Lady Marie Stubbs greeted every pupil personally when the school reopened and shook them by the hand. She involved them on an interpersonal basis by getting each pupil to write up a personal learning plan for themselves and consulted them on broader plans for the school. A rota of pupils was taught how to manage the reception desk for the school. When some teachers refused to attend a celebratory ball for pupils finishing their GCSEs, Stubbs simply drafted in qualified teachers from amongst her family and the party went ahead.[8]

The issue of physical spread throughout an organisation also brings other dimensions into consideration. If, for instance, the change is limited to one functional division which is located within one nation state and employs similar types of staff, then the change process is less complex than trying to lead a change over a multidivisional global corporation. The case on Tarmac in Chapter 4 which details the implementation of a change initiative across 11 different divisions illustrates the complexity of leading change in such circumstances.

3.4 PRESERVATION

Preservation is the extent to which it is essential to maintain continuity in certain practices or preserve specific assets, either because they constitute invaluable resources, or because they contribute towards a valued stability of culture or identity within an organisation (Figure 3.4). Assets include tangibles such as money, buildings and technology but also include intangibles such as know-how, and staff loyalty or pride in the employer or product.

3.4.1 Assessing preservation

A key criterion for the change agent to consider is the extent to which there is a need to preserve the status quo within an organisation. There are two aspects to preservation. The first is to be clear about what the organisation's assets are, both tangible and intangible. The second is to decide upon what should or should not be preserved in a change process.

Tangible assets are to do with physical, human and financial resources. These can be identified from a simple resource audit, which lists the assets in each category.[9] Intangible assets are more to do with know-how, or the 'tacit knowledge' of particular

Figure 3.4   Contextual feature: preservation

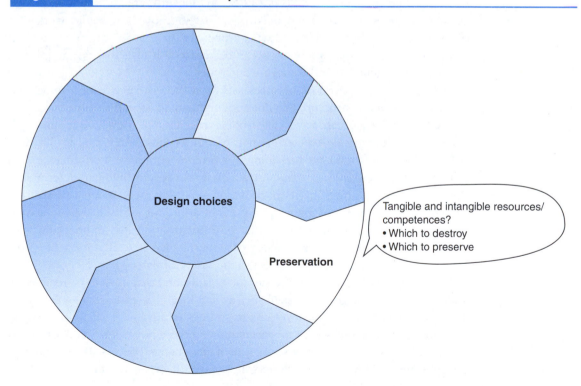

staff. Tacit knowledge is about knowing more than you can tell – it is informal, not codified and therefore difficult to talk about. This knowledge could be about understanding, for example, customers or causes of organisational success, and is often acquired through experience. Since tacit knowledge is not formally held within an organisation in the form of standard operating procedures or practices, it is hard to imitate and pass on to others. When this informal knowledge gives competitive advantage, it is often referred to as an organisation's core competence.[10] It is important that all resources that contribute to an organisation's competitive advantage are retained during the change process, but it is particularly important that the change process does not lead to the loss of the more intangible resources that are unique and difficult to imitate, and often embedded in an organisation's culture.

Some of the downsizing that went on in the early 1990s resulted in the precipitous removal of more experienced managers from corporations. They were often perceived as an easy target for redundancy because of their age and pension holdings. However, their hasty removal from the organisation often resulted in a loss of tacit knowledge. Cable and Wireless in the early 2000s were forced to implement a severe redundancy programme. Prior to this, much of the communication within the company had thrived on informal communication between friends and colleagues. After the downsizing, people found that much of the decision making and communication within the company was slowed down because the informal networks that had existed before had been broken up by downsizing.[11] Many companies continue to risk losing expertise through downsizing and cost-cutting exercises, and the associated costs can be significantly greater when such cuts cause companies to lose experienced people who know how things work. If a change agent does not understand what aspects of the existing organisation need to be preserved, or how such assets can be replaced if lost, the change process may have unanticipated and damaging outcomes.

In extreme cases, the loss of specialists, and the emergence of a remaining middle management structure that does not understand its staff's daily operational routines and rituals, can have catastrophic results. The newly appointed HR Director for Network Rail, Peter Bennet, recounted how, on taking up his new post in 2003, he found he was joining a broken company. Performance was abysmal and the rail infrastructure for which it was responsible had deteriorated through underinvestment by its previous owners, Railtrack. When nationalised, British Rail had several problems as an organisation but safety had been a well-embedded value. In Bennet's view, the post-privatisation loss of specialist staff and the introduction of poorly trained new recruits led to a situation where this loss of corporate memory was critical to the safety of passengers.[12]

There may also be cultural aspects of the organisation that need to be retained in addition to particular groups of staff, such as staff loyalty, a team spirit, or extensive staff collaboration which in turn leads to sources of advantage such as creativity or better customer service. If an organisation's competitive position is based on its staff's creativity or customer service, then any change process that unwittingly destroys these features of the culture will damage the organisation.

The extent of preservation is in part dependent on the scope of change. Arguably, the more that has to be retained, the less the scope of change. Yet it is necessary to address preservation as a separate question. If an organisation needs to undergo transformation, it is possible to overlook the existing sources of competitive advantage that reside within the organisation. The baby gets thrown out with the bath water.

A cultural web analysis can help identify some of the softer organisational aspects that need to be retained. Therefore such an analysis needs to be used in two ways – to consider first, what aspects of the organisation need to be changed, and second, what aspects of the organisation need to be specifically *retained,* either because they contribute to competitiveness or because they can be used to facilitate the change process.

3.4.2 Preservation and design choices

If preservation of hard-to-replace assets is important, particularly intangible assets embedded in the existing culture, then a number of design choices become clear. For instance, *revolution* in which many aspects of the organisation are changed simultaneously would be a risky change path. Similarly, a *target of outputs* could be dangerous as this could lead to many unintended behavioural side effects.

If preservation is more to do with the retention of particular staff groups, particularly if these people are seen as highly desirable assets in the external labour market, this has implications for the *style of change*. To avoid alienating them, a *collaborative or educative* style of change may be a safer route than a directive approach. In addition, if the staff group concerned is a group that values their autonomy and independence, such as university lecturers, then *direction* and prescription of *behaviours* or *values* is likely to be inappropriate, and it might be that a *change target* of *outputs* would then be appropriate. Illustration 3.3. describes a change initiative at the Hammersmith Hospitals NHS Trust which deployed very high levels of collaboration in the way it designed change to overcome issues of staff preservation, using an approach called Appreciative Inquiry.

On the other hand, organisations seeking true transformational change will have to give up, or even destroy, features of organisational life that in the past might have been assets but now represent barriers to change. The emotional attachment to such features may make this hard to do. Managerial and staff mind-sets about what leads to success, and about what is the right way of doing things, may need to be abandoned. This is about 'unlearning'. Unlearning implies that people have to throw out unhelpful behaviours or ways of thinking to make room for new ways of thinking. Whilst this can be achieved through *training and development,* if these old ways of thinking have become taken-for-granted assumptions for individuals, then challenging them and giving them up can be a painful process for staff. This may mean that change needs to follow a more *top-down, directive* approach.

Illustration 3.3

Preserving what you've got: the role of Appreciative Inquiry in a hospital trust

In 2001 Derek Smith was appointed Chief Executive of the Hammersmith Hospitals NHS Trust in West London and set about creating a new vision for the future of the Trust based around the values of this public sector body. Rather than seek to impose a set of values on this diverse professional and vocational workforce, the new Head of Organisation Development persuaded the CE and her colleagues to adopt a more unusual approach to change based around Appreciative Inquiry (AI). AI is an approach to organisational change that is based on the idea that if you start by asking people what works well in the organisation, then you can build on those ideas, learn how to replicate them and change through positive behaviour. A benefit of the approach is that through the use of internal facilitators, expertise and knowledge are developed in-house so that in effect the change process builds the organisational development capability of the Trust at the same time as instigating change.

A major business school trained 40 internal facilitators in how to lead one-hour workshops across the organisation. Thirty project champions were also identified from across the whole organisation. They were identified as people who commanded respect, were good at influencing and were well networked within the Trust. The CE then sent out 2,000 individual invitations to staff, and about 500 of those invited opted to attend a workshop. The workshops used mixed groups from across all the clinical directorates but people were **not** allowed to introduce

themselves using their job title – only their name and the department they were from. This reduced the restrictions of hierarchy. People were asked in pairs to share examples of when they felt good about themselves at work or good about the Trust itself. These stories were collated by the facilitators and then analysed for common themes. Four themes were identified:

- The centrality of patients
- The importance of teamwork in delivering high-quality care
- An energised atmosphere
- An emphasis on innovation

The central OD team then checked with staff across the Trust that these four core values resonated with people's experience through the normal communication channels of team meetings. By July 2004 the values were endorsed by the Trust's board and a range of different media were used to communicate the values across the Trust, including interactive websites and also paintings which were used to communicate ideas with staff for whom English might have been a second language. Since then, AI as a process has been used to facilitate a number of different issues within the hospital. The values generated through the process are used to help the induction of staff. The financial performance of the Trust has also improved. The senior management team believe that seeking to preserve and develop their existing competencies through AI as a change process has contributed to that improvement.

Adapted from Syedain, H. (22 March 2007) 'Appreciative action', *People Management,* pp. 31–33

If redundant practices are deeply embedded within an organisation, particularly if there is little time for change, the imposition of changes to working practices via structures and systems may be necessary, accompanied by visible destruction of aspects of the organisation that symbolised the past.

3.5 DIVERSITY

Diversity is to do with the degree of diversity that exists among the staff group(s) affected by change (Figure 3.5). Essentially it is asking the question: 'Is the organisation heterogeneous or homogeneous?' Change may affect groups or divisions with different subcultures, or different national cultures. Staff may also differ in the way they identify with the organisation – through their team, job, department, division or the whole organisation. Professional groups may identify more with their profession than their employing organisation. For multinational organisations, the task of implementing change over many different geographic divisions has always been a challenge.

Figure 3.5   **Contextual feature: diversity**

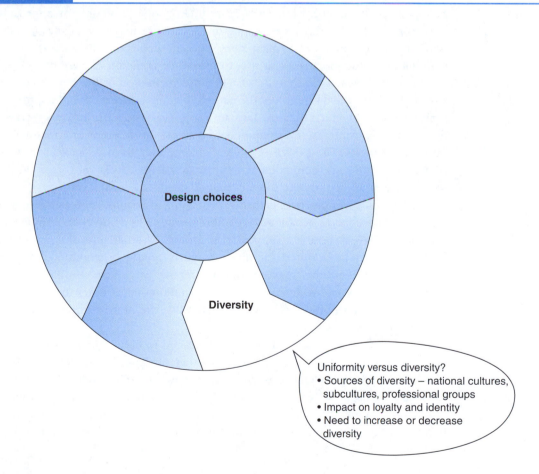

3.5.1 Assessing diversity

Many change texts assume that organisations are homogeneous. This is usually far from the truth. There are three aspects to diversity that can impact on the appropriateness of any change approach:

- The *extent* to which there is uniformity or diversity within an organisation. Diversity can occur within an organisation because of the existence of different *national cultures,* different *subcultures,* or different *professional* or *occupational groups* between divisions and departments.
- The *impact* of these differences on staff loyalty and commitment to the overall organisation.
- The extent to which the change agent wishes to *reduce* or *increase* levels of diversity as part of the intended outcomes of the change process.

If a corporation is spread over several different countries, then issues of diverse *national cultures* must be taken into account. A change initiative designed in California may be quite unacceptable to a southeast Asian national culture. The issue of cross-cultural management becomes less of an issue in truly global corporations where the culture of their staff is so international that common approaches are possible despite different geographic locations. However, truly global or transnational corporations remain rare. The more diverse the operations and national units, the more difficult it is to introduce common change processes at anything more than a visionary level. The implementation of the new vision may have to be left to the discretion of the geographic unit concerned. In Chapter 4 we look at the way in which the firm Tarmac, a supplier of building and raw materials, implemented a centralised change initiative across 11 different international and business divisions. The design of such a change may have to look at trade-offs between getting some commonality in approach across divisions versus allowing some customisation of design to meet unique needs at a local level.

Another source of diversity is that of *professional groups,* such as doctors and nurses in a hospital, or academics and administrators in a university. Any change process will have to be able to appeal to all groups. Alternatively, different change strategies might be adopted for different parts of the organisation: 'different strokes for different folks' may be a more effective way of persuading people to change than corporate-wide change implementation that assumes that employees are all the same. The more subcultures that exist, the more complex the design process becomes.

Diversity may also mean that change is required to build a more united organisation. See Illustration 3.4. The Natural History Museum in London launched a change initiative called 'One Museum' in an attempt to build a more unifying orientation amongst staff within the institute who were loyal to their particular scientific discipline or department within the Museum but less engaged by the overall mission of the place. The change initiative was designed to create a loyalty to the

Illustration 3.4

Behind the scenes: unifying changes at the Natural History Museum

The Natural History Museum in London is a well-known establishment housing skeletons of dinosaurs and Jurassic Park-style animatronics and welcoming over 3.3 million visitors each year. In 2005 its gross income was £59.7 million. In May 2004 the new Director, Mike Dixon, faced the challenge of attracting even more visitors and generating additional forms of income but also the challenge of uniting a diverse workforce behind the goal.

The Natural History Museum is both a research institute and a museum. It employs 850 people, 350 of whom are scientists and another 350 of whom are responsible for exhibitions of collections. In addition, other staff groups include security staff, cleaners and central functions such as marketing, finance, fundraising and human resources. In 2005 alone the Museum welcomed 9,000 visiting scientists. There are also 250 volunteers who make up the equivalent of 42 full-time staff.

As with many academic institutions, one of the challenges facing the new executive team was to build upon the existing sense of professional identity focused around people's scientific speciality but also to create a more unified sense of common purpose. The new Director championed the idea that the Museum

was bigger than the sum of its parts, through the idea that being a 'corporate' citizen of the Natural History Museum was as important as being an excellent citizen of the botany department. He launched a change programme, 'One Museum', to capture this idea. The aim was to ensure that whether employed as a cleaner or a curator, all employees were united in their aim to make the Museum succeed as a whole.

The Museum undertook a significant rebranding exercise and encouraged the introduction of cross-departmental project teams to work together on One Museum initiatives. The people agenda was important to the achievement of this change programme. A quarter of a million pounds was spent on training and benefits for staff such as home computers and childcare vouchers. A new pay deal was struck which particularly focused on staff at the lower end of the pay scale. The organisation was also restructured. The HR Director summed up the success of the programme as: 'Some people you will never convince. Some people will say "Yeah, okay I understand it" and some people "Yes absolutely!" Some people are less happy, some have had to leave but for most people it's "One Museum is a pretty good thing and I'm equally well treated."'

Extracted from Smedley, T. (17 May 2007) 'Natural evolution', *People Management*.

vision and values of the whole Museum's activities, a loyalty that was a necessary foundation for the implementation of other centralised change programmes that were waiting to be rolled out. In this way the new Director was trying to shape the organisational context in order to increase the organisation's receptivity for change.

Different sources of diversity in turn affect employee loyalties and commitment. If the source of diversity is national culture, to what extent would a local employee in a developing country agree to a corporate change if he or she felt that it threatened the national security or safety of his or her country? Similarly, staff who are members of professional or vocational bodies, such as lawyers and doctors, may put their allegiance to their professional norms, values and professional bodies before their allegiance to any one particular organisation. Alternatively, employees may show more loyalty to their trade or staff union. The very existence of a tradition such as collective bargaining within an organisation should alert change agents or managers to the possible existence of diversity within the workforce.

At a more basic level, staff may identify more with their immediate work or peer group rather than the notion of their whole employing organisation. Sometimes head office staff identify more with an organisation than geographically dispersed field staff. Research shows that within some large corporations, there has been a significant decline over the last decade in the loyalty felt towards both the corporation and the senior management team. However, loyalty to the immediate boss has not declined.[13] In these circumstances, where staff loyalty favours the local manager, it is important to ensure that these managers are fully committed to the aims and objectives of any change programme they are being asked to implement. This is a major factor in creating a climate of 'Engagement' and is a theme we return to in Chapter 7. The key issue is that senior managers must not assume that the rest of the staff shares their strong allegiance to the employing organisation. Change agents should not assume that the people feel that the 'organisation' is worth the pain of their individual change.

Having identified the levels of diversity or uniformity within an organisation, the change agent may consider addressing these as part of the change process. An organisation may be too diverse, with insufficient unifying elements, for commercial effectiveness or the maintenance of management control. This can often happen as a result of rapid growth or increasing internationalisation where units start to grasp too much autonomy from the centre. Alternatively it may result from many mergers and acquisitions and inadequate periods of consolidation, which in turn enables employees to retain the identity and cultures of their old organisations. Or it can be the result of strong professional identities being encouraged within the organisation. Illustration 3.8 tells the story of a group of research and development (R&D) scientists, employed by a US multinational company named 'Pelican', and their reactions to the corporate California centre's attempts to bring the scientists in the Laboratories (Pelican Labs) more in-line with management control systems operating throughout the rest of the corporation. In Pelican Labs there was a strong negative reaction by the scientists to these centralised initiatives. This resulted in a series of power plays as the scientists withheld or manipulated the knowledge base they had, which the company wished to possess. The way the change was designed failed to create the desired unity of purpose, and in fact, only created a stronger sense of professional identity within the R&D division.

Conversely, an organisation may have become too uniform, with conflict or dissent eradicated from everyday working behaviours. Alternative ideas are not considered and different personality types are either not allowed to enter the organisation or are ejected once inside. The result can be a company of clones who all think and behave alike and have fixed views on how business should be conducted. Whilst their views fit the marketplace, the business may succeed. However, if the market changes, they may struggle to change in order to meet new forms of customer or competitor demand. Here the change issue becomes one of promoting diversity within the organisation.

3.5.2 Diversity and design choices

A company's approach to managing diversity is increasingly key as the levels of internationalism increase. In reality there are huge variations in approach, depending upon the company's history and business strategy, and therefore its desired levels of centralisation, coordination and decentralisation. Centralisation refers to focusing on activities carried out at the global level, and decentralisation to activities carried out at the local subsidiary level. Coordination refers to a middle ground, balancing those activities that would best be undertaken by local subsidiaries with those managed by global or regional centres.[14]

If there are *high levels of diversity* based around different national cultures, then a *target-* or *value*-led change, if time allows, can cross these boundaries. Likewise, common output *targets* or policies may be prescribed across the globe. The case of the international furniture store IKEA shows clearly how centralised policies can be used as a means of supporting the global corporate culture. IKEA employs 84,000 people across the world and has a very strongly centralised corporate culture and product range, despite its very decentralised approach to store management and HRM. The IKEA 'HR Idea' provides a central philosophy underlying all HRM activities, rather than prescribing particular HRM activities which all stores must undertake. In IKEA, it is the philosophy underlying the practices which is the same in all locations, providing a common platform. However, actual practices vary considerably based on numerous factors, such as the age of a store, how active the HR manager is, how advanced HRM is, trade-union influence, employment legislation and local culture.[15]

A high level of diversity also has implications for change *roles*. In a large corporation, either national or international, local staff may identify more with the head of their business division than the overall Chief Executive of the whole corporation. Therefore in identifying change champions, it may be wise to devolve responsibility down to business unit heads. On the other hand, a strong organisational identity may mean that the Chief Executive is seen as a leader for all staff, and therefore is the natural choice for the role of championing change.

Diversity can also affect the *change path*. When undertaking a merger or acquisition, the initial change phase may concentrate on unifying the cultures of the two organisations involved. Similarly, if an organisation already has sub-cultures within it as a result of, for example, previous acquisitions or mergers, and this diversity needs to be reduced for the planned changes to work, then again the initial change phase may involve interventions aimed at unifying the different cultures.

The presence of diverse professional or vocational identities means that any change process has to take that diversity into account, particularly if the groups are powerful. A *role* could be created for a professional representative within the change design team, in the same way that union involvement would be sought to increase the acceptability of proposed changes. Many hospitals involve representatives from the different professional groups, such as consultants and nurses, in change teams. If this is not possible, then a change *style* that incorporates education and collaboration may be necessary to engender a better sense of ownership for change among the different groups. Behavioural prescription, as we argue above, is also less likely to be received well by professionals because they often have a great need for high levels of autonomy, as seen in the Pelican Labs example (see Illustration 3.8) However, this may point to the need for a mix of change styles. Whilst a directive style may be inappropriate for professional groups within an organisation, it may be appropriate for administrative staff groups.

3.6 CAPABILITY

Capability assesses how capable the organisation is at managing change (Figure 3.6). Capability should not be confused with experience or with readiness. Many organisations experience change but neither handle it well nor learn from their mistakes. To use an analogy, two people take a long-haul airline journey – one person prepares for the journey carefully by taking into consideration measures such as health and well-being, efficiency issues such as size and weight of luggage, and logistics so that they arrive at the airport on time and in a good frame of mind to enjoy the journey. The other person fails to adequately prepare for the flight, packs so many things that they take too much luggage, dresses in uncomfortable clothes and drinks too much alcohol before takeoff. Both people are making the same journey but one is a capable and experienced traveller who arrives at their destination as refreshed as possible, whereas the other has an awful journey and arrives worn-out and tired. Change is much the same – two firms can embark upon a similar change journey, but one is capable at change management and the other is not.

It is also important to distinguish between capability for different types and ways of delivering change. An organisation, and the individuals within it, may be very good at delivering operational change, such as rolling out new operating procedures, or sharing best practice from one part of the organisation to another. However, this does not give the organisation a capability in more transformational change. Furthermore, delivering change as a planned and deliberate intervention requires one set of capabilities, and delivering change on a more continuous basis to keep pace with a changing environment

Figure 3.6   Contextual feature: capability

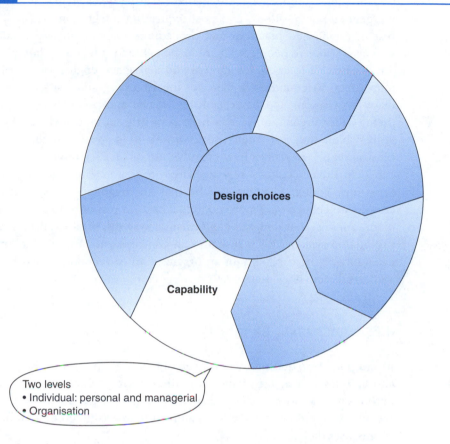

Design choices

Capability

Two levels
• Individual: personal and managerial
• Organisation

requires a different set. To push the air travel analogy further: a person may be very experienced and competent at short-haul travel, but if they approach their first long-haul journey of 18 hours with the same level of preparation they use for a two-hour flight, they may find they are ill-prepared for a journey of this length.

To assess change capability it is useful to differentiate between two forms of capability. One form of capability resides at the level of the individual. How flexible and adaptable are managers and non-managerial staff in terms of their skills, behaviours and attitudes? The more adaptable the staff, the more able they will be at handling personal and organisational transition. Some employers specifically target their recruitment at attracting people who display these personal attributes. The frenetic pace of many investment banks is possible because the banks only select people who display adaptability. All levels of employees will be expected to travel, work long hours when necessary and move about departments within the bank with little difficulty. Such employers often are more interested in finding highly flexible and intelligent people than in recruiting to specific job descriptions.

The second form of capability is located within the organisation itself. Organisations can, for example, be expert at particular types of change, such as mergers and acquisitions, and post-acquisition integration. This capability may rest in established practices and procedures for handling acquisitions, and in specialist teams of people who are responsible for the integration process. GKN, for example, a focused automotive and aerospace engineering group active in more than 30 countries in Europe, the Americas and Asia-Pacific, undertakes many acquisitions and has established teams and procedures for dealing with them. Other organisations may have sophisticated and well-developed HR systems which they can then use as levers to deliver change. Chapter 6 (see Illustration 6.5) describes how effective use of a leadership development scheme can help drive a cultural change within the professional services organisation Ernst and Young. It might also be that an organisation's systems allow it to coordinate change on a more continual basis in response to a changing environment. These systems might be information systems, business planning systems or production systems. Such systems can contribute to an organisation's 'dynamic capability',[16] the capability of an organisation to reconfigure existing processes and create new ones, to deliver on-going competitive advantage.[17]

3.6.1 Assessing capability

It is important to question whether an organisation possesses the necessary skills and abilities to manage change on either an individual or organisational level before embarking on change design and implementation. Often, organisations are overly ambitious in their plans and fail to assess their competence to deliver sophisticated change.

The first aspect of capability at the individual level is *personal capability,* the ability of individuals in an organisation to manage change within themselves. Anyone who has lived through a personal crisis such as a bereavement or divorce will understand that personal change can be an overwhelming experience. However, the more reflective the individual, the better they can expect to learn from the experience, and hopefully then be able to manage the process more effectively if it recurs. The more an individual has experienced change, and reflected on it, the higher their personal capability for change should be. Various models for understanding the process of personal transition are described in Chapter 5.

Some organisations use personal development interventions, such as coaching or Senior Executive Development programmes, to help their managers develop a change capability. These interventions usually incorporate some form of experiential learning, through which individual staff members can develop a competence for handling change at a personal level. The sponsoring organisations know they gain if their staff become more capable of managing the personal impact of change. Staff with a personal capability for change may show less resistance to change, or may need less persuasion from their peers or managers to undertake change. Resistance at an individual level is often not directed at the change but towards the change process itself.

The second aspect of capability at the individual level is *managerial capability*. How able are line and general managers to counsel and help their staff through the process of change (see Chapter 5)? Does the organisation's management possess the appropriate communication skills to convey a clarity about the change and a commitment to their staff? Do they possess change-counselling skills? Are any managers experienced in dealing with a number of different change initiatives at one time? Does the organisation know which managers within their staff have a high degree of competence at managing change?

Research has concluded that line manager capability is a key differentiator in accounting for the differences between success and failure in the different change histories of companies.[18] In companies that successfully transformed or changed, the researchers found:

- Line managers followed through consistently on change initiatives, whereas in companies that struggled with change, line manager response was inconsistent.

- There was a focus on a few clustered and coherent interventions. Thus, their line managers were not faced with a bewildering array of change initiatives.

- Managers were assessed and held accountable for managing change and were also rewarded for their efforts in this area.

At the *organisational* level, specialist change units can be established anywhere within an organisation. Some change experts may be located within strategic planning units, Chief Executive Offices, Human Resource functions or specialist change units called Organisational Development departments. As well as displaying expertise within the broad subject of change, they may be specialists in their own right in areas such as management development, top team development, management of high-potential or fast-track staff, or internal communications. All these functions contribute to an organisation's overall capability in handling change. Illustration 3.5 describes the creation of an innovation unit within the television company ITV in the UK to enhance organisational capabilities in this area.

By their very nature, *big-bang* change programmes attract greater attention. Research has shown that companies who possess a competence at this level also display certain other skills.[19] They know which levers to pull in order to achieve rapid change. Senior managers know which change initiatives can instantly tap into sources of motivation. For instance, investment bankers are primarily motivated by rewards and bonus systems. Adjusting the criteria by which bonuses are achieved is a rapid way of delivering behavioural or output change. These are, therefore, potentially key levers in achieving change within investment banks.

Different levers may well be more important in other organisations. Research suggests that a capability in more continuous, incremental change is based upon

Illustration 3.5

Illustration 3.5   *change in action*

Building capability for change and innovation at ITV

The newly appointed Executive Chairman for ITV in the UK, Michael Grade, in 2007 said that the television company needed to be more innovative. Pre-tax profits had fallen from £311 million in 2005 to £288 million in 2006. The marketplace was becoming more complex, with research suggesting that the 16–24-year-old age group is spending more time on their computers than watching TV.

An earlier cultural audit of the company had revealed that, compared with benchmark companies such as 3M, MTV, Disney, Pixar or Google, ITV was not as well placed to deliver innovation as some of those other organisations. Sharing knowledge across the business was not as well developed. It was also found that other companies had a centralised innovation unit that spread ideas and knowledge across divisions and were much better at encouraging people from different backgrounds and cultures to work together to implement innovation and change. ITV determined that they would also develop such a capability at the centre alongside the delivery of cultural change initiatives to support the generation of a more innovative climate.

A central innovation unit, Imagine, was shaped over the process of a year. Its head,

Cortizo-Burgess, said, 'If someone asks what is going on in TV, Imagine will come back with the latest cultural trends or what is happening in technology.' Keeping in constant contact with changes in the external environment is seen as critical; but linkages internally are also important. Secondments from across the various departments will ensure that Imagine is not seen as a rarefied think tank divorced from the main business. The unit is housed within one of the main sites in London, with a 'media wall' of about 20 screens, private pod areas for thinking time, interactive media and presentation facilities.

One of the other change initiatives, called Realise, targets 140 managers and works with them in workshops and individually to unlock their creativity and inspire their teams. Piloted before roll-out, this programme will be run by a team from Imagine supported by HR. Another intervention is the reinvention of the company's ideas scheme under the banner 'Create'. Again, workshops will be held and training sessions aimed to help unleash people's creative abilities. All of these initiatives should develop the new media ideas for the future and build capability for constant reinvention throughout the organisation.

Adapted from Evans, R. (22 March 2007) 'Telly Vision', *People Management,* pp. 24–26. Reproduced with permission.

a set of different skills: constantly scanning the external environment; using management systems as information and communication systems; promoting flexible organisational structures; and maintaining a relatively stable set of cultural values for the purpose of consistency.[20] This is, of course, fine as long as the changes required do not challenge the core values.

The People Process (see Chapter 6, section 6.5.2) model can be used to assess levels of change capability within an organisation.[21] Specifically it checks out transformational competence in three areas – organisational transformation, transformation of future leaders, and the ability to transform the workforce. This model assesses the strength of linkage between individual behaviour and corporate strategy through the sophisticated use of people management processes and systems. For more details of this framework and how to use it, see Chapter 6.

Capability is a difficult feature to assess in the short term. At an individual level there exists a plethora of psychometric tests that can indicate change capabilities, particularly among managerial staff. At the level of the organisation, it may simply require a database of skills and different contractual arrangements. Surprisingly enough, depending on the size of the organisation, a simple questionnaire or focus group sessions with staff may uncover valuable information in this area. Some organisations engage in capability reviews which extend beyond the area of change management but include change within its remit. Following a capability review in 2006, the UK Government's Department for Work and Pensions appointed a director of change management to support the executive team. The review evaluated the department's future capability to deliver the government's agenda in three areas: leadership, strategy and delivery.[22]

3.6.2 Capability and design choices

A change agent should not design an implementation process that the organisation is not capable of delivering. Levels of change capability affect the level of sophistication with which change can be tackled. As a result of their evaluation of their capability, some organisations choose to increase their competence in this area first before embarking upon their desired change. Chief executives may seek to shape the context so that it becomes more receptive to their planned change. In Chapter 4 the case study of Scienceco, an Irish manufacturing division of an American multinational, shows how after a review of the organisation's capability for change, senior management chose to instigate frontline managerial training in leading and managing change in order to raise their competence levels for handling the implementation of new production processes. In so doing, they shaped their organisational context to make it more capable of handling more profound change.

Capability influences the choice of *change path*. Transformational change, whether evolution or revolution, is harder to achieve. This may mean that whilst transformation is the preferred change path for an organisation, it is not an option because the organisation lacks the capabilities listed in the previous section. The organisation needs to start with adaptation or reconstruction first. For instance, earlier change may entail developing managerial capability. Managers may need to be taken through training and planned personal development initiatives to enhance their understanding of change and change management techniques. If the ultimate aim is evolution, business planning systems, including performance management systems, may need to be established to aid an incremental approach.

When considering *change targets,* value-led change is probably the hardest form of change to achieve as it requires skill to purposefully and successfully penetrate the values and attitudes of staff and to change them. At the very least the organisation would need to be able to demonstrate an Organisational Development capability, with perhaps a team of development specialists who have a knowledge of personal change. Some organisations have change consultancy teams with such capabilities who act as internal contractors within the organisations. A *change style* of *collaboration,* for example, may also require particular skills such as facilitation. Capability, therefore, also affects the choice of *change roles*. Consultants may need to be involved in a change process to compensate for a lack of change capability within an organisation.

Capability can affect the choice of *change levers*. Symbolism can be used as a powerful change lever, but in inexperienced hands symbolic change can be counterproductive (see Chapter 6). Similarly, using Human Resource Management systems as change levers, such as recruitment and selection or reward systems, requires the staff in the Human Resources function to possess both an operational excellence in these areas and a strategic understanding of these systems' power as change mechanisms (again, see Chapter 6). In addition, as stressed above, if an organisation lacks the necessary levels of individual capability, training and personal development interventions aimed at building this capability in individuals may be introduced such as the transition curve discussed in Chapter 5.

Unfortunately, the easiest options, such as top-down and directive change, often seem the most attractive. The problem is that these options may not be the most appropriate way to inculcate change within a specific organisation. The research on change is littered with examples of organisations who either implemented inappropriate change designs or attempted change designs that were too sophisticated for their levels of change competence. This is also why many of the change initiatives that are heralded as transformational actually result in reconstructive change.

3.7 CAPACITY

Capacity considers how much resource the organisation can invest in the proposed change both in terms of *cash* and *staff*. How much *time* managers have to devote to change is also an issue (see Figure 3.7). This has become a more critical factor in recent years for a number of reasons. One is that change management activity in organisations has increased as the external environment moves at a faster pace and with greater complexity. This has resulted in many senior managers increasing the number of change initiatives that are running within the organisation at any one time. However, there is substantial research evidence to show that organisations have not necessarily simultaneously increased their capacity-building activities to match the increase in initiatives.

Figure 3.7   Contextual feature: capacity

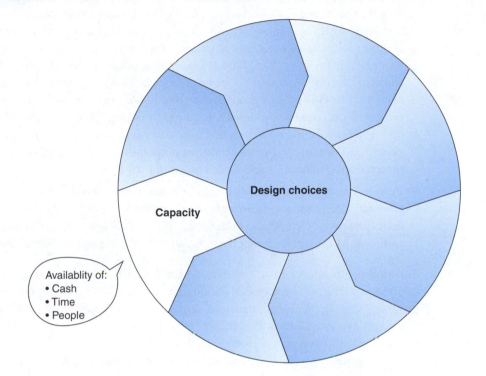

3.7.1 Assessing capacity

Many of the change programmes written up as showcase pieces feature large corporations undertaking change. The danger is that small- to medium-sized enterprises try to mimic these larger programmes but without the same capacity available for investment in initiatives. The result can be overambitious changes announced at senior management level which then fizzle out at lower levels because there is no means to manage a big-bang change. It is therefore necessary to consider which key resources are limited in any specific change scenario.

Capacity can be divided into three main areas – cash, time and people:

- *Cash*: Any change interventions that involve management development programmes, particularly off-site, are likely to be expensive and require considerable investment. Physical change assets, such as new technology, can also be expensive. Symbolic change, such as the relocation of offices or redesigning existing office layouts, can also require cash investment.

- *Time*: During change, time is a very valuable resource. Difficult questions need to be addressed about how much time is available for senior managers to devote to leading the change. Middle managers often feel squeezed by the pressures of change. All too often they are expected to implement several different change initiatives whilst at the same time continuing to deliver on all their normal performance targets. If a change agent wants line or general managers to give attention to change initiatives, then he or she needs to consider creating time for them to do so. Some organisations remove managers' responsibility for certain routine tasks for a limited period of time in order to create time for the implementation of change. Boston Consulting Group in the US argue that the amount of effort required to make a change happen should be taken into account. The consultancy group argues that if more than 10 per cent extra work on top of everyone's workload is required, it is likely that the project will run into trouble, meeting resistance and time shortages. They advise employing temporary staff or outsourcing some routine responsibilities or tasks to free up some time for staff.[23] These issues are discussed in Chapter 7.

● *People*: The issue of capability has already been considered, but quantity is also relevant. Are there sufficient people or managers who are competent in the management of change and committed to the change itself? Are these people sufficient to create the momentum needed for the change to be carried out?

Illustration 3.6 shows how capacity and scope are very much interlinked as contextual features. The scope of the change for the UK's National Health Service proposed by the Wanless report in 2002 required a huge injection of cash. However, five years later, despite increasing government investment, the Health Service had not been transformed at the pace that was desired.

Recent research in the UK suggests that senior managers are not thinking about these issues in sufficient depth before the launch of programmes.[24] Research shows that the number of managers affected by change, and multiple forms of change, is increasing in both the private and public sectors. Furthermore, there is a clear relationship between the type of organisational change experienced and the well-being of managers. Overall, many managers thought their workloads were unmanageable within their current working hours. Yet many change agenda continue to be demanding in circumstances where the capacity and capability of an organisation to implement such breadth and depth of strategic change in the timescales required is debatable. Research suggests that it is the middle managers who are bearing the strain of such strategic change.[25] The role of middle managers in change implementation is discussed in more depth in Chapter 7.

Research also suggests that people have a finite capacity for change. Organisations need to think about how to avoid '*Repetitive change syndrome*': excessive levels of change-related pain lead, in simple words, to 'more pain, less change'.[26] Symptoms of this syndrome include an overload of initiatives or a succession of change initiatives, which leads to an increased sense of uncertainty as people know that 'everything will change in six months'. This may be coupled with change-related chaos, whereby the overload of initiatives leads to burnout, and cynicism towards future changes.

In summary, an organisation that repeatedly fails to sufficiently invest in resourcing the implementation of a change programme to match the programme's scope in terms of cash, time and people will find that over time, its overall receptivity to

Illustration 3.6

Capacity: an on-going problem for the UK's National Health Service?

A major review to examine health care funding needs for the next 20 years was led by Sir Derek Wanless and published by the Treasury in April 2002. Securing Our Future Health: Taking a Long Term View was commissioned by Gordon Brown, the then Chancellor of the Exchequer, to help close the gaps in performance both within the United Kingdom and between the United Kingdom and other developed countries. The 2002 review made it clear that spending the recommended amounts would not succeed in transforming the health service unless it was accompanied by radical reform to tackle such underlying problems as excessive waiting times, poor access to services, poor quality of care and poor outcomes.

In 2007 the King's Fund, an independent charitable foundation, asked Sir Derek Wanless to again lead a team to review NHS spending five years on from his original report. Sir Derek reported that in the five years since 2002, there had been unprecedented levels of government investment in the NHS – there was an average annual real term growth of 7.4 per cent over the five years to 2007–2008. Over that period, real spending on the NHS rose by nearly 50 per cent – a total cash increase of £43.2 billion – while the proportion of the United Kingdom's gross domestic product (GDP) devoted to health care spending had grown to 9–10 per cent, close to the European Union average.

Additional UK NHS funding from 2002–2003 onwards had broadly matched the recommendations of the 2002 review for the first five years of its spending trajectories. This additional funding for the NHS over the five years enabled the service to invest in substantially increased resources – particularly labour. Staff numbers were at their highest for many years and have exceeded commitments made in the NHS Plan and adopted by the 2002 review.

However, despite this considerable increase in investment the 2007 review estimated that further increases in the number of doctors would be needed before the end of this decade to address anticipated extra demand. There had been substantial replacement and upgrading of buildings but no progress on reducing the maintenance backlog, and there was some way to go on upgrading primary care premises and hospitals. The review also noted that problems and delays in the area of NHS ICT infrastructure had the potential to jeopardise the productivity gains envisaged by the 2002 review. It noted that a future commitment not only to implementing core ICT systems but also to realising patient benefits and productivity gains was essential. The review also pointed out that the process of organisational change had been costly, not just financially but in terms of disruption, loss of experienced staff and changes in working relationships both within the NHS and with external organisations

The report acknowledged that significant investment had been made in the NHS as a whole yet the on-going cost of transformation was still a challenge. The report concluded that even higher levels of funding would be needed over the next two decades to deliver the high-quality services envisaged by the 2002 Wanless review.

Adapted from the House of Commons Research Paper. (3 May 2002) 'NHS funding and reform: the Wanless Report' and Wanless et al. (2007) 'Our future health secured? A review of NHS funding and performance', Kings Fund.

change is affected. This reduction in receptivity impacts on the level of readiness for change within the organisation, which we go on to discuss in the next section.

3.7.2 Capacity and design choices

Cash capacity affects the choice of *change path*. Big-bang programmes may be costly. Incremental change may require less up-front investment, in terms of cash and resources, but only if the management system infrastructure and line manager capability is already in place. If not, then substantial investment will be needed to build up the systems and capability.

Likewise, value-led change, if it is to be successful, involves a heavy investment in the participative/collaborative/educative change levers that will need to be used to achieve the *target* of value-driven change. Investment is needed in the form of both managerial time and money. Changing outputs or behaviours is much cheaper in terms of investing time and money but may not deliver the change that is needed.

Higher levels of capacity, in terms of time, cash and people, are needed for collaborative, educative or participative *styles* of change. Less time and money is needed in the short term for directive styles of change – although there is always the risk that managing the resistance to extreme forms of direction may be more costly in the longer term.

Choosing the right people for the key *roles* in change management also raises questions of capacity. The Chief Executive may be the company's most charismatic leader, but if he or she simply has no time to devote to the leadership of the change process, then alternative candidates need to be considered. If the company has little time but does have cash, then there is the option of bringing in an external change consultancy to help manage the change, or assembling an internal change action team to lead it through the organisation.

3.8 READINESS

Readiness for change exists at two levels. The first is the extent to which staff are aware of the need for change. The second is the amount of personal commitment there is towards changing individual skills, attitudes, behaviours or work practices (Figure 3.8). In addition, the concept of readiness can be divided into two forms: one form of readiness is the receptivity to a particular change initiative or programme – a piece of deliberate, planned change. A second form is the idea of on-going readiness for change, sometimes called agility or engagement.[27] Both of these are critical features within the change context, and accurate assessment of staff readiness at the earliest opportunity can make a fundamental difference to the design of the change, and therefore the likelihood of success.

Figure 3.8 Contextual feature: readiness

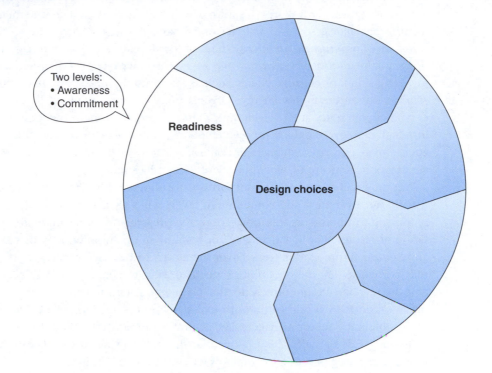

Two levels:
• Awareness
• Commitment

Readiness

Design choices

3.8.1 Assessing readiness for change

When launching a particular change initiative, change agents need to understand the degree to which employees are aware that change is necessary, and the degree of motivation staff feel towards change. Staff can be aware at a rational level of the need for change but be unprepared at an emotional level to embrace change personally. Low awareness of the need for change is primarily a reflection of the inadequacy of communication in an organisation about the need for change since achieving intellectual awareness through communication is relatively easy, whereas commitment to change exists at a very personal level and is harder to create. It is linked to the idea of personal transition, which is explored further in Chapter 5, along with how to generate readiness for change. Low commitment can exist for a variety of reasons but many of them stem from self-interest. At a simple level, the change may be disadvantageous to the individual. For instance, it may lead to a loss of power or status, or potentially a loss of job. At a deeper level, the individual may fear the prospect of change. Research has shown that employees can be ambivalent about change – they can think that the proposed change is a good idea but at the same time be frightened by the thought of what is involved.[28]

The concepts of 'organisational energy' might help to express what a high readiness for change might look like. One role of leadership is to ensure that the company's mission and strategy capture people's excitement and engage their intellectual capabilities, so as to unleash organisational energy.[29] The intersection of *intensity of organisational energy* (high or low level of activity, alertness, interaction) and the *quality of organisational energy* (positive energy such as enthusiasm, joy, satisfaction; or negative energy such as fear, frustration, sorrow) determine the state of an organisation's energy. Organisations can be described as occupying certain energy zones at any given time. One such energy zone is the 'passion zone' in which employees exhibit positive emotions, enthusiasm and excitement. In this zone employees may exhibit high readiness. The concept of the passion zone is similar to the concept of 'Hot Spots' described in Illustration 3.7.

Not only will there be different forms of readiness within an organisation, but usually the awareness and commitment levels will vary according to the level of employee within the organisation. This often presents problems in the implementation of change. For instance, a senior team of an organisation may be expert at anticipating future market trends over the next 5 to 10 years. As a result, the team may recognise that the organisation needs to start to change now in order to be able to respond competitively to the changing environment. However, if the organisation is in good health, with excellent profits and high staff satisfaction, the problem the senior managers face is how to demonstrate the need for change to lower levels of staff. This is similar to the problem faced by Glaxo when its blockbuster drug was due to come off patent in the mid 1990s.[30]

Paradoxically, sometimes a high readiness for change may raise expectations for speed and effectiveness of change programmes within customers and staff that managers then fail to deliver against. For instance, the concept of privatisation of nationalised industries is often sold to the electorate on the promise of immediate improvements in cost-effectiveness and customer service. Yet often the paradigmatic change that is required within these sorts of organisations can take years to implement, and in the interim the customer base can get frustrated or feel cheated by the slow response.

The second form of readiness for change, a constant agility, a receptivity for continuous re-creation of the organisation on an on-going basis,[31] is similar to the concept of 'employee engagement'. This is an idea that has been gaining momentum over recent years in response to the concern generated over the reports of high levels of work overload, stress and fatigue associated with continuous change. (See section 3.6.) The Chartered Institute of Personnel and Development in the UK define employee engagement as a 'passion for work', feeling positive about your job and being prepared to go the extra mile to make sure you do the job to the best of your ability.[32] High levels of engagement have been found to be associated with a range of beneficial outcomes including high performance but also a higher receptivity to change amongst employees.[33] However, engagement is an on-going organisational state, not something that is whipped up when a change programme is about to be launched. We discuss this concept in greater detail in Chapter 7.

Illustration 3.7

change in action

Igniting purpose: a high readiness for change

'Hot Spots' is a concept developed by Linda Gratton to describe how various companies have managed to create energy and readiness for change and innovation. A 'Hot Spot' is 'a moment when people are working together in exceptionally creative and collaborative ways . . . Hot spots occur when the energy within and between people flares – when mundane everyday activities are set aside for engaged work that is exciting and challenging. It is at times like these that ideas become contagious and new possibilities appear.' To create 'Hot Spots' you need 'a belief, a passion, a point of view, a question that is often challenging and audacious'. Therefore to ignite people's energy you need one of three things:

- *An igniting vision*: For example, the creation of Wikipedia by Jimmy Wales, with his appeal to imagine a world in which every single person is given free access to the sum of all human knowledge. With this vision he created a community with more than 100,000 volunteer contributors from around the world.
- *An igniting question:* For example, BP asked the question 'How can a large oil company create value in the world rather than simply being an exploiter of natural resources?' This simple but appealing question set in train many different initiatives, many of which were combined under the commitment to making

BP a force for good. Here an emotional commitment was being created to change the operations of the company for the future.

- *An igniting task*: For example, BT's Chief Executive of the retail division unleashed a readiness for change through a simple initiative called the Challenge Cup. Pierre Danon set teams to the question of how to make a positive difference to the customer's experience. One team would be crowned champions of the task challenge task. Any employee could participate but they had to form a team of eight people and appoint a team coach and a sponsor. The idea was that people just volunteered to take part. The first year it ran, there were 450 teams. The second year, 2005, there were 540 entries, and 300 teams made it through to quarterfinals. The results? In the short term there have been impressive productivity improvements which the company estimates to be about £42 million. In the longer term BT feels that it has increased employee engagement and enthusiasm for change and innovation.

Gratton concludes that igniting tasks must be meaningful to employees and resonate with employees' sense of values. They must also have impact on others and on the company and create opportunities for learning and personal growth.

Adapted from Gratton, L. (2007) 'Hot Spots: why some companies buzz with energy and innovation – and others don't', Financial Times/Prentice Hall.

3.8.2 Readiness and design choices

A low readiness for change has implications for the *change path* selected. If an organisation has a complacent workforce, the change may need to take a change *path* that is big-bang in nature but only achieves (deliberately) realignment rather than transformation for the organisation. This high-impact change design may be necessary in order to shake staff out of their complacency in readiness for a subsequent more fundamental change initiative. This is what was done at Glaxo at the beginning of the 1990s to achieve some level of readiness amongst staff.[34]

If personal change is not perceived as necessary by staff, this also impacts *the change style*. If time allows, the change agent may need to lead a participative or collaborative campaign that engages the personalities of the staff involved. Merely directing staff to change may be insufficient. Likewise if there is low readiness for change, it may be impossible to expect change to *start* at the bottom of the organisation and percolate upwards. Instead, top-down change may be necessary to kick-start the process. Alternatively, change agents could consider using pockets of good practice or pilot sites to start change initiatives. These pilot sites could symbolically act as role models for the rest of the organisation. Chapter 5 discusses these issues and tactics for developing readiness in more detail.

A low readiness for change is likely to necessitate a *change role* of strong championship. Anyone who is to lead the change must demonstrate two things to the rest of the organisation: an absolute belief or passion in the need for change and a commitment to change themselves. The change leader must also demonstrate the visible manifestation of that change to all staff in the organisation. Therefore, senior managers who are potential change champions need to be assessed against these criteria. Otherwise, they may espouse the need to change to the rest of the organisation, whilst contradicting what they espouse by not changing their own working practices.

Change levers to be considered when there is low readiness for change include personal development courses for senior managers and other levels of staff which are designed to encourage them to recognise the need for change. Where staff understand the meaning of the change but perceive little gain from it, the change agent may need to accept that some staff will not change and therefore contemplate voluntary or compulsory exits from the organisation.

When the organisation displays a high readiness for change, then change champions may find themselves pushing on an open door. The menu of design choices is increased.

3.9 POWER

A consideration of power examines where power is vested within an organisation (Figure 3.9). It is to do with the identification of the major stakeholders (within and outside the organisation) and individuals or departments that hold power in the organisation. Power can exist formally or informally within the organisation. Other issues include whose support must be canvassed and how much discretion the change unit holds.

Figure 3.9 | **Contextual feature: power**

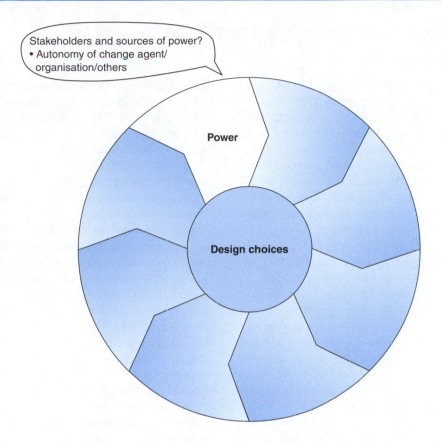

3.9.1 Assessing power

Power can be understood on many levels. Here it is considered from two perspectives – the personal power exercised within organisations by individuals or groups of people, and the power of the organisation to determine its own future.

Understanding the personal power and politics within an organisation, and identifying the major power brokers, is critical. The best choice in design terms may not be achievable because of powerful coalitions who may block the change because of their own agendas. To give a practical illustration, in the health service the medical consultants are powerful figures. Any change agent within a hospital needs to be able to convince a critical mass of consultants that the change is necessary in order to get processes implemented. Similarly Illustration 3.8 shows the power of Research and Development scientists in Pelican Labs to block and resist the imposition of new management control systems imposed upon them by the corporate centre.

In organisational terms, many change texts assume that an organisation's management team have full latitude of discretion in terms of the choices they

Illustration 3.8

The power of knowledge: resistance to change at Pelican Labs

Pelican is a computer company with a 60-year history. At the beginning of the 1990s, it employed 100,000 staff worldwide, including 20,000 in Europe. Competing on quality rather than price, the company had an extremely strong history and culture based around the traditions of scientific research, teamwork and a collective culture. The role and activities of the Research and Development Laboratories (R&D Labs) across the world reflected that legacy. Whilst the company had continually changed throughout its history, there was a tradition of granting the R&D division an immunity from some of the corporate changes designed for other divisions within the organisation.

In the mid-1990s the company started to take a dip in performance as change in the external marketplace accelerated in terms in pace and complexity. A new CEO was appointed from outside the company, something that had never happened before. The new CEO set about implementing a number of significant changes in the way the company operated, including restructurings and the implementation of new control systems. The R&D Labs in the UK found themselves reporting into a Global Head of R&D based in California, whereas before they had reported to the national head in the UK.

One of the management control systems introduced at the same time was the practice of 'forced ranking' in performance evaluations. Whilst the company had a strong tradition of evaluating performance, forced ranking was a new development for the company. Forced ranking required the line manager to force his/her team evaluations into a normal distribution regardless of their actual relative performance to each other. So, for instance, 10 per cent of each team would have to be ranked into the bottom

ranking regardless of whether their actual performance reflected that. If someone stayed in that bottom 10 per cent for two consecutive years, they could face the possibility of losing their job for poor performance.

The reaction of the R&D scientists in Pelican Labs in the UK was very negative: 'Forced ranking is an utter nonsense, a nightmare in this environment.' The scientists pointed out that much of innovation is pure luck. They said that a scientist could work hard for years with no success whereas a colleague might chance upon something that rapidly delivered success. Due to the opportunistic nature of idea generation, they perceived a ranking of individual performance in this way as inappropriate and destructive. They also found it somewhat easy to dash the mechanics of such a system: 'We have a specialist Maths group and they will sit down and tell you why these distributions are incorrect in probabilistic terms and how to bend the figures around.'

Management in R&D environments generally is different because it is difficult to impose any central systems on such a community. The most any manager can hope for is that through influence, encouragement and coaching they can persuade these bright, intelligent and highly employable people to adopt certain corporate initiatives. As one scientist explained: 'Our managers have a tough time because they don't know how to control us.' So in Pelican Labs, if the managers wanted to take a more interventionist role as required of them by California, it was difficult because they didn't necessarily have the knowledge to understand all that was going in their teams and it was that knowledge that was the valuable asset within the company. 'In a research environment people don't even know what the options are on the project if the research staff won't tell them. So here the power is held below by the people who have the knowledge, by the researchers with the bright ideas. At the end of the day it is those bright ideas that are going to save the organisation.'

The scientists themselves had the power to decide whether or not to share that knowledge with the corporation or simply keep it in their heads, believing that, 'The managers are there to serve this technical community, not the other way round.' Therefore it was very difficult for managers to impose any centralised change initiatives. Corporate presentations given by senior people from outside the Labs would be logically and critically challenged openly. Some scientists simply chose to ignore what was going on, particularly those initiatives they did not respect. Others spoke of middle managers protecting the research activity by presenting back to California what California wanted to hear but letting lower levels pursue their own activities.

Adapted from Gleadle, P., Hope Hailey, V. and Balogun, J. (2003) 'The Process of Identity Regulation in Knowledge Intensive Firms – The Case of Pelican Labs'. Paper presented to the EGOS conference, Copenhagen.

can make about change. In reality, many organisations are constrained in what they can undertake by their relationship with other institutions. This is particularly true of public sector organisations contemplating change. They may not be allowed to choose the obvious or best course of action because of constraints placed on them by their political masters – see Illustration 3.6 above on HMRC. However, this lack of room for manoeuvre is not restricted to sectors with government involvement. In private sector organisations change agents face other constraints on their decision making because of forces beyond the organisation. For instance, membership of a group of companies can be a constraint.

Shareholders or institutions like the stock market can also have an impact on change. A useful way of assessing who has power and their position on the proposed change is to use stakeholder analysis (see Chapter 7). A stakeholder analysis enables a change agent to consider what they can do to gain support for their proposed changes from those who hold power and are against the changes or are ambivalent to them. It also enables a change agent to consider how weaker stakeholders can be used to help endorse change.

3.9.2 Power and design choices

Power, or lack of it, can influence the choice of change *path* taken. A business division may badly need transformational change, but its managers can be prevented from embarking upon such a route because other more powerful divisions, or the group's centre, block their actions. Equally, a powerful parent can be a strong facilitator of change.

Powerful individuals may block the change path in the same way. A powerful chief executive who feels a potential threat from the proposed change can squash a plan for transformation in favour of more modest realignment routes. Equally, an overly powerful change agent or executive can insist on a change process which is disproportionately large in comparison to the problem the organisation is trying to address. However, the agent or executive concerned may see this as a way of raising their profile and visibility within the organisation and the wider business community.

Powerful individuals, such as managing directors or chief executives, can push through directive change. However, where the agent has identified powerful groups within the organisation whose support and commitment need to be retained, then a more collaborative style is appropriate. Paradoxically, highly powerful individuals such as chief executive officers who take a leadership role can be counterproductive when the *target* for change is values and the culture they are trying to remove is one based on blame and fear. If the CEO is seen as a bully but leads the change, staff will merely start to mimic the desired values because they feel threatened. This will not lead to significant change and the issue will never be addressed due to the atmosphere of fear.

Power is critical when assigning *roles* within a change process. If a change champion is to be appointed, then the change agent needs to pick a powerful individual or provide an individual with powerful backing. Then they also need to consider other stakeholder groups and whether or not to incorporate them in some way into the change process, particularly if these groups could be obstructive. In the case of the Clerical Medical Investment Group's transformation programme in 2000 (see Illustration 2.4), a change action team was used to develop the pilot scheme for the customer relationship management change initiative. The team was deliberately made up of some people who vigorously opposed the proposed changes and others who were positive supporters of the change. By ensuring that they worked together to design an implementation strategy, two powerful groups were symbolically and practically combined into one task force.

Specific *levers* to deal with power include techniques such as breaking and reforming both formal and informal power structures within organisations; using the existence of cliques, networks and those with influence to gain buy-in for change; and drawing on resistance management techniques (see Chapter 7).

3.10 SUMMARY

In this chapter we have discussed the need to analyse the change context in order to avoid using inappropriate change formulae. We show how the contextual analysis is the key to successful change since it is the context that should drive the design choices that are made rather than personal bias on the part of the change agent. In particular this chapter has:

- Explained the use of the change kaleidoscope as a diagnostic framework for mapping the change context.
- Described each of the eight contextual features from the kaleidoscope of time, scope, preservation, diversity, capability, capacity, readiness for change and power.
- Discussed the design implications of each of the contextual features.
- Outlined the various diagnostic frameworks that can be used to understand these contextual features.

The next chapter explores the interaction between these features of change context and the design choices through several case studies and focuses on how change agents can develop and exercise *contextual judgement,* the ability to recognise what is unique and specific about their context and design change accordingly. Having considered the range of design choices open to change agents in Chapter 2, and in this chapter how context affects which of these design changes are more or less appropriate, Chapter 4 says more about how, after having carried out a detailed analysis of the organisational change context through the contextual features, it is then necessary to determine which aspects of the current context are most critical, and how this affects the design choices made.

REFERENCES

1. For more information on this research, see Gratton, L., Hope Hailey, V., Stiles, P. and Truss, C. (2004) *Lessons from the Leading Edge,* Oxford: Oxford University Press.
2. For a review of literature examining the relationship between speed and innovation, see Kessler, E. and Chakrabarti, A. (1996) 'Innovation speed: a conceptual model of context, antecedents and outcomes', *Academy of Management Review,* 21(4), pp. 1143–91.
3. See Cottell, C. (12 July 2007) 'Commission accomplished', *People Management,* pp. 34–38.
4. The term *burning platform* is a popular term used for a compelling reason and vision to change.
5. See Hope Hailey, V. and Hendry, J. (1995) 'Corporate cultural change: is it relevant for organisations in the 1990's?', *Human Resource Management Journal,* 5 (4). 1995. Also, Collier, N., Hope Hailey, V. and Balogun, J. (2003) 'Transforming Glaxo Wellcome through the 1990s', in *Exploring Strategic Change,* 2nd edn, Balogun, J. and Hope Hailey, V. (eds).
6. See Johnson, R. (22 February 2007) 'The nicer splice', *People Management,* pp. 36–38.
7. See Hope Hailey, V., Balogun, J., Kelliher, C., Farndale, E. and Abotson, S. (2006) Change Management Consortium report on HMRC – September. Cass Business School.
8. See Hope, K. (23 March 2006) 'Lessons learnt', *People Management,* pp. 30–32.
9. For more details on how to carry out a resource audit, see Chapter 4 of *Exploring Corporate Strategy,* 7th edn.

10. For more information on tacit capabilities, see Barney, J.B. (1995) 'Looking inside for competitive advantage', *Academy of Management Executive,* IX (4), 49–61, and Prahalad, C.K. and Hamel, G. (1990) 'The core competence of the corporation', *Harvard Business Review,* 68 (3), 79–91. Chapter 4 of *Exploring Corporate Strategy,* 6th edn, also discusses how to identify more intangible resources.

11. See Change Management Consortium Report. (2003) 'Cable and Wireless'. Cranfield School of Management.

12. See Johnson, R. (1 June 2006) 'Back on track' *People Management,* pp. 24–26.

13. Farndale, E. and Hope Hailey, V. (2007) 'Managing Trust in Times of Turbulent Change'. Paper presented at the ESRC Seminar Series on Trust, (June), Oxford Brookes University.

14. See Evans, P., Pucik, V. and Barsoux, J. (2002) *The Global Challenge. Frameworks for International Human Resource Management.* New York: McGraw-Hill.

15. See Farndale, E. and Paauwe, J. (2005) 'The Role of Corporate HR Functions in MNCs: The Interplay Between Corporate, Regional and Subsidiary Levels'. Paper presented at the IHRM conference in Seville.

16. Teece, D., Pisano, G. and Shuen, A. (1997) 'Dynamic capabilities and strategic management', *Strategic Management Journal,* 18 (7), 509–33.

17. See Wright, P.M. and Snell, S. (1998) 'Towards a unifying framework for exploring fit and flexibility in Strategic Human Resource Management', *Academy of Management Review,* 23 (4), 756–72.

18. See Gratton, L., Hope Hailey, V., Stiles, P. and Truss, C. (1999) *Strategic Human Resource Management,* Oxford: Oxford University Press.

19. See Hope Hailey, V. (2004) 'What really matters in HRM and business performance – organisational agility as an alternative perspective', in *Next Generation Business Thinkers Series,* Chowdhury, S. (ed) John Wiley.

20. Shafer, R.A., Dyer, L. et al. (2001) 'Crafting a human resource strategy to foster organisational agility', *Human Resource Management,* 40 (3), pp. 197–211.

21. See reference 19.

22. See Phillips, L. (26 October 2006) 'New director drives reform at the DWP', *People Management,* p. 9.

23. See Sirkin, H. Keenan, P. and Jackson, A. (2005) 'The hard side of change management', *Harvard Business Review* (Oct).

24. See Worrall, L. and Cooper, C. (2006) *The Quality of Working Life: Managers' Health and Well-Being,* London: Chartered Management Institute.

25. See reference 7.

26. See Abrahamson, E. (1 April 2001) 'Change without pain', *Harvard Business Review.*

27. See reference 19 above.

28. Piderit, S.K. (2000) 'Rethinking resistance and recognizing ambivalence', *Academy of Management Review,* 25 (4), 783–94.

29. See Bruch, H. and Ghoshal, S. (2003) 'Unleashing Organisational Energy', MIT Sloan Management Review No. 45.

30. See reference 5.

31. See reference 19, and also Pettigrew, A. et al. (2003) *Innovative Forms of Organising,* Sage Publications. For a review of employee engagement, see Vance, R.J. (2006) *Employee Engagement and Commitment,* Alexandria: Strategic Human Resource Management Foundation.

32. Truss, K., Soane, E., Yvonne, C., Edwards, L., Wisdom, K., Croll, A. and Burnett, J. (2006) *Working Life: Employee Attitudes to Engagement 2006,* CIPD.

33. Dicke, C. (2007) 'Employee Engagement and Change Management' (May). Paper presented at the Centre for Advanced Human Resource Studies Workshop on 'Employee Engagement: What Do We Really Know? What Do We Need to Know to Take Action?', Paris.

34. See reference 5.

WORK ASSIGNMENTS

3.1. There are many textbooks and articles on 'how to do change'. Read two or three of these to identify the different change recipes advocated.

3.2. Consider an organisation with which you are familiar. Identify the aspects of the organisation that would need to be preserved in any change initiative and explain why.

3.3. Identify an organisation with low diversity and another organisation with high diversity. What are the implications for implementing change in both of these organisations?

3.4. How can you evaluate change capability within an organisation? What sources of information, for example, could you draw on?

3.5. How does a lack of capacity (cash/people/time) limit your design choices?

3.6. How might a change agent heighten readiness using technical, political, cultural and interpersonal interventions?

Analysing the change context: exercising change judgement

4.1 INTRODUCTION

The previous chapter explained how to analyse the change context using the change kaleidoscope. It explained in some detail how to assess the eight contextual features of the kaleidoscope (time, scope, preservation, diversity, capability, readiness, capacity and power) and how the nature of these contextual features impacts on the design choices (change path, start-point, style, target, levers and roles) discussed in Chapter 2. This chapter builds on the previous two chapters to say more about *contextual judgement,* the ability of change agents to recognise what is unique and specific about their current change context and design change accordingly. As this book has already stressed, it is important for a change agent to remember that even organisations that seem very similar are often, in reality, very different. In addition, even the use of past experience within the same company can be dangerous. What worked well at one time may be a poor indicator of what will work well in the current context. This is not to say that previous experience is irrelevant. However, change agents need to remember what was unique about a specific change situation and what was generalisable or replicable in other organisations or at other times. Similarly, they need to appreciate and acknowledge what is *unique* and *specific* about the current context in which they are working. This 'reading of contexts' is increasingly recognised as one of the key competencies of successful leaders, 'who understand that there are no universals'.[1] We, as the authors of this book, similarly argue that there are 'no universals' and that the art of 'situation sensing' is becoming increasingly critical for leaders as organisational complexity increases.

This chapter uses three extended case studies to develop the readers' understanding of how to use the change kaleidoscope to aid the exercise of change judgement. Its purpose is to help the reader to identify the critical contextual features in each case and understand their implications for the design choices. It is deliberately different in style from the other chapters due to the nature of the material used. The descriptions are as rich in contextual features as space permits, although in a real situation the change agent would seek much more detail. Each change feature within the kaleidoscope is analysed in every case. Through this analysis the chapter examines:

- How to understand change context using the change kaleidoscope.
- How to identify which contextual features are critical.
- How to link the analysis of context to the decisions made about change.

The cases are chosen to illustrate different aspects of change. The first case, Tarmac, looks at how a centralised change programme was implemented across several international divisions of the company. The second case, Scienceco, looks at an Irish manufacturing division of an American multinational. It details how the senior management team analysed their divisional context in anticipation of future changes and then sought to shape that context in order to make the organisation more receptive to change. The third case, Bayer Diagnostics Europe, looks at a change programme which aims to deliver greater integration and consistency across the European region.

4.2 TARMAC

This case looks at the change implemented across the whole of an international company – Tarmac. At the time of the case study, Tarmac was owned by the mining group Anglo-American. Tarmac produces construction materials such as rock, asphalt, sand, gravel and concrete, and therefore, like its parent company, it is involved in a great deal of quarrying and other extraction processes. The case describes the implementation of an Anglo-driven health and safety change programme across 10 different business and international Tarmac divisions. (See Illustration 4.1.) The case brings out the problems faced by complex international corporations that are seeking to establish common practices across diverse and decentralised business divisions.

This case shows how Tarmac overcame the constraints of power and diversity through an effective change design which balanced the need for universal adoption of the objectives of the change programme but also allowed for customisation of design at the local level. The case shows that, whilst there was only one change programme, it actually had two distinct phases in its change path: reconstruction and evolution. It shows how the design choices taken in the first phase of change helped to reshape the change context so that the organisation was much more receptive to the more fundamental change ultimately required by the time the company passed into the second evolutionary phase. The case also illustrates how a range of change levers – technical, political, cultural and interpersonal – worked together to produce a consistent and complementary battery of interventions over a prolonged period of time. Critically, the case demonstrates how a seemingly technical change around safety targets can actually require and result in a fundamental shift in attitudes and behaviours across a company.

The study looks at the change programme from three different perspectives: the experience of the Tarmac Central division in the UK and the Tarmac France division, and also the experience of Tarmac as a whole company.

Illustration 4.1   *change in action*

Zero tolerance at Tarmac: implementing an international change programme

History and structure of the company

As a company, Tarmac produces construction materials in the UK, Continental Europe, the Middle East and the Far East. The construction materials operations principally involve the production of crushed rock, sand and gravel; asphalt; ready-mixed concrete and mortar; concrete products; lime; and cement. Key customer groups include civil and building industry contractors, merchants and distributors, industrial users and DIY consumers. The production process involves the extraction, processing and delivery of these mineral resources. The company was established in 1903 and nearly a hundred years later was acquired by the Anglo-American plc in 2000.

In 2002 Tarmac UK had over 500 production units and was split into four regional business units: Tarmac Northern, Tarmac Central, Tarmac Western and Tarmac Southern. Within the UK unit there were also three other business divisions: Tarmac Concrete Products, Tarmac National Contracting and Tarmac Recycling. In addition to Tarmac UK, there was also an international division called Tarmac Group Europe, Middle East and Asia. This case study focuses on the whole of Tarmac UK plus three parts of the international division: Tarmac France, which incorporated France and Belgium; Tarmac Central Europe, which comprised Germany, Poland and the Czech Republic; and Steetley Iberia, which was the Tarmac Group's Spanish subsidiary. Much of the international expansion had been done through acquisition. For instance, Tarmac

France consisted of two main businesses, Tarmac Materiaux de Construction, which manufactured concrete products, and Tarmac Granulats, which produced aggregates. So, within both the UK group and the International group, there was a huge amount of diversity. There was also a large amount of decentralisation of strategy and decision making across all the different business divisions.

The culture of the group reflected this high level of decentralisation. An interview survey of senior managers at the centre concluded that within Tarmac UK, 'new concepts take quite a bit of time to be established' and that the main barrier to change was the highly decentralised organisational structure. Senior people at the centre reflected that an important necessity was to win over 'hearts and minds' for change to happen. Decision making within the group was achieved by agreement with the Managing Directors, supported by the Shared Services Division, who assisted each division and acted as a resource-promoting standard company practice. Senior directors also reflected that strategy was currently 'invisible' with the emphasis in the divisions upon the day-to-day business. A member of the corporate strategy team thought that complacency was one of the major barriers to achieving change. One of the directors commented that some of the business divisions' Managing Directors acted like 'barons – if they don't want to do something it doesn't happen'. They also reflected that within the businesses it was possible to 'do what you like'. Many said a new outlook was required and that the company needed to 'Be more open to new ideas and opportunities, work together more effectively, introduce team working across businesses and functions, introduce empowerment as a reality not a slogan, with greater openness and honesty.' When asked what they would identify as the most important blockers to change, most senior managers said that 'people' were the most important blockers to change as management were not incentivised to change current practices. Tarmac was described as a 'low risk culture restricting change and innovation'.

Another senior manager observed that the balance of power varied region by region and that within the international divisions there was a more complex situation. Many of the units within this division were recent acquisitions. In some cases, but not all, they were much smaller business units. Therefore, whilst the businesses in the UK had the challenge of entrenched practices with a strong history behind them, in Europe the issues included: cross-cultural management, the arrival of recent acquisitions into the Tarmac Group and the differing sizes of units depending upon specific countries.

Health and safety within Tarmac

In 2001 the Anglo-American Group declared targets for improving their record in safety, health and environmental areas across all their businesses. This case study focuses only on the safety aspects. The CEO for the Anglo Group stated that the Group's number of fatalities recorded for previous years was unacceptable and that all businesses in the group would have to adhere to Group targets. Why was this so important? In 2001 the Anglo-American Group as a whole reported that 42 employees and 16 contractors lost their lives whilst working for various business divisions The City was not happy with Anglo's record as a whole and so the Anglo Group CEO was

under pressure to ensure that the company's record in health, safety and environmental practices matched the expectations of shareholders in the twenty-first century.

Tarmac's record within the Anglo Group was comparatively good. Nevertheless, in the 2002 report Tarmac reported that, since its acquisition by Anglo in 2000, it had recorded three fatalities. So the CEO of Tarmac in turn launched the following policy statement in the Safety, Health and Environment reports for 2001 and 2002:

'The Tarmac Group will strive to achieve and maintain the highest standards of safety and health for all employees, contractors and members of the public who may be affected by its activities and will pursue continuous improvement in all areas.'

To make this happen, Tarmac launched the Anglo-branded change target, which was called OTTO and stood for 'Zero Tolerance Target Zero'. The target of the change programme was to achieve 'Zero Lost Time Injuries by 2005' and a 50 per cent year-on-year reduction in Lost Time Injuries. Zero Tolerance was defined as:

- No one observes an unsafe situation without taking appropriate action.
- No one observes someone behaving in an unsafe manner without requiring them to stop.
- No one allows a colleague to work in unsafe conditions.

It was noted at the time that OTTO represented 'a significant challenge' and required a 'quantum leap forward' in safety attitudes and behaviour by every single person who entered a Tarmac-controlled site. The CEO announced that his personal message to all employees was this: *'No job is so important that it cannot be done safely.'* The CEO also talked about 'creating a culture' where everyone acted and believed in the importance of the new safety standards. Whilst the CEO could seek to influence the behaviour of Tarmac's managers and employees, there was also the challenge of large numbers of people operating within Tarmac sites who were not directly employed by Tarmac – these were the various transport *contractors* who were constantly on-site collecting or delivering materials.

The roll-out of the central change programme

All businesses and divisions were given a target of 2002 to reduce lost time injury frequency (LTIF) by 50 per cent, using their 2001 performance as a baseline. The focus was on eliminating injuries and ensuring that, when they did occur, every assistance was given to employees to ensure their speedy return to work. In addition Tarmac supported the government's initiative (Health and Safety Executive – HSE) in this area. The government's aim was to 'halve the number of accidents in the quarrying industry' by 2005. The company contracted the consultancy services group DuPont to help them with the roll-out.

In addition, the company declared that various policies would be put in place to support OTTO. The report stated that in order to achieve these aims, the Company would:

- Demonstrate visible commitment by all line managers carrying out regular safety task audits.
- Adopt a behavioural approach to the management of safety and health.
- Seek to eliminate at-risk behaviour.
- Achieve and maintain conditions of work which are healthy and safe.
- Provide adequate welfare facilities for our employees.
- Seek to eliminate incidents and dangerous occurrences.

- Carry out appropriate health screening of employees every three years.
- Provide effective instruction, training and supervision.
- Ensure that persons employed are both physically and mentally fit and competent for their duties.
- Ensure that employees are fully aware of their responsibilities regarding safety, health and welfare.
- Identify hazards and assess risks and eliminate where practicable.
- Involve employees at all levels by establishing local SHE committees.
- Provide and maintain safe plants and equipment.
- Continuously review and revise policy.
- Provide adequate resources to ensure full compliance of the above.

Specific initiatives to support the transition included:

Contractors' safety passport for quarries: Launched by a Safety Consultancy, EPIC, in conjunction with the HSE, the scheme aimed to ensure that all contractors had a minimum understanding of safety, health and environmental issues. Tarmac issued a notice to all its contractors, saying that it needed them to hold this passport by December 2003. The company wrote to 2,700 companies between 2001 and the end of 2002.

Safety Task Auditing: A professor who was a safety expert was commissioned by the Anglo Group to carry out a review of safety across the whole Anglo Group. On of his conclusions was that if the Group wanted to improve safety performance, then they needed to focus on 'unsafe behaviour', as this was the main cause of 90 per cent of workforce injuries. He concluded that if OTTO was to be achieved, the focus had to be on people. As a result of his work, 'Safety Task Auditing' was introduced. It was piloted in

Tarmac Central in 2001 and then rolled out across the whole Group after that. Task Auditing involved observing people at work, discussing what they were doing and the way the work was being carried out, identifying safe and unsafe acts, gaining employee commitment to work safely in the future and praising safe working. All line managers from the CEO downwards were trained in Task Auditing techniques, and targets were set for the number of task audits that had to be completed each month. The CEO and all the MDs had to commit to spending at least eight hours a week on Task Auditing. A consequence of this was something that became known as 'visible felt leadership'. The fact that senior managers and the CEO were *seen* at the sites *doing* the auditing was felt to be very important in communicating the importance of the change. One story which went into the company folklore was of a time when the Chief Executive Officer, a charming, well-spoken man, was at a particular site and a contractor drove in and used a procedure which contradicted all safety rules. Without explaining who he was, the CEO, in full view of all the workforce, went over to the contractor and spoke to him in his cab and explained why his behaviour and actions were contradicting company procedures. The story goes that the contractor turned round and gave the CEO a mouthful of abuse before somebody came up and explained to him that he was swearing at the CEO of Tarmac! This story was told again and again around the company.

The Golden Rules: Tarmac had always supported the EU Week for Safety and Health, but in 2002 used the week to launch two initiatives. One was a Transport Initiative, which audited whether transport used on Tarmac sites, whether owned or contracted, had appropriate safety mechanisms such as CCTV for reversing and tipping. The other initiative was the Group-wide launch of 'The Golden Rules'. The Golden Rules developed safety procedures which were to be strictly applied and enforced at all locations. A training video was produced with an introduction from the CEO. The video was translated into 10 main languages. A safety calendar for 2003 was produced, and the launch of the Golden Rules continued well into 2003. The calendar and its illustrations were used as a prop to conduct refresher training courses throughout the year.

Publicity for particular events: Certain outreach events were advertised throughout the company. One example was an event in 2002 involving a local primary school who visited one of the Tarmac sites and produced safety posters for the site. In return the supervisor from the site visited the school and conducted a safety audit! By 2003 the school initiative had developed to include a cartoon character called Otto the Otter. Another example of publicity material was the communication of the safety auditing conducted at Shared Services in the Midlands. Whilst the site consisted of a set of office blocks, it was made clear to the rest of the company that this too was subject to the new Golden Rules. One quarry in Yorkshire won the Anglo-American CEO's Safety Award for small sites, and several Tarmac operations won external safety awards. A road safety policy was also publicised in 2003 and businesses within the Group continued to win both Anglo-American Group awards for safety and also external awards from within the industry as a whole.

Communication: Communication initiatives were increased during the change. In 2002 there was a fatal injury to a Belgian factory worker who was crushed between a forklift truck and a 1.5 tonne steel mould. It was discovered that the operative had improvised a method for lifting the mould and had not been following safety procedures. The fact that the individual had not been following the Golden Rules was communicated across the company. In 2003 safety booklets were produced in some divisions to emphasise safety in the home.

Divisional reactions to the changes

Although data was collected on all 10 divisions, the case focuses on the reactions of just two of those divisions, Tarmac Central (UK) and Tarmac France.

Tarmac Central

The majority of staff surveyed in the Central business division had a clear view that the purpose of the change was to 'bring people home safely and to reduce accident levels'. Whilst most saw that a safety culture was already in place before the change, they recognised that the change was necessary to bring the company in-line with the increase in safety awareness throughout the industry. A few saw a secondary purpose being the company's desire to avoid litigation. In terms of the specific outcomes of the change, staff were clear that Target Zero meant that there were to be zero accidents at the end of five years. However, as the process began to be rolled out, those surveyed said that they saw that the change was 'aiming to alter a culture' by trying to bring common standards to a newly amalgamated group. They did not perceive that the change would end until the end of 2005.

Staff said that initially they did not perceive the change to be that urgent but with the benefit of hindsight, they understood the urgency. All parts of the workplace were affected, but it was recognised that operational workplaces were affected far more than offices. However, it was perceived that all levels of *people* were affected. Staff in Central perceived the change to be quite 'radical' because they said 'it affected the basic way we go about our work'. There were far more risk assessments and a greater pressure to make the job safer. They also said that the evidence that the company was willing to spend money on the initiative communicated that it was a fundamental and important change. There was a universal feeling that it was almost a case of 'money no object' when requests were made to spend money on plant and equipment connected with safety.

People spoke about the need to get rid of 'a cavalier attitude and culture', which meant getting rid of the acceptance that accidents 'happened' and discarding a 'production-first' ethos. All levels of staff remarked that before the change programme was launched there were big differences between various sites within Tarmac Central and that attitudes to safety had varied from site to site depending upon the attitude of the site managers.

Staff did not feel that there had been major changes to the organisational structure, but new posts had been created for safety advisers in the division. What did change was the amount of time operational managers spent on the Health and Safety component of their job: time spent on SHE apparently doubled. Despite the minimal structural changes, change was described as 'very visible' in other ways. For instance, safety was always placed at the top of the agenda for meetings, and directors and senior managers were seen to lead meetings on the subject. Logos were changed and the day-to-day language changed in the sites to incorporate all the new initiatives. Uniforms were changed, and safety messages were also put into wage packets; put on mugs, pens and pads; and incorporated into signage. Staff felt this all had a great impact. There was much more discussion around safety figures, and news of any Lost Time for Injury travelled rapidly around the organisation.

As the change programme progressed, people felt staff loyalty to the company actually increased. This was because a consequence of the change programme was that staff felt more empowered because of their ability to challenge unsafe practices, and they also felt that the company had made a real effort to communicate with them. The impact of this empowerment was profound upon lower levels, and it was seen as one of the reasons this change process had been successful. The employees felt that the issue now was maintaining that sense of empowerment in other areas – not just safety. They also felt that the change process had been 'seen through', whereas other change initiatives had been left to fall by the wayside.

Staff were particularly taken with the impact of all the different communication tools and techniques that had been used to reinforce the corporate message. At the start of the process, staff felt the communication style was very directive – the change was to happen and it was not up for negotiation. (The pressure from Anglo was associated with this approach.) However, as the process was rolled out staff felt the emphasis shifted to a more collaborative approach through seeking staff opinions and involvement in the change. In particular they mentioned the face-to-face team briefings, Toolbox Talks and Task Auditing, as particularly successful. The communication papers on the notice boards were not seen as effective.

The fact that numerical safety targets were written into the performance management system was seen to have helped, but people felt that it was the emphasis in the programme upon behaviours which had made a difference. Some people thought, though, that something deeper had happened – one operative said he'd changed his whole approach after 35 years of working at Tarmac. It was noted that site managers, supervisors and operations managers had all carried a heavy part of the workload in making the change happen. Whilst staff recognised that money had been made available, the extra time necessary to make the change happen was put in by the site managers through their own personal commitment – 'the managers have had to carry the change process'. (Few mentioned the role of the external consultants.) As a result of this, the staff surveyed said that initially people complied with the things which needed doing regarding the change but that commitment increased as they realised that the company was serious about OTTO's

implementation. Comments were made that it was the 'upkeep of pressure on the process' which was more important to the effective implementation than the initial launch, although they recognised that the launch itself had been impressive.

The division had been given overall objectives that were being applied to the Group as a whole, but they did recognise that the methods by which these objectives were achieved varied slightly. So there was some autonomy but there were also standard procedures which had to be adhered to. As sites implemented the change, examples of good practice spread across the division, although this was not planned – it just happened.

Resistance came from the older workers and from contractors and hauliers. The change programme cost the contractors and hauliers money and time which they had to pay for themselves, whereas it didn't personally cost the company employees any money. Halfway through the programme, greater emphasis was given to the contractors and hauliers, and staff felt that the change could have gone even quicker if greater emphasis had been given to these contract groups at the outset.

Tarmac France

The French businesses were described as having an 'authoritarian approach' – considering people as incapable of thought. One person said that 'the overriding theme was that of the attitude of management towards employees: that they were there to carry out tasks and not reflect upon them'. People commented that there was an 'entrenched' view that the need to produce counted above all else. There was apparently a poor communication structure and a great deal of routinised behaviour which was described as akin to 'sclerosis'. Employees felt that there was a lack of consultation and explanation and an inappropriate sense of priorities, one example of which was the fact that maintenance was carried on without halting the plant. Morale was an issue.

When the change was introduced, the tight time frame and the demanding targets set for the change were seen as a positive influence because they created a sense of urgency for change amongst the senior managers. The setting of clear, common and easily measurable objectives assisted in bringing about a change in attitude in the upper levels, but even then it was said that it took them six months to accept that this change was really going to happen. As these senior managers felt the pressure, they directed the message down through the different levels of the organisation in an authoritarian way, typical of their management style. Lower levels of staff said that it took a while for the seriousness of the issue to filter down. Middle managers became closely involved in the gradual process of putting in day-to-day improvements from late 2001 onwards, and there was a certain amount of variation of approach at the area level as the implementation of objectives varied according to local needs and management styles. One senior manager commented that 'senior management communicated the message and middle management implemented it'. In particular the responsibility for safety improvement was given to the production managers rather than the specialist safety units, with the result that safety and production were not seen as separate concerns. The urgency for the change was highlighted following the fatal accident in Belgium in 2002, which was seen as a 'wake-up call' to the group and made safety become of maximum importance.

Tarmac France described the change as both deep and broad since it 'stretched vertically down hierarchies, impacted on almost all tasks including production and maintenance and involved a profound cultural shift'. The French middle managers specifically commented that prior to the change, they lacked a structure through which they could make improvements, although senior managers seemed keen to preserve the current management structure. They said that the capability for change was there within the organisation, but what was important was the creation of the right environment in which these changes could take place. However, employees reported that initially they were sceptical about the provision of resources – they feared that any suggestion for safety improvements would be disregarded and not actioned because it would involve spending money. As a result, at first employees did not speak up and initiative was 'stifled'.

In the end, as in Tarmac Central UK, there seemed to be no restrictions in terms of financial, technical or management resources, and this investment created the appropriate environment. In addition, employees started to see that management's words were being 'backed up by actions', with the widespread investment in technical improvements to the safety environment. Employees started to be consulted on a day-to-day basis by line managers as well as through the task audits and the safety 'circle' teams that were established. This resulted in improved motivation generally and the more collaborative style meant that the workforce started to reflect on their actions and the consequences of those actions, and safety started to improve. The fatality in Belgium resulted in senior managers visiting sites and talking about the accident and then reiterating the importance of safety. Safety films were shown to the various sites. All of this meant that the everyday 'routines' of work started to be 'broken', which allowed change to happen. In particular the two-way communication had a huge impact on employees. Employees said that they were self-disciplining, more responsible for their actions and therefore more confident about themselves. Employees felt that it was the improved two-way communication, laterally and vertically, that had led to a change in behaviour and fewer 'unsafe acts'. Others commented, like other parts of the Tarmac Group, that this 'visible felt leadership' was a critical lever in the change.

Overall, senior managers felt that the first six months had seen 70 per cent of the effort focused on technical changes, with only 30 per cent on cultural aspects of the change, but that thereafter the balance had been switched.

Senior people felt that the Golden Rules and the Task Audits were the most critical change levers. Some employees felt that the training for task auditing had been insufficient in some cases and others said that some recognition and celebration of the improved performance would be welcome.

Overall, management felt they had been allowed to adopt a tailored approach to implementation, but with clear and measurable goals which were common across the group. They said that credibility for the initiative was secured through a constant reinforcement of the message, which was said to leave no room for doubt or compromise. In general, motivation and a sense of involvement had improved as a result of changes in communication and training. Employees tended to now reflect before acting. Senior managers said that the moral dimension helped – improved safety was in everybody's interests and was easier to 'sell' than profit-driven initiatives. Lastly, senior managers commented that the general approach to all work had improved and that the results of the change had served as a platform for positive changes in other areas such as quality and the environment.

Group Approach

When considering the approach across the whole group, there was agreement that the change had started top-down with a clear, directive – some said coercive – style set by the Group's senior management. The health and safety theme was accessible, visible, clear and measurable and this was seen to be of critical importance. The initial statement of the CEOs – 'No job is so important that it cannot be done safely' – was seen to have huge impact. The fact that it affected everyone in the Group was seen as a critical

contributor to its success, as no one could be passive in the change.

In most parts of the Group, the directive approach had given way to a more participative and empowered style of communication after the initial stage of change. The senior managers and the divisional MDs were seen as the leaders of the change. All agreed that the scope was broad and deep and that the target for the change had at first been employee behaviours but that over time, people's values had also changed. People said there had been 'relentless communication', and both 'bonuses' and 'bollockings' had been tied into the change process as levers for change.

Europe did feel that it had been more difficult for its various sites because the businesses were at differing levels of sophistication in safety provision and change capability. This was because some businesses had only joined the Group recently. Some found the scale of the change was too much too soon for them and felt the timescale was too rapid for them. Some felt that newer entrants to the Group should have been accorded greater funds and attention than more mature businesses. Whilst everyone implemented the change, the change paths did vary according to the unit, and the exact nature of the implementation might have also varied. Overall people felt that it was a major cultural change because of the changes it had brought about in terms of communication, management style and empowerment.

Results of the change

At the end of 2003, the Tarmac Group as a whole had recorded a 75 per cent improvement on their record in 2000. In 2003 89 per cent of their 697 locations were accident-free. Tarmac Iberia recorded 'disappointing results'. Using the UK's Health and Safety Executive's measures, Tarmac recorded a 77 per cent improvement rate, twice the rate achieved by the industry sector as a whole. However, three prosecutions were also brought by the UK's Health and Safety Executive in 2003 into Tarmac Concrete Products and Tarmac Central.

In 2003, from a focus group of senior managers from across all the divisions, both UK and international, 50 per cent said that health and safety issues were the most critical issues they faced, with the other 50 per cent saying that achieving budget in a competitive marketplace was also important. Forty-four per cent said that the key challenges facing Tarmac were health and safety issues, whereas only 34 per cent said it was the competition. When asked about the potentially changing elements of the external environment, 83 per cent mentioned the new legislation the company had to operate within. This included the European Working Time Directive, European product standards, environmental legislation and health and safety directives.

The results from the 2003 Employee Attitude survey showed that over three-quarters of staff were highly committed to helping Tarmac succeed. A high proportion of staff (92 per cent) agreed that they trusted Tarmac's senior managers, and only 20 per cent disagreed, saying that Tarmac's senior managers hadn't put enough time and effort into communicating the Division's goals and priorities. Fifty per cent of staff disagreed that Tarmac as a whole was good at sharing best practice, and only 34 per cent rated Tarmac as good at communicating. The three things people rated as most important in terms of communication were Safety, then Strategy and Future Direction and finally Financial Performance. The survey showed there was a strong desire for more involvement and that staff found face-to-face channels of communication particularly valuable.

4.2.1 The kaleidoscope of Tarmac Central UK

Time was not initially recognised as urgent at the start of the change process. In a highly decentralised company operating across many different international regions, many of whose operating units had only recently been acquired into the group, it was perhaps difficult for lower levels of staff in 1 of 10 divisions to understand that the parent company had set the business some tight deadlines for achieving this change. The *scope* of the change was recognised, however, at management levels. Managers saw that it affected the whole division and that it was a deep change requiring a transformation in the 'basic way we go about our work'. In addition the senior divisional managers wanted to keep certain operating practices but did not want to *preserve* their 'cavalier attitude and culture' towards safety and the general 'production-first' ethos. There was also an embedded *diversity* of approach to health and safety amongst the various sites, even though the divisional culture itself was fairly homogeneous. In terms of *capability* the division did not have any organisational change expert or expertise. This left the division heavily reliant upon the skills and capabilities of their site managers and on the communication of objectives in a manner that made them clear to lower levels of staff and contractors.

A positive feature of the change context was the consensus in terms of *capacity* that 'money was no object'. Managers and non-managerial staff could see that the company was willing to invest heavily in the implementation of the programme in terms of plant and equipment, although the managerial time was a constraint. Managers said that the corporate centre had not anticipated the amount of managerial time that would be consumed by the implementation of OTTO.

Generally there was little awareness that a change was necessary, as safety procedures had always been in place and many people felt that the attitudes to safety were 'good enough'. However, the tight timescales imposed with the drive from Anglo did generate a willingness to act in the senior managers and some level of *readiness*. Following the eye-catching launch of the change, awareness of the need to change was achieved through the exercise of clear direction from the group, and commitment gradually started to emerge and grow as employees realised that the company was serious and the initiative was going to be sustained. Employees also started to see that there were benefits for them as over time, the change programme was perceived as actually empowering lower levels. A high readiness for change was therefore developed over time.

Examination of the *power* dynamics is interesting. Anglo was a powerful force behind the change and the corporate centre at Tarmac was given little choice but to ensure that the parent company's objectives were communicated and implemented. However, there was still a powerful culture of decentralisation and autonomy within the divisions. Another powerful group were the stakeholders who were not employed by Tarmac – the hauliers and contractors. The change needed to affect them too.

4.2.2 Key contextual features for Tarmac Central

See Figure 4.1.

4.2.3 Design implications for Tarmac Central

Change path

The change process had two phases. These were not the result of a formal design but emerged in the course of the implementation of the change. The first phase was reconstruction and was concerned with the establishment of the clear targets for change as measured through LTIF, the safety targets established in conjunction with the national Health and Safety Executive and the publication of the Golden Rules. Communication initiatives were also put in place in this phase.

| Figure 4.1 | Key contextual features for Tarmac Central |

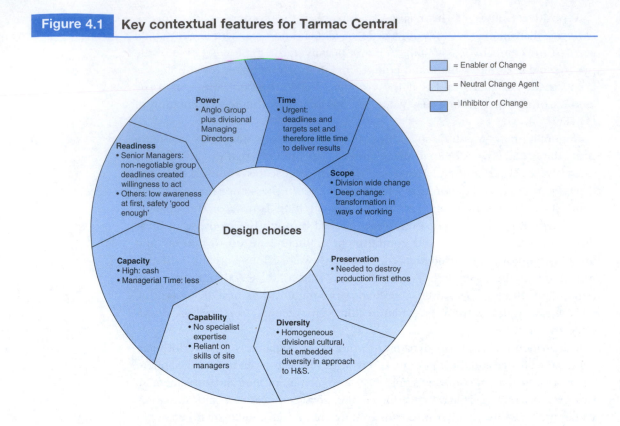

Change moved into the second phase as people's attitudes and behaviours started to change in an evolutionary fashion through the use of more cultural and symbolic interventions. As attitudes and behaviours changed, staff started to use phrases such as 'radical change' to represent their day-to-day experience.

Change start-point

In line with the two phases of change, the reconstruction phase started top-down. With low readiness for change, there was little hope that adherence to the new safety targets would emerge over time, certainly not in time for senior managers to reach the targets set for them by the corporate centre. However, whilst the technical levers were imposed top-down and the initial communication was also top-down, as the cultural change began to emerge, more autonomy was given to the division to allow for variation in approach and to take advantage of a developing managerial capability to deliver change. A more bottom-up approach was established once the discipline of common standards and targets had been established, consistent with a more evolutionary phase of change. Managers reported that pockets of good practice started to emerge within the different sites, and in turn this created the emergence of a natural collection of local stories about changes to day-to-day working practices.

Change style

The style again was split into two phases, with direction dominating during the reconstructive phase as appropriate, given the low readiness and speed required with a shift to a more collaborative and educative approach in the second phase. Some managers felt that the measurement of LTIF had been a fear factor which had been deployed in quite a coercive way initially. In the second phase, employees were encouraged to speak up and have their voice heard, particularly through the use of safety briefings, task auditing, etc. The fact that this style was different to anything that had been experienced before in the Division helped to develop a shift in attitudes and behaviours. Therefore the style of the change was producing a transformation, in addition to the actual content of the change programme itself.

Change target

Again consistent with a reconstruction, the first phase used outputs as the change targets through the imposition of LTIF objectives, OTTO targets and Health and Safety Executive targets. However, the publication of the Golden Rules in this first stage also heralded the attention that behaviours were to be given. A focus on behavioural change then dominated the second phase, and over time a change in values was achieved, although this was never a direct target in either phase.

Change levers

As the discussion of other design choices has revealed, in the first phase the levers used were primarily technical levers around targets, objectives and changes in measurement systems. The publication of the Golden Rules acted as a bridgehead between the technical interventions of the reconstruction phase and the deployment of more cultural and interpersonal levers in the phase of evolutionary cultural change. Many companies would have just published the Golden Rules as a behavioural mantra. At Tarmac, by comparison, Central backed this up with managerial attention to achieving shifts in day-to-day practice, which resulted in a shift in mind-sets. Arguably, however, Tarmac deployed these cultural levers because the targets set by Anglo and Tarmac's corporate centre were so demanding that they could only be achieved through fundamental change. Hard technical targets ensured that softer levers had to be deployed, since achievement of the technical targets ultimately required behavioural and attitudinal change. In turn, the deployment of the softer inter- ventions would not have been possible without the willingness by the company to invest in the change process. Thus it was a combination of the hard targets and the investment that made the behavioural and attitudinal change both necessary and possible.

Change roles

Staff within the Central Division identified their Managing Director as the leader of change. However, other change agents included the external consultants used to advise the whole company, the CEO of Tarmac and the CEO of Anglo. The two CEOs launched the change programme, but the power of these significant change agents was hidden from divisional staff in the second phase. This fitted the tradition of decentralisation and autonomy within the divisions. In addition, staff in Tarmac generally identified with their local managers and Divisional senior managers, and it was their leadership that delivered the attitudinal and behavioural change.

Summary of Tarmac Central

What is particularly impressive about this change is the way the design of change was reconfigured to match the different phases of change, with far more emphasis on the softer cultural and interpersonal levers in the second phase of evolutionary change, which also took advantage of the growing readiness and capability for change following the initial reconstruction. However, it was also significant that in both stages of change, hard outputs and targets were set as a means of evaluating the change on a continuous basis. This was necessary because of the time deadline set for the company by the Anglo Group CEO.

4.2.4 The kaleidoscope for Tarmac France

In conducting a kaleidoscope analysis for the French division, it is important to appreciate the different history of the company and the way this affected their general receptivity to change. The various units within the Divisions had become part of Tarmac relatively recently, and their exposure to the Anglo parent company was even less. Arguably there was an even greater cynicism about the corporation's commitment to change and, as their attention to safety was more underdeveloped than Central's, it affected timescales for implementation and the scoping of the change.

Managers within the French division, which included Belgian sites as well, felt the *time*scale for the delivery of the change was tight, especially considering what they saw as the huge *scope* of the change that had to be delivered if the targets were to be achieved. The change had to be both broad and deep in penetration. This was underlined by the fact that the Division felt there was little that needed to be *preserved* within the old culture and structure. In particular it was felt that the company needed to get rid of their authoritarian approach and the tendency to focus solely on production. Although there was variation in culture and style, not least two different national cultures, *diversity* could not be allowed to deflect the company from imposing common goals and objectives. Change *capability* was mixed across the Division. However, one of the positive drivers for change was the fact that the money (*capacity*) was made available from within the whole group to support the change in France. This affected the levels of *readiness* within the division. At first there was cynicism resulting in low levels of readiness for change amongst non-managerial levels of staff. They believed that requests for investment would not be successful. The fact that money was invested turned the climate of disbelief into a climate of awareness that change was going to happen, although other design decisions were also important in this respect. At the start of the change, *power* was firmly vested in senior management.

4.2.5 Key contextual features for Tarmac France

See Figure 4.2.

Figure 4.2 **Key contextual features for Tarmac France**

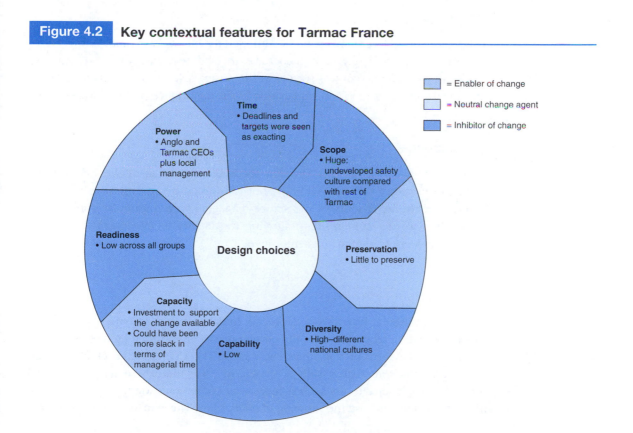

4.2.6 Design implications for Tarmac France

Change path

Although the intended change path was reconstruction followed by evolution, it was not clear whether this division had achieved a full transformational change at the time of the research. This is perhaps not surprising, given the more entrenched levels of inertia and authoritarian culture within this Division. The fact that it took a fatal accident in this Division to actually alert staff to the seriousness of the change objectives reflects the high levels of complacency that existed. Certain units reported a feeling of increased responsibility at the time of the research, but this was not a universal phenomenon, implying that more work was necessary to successfully complete a transformational change.

Change start-point

Given the low levels of readiness and capability for change, the start-point for the change had to be top- down.

Change style

This was a critical lever in many ways. Although the change style initially was highly directive, and some described it as coercive, the shift towards a more collaborative and consultative approach was seen as key in raising levels of readiness for change. Improved communication and explanation of the importance of the change helped.

Change target

As with Tarmac Central, this Division focused on outputs as the initial target through the use of OTTO, LTIF, etc., but reinforced by an emphasis on behaviours. Here the behaviours of the senior managers were particularly important. Their visits to the various sites following the fatality enabled staff to see that behaviours were changing at a senior level.

Change levers

A variety of different levers were deployed. Initially, as in the Central Division and consistent with a reconstruction, the emphasis was on introducing technical interventions in the form of objectives such as OTTO, LTIF and the Golden Rules. However, consistent with a shift to evolution, over time these were reinforced through interpersonal levers such as increasing communication through task auditing and briefings and also the showing of safety films. The managers' site visits were also hugely symbolic, as was the handing over of leadership for the change to middle managers.

Change roles

As noted above, it was initially led by the senior management with what was described as 'unconditional support' from the Managing Director. Middle management led the change in the later stages.

Summary

In general the design choices in Tarmac France fitted the context and fitted two different phases of reconstruction and evolution. However, the Division could be described as a more constrained context than the Central Division in the UK. There were several factors contributing to this: it was a more geographically distributed and culturally diverse division than its counterparts in the UK, and it also had a less developed safety culture. Thus the scope of the change was broader and deeper, requiring more effort. The Division thought it could have been given even more investment in recognition of this larger scope.

4.2.7 The kaleidoscope for Tarmac Group overall

At one level it is possible to consider and build a kaleidoscope for the Tarmac group overall. *Time,* for example, was generally seen as urgent leading to a short timescale for what was a transformational change. The change was also typically seen as 'all-encompassing' and requiring broad change across all of the business units. It was recognised that the change needed to affect every employee within every business across every country. Having said that, however, the depth of change needed by individual business units was different, as existing safety cultures varied in their levels of sophistication. So for some countries in the European region, such as France, and for some of the smaller businesses within the UK Division, for instance, the depth of the change was greater than in the large main UK Tarmac divisions. This affected how fast they could move and how much they could achieve in the short timescales. Whilst the *diversity* of the organisation was not allowed to hinder the universal application of the objectives of the SHE change initiative, and business divisions were not allowed to play the 'not invented here' card to wriggle out of change, the diversity does make it difficult to draw singular conclusions about the contextual features of the kaleidoscope for the Tarmac Group overall. This illustrates that in complex multi-divisional organisations, the analysis of context may need to be done on a division by division basis.

The diversity of the business divisions in terms of change context was also reflected in capacity and readiness. *Capacity* for change was consistently created through the availability of large amounts of cash investment, although managerial time remained a constrained resource, particularly for those middle managers tasked with the day-to-day implementation of the change. Thus some businesses, such as France, felt that they should have had more investment of time and resources given the greater depth of change required. In contrast, the Shared Services Division at the centre of the Tarmac group, a purely managerial and administrative unit, reported that they had plenty of cash and time. In terms of *readiness,* across the group generally at the beginning of the change programme, people were aware of the importance of the change, but probably not of the speed and extent required by the parent group. The targets and deadlines imposed upon Tarmac by the Group did create a sense of urgency amongst the divisional senior teams, but to varying degrees.

4.2.8 Design implications for Tarmac Group

Change path

Despite the differences in context by division, the consistent need for transformational change driven by the imposition of tight targets and deadlines led to a predominant change path across the divisions similar to that seen in Tarmac Central: a period of reconstructive change followed by a phase of more transformative evolutionary change. However, this was not a universal experience. In Tarmac France, their intention was to deliver transformational change but at the time of the research, they had yet to embed the new behaviours and values across the whole organisation. In contrast, the Shared Services Division did not experience such significant shifts in empowerment as they had a more consultative tradition at the start of the change process. Given the breadth and depth of diversity across the group, it would not have been surprising for different paths to have been taken even if there was a shared destination.

Change start-point

For all divisions the change started top-down, primarily due to the initial low readiness for change and the need for speed, but was followed by some bottom-up activity. The top set clear boundaries and targets but once these were established, freed up managers across the divisions to implement the second phase of change in a more bottom-up fashion.

Change style

All divisions reported that the change style initially was directive, and in some divisions, coercive. This was necessary to set a clear, common set of objectives across the divisions, particularly given the high levels of diversity. However, over time the style shifted to one that was more educative, collaborative and participative. In particular people remarked upon the fact that the second phase of the change programme made it a much more active rather than passive experience. As staff were empowered to challenge breaches of safety on an everyday basis at any level, this secured their involvement. People felt that if should 'spot something that wasn't right', then they could seek to change it.

Change target

The majority of staff believed behavioural change was the ultimate target but felt that the clear statement of objectives through LTIF, the Golden Rules, Safety Task Auditing, OTTO and the Health and Safety initiatives meant that there were measurable outputs driving that behavioural change, particularly in the first reconstructive phase of change.

Change levers

Perhaps one of the most impressive characteristics of the Tarmac change programme was their use of a wide range of change levers during the different phases of change. An initial use of primarily technical and interpersonal levers in the reconstructive phase was extended to a range of technical, cultural, political and interpersonal interventions as change progressed, consistent with the need to achieve and embed a transformation. In terms of technical interventions, the new safety procedures and systems were supplemented with new measurement systems and the introduction of new reward and incentive systems. Success or failure was linked to bonus payments, thereby ensuring both positive and negative incentives at all levels. At a political level, meeting agendas were changed to ensure that the SHE change initiative was always the first topic to be discussed. Culturally, stories about senior management interventions with lorry drivers or contractors were used to spread the word about the commitment of directors across the company. At an interpersonal level, there was an impressive and intelligent use of communication. People said that the very first statement about OTTO had impact since the branding of the programme was good. People reported that there was a relentless use of communication, ranging from face-to-face interaction to task audits and team briefings. In particular, staff talked about the impact of 'visible felt leadership': the fact that senior management got out and about and talked to staff, referred to as 'managers out and about in their safety kit'! Staff said that the improvement in communication was a major cultural change in its own right.

It resulted in staff believing that their opinions meant more and this led to a better dialogue between staff and managers on a whole range of topics, not just those related to safety. In the office-based Shared Services Division, these levers had less impact because the shift in style was not as radical for their culture.

Change roles

Symbolically the Managing Directors were seen as the main change agents at the start of the change, which was necessary at the outset given their position of power within a traditional autocratic culture. Over time, leadership passed down to the local management levels, which was again appropriate as they were able to draw upon local loyalties and identities. The senior managers themselves cited the impact of the Tarmac CEO's leadership upon their motivation to change and some also saw the parent group's CEO as a powerful change agent. External consultants were used for advice and for establishing the common methodology across the group. However, their influence seemed to be hidden from the great majority of staff. This ensured ownership within the businesses rather than the change being seen as a consultant-led process.

4.2.9 Tarmac case summary

Across the Tarmac international group there was a certain consistency in the design choices made even though the design for the second stage of change, the evolutionary phase, was devolved down to divisional level. (See Figure 4.3.) Initially the reconstructive stage used a directive and top-down approach, with the managers in the evolutionary phase adopting a more participative approach. At the

| Figure 4.3 | Design choices for Tarmac Group |

start of the change, the low readiness for change among non-managerial staff, and in some cases divisional senior managers, combined with a low capability for change, meant that a top-down directive design was appropriate and even necessary to kick-start the implementation! In the second stage, however, once there was more acceptance and readiness for the SHE initiative, as the early target-focused initiatives facilitated a reconfiguration of the context, and experience of change and therefore capability grew, a more participative approach was possible for both managers and non-managerial staff. In effect the centre let the divisional managers be seen to lead the change, which suited the decentralised decision making of the corporation and the fact that there were many hundreds of sites spread over the world. A centralised approach to transformation would have been interpreted as the Group's central managers imposing a set of values upon local staff. This would have met resistance from manager and non-managerial staff. As change progressed there was a good use of cultural and interpersonal levers to support the second stage of change. The increase in two-way communication produced beneficial outcomes in its own right. Commitment and loyalty to the company increased.

Although the change was a success, there are some lessons that can be learnt. One is about the difficulty of changing people who are not directly employed by the organisation – in Tarmac's case, the hauliers and contractors who constantly visited their sites and were very much part of the everyday life of the company. As offshoring and outsourcing continues, this issue of influencing beyond organisational boundaries is key for organisations.

4.3 SCIENCECO

The Scienceco case (see Illustration 4.2) illustrates how senior managers can shape their organisation's context proactively in order to make it more receptive to anticipated future change. In general, the higher an organisation's receptivity to change, the greater the chance of successful implementation. The senior team at Scienceco anticipated the need for larger-scale change in the near future and therefore put in place a series of initiatives to help the organisation be more receptive to this longer-term transformation.

4.3.1 The kaleidoscope for Scienceco in 2003

Time was not a huge constraint for the plant but there was a need to act in the medium term. The *scope* of the change was not particularly deep but it was aimed at the whole plant. The senior team wished to *preserve* the good industrial relations climate but at the same time destroy the practice of using the trade unions as the main vehicles for communication and employee voice. There was also a need to destroy the overreliance on the paternalistic senior team at the

Illustration 4.2   change in action

Shaping the context for change at Scienceco

Scienceco is a large, multinational scientific instrument company whose head office is on the west coast of the US. It has manufacturing plants in the US, UK, Ireland, Eastern Europe and China. The group operates in such a way that each plant competes against the others for new investment, both for new products to be produced but also for more efficient machinery for producing existing products.

This case focuses upon the Irish plant, which was established in the late 1970s and, in 2004, employed 1,700 employees and contributed to 20 per cent of the group's net sales. The geographic area had been designated as a priority zone for economic regeneration within the European Union and as a result, financial incentives are available to companies investing in the area. The plant was extremely important to the local economy and its CEO enjoyed his role as a popular figurehead within the local community, in many ways a paternalistic figure and a representative of the management style at the plant. Scienceco was seen as a good employer, as they paid above-average wages and also offered a good range of employee benefits. There were many people at the Irish plant who had never worked for any other employer and there were not many alternative employers within the area. The company funded many local community activities including hospitals, schools and sports provisions.

The Irish plant was also highly unionized: 85–90 percent of the 1,600 operatives were trade-union members. There was a joint union-management partnership forum which was completely in tune with the promotion of partnership in employee relations favoured by the Irish government at the time. There had been no industrial action in the plant's history, but some managers felt that this was a result of the approach adopted by the collective-bargaining managers, dubbed by some as 'cheque book management'. Local managers believed that the parent company in the US would be very sensitive to any industrial action and that such action might jeopardise the chances of future investment for new products. As a result there had been a history of buying off employee resistance by making concessions to employee demands. However, this approach could only be sustained if growth was sustained.

Anticipating change

In 2003 the senior management team at the Irish plant started to examine a number of issues within the Group's operations that were impacting upon the Irish context. One was the fact that one of their production processes was supplying a declining market. A second factor was the on-going discussion with the US head office about investment in new machinery which would allow a higher degree of automation within the main production process. This would allow the plant to become more competitive against the Scienceco plants situated in lower-cost economies. Whilst this was good news for the long-term future of the plant, in the short term it would mean that a third of the operative staff might be made redundant. A third factor was the intention to introduce a 'lean processing' approach into the production process following the success of its innovator, Toyota.

The management decided to investigate the plant's receptivity to change and commissioned an external evaluation of its change capability, which it considered alongside the comparative data generated from Scienceco's global internal attitude survey. The two data sources revealed some common themes.

First the research revealed that supervisory ratios were a significant issue. Operatives reported that there were too few supervisors reporting into very few production managers. This was a result of a teamworking initiative which had been introduced a few years previously and had resulted in an increase in spans of control. As a result, operatives felt that the organisation did not wish to hear their views nor sought their involvement. It also resulted in a lack of performance feedback to operatives, particularly feedback of a positive nature. Only 23 per cent staff agreed that management were good at responding to employee suggestions, and similarly only 20 per cent agreed that senior management were sincere in listening to employees. Thirty per cent of the staff believed there had been a decline in recognition for contribution over the previous two years. One operative commented: 'If you are going to change something it needs buy in and people's opinions. Not only listening to opinions but they need to be valued.' Only 23 per cent of all respondents agreed that senior management were well informed about what lower levels thought.

Nevertheless, overall 71 per cent agreed that they really cared about the fate of the organisation. Demographic analysis revealed more variation. Employees with the longest length of service felt most betrayed by the company in terms of culture and work intensification even though their terms and conditions remained very favourable compared to other employers in the area. Older staff complained that as the plant had grown, the old family culture had been lost and a 'them and us' culture had emerged: 'Start treating the people on the floor the way they used to treat them . . . all on an equal level. Then we can actually say to people that we are one big happy family.'

However, from a senior management perspective, they saw themselves as being very concerned about the future of the plant and, in some ways, trying to protect the community from the realities of operating in a more competitive global economy: 'In my own mind when we are pushing production, people, figures and pushing people, it is good for the plant and good for the majority of the people.'

The organisational response

The senior team decided that there were aspects of the context that could be changed in advance of the anticipated changes being implemented. In particular they believed that they could directly change two areas: communication and the role of frontline supervisors and production managers. They decided to increase communication and improve management capability and capacity within the plant in order to build their change management capability. This also meant that senior management could alter the employees' reliance on the unions as their main conduit for communications and thereby redress the balance of power.

A number of initiatives were introduced. In the area of communication, the team started to push the idea of 'conversation' rather than communication. Thirty-six 'town hall' communication sessions were implemented in the first year with either the CEO or his deputy hosting the sessions. Breakfast meetings were hosted for frontline supervisors to discuss current issues on the shop floor with the CEO or another member of the senior team. Brown bag lunches were also introduced for managers and supervisors and at all of these meetings, up-to-date results of the corporate attitude survey were shared and action plans were drawn up amongst the managerial teams.

The number of shop floor supervisors was increased and 'new blood' was introduced into the culture by some of these vacancies being filled by external recruitment. All supervisors were encouraged to focus on improving employee relations and increasing employee engagement. A group-wide initiative was also implemented within the Irish plant: 'Back to the floor'. This encouraged supervisors to engage in more direct contact with employees and to informally gain a better sense of attitudes and motivations. The introduction of lean processing techniques also allowed the team to emphasise that the new goal was to support frontline managers rather than disempower them. Finally, a Leadership Development programme was introduced in conjunction with a UK-based management training college. The initial focus for this programme was the frontline manager, and it aimed to shift them towards a relationship rather than a rules-based leadership style. Action Learning groups and coaching were also introduced to support the transfer of off-site learning.

Rewarding anticipation

In the end, the senior team's attention to capacity and capability building paid off in an unexpected form. Whilst the anticipated automation to the main production process did go ahead, the Group was impressed by the improvements instigated by the senior team, and a new production process was opened within the plant. This allowed the majority of the people rendered redundant by the automation of the established process to be redeployed onto the new production unit.

plant and seek to empower line managers. The *diversity* of the organisation was not huge, although there was slight variation in attitudes between employees with longer lengths of service and those who had joined the company more recently.

Whilst this therefore seems like a reasonable, positive context for change, *capability* for change was not high, as the company had previously gained employee assent by using cheque book management to buy compliance with change. There was little tradition of managers influencing or coaching employees through transition. There was, however, an organisation development manager within the HR team. *Capacity* was also low. The large spans of control for shop floor supervisors meant that they had neither time nor the numbers to engage in practising good communication. In addition, *readiness* for change was low. Staff were protected from the realities of global competition by the senior team. They were equally unaware of the threat of automation and the possibilities of redundancies, since the senior team had not exposed them to the group's strategic reality.

The senior team was constrained in terms of *power*. The trade unions were powerful, as they could threaten strike action. The Scienceco group was also very powerful since it determined the levels of investment between plants based on their achievement of performance targets. In addition, the local community was influential: the CEO had made himself a 'local hero' and he did not want to tarnish that image within the town. Finally, the Irish government held a certain degree of influence as it actively promoted partnership with trade unions as a political model. It would therefore have been against any adverse publicity that would deter any other US multinationals from investing in the country.

4.3.2 Key contextual features for Scienceco in 2003

See Figure 4.4.

4.3.3 Design implications for Scienceco in 2003

Change path

These initiatives were aimed at improving capability for change and so the path was reconstruction

---

Figure 4.4   Key contextual features for Scienceco in 2003

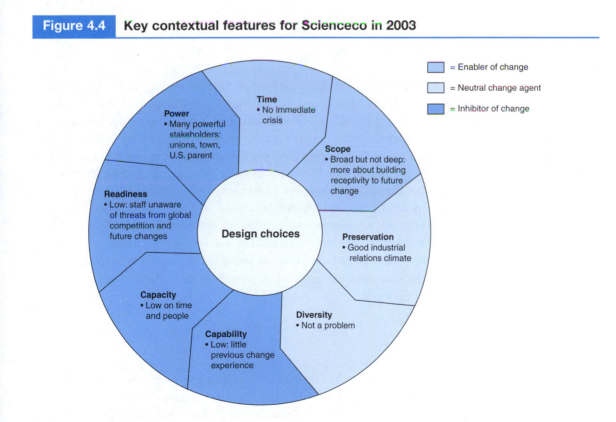

Change start-point

The initial changes had to be brought in top-down, as there was little readiness for change, nor was there any capacity or capability for change.

Change style

Given that the aim of the change was to build the managerial and supervisory capability to engage and communicate with employees, the medium had to match the message. Therefore a very participative and collaborative style was used to introduce the new communication mechanisms and new supervisory training.

Change target

The target was clearly behavioural. Increased communication and employee engagement required a change in behaviours of supervisors and managers, which in turn would lead to a change in behaviours of the lower levels of staff.

Change levers

An initial examination of the changes at Scienceco suggests that change levers focused on the interpersonal subsystem, with many communication interventions, frontline manager training and Action Learning groups and coaching. However, a deeper examination reveals a mix of interventions. Increasing the number of supervisors on the shop floor was a technical intervention. The introduction of lean processing was also a technical intervention, as it introduced new systems, but it was also cultural since it required new work routines, as did the requirement for supervisors to focus on employee relations, engagement and the 'back to the floor initiative'. Many of the communication initiatives were also cultural levers aimed at changing the softer aspects of the organisation at the level of the everyday experience of employees. This was an appropriate mix of levers, given that the change target was behaviours.

Change roles

The senior team took the leadership role and deliberately aimed to empower other levels of leadership through the change initiatives. The unions were not given a change role since ultimately the change was about changing the balance of power.

4.3.4 The kaleidoscope at Scienceco in 2005

Following the implementation of these changes, Scienceco had effectively reshaped the organisational context. Whilst time was more urgent in 2005, they had successfully increased the organisation's capability and capacity for change whilst maintaining the good industrial relations climate. They had also changed the power balance at the plant, with supervisors and management having better channels of communication with employees, and thereby reducing the power of the trade unions to some small degree. Readiness for change had been increased at supervisory and managerial levels. This meant that the company was in better shape to implement the changes that accompanied the introduction of the new production process.

See Figure 4.5.

4.4 BAYER DIAGNOSTICS EUROPE

This case study examines one company's strategy to address a shift in market trends across Europe and also to seize an opportunity to create a pan-European organisation (see Illustration 4.3). The objectives for the change process were to (1) create greater organisational and cultural cohesion, (2) achieve cost savings and (3) improve customer service.

| Figure 4.5 | Key contextual features for Scienceco in 2005 |

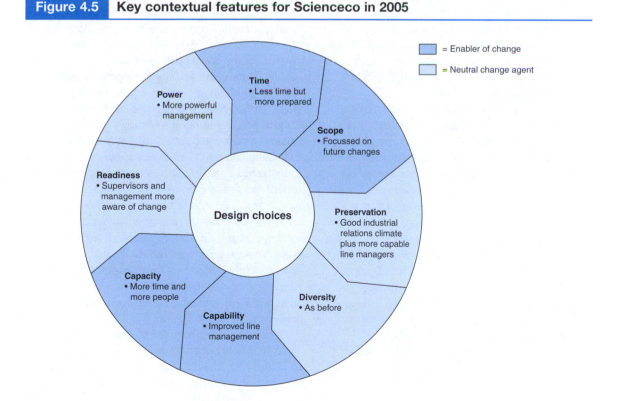

Illustration 4.3

change in action

Bayer Diagnostics Europe: a case study on pan-Europeanisation

In late 1998, Chris Tobin, then a senior manager in Bayer Pharmaceuticals, was promoted to Senior Vice-President, heading Bayer Diagnostics Europe (Bayer DS EU), another division within the Bayer AG organisation. Bayer DS EU comprised 20 national operations, had 1,800 employees and an annual turnover of € 600 million. His appointment was made against a background of patchy performance across the various countries. Chris Tobin's remit was clear: to radically improve Bayer DS EU's performance and put in place a strategic model that would serve as the foundation for sustainable growth.

The European market was changing. There was a trend towards European convergence. Customer needs in different European countries were becoming more similar, illustrating significant convergence of market needs. This heralded a likely move away from fragmented, nationally independent markets. The reasons for such an erosion of cultural and national distinctions were converging European legislation, greater cross-border transparency and increasingly similar national standards and behaviour.

Further, as a consequence of technological advancement, diagnostic health care providers throughout Europe were engaged in a process of consolidation of their laboratory sites. Rather than investing in small, dedicated laboratories and technologies, health care providers were investing in fewer, automated, full-scope laboratories. Such a shift was also manifested in product development, where the industry was showing a trend of increasing commoditisation, resulting in greater uniformity in products across Europe.

As a result, Bayer Diagnostics was facing a changing market, moving away from fragmented, nationally based domains towards greater convergence and consolidation. Therefore, the drivers for Bayer Diagnostics'

pan-Europeanisation were market convergence, greater price transparency, increasing commoditisation of products and much more intense competition. These factors identified a two-pronged need for change: greater consistency in operations and functions across all European entities, and a new approach for adding value beyond the traditional product offering.

The initial approach for Europe was to be focused on adding a greater dimension of integration and control of the different constituent countries, whilst not losing the level of local responsiveness and operation currently in place. A small central team was envisaged, with the aim of adding value through stretching performance, sharing ideas across Europe and leveraging the scale that a combined European organisation could provide. These measures were aimed at creating '*a Centre that was staffed by a small team focused on long term, allowing countries to run their business*'. The approach was to be communicated as '*regional leadership*'.

How Chris Tobin and his management team were to go about implementing the strategy was clearly critical. A great deal of attention was paid to rolling out the strategy and the '**Vision' phase** successfully. Right from the beginning, in early 1999, a **European Leadership Team** (ELT) was formed, with the top 90 managers from all the European operations. This was to constitute the driving body for formulating and implementing the strategic plan for Europeanisation. The ELT would meet regularly, providing the forum for communicating the Vision and establishing the new European culture. The ELT was based on trust and participation, and reduced the need for an implementation team.

One of the key drivers for change was the need to create consistency among all European operations. This was to be achieved through various initiatives designed around '**best practice**' – taking procedures and practices from the countries with the best performance and applying them across Europe. This was to be achieved through part-time cross-national teams, drawn from the ELT, looking at functions from a Europe-wide perspective.

A key development resulting from the establishment of the Centre was the opportunity to measure, control and set consistent targets for all the European countries – something that had not been possible previously. The Centre therefore gave itself the task of setting **stretch targets** for its ELT members, and encouraging clearer, more frequent communication among countries. This afforded the Centre a greater degree of authority over planning and control.

Other new initiatives resulting from the strategy changes were focused on people development. A **Leadership Development Programme** was introduced, aimed at providing better training and support for members of the ELT. This was supported by a **rewards system** that was introduced in parallel with the change initiatives. Finally, from early on in the change, the ELT designed a '**balanced scorecard**', providing the first opportunity to apply a uniform system throughout Europe that allowed greater visibility within operations.

Despite progress achieved by initiatives emerging from the early phase of change, in June 1999 Chris Tobin received a '**provocation**' from Bayer President Rolf Classon, challenging why Europe needed significantly more people to run its business than the USA, despite very similar levels of sales. In response to this, the DS EU Centre developed proposals for a more integrated European approach.

The philosophy for Europeanisation therefore encouraged national operations to focus their efforts on customer-facing activities, whilst the expanded Centre pooled non-core back-office activities and took greater ownership of systems and processes. The rationale behind this structure lay in the recognition that to delight a customer in a distinctive market (Europe was converging, but was still not one homogeneous market), customer service needed to be tailored to meet national characteristics, and the best people to do that were at a local level. Also, sales and operational marketing activities were the functions best represented at national levels. On the other hand, business management activities, such as warehousing, accounting, strategic planning and HR, could all be pooled, as they didn't reflect the country offices' core competences. There was duplication of resources and processes in the country operations that could be cut.

The result of this strategic development was that the Centre would have two roles – one to provide strategic guidance without interfering in operational activities, the other to provide 'shared services' for the 'back-office' functions where economies of scale could be achieved. In this way the Centre hoped to avoid the ivory tower phenomenon of some headquarters, by offering a shared services structure, rather than centralisation.

Despite the networks that had been created and the opening up of communications across European countries, the Europeanisation philosophy was resisted by a number of the country organisations who genuinely believed that moving any functions out of their countries would be detrimental to their ability to service customers.

However, in June 2000, Bayer Diagnostics globally ran into trouble with significant additional costs due to exchange rate changes. In response to this, Bayer Diagnostics launched **Project CURE,** a far-reaching turnaround exercise. In Europe, Project CURE focused on customer profitability and implementing the integrated European structure for marketing, supply chain, customer support and back-office operations. In light of the imperative to turn around the performance of Bayer Diagnostics, Europeanisation and the tough new targets set by the Centre for each country operation met little resistance.

One of the early visible successes emerging from Project CURE was the project on 'Customer Profitability'. An index of Bayer DS EU's customers' profitability was drawn up across Europe. Customer profitability proved to be subject to a Pareto effect, whereby 80 per cent of the profits were derived from 20 per cent of customers whilst some 15 per cent of customers were loss making to the organisation. Bayer DS EU adjusted their management of those customers and developed a process for monitoring all customer accounts. This project provided a valuable source of revenue improvement and, for the first time, a clear and consistent customer management strategy across Europe. The Customer Profitability Project would not have been possible if the networks initiated in 1999 had not been established.

During Project CURE, the strategic **centralisation of European marketing** was completed, resulting in marketing directors overseeing from the Centre the emergence of consistent and structured strategies across Europe. Where previously each country was responsible for designing and running its own marketing approach (resulting even in different product packaging), the centralised marketing team ensured that a consistent strategy was devised, allowing local marketing teams to tailor the strategy to their domestic needs.

By 2001 a new phase of the change transformation was initiated. **Project Enterprise,** an investment in enabling technology, was designed to implement a common IT system across Europe. The change would introduce consistent and transparent standards, along with consistent management information, across all European operations and, importantly, enable a reduction in the number of warehouses in Europe from 16 to just 2, serving northern and southern Europe.

All the above initiatives were designed to pull the Bayer DS EU organisation irrevocably towards a pan-European structure and culture through three distinct levers identified by senior management at the start. These levers were stretching people and performance (e.g., stretch targets, ELT and Leadership Development Training), sharing best practices (e.g., centralised marketing and Customer Profitability) and leveraging economies of scale (Projects CURE and Enterprise).

Since the change project for pan-Europeanisation was initiated in early 1999, Bayer DS EU have managed to increase their profit margin and market share. Chris Tobin and his management team attribute much of this success to the on-going change programme, and in particular the initiatives associated with Project CURE.

At the time of writing, Project Enterprise, the common IT system, has been implemented in the Iberia, Benelux and France branches.

In the last year, Bayer AG, Bayer DS EU's parent company, announced plans to merge its five distinct health care divisions (Diagnostics, Pharmaceuticals, Animal Health, Consumer Care, Biological Products) into one entity, Bayer HealthCare. This new change will provide yet more opportunities and further challenges to DS EU to improve its contribution to the Bayer business, yet again testing its ability to effectively manage transition.

Therefore, in late 2002, after almost four years, Bayer DS EU was still in the midst of change. There have been some clear successes. However, question marks still remain over the future role of the Centre in pooling resources and functions, and synthesising Europe's strategy with that of global strategy.

4.4.1 The kaleidoscope of Bayer Diagnostics

Illustration 4.3 shows that *time* was not a major problem for Bayer DS EU in the late 1990s, as the change process had about three to five years to deliver the change. Nevertheless, presumably the falling performance of Bayer Diagnostics overall resulted in an awareness that some immediate cost savings were necessary. Therefore there was initial pressure to do 'something', with a longer-term *scope* of more transformational change.

In fact, the changes put in place by Chris Tobin targeted the senior managers and back-office operations, but not the front-office sales personnel. He wanted to impact as little as possible the people at the coalface. Customer-facing staff were allowed to continue to operate, more or less, as they always had, to maintain local customer responsiveness. The intent was to shift the senior managers and the individual back-office operations in each country away from existing assumptions of independence, autonomy and locally developed procedures, to integration, centralised decision making/control, and shared common services. The *scope* was also broad as well as deep. It affected all European operations. In the longer term the change also affected the operation of Bayer Diagnostics worldwide, as global operations needed to be adjusted to meet the demands of a pan-European organisation. The extent to which this was apparent at the outset of the restructure is unclear. By mid-2002 the impact on worldwide operations was being felt. Similarly by 2002, it was necessary to think about the front-office European operations.

Bayer wanted to *preserve* the brand and product quality and also staff commitment. The biggest threat to the change lay in the *diversity* of the European organisation. There was large heterogeneity in terms of national culture but also in terms of size and maturity of the different country units. The branches also operated independently of each other. The change meant that each country lost power, headcount and ability to set its own strategy. This was the most significant barrier to change. The *capability* for change was mixed across the company, and the internal economic pressures experienced by Bayer Diagnostics worldwide meant there was little *capacity* with which to run the change.

Although there was rational acceptance of the strategy, there was questionable emotional *readiness* for change. That is understandable, given that the countries, and the individuals within them, had much to lose in terms of power, status, budget and control. Some of the managers were long-serving members of staff. Since there was no burning platform for change, these personal feelings acted as restraints on the whole change process.

The *power* was one of the most positive influences upon the change context. Chris Tobin had clear authority at the outset of the change, and was fortunate to have support from Bayer HQ.

4.4.2 Key contextual features of Bayer Diagnostics

See Figure 4.6.

4.4.3 Design implications for Bayer Diagnostics

To appreciate the full design implications for Bayer DS EU, it is necessary to take into account the findings from a change progress evaluation in mid-2002 by an independent consultant. The majority of managers accepted the strategy and vision. People felt the new direction was a breath of fresh air and Chris Tobin's leadership style was perceived to be participative. The early ELT meetings were seen as useful in encouraging a common culture and networking among managers. Likewise the LDC training was well received, and, most unusually for a change process, communication was unanimously praised. The smaller European divisions viewed the concept of best practice very positively.

Inevitably, concerns were expressed. Some felt that the strategy and structure had been developed too fast. The new Centre came in for criticism with remarks such as 'it takes but does not give' from its location in the UK. Not all the units had seen immediate benefits from the centralised marketing. Some interviewees

Figure 4.6   **Key contextual features for Bayer Diagnostics in 1999**

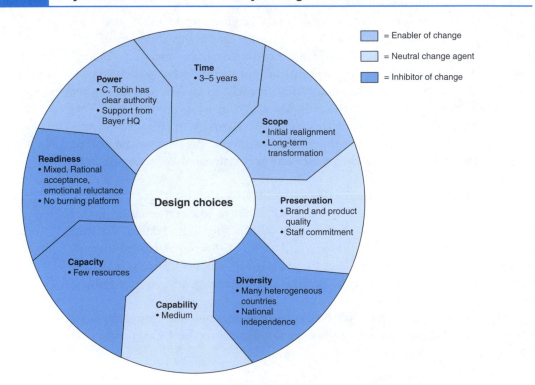

still felt confused over the new roles – 'Who is my boss?' Similarly the problems of the diversity of Europe were still there, although to a lesser extent.

There was a danger that the change could lose momentum as communication started to tail off. The consultant concluded that whilst the change had been a success, there was now a need to focus on some softer levers for change. He also recommended that new initiatives, such as the ELT, be subject to constant development and evaluation as needs changed over time.

Change path

There was time for the changes to be evolutionary in nature and, as part of the change process, to build required levels of readiness and capability. However, at the time of the evaluation of the change, there remained a need to sustain the change path by introducing new, softer elements to achieve the full back-office transformation.

Start-point

The change start-point was top-down. Given the diversity and mixed readiness within the business, it would have been difficult to adopt any other approach. However, the top-down approach was criticised in terms of 'best practice' as managers felt that it had been developed too quickly with insufficient internal benchmarking. Likewise, Project Enterprise was criticised for the way it was implemented, as it was seen as too uniform and not tailored to meet local needs.

Change style

Within the top-down approach, the CEO, Chris Tobin, practised a very participative style of leadership which drew in key stakeholders from the diverse European units. This helped him to gain general acceptance for the new strategy. The ELT meetings and the cross-functional teams were used to ensure that the ELT members felt involved. However, given the diversity within Europe, perhaps he could have adapted the style to a more collaborative approach over time, particularly over difficult issues such as 'best practice' or 'Project Enterprise'. Time was not a sufficient issue to rule out collaboration.

Change roles

The CEO took the change leadership role for himself. Given his past reputation for a participative style of management and the extent of diversity he needed to harness, this was clearly the right decision for a change that would inevitably not please all of the people all of the time. An external consultant who provided challenge and objectivity throughout the process assisted him. However, there was evidence that the cross-functional working teams needed to be supported in their work in the field.

Change target

The target for the change combined both outputs and behaviours, which matched the project deliverables on costs and the capacity constraints on the change process, but potentially limited the extent of transformation. As cost reductions needed to be delivered, new outputs were defined early on through stretch targets in performance. The restructuring and job redesign resulting from the establishment of the Centre and the shared services meant that over time, behaviours would change. These changes were supported by initiatives such as Leadership Training and the ELT meetings. However, this behavioural change was mainly required at a senior managerial level – many of the lower levels of staff remained unaffected.

Change levers

The levers used appear to have been primarily technical – structures and systems. These interventions were important in bringing together and reducing some of the diversity in operations – a key aim of the changes. There is some evidence of interpersonal levers in the Leadership development and the ELT. Clearly the technical changes were communicated well and this helped their implementation, as did Chris Tobin's style of leadership.

However, some change challenges remained post-2002. Softer symbolic aspects were missed from the change levers. For instance, the Centre was criticised for being too 'anglicised' in its approach. The location of central offices sends a very powerful message to employees. The repercussions of it being offshore from mainland Europe are reflected in these criticisms.

Perhaps more could have been done symbolically to erode the idea of a 'British' regional office. Furthermore, more cultural changes need to be introduced to sustain the change so that it becomes fully embedded. This may require an accompanying shift in the target of the interventions.

4.5 SUMMARY

This chapter has explored the use of the change kaleidoscope through three extended case studies of companies undergoing change. These cases have illustrated both the complexity of change and the interrelated nature of all the kaleidoscope features. None of the individual features can be considered in isolation from the other seven aspects of context. Furthermore, the contextual features may differ within one company, as seen in the international case of Tarmac. The Scienceco case illustrates the idea of shaping a context to make it more receptive to change *before* the commencement of any transformation. Thus the pattern of features at one time will be altered by the changes put in place at any other time, and this means the features, therefore, have to be reassessed before choices are made about future changes.

In particular the chapter has considered three main areas:

- How to use the change kaleidoscope to understand the change context in depth.

- How to identify the key contextual features in any change situation that influence the design choices and therefore the change approach. As the case studies illustrate, certain contextual features may be critical in one organisation and of minor significance in another.

- How to link the assessment of the contextual features through to the design of change.

Having established the link between change context and change design choices, the next three chapters explore the design and management of the transition process.

REFERENCE

1. For more information see Goffe, R. and Jones, G. (2006) *Why Should Anyone Be Led by You?* Harvard Business School Press. They discuss the need for leaders to be able to read their organisation's context and know how to change it to support their intended change initiatives, and describe what they call 'situation sensing' in some detail.

WORK ASSIGNMENTS

4.1. For the Scienceco case, what should the design choices be for the next phase of change?

4.2. Using the example of the Tarmac case, discuss the difficulties of influencing critical stakeholders, such as contractors, who are not employed by the organisation.

4.3. Drawing on the Bayer or Tarmac case studies in this chapter, what lessons can be learned about managing change in a multinational enterprise?

4.4. Compare the three case studies in this chapter and reflect on why the design choices taken were appropriate or inappropriate. Were there other options that you would have considered?

Transforming a public sector communications agency

Rees Ward • Derrick Neal • Veronica Hope Hailey • Julia Balogun

This case describes the creation of the DCSA. It can be used to help students and other readers of the book deepen their understanding of how to apply the change kaleidoscope in practice, and how to develop change judgement. Assignment questions are at the end of the case.

The Ministry of Defence (MoD) is a particularly complex public sector organisation which has to contend with rapid changes and demands on its ability to deliver its military capabilities in war fighting or peacekeeping or, indeed, in support of the government in dealing with domestic crises. Whilst it is not as large as some other public sector departments such as Health and Education, it has many constituent parts that have to function with a level of coherence greater than that found elsewhere in the public sector. Failure to achieve this puts lives at risk daily.

In order to understand the importance of the role played by the Defence Communications Services Agency (DCSA), it is helpful to position the agency within the MoD as a whole. Figure 1 shows many, but not all, of the key organisations that formed the MoD as of January 2005 (to make the figure exhaustive would only serve to complicate matters), and where DCSA sits relative to the Military/Political process and the Front Line of operations. It is through efficient/effective management in the Business Space that successful military operations can be conducted. The totality of the elements within the figure supports some 600,000 staff, of which about 50 per cent are accounted for within the Defence Industry through prime contractors and small- and medium-sized enterprises (SMEs).

The DCSA needs to be able to operate in a sufficiently dynamic manner so that it can deliver real-time information to the military commander (forward facing) where lives may be at risk. Equally, the DCSA also works through industry (managing contracts for the provision of services and products) in a professional and effective manner to help facilitate the operation of organisations such as the Defence Procurement Agency (DPA) and the Defence Logistics Organisation (DLO), in order for them to deliver their contribution to the provision of military capability.

Therefore, the DCSA has a central role in facilitating the MoD's delivery of effects-based operations in support of the government agenda. When it is

Figure 1	Elements and relationships within the MoD

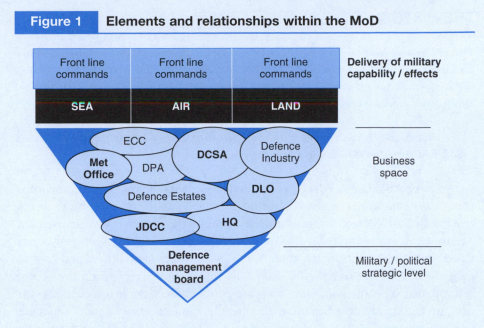

not doing that, it is directly supporting the other organisations that constitute the MoD to ensure that the Business Space can function. The drivers behind the DCSA are numerous, but two key drivers need to be considered:

1. The nature of military operations has been going through major change, with UK military staff increasingly deployed on a wide variety of operations throughout the world. The conflicts in which the military are engaged have changed substantially in character. What is now required is timely and fused information which allows for rapid and accurate decision making. All of these factors lead to the military commander needing highly reliable, fast and flexible communications and information system structures. Given the dramatic increase in the volume of information, it is also necessary for the commander to have technology and applications that can help him/her synthesise the raw data in order to make robust decisions.

2. Network Enabled Capability (NEC) was born and given a high profile in 2002 and will continue to be a major driver now and into the future. The terrorist attacks on the World Trade Centre and the Pentagon highlighted vulnerabilities in the MoD's posture for Business Continuity (BC), and the recent attacks in London highlight the importance of intelligence gathering and knowledge management. In the event of a major attack in the UK involving agents other than explosives, it will be essential that all emergency services have a coherent infrastructure that delivers maximum efficiency in communications and information systems.

THE HISTORY

The DCSA was formed on 1 April 1998 as a Defence Agency of the MoD, a ministerial decision recommended by the Finance Planning and Management Group (FPMG), the forerunner to the Defence Management Board (DMB).[1] The original aim for the Agency was limited in scope:

> *. . . to provide its customers with the optimum end-to-end wide area information transfer services to meet Defence needs.*

The three Single Services who controlled their own communications and information systems were concerned, not unreasonably, about transferring their systems and their control to an unproven agency. This original aim focused the Agency primarily at the Network/Transmission layer,[2] and the Agency was provided with the assets from the three Services and other centrally owned components to deliver that layer.[3] Unfortunately, this pragmatic approach put to one side the major people issues in which the people who were involved in the vertical integration of networks, infrastructure and applications were now separated into different organisations. Although some visionaries could see that the Agency should encompass all three layers of activity, at that stage, it was clear that the major stakeholders would not accept the enlarged scope. It was not until mid-2001 that the DMB agreed that all of the Infrastructure layer should transfer to the Agency; the totality of the application layer has still to be decided.

As is common with major changes in structures and reallocation of funding, the formation of the Agency was not universally welcomed. On one hand it was clear that the various elements shown in Figure 1 were developing systems which met their own needs and were integrated vertically within their own organisations to provide the required information, but this approach had led to incoherence and inefficiency of delivery across the MoD. This was a classic manifestation of stovepipe development. For example, at the Network/Transmission level, there

---

[1]The Defence Management Board (DMB) is, in effect, the Board of Directors for the MoD, and it is responsible for setting and assessing the strategic direction of the MoD.

[2]The Communication Information Systems (CIS) world may be characterised by three layers. The base layer is the Network/Transmission layer consisting of satellite and long-haul radio bearers and landlines – e.g., copper or fibre-optic cables. The middle layer is the Infrastructure layer consisting of desktop computers, laptops and their associated servers, which are linked together by the Network/Transmission layer. The top layer is the applications layer consisting of software applications which run on the infrastructure.

[3]The initial components of the Agency were: HQ DCSA and DCSA Service Management Centre, DCSA (Germany), Defence Fixed Telecommunications Service (DFTS) handling UK-based transmission networks and telephony, 9 SU-handling long-haul communications, 1,001 SU-handling satellite communications, Defence Communications Centre (DCC), Naval Shore Telecommunications Network (NSTN) handling, Royal Naval Radio Services handling HF to VLF services, and Intelligence Message Handling System (DIMHS).

were 19 networks, 4 HQs and 7 Network Control Centres. At the Infrastructure level, there were 300+ systems managed through 500+ contracts. At the application level, the number of applications in use across Defence was almost incalculable. In the Logistics area alone, there were an estimated 1,200 applications.

Most of the MoD procurement and delivery of equipment and services operates through Integrated Project Teams (IPTs). An Integrated Project Team is a group containing the correct balance of skills to manage an equipment or system delivery programme from concept, development and manufacture through to deployment in service. Sitting within the Equipment Capability Customer (ECC) are about 10 capability areas (known as Directors of Equipment Capability [DECs]). Approximately 150 IPTs respond to the DECs' requirements to provide the MoD with its fighting capability both now and into the future. Each team typically has its own culture and focus. For example, some IPTs within the DCSA were based and hosted by another agency at a different site but were still part of the DCSA. About a dozen IPTs were DCSA-hosted and have a focus on products or services associated with information management and/or communications. In addition, some IPTs were relatively small in number and were managing contracts with an industry supplier. Other IPTs were more than 500-strong and, again, had their own identity and culture.

Parts of the MoD shown in Figure 1 were generally reluctant to lose control of their assets which were vital enablers for the delivery of the outputs. There was also suspicion of a new and untried organisation which would have more Defence-wide goals rather than the more narrowly focused individual goals for the various key budget holders. At vesting day, most of the centrally owned assets were transferred, but two of the Front Line Services decided that total transfer was too risky and held back some assets.

Within various parts of the MoD there was great resentment from lower levels. Civilian staff felt that they had been abandoned by the Front Line Service with which they had identified, and there was considerable concern and uncertainty over jobs because of the clear intent of the DCSA to rationalise and drive out inefficiencies. Likewise, the military staff felt that they had been removed from their 'protected' single-service environment and culture and had been 'given away' to an unknown regime with a different agenda and set of values.

By early 2002 the Agency had already acquired all of the Network/Transmission layer assets. With the mandate to acquire the Infrastructure assets, the Agency staff were systematically acquiring them from across Defence. These transfers were very challenging as there was a reluctance to transfer the full funding and all the staff with the physical assets. Additionally, continuity of service through transition and personnel management had to be carefully managed. It had been agreed in principle that corporate applications should also be transferred to the Agency, but these transfers were very difficult to achieve.

Customers were reluctant to agree to the transfers without a clear and measurable statement of the service that they would be guaranteed in return. This was particularly difficult as most Customers could not state what they required and to what quality, beyond the fact that they were broadly content with what they were generating themselves. Development of Customer Supplier Agreements (CSAs), Service Level Agreements (SLAs) and Internal Business Agreements (IBAs) received renewed emphasis. CSAs were possibly the least mature and required a significant injection of effort. This new approach was not welcomed in some quarters in the Customer community nor by the newly transferred members of the Agency who were already feeling resentful. Embedding these new customer-focused behaviours (such as keeping promises to the customer to deliver a service to the time, cost and quality agreed; and being responsive to a customer's legitimate changing requirements) throughout the organisation represented a significant challenge.

The Agency continued to pursue its strategic goal of rationalisation of assets and staff to create efficiencies. However, there was some concern that the Agency was not capable of responding with sufficient speed and agility to match the tempo required in operational conditions. The acquisition tempo of day-to-day business for the IPTs did not appear to meet the needs of very rapid planning and execution of operations.

Within the DCSA, there were 10 IPTs with a focus on products or services associated with information management and/or communications. In all cases where the product or service being provided was of a communications or IT nature, the DCSA increasingly had a role and responsibility to ensure compliance and coherence within the needs of defence as a whole. This emphasis increased with the trends mentioned earlier of military actions requiring a Network Enabled Capability. It was on the back of this dynamic that the DCSA embarked on a very difficult challenge – to give communications and information management within the MoD a sense of identity, purpose, credibility and robustness. The change programme within the DCSA had to ensure that the organisation was able to meet the needs and demands of a range of stakeholders, including the operational commander, the MoD head office, the defence industry and of course the political masters of the day.

A single Agency Change Programme was set up in April 2002 with five work streams taking forward 29 key initiatives of the 55 initiatives that had been identified as running in the Agency. Delivering these changes was hampered by the fragmented nature of the Agency, which was spread over 71 locations and employed in excess of 5,000 staff. To minimise disruption of outputs during the transition, there were no major staff movements. In addition to rationalising systems, structures and processes to provide the DCSA with the necessary agility, the downside was that whilst the numbers employed in the DCSA were set to increase from about 5,000 in 2002 to about 7,000 in 2007, it was envisaged that between 2007 and 2009, some 3,000 staff would move out of the DCSA. It was announced that in some cases staff were to take retirement of one form or another; in other cases they would be found alternative opportunities either within the MoD or outside of the Department, and others would be 'outsourced' to the commercial sector.

THE DCSA CHANGE PROGRAMME 2003–2005

The DCSA Change Programme was launched in early 2002 as the key instrument for implementing effective business change, and the new Vision for the Agency was established as: *Information anytime, anywhere – transforming Defence effectiveness*. Lack of progress with the Change Programme was recognised in mid-2003 and a decision was taken to inject substantially larger resources into the effort to develop momentum. The Programme was driven at pace across the Agency to deliver significant improvements in the DCSA's ability to meet future communications and information services needs of UK Defence. The Programme was seen as ambitious and was personally led by the Chief Executive, and was directly supported by the Agency's top management team. It comprised five core work streams. Each was led by a corporate director who drew on support from across the Agency as required. The DCSA Programme Management Office (PMO) directly supported the Change Programme activity and provided monthly reports on progress to all key stakeholders. The Programme was managed in accordance with the Office of Government Commence Managing Successful Programmes (MSP) methodology.

There were two key, customer-orientated work streams — 'Delivering Operational Effectiveness' (DOE) and 'Coherent Solutions'. The DOE and Coherent Solutions Workstreams aimed to join together the CIS and ICS provided through the Agency to UK Defence and to deliver them on a truly end-to-end basis.

DOE was the main point of effort within the DCSA Change Programme. Its purpose was to radically improve the customer focus of the Agency, making the Agency more agile and responsive to customer needs by simplifying customer-facing Agency processes, making the DCSA easier to deal with, and improving delivery of agreed outputs.

The main focus of Coherent Solutions was to drive technical coherence across the Agency's value chain, ensuring operational integrity and enabling new systems to be incorporated in a timely manner across the Defence. By working with the Agency's IPTs and industry service providers, the Coherent Solutions Workstream aimed to underpin the delivery of end-to-end CIS by mapping the existing Defence Network, maintaining configuration control, performing release authority and ensuring that new CIS capabilities followed a common architecture approach.

The Optimised Acquisition Workstream was set up to work in partnership with IPTs to apply modern acquisition techniques, such as Procurement reform and e-Business and Lean Support, to transform the relationship between the Agency and its commercial suppliers. Through the introduction of best practice purchasing and advancing supply chain tools, techniques and methodology, the Optimised Acquisition Workstream was charged with delivering significant efficiency benefits as the Agency maximised the corporate buying power of Defence in the commercial IT market.

Two further work streams completed the core Change Programme activity: Right People, Right Skills, Right Environment (R3), and Rationalised CIS support (CISR). The focus for these work streams was to manage the changes impacting the Agency's staff, ensuring that the Agency retained the right people with the right skills for current and future needs. A key element of the R3 work stream was the redevelopment of the DCSA Headquarters site at Corsham to provide modern accommodation for the future Agency.

Allied to this, and in support of the Agency's drive from a 'Provider' organisation to a 'Decider' organisation[4] was a programme of significant cultural development across the Agency. This included embedding the new DCSA values and behaviours. The aim was to discard the destructive interculture rivalry, the mistrust of senior management and the undue emphasis on position and status. However, the Agency wanted to retain the enthusiasm of the military, engineering and administrative staff; the existing communications and IS expertise; the military ethos; and the civil servant's tradition of impartiality. In addition, the Agency wanted to create a new culture where people were clear about their responsibility, and were performance focused, with more concern for results than process. The Agency also wanted to promote real teamworking at all levels and to achieve a situation where people would cede IPT needs to the corporate needs of the DCSA where appropriate. The CEO spoke about creating a sense of community and the need to be a 'learning organisation' where they would strive to learn and improve on a continuous basis. The Agency also set about introducing flexible working practices best suited to the modern, forward-looking Agency, and overseeing the implementation of the wider MoD People Programme across the DCSA.

STAFF PERCEPTION

A piece of academic research conducted in 2004 revealed that there appeared to be a certain amount of disconnect between the strategic direction in which the DCSA was moving, and the experience felt or 'lived' by the employees, almost as though the organisation was going through a transformation whilst the people were feeling 'left behind'. There were various reasons for this.

Change fatigue

The first reason appeared to be a form of **change fatigue**, possibly caused by a lack of understanding why change initiatives took place, and how they contributed to the overall strategy. A common complaint was that there were too

---

[4]A 'Provider' organisation delivers products and services using internal resources. A 'Decider' organisation determines what needs to be provided but uses external resources to deliver the products and services.

many change initiatives and that there was very little time to draw breath, let alone evaluate their effect, before another initiative was brought in. There was also a level of cynicism exhibited around this subject:

I think we change a bit too quickly because we haven't actually finished one phase, then we're into another one. My own view is that you don't get a chance to actually evaluate what you've just achieved before there's another change. And that's not always because of the organisation itself, that's I think, quite often politically driven by our masters, we're here to do their bidding. (Junior Staff Member)

There's still an element of resistance, inevitably people don't like change anyway but there is a resistance to change, there is a weariness about change. And I don't think enough has been done to recognise that that weariness has got to be addressed at the same time as pressing ahead of the changes that need to be made. (Senior Manager)

Whether you're talking high level or matter of fact level, you just seem to get bombarded with constant change and it's virtually impossible to keep up with it. (Middle Manager)

Closely related to this complaint was the pervasive saying of 'change for change's sake', where employees felt that new initiatives were brought in just for their own sake, and they did not add any specific value or benefit to the way that the job was carried out.

Change resistance

Another aspect picked up, and closely entwined with the inability or unwillingness to appreciate the big picture, was that there were pockets of **change resistance** from some people within the IPTs, and even hostility, and some admitted that the DCSA was subject to a certain amount of what was termed 'backlash' behaviour.

There's quite a lot of cynicism around too: what is this actually going to do for me, what's it going to actually do for what I get out of the job? (Senior Manager)

It was often commented that people were reluctant to change, were unable to change, or simply refused to change. Part of this was attributable to the culture where risk-taking behaviour was low, and where employees were generally portrayed as conservative and not readily adaptable or flexible.

There are several people in our section for whom change is just a taboo, it's [like] they won't even move from one end of the desk to another end of the desk, it can be that bad. (Middle Manager)

It was interesting that few people personally felt that their jobs were at risk although they acknowledged that there would be **job losses**. Most people felt that the job losses would be absorbed by volunteers nearing retirement. People also perceived a contradiction in the strategy of slimming down the MoD by reducing headcount, only to replace people with more expensive contractors who appeared to stay for long periods of time.

> *The numbers seem to have crept back up to where they were before and you can't work out what these people are doing...we have to contract out the design assurance which used to be in-house, and I'm not convinced that we pay any less for it, we just pay consultancies.*
>
> (Middle Manager, IPT)

A survey showed that 82 per cent of current employees did not expect to be with the DCSA beyond five years. Of these, 38 per cent indicated that this would be due to retirement.

Identity

It was perceived that the **DCSA lacked a strong identity** and that members of IPTs went about their business *despite* the DCSA rather than being guided by it. The term **stovepipe mentality** was a common expression, intimating that IPTs operated independently and territorially, in contradiction to the ethos of the DCSA being an organisation that incorporated a number of different IPTs, all of which should be interconnected and interdependent.

> *It seems to be that sort of agency that it's made up of a stove pipe IPTs that were pulled together, trying to get coherency across the top has been quite a challenge I think.* (Senior Manager)

Some employees appeared to **mourn a *loss* of identity**, having previously been aligned to the Army, Navy or RAF. There was also some comment about the way that the MoD was becoming civilianised, and its original identity eroded.

There were also issues surrounding the way that the IPTs identified with the DCSA:

> *There are only so many hours in the day and we already have a poor work life balance culture, and if I put a significant amount more time personally into driving forward the corporate part of the agency then the only way I could [do] that would be to provide more resource for the team. I don't have the resource to do that, so my balance is balancing the core outputs of my team versus the corporate work.* (Senior Manager)

> *I think the problem you've got is an IPT vision, and a DCSA vision and it's hard to keep them all straight.* (Junior Staff)

Conflict in purpose and values

There appeared to be a tension and conflict in what was really valued by the organisation. The military were often critical that civilians overlooked the 'real' purpose of their role because everything was shrouded in 'business-speak', and their job of providing communication to those at the 'sharp end' was often ignored. One reason given for this was that civilians did not have experience out in the field, and could not appreciate how fundamental this was, and that the failure to provide the right communication to the right people could result in loss of lives:

> *This is one of the biggest problems that I believe the DCSA has, they are trying to bill themselves and portray themselves as almost a commercial organisation running on a private sector ethos.*   (Junior Staff Member)

In contradiction to this, civilians felt that the military always wanted to get things done so urgently that cost was often a factor overlooked, and that sometimes alternative quotes for work were not requested. Therefore there was a tension between cost and action, with most people only considering part of the equation. The survey showed that more than 60 per cent of employees did not perceive a common sense of purpose. However, a small number of people could articulate how the DCSA needed to operate both efficiently and within a constrained budget:

> *We've got to provide something that's going to be economic to the taxpayer and effective for the job that we're going to do.*
> (Junior Staff Member, IPT)

THE SITUATION AT THE END OF 2005

At the end of 2005, the Agency was well into a transformational change programme, although the transformation meant different things to different people in the Agency. The senior team had a clear picture of where they needed to take the organisation but many of the lower levels of staff and below were not so sure, and a degree of suspicion still existed throughout the organisation. Change was something that was being done to them rather than a process where they could take the initiative, and this was reinforced by their perception that they had to deal with the change issues in addition to completing the day job. For some staff it was 'business as usual'. The influx of programmes, funding and people was such that the DCSA was in a constant state of flux with major changes still to occur, as shown in the manpower profile in Figure 2.

Much had been achieved in the preceding years, and yet there were still more changes to be delivered. However, 2005 seemed a good time to take stock and reconsider how to drive the change forward into its next stage of development.

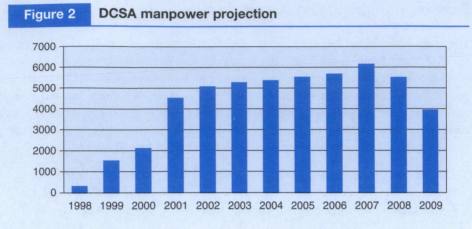

Figure 2   DCSA manpower projection

ASSIGNMENT QUESTIONS

1 Using the kaleidoscope framework, do a contextual analysis of the DCSA in 2002. What were the positive features within the change context and what features were barriers to the achievement of change? Which barriers were most critical?

2 How well did the design of the change programme address those barriers to change?

3 Construct a contextual analysis for DCSA as it is described at the end of this case study. To what extent is the change context more positive and receptive to change at the end of the case?

4 If you were advising the Chief Executive on the Change Programme, what would you recommend for them to do next to drive the change forwards? What do you consider to be the critical issues they should focus on in the next stage of change?

5

Designing the transition: the implementation path

5.1 INTRODUCTION

So far, this book has discussed the initial planning and design for change implementation. Chapter 2 introduced the range of design choices open to organisations implementing change. Chapters 3 and 4 discussed how to assess the key contextual features of the change situation, and how to use these factors to judge what change approach to take. As yet, little has been said about the design of the more detailed steps to achieve the implementation of the desired change approach or, for that matter, once change gets underway, how to manage the implementation. This is the focus of Chapters 5–7: the design and management of the actual transition, with a particular emphasis on managing complex evolutions:

- The notion of three change states – the *current* (where the organisation is now), the *future* (where the organisation wants to be), and the *transition* (how to get to the future state) – is revisited.

- The concept of a change *vision* is introduced, and it is explained how this aspect of the future state needs to be considered before moving on to design the transition.

- The need to diagnose barriers to change that may be encountered during the transition is discussed. Barriers arise primarily from organisational culture and stakeholders.

- The notion of the transition state is expanded to explain how it encompasses three change phases – mobilise, move and sustain.

- The concept of the transition curve is explained to illustrate how the organisational transition process of mobilise, move and sustain is underpinned by the personal transitions of individuals within an organisation.

- Creating mobilisation, or developing readiness for change, is discussed along with a series of techniques for achieving this.

- Consideration is given to how to design a series of change interventions, and how to sequence their deployment, to achieve the chosen change approach and move the organisation through the transition from mobilisation to ultimately sustaining the changes.

Chapter 6 extends the discussion of the range of *change interventions* that can be deployed during the transition state to achieve the desired end result. The special *management* and *resource requirements* of the transition state are discussed in Chapter 7.

5.2 THE THREE CHANGE STATES: THE CURRENT, THE FUTURE AND THE TRANSITION

Chapter 1 introduced the concept of three change states[1] (see Figure 5.1). Whilst this text assumes that readers have already mastered the techniques to enable them to diagnose the current and future organisational states from other texts, before this chapter moves on to consider the detailed design of the transition, it is necessary to revisit the analysis of the start and end points of change. In particular, it is necessary to give consideration to developing a vision or picture of the desired future organisational state, and to diagnosing the barriers to change that exist in the current state.

5.3 THE FUTURE STATE – DEVELOPING A VISION

Since the 1980s, there has been an increasing emphasis on the need for a powerful change 'vision', or picture of the future, if change is to be successful. Transformational change in particular usually consists of a number of projects and initiatives. Without a unifying vision, these initiatives can appear to be unrelated, confusing and piece-meal. Employees can struggle to understand what they are trying to achieve and what the future organisation looks like. A vision gives change recipients a target to aim for, and the incentive and energy for change. It should also generate commitment to change.

Figure 5.1   Three change states

To achieve change it is necessary to:

1 Assess the current organisational situation.
2 Define the desired future organisational state.
3 Determine how to get there.

A vision is usually a qualitative expression of the desired future state. There are various descriptions of what constitutes a good vision, but generally three aspects are mentioned. A vision encapsulates: what the organisation is trying to achieve; a rationale for the changes to be undertaken; and a picture of what the future organisation will 'look like', which incorporates something about the values of the new organisation and what is expected of employees. A good vision statement should also be exciting and challenging. In addition, visions need to appeal to the majority of an organisation's stakeholders, and comprise realistic and attainable goals.[2]

5.3.1 Vision statements

For many organisations, since a vision is about explaining to people where the organisation is going, having a vision means having a vision statement. The popularity of vision statements stems from some famous examples that are cited as central to the successes achieved by the organisations that used them. Komatsu, the Japanese earth-moving equipment manufacturer, is famous for the intent to 'Encircle Caterpillar'. Caterpillar was the industry leader in Komatsu's sector at the time. Similarly, Honda wanted to become a second Ford, a pioneer in the automotive industry. These statements show that using examples, metaphors or analogies can help to succinctly express to employees what is required without using jargon. On the other hand, these vision statements were developed with a long time horizon in mind. It is more common to develop a vision statement addressed more specifically to a particular change initiative. So, for example, Claridge's, the famous London hotel, was in decline in the late 1990s. The executive team started a change process with a vision to be 'the first choice for any guest coming to London looking for style and quality service, and the first-choice employer.'[3]

Giving employees a vision is a critical part of the change process. How can people change if they don't understand what they have got to change to? Yet many people are cynical about vision statements, despite their popularity. Vision statements can be woolly and generic. Employees often feel that they are a PR exercise rather than a genuine attempt to communicate the goals of change. In addition, words are open to differing interpretations. To return to the Claridge's vision above – what do words like 'style', 'quality service', and 'first-choice employer' mean? What matters is a common understanding of what the vision is about, rather than the words used.

5.3.2 Communicating a vision

A vision should be expressed in such a way that it can be communicated effectively to employees in a way that is memorable. Employees will find it difficult to remember overly long and complex messages. Few individuals are able to remember even a page of detail, so a memorable vision statement is likely to be short and to the point. Furthermore, employees need to understand how they can help make the vision happen – they need to be able to link what they do on an everyday basis to the achievement of the vision.[4] Vision statements are, therefore, only one way of expressing the change goals and aspirations of an organisation. There are many other and potentially more effective means of communicating and expressing a vision.

Visions can alternatively be communicated through pictures. One technique is the 'strategy canvas', where a one-page picture showing both the current and future states is developed and used to share the vision with an organisation's employees.[5] Then instead of communicating a vision statement, the vision can be shared through conversations based around the big-picture elements of the future, such as what the future organisation will look like, how this future was generated, and practicalities to do with the types of jobs available.[6]

The process used to develop a vision can be as important as the vision itself. A more participative process in which employees are involved, and in which two-way dialogue and discussion is used to foster a shared understanding of what the vision is about, may lead to a more effective vision. The words of the agreed vision statement may be no less woolly, but there should be more clarity about the expectations of employees and the changes the company is embarking on. This was the approach taken by City & Guilds, a charity which is the UK's leading vocational examinations body. See Illustration 5.1.

Another increasingly popular approach is that of storytelling. Parcelforce used this technique to sustain a change process put in place in 2001 to turn the company into a profitable concern from one losing £200 million a year. By 2005, following major 'surgery', Parcelforce Worldwide achieved breakeven, but then the challenge was to maintain the momentum now that the burning platform for change had gone. They decided to use storytelling. A story map was created that, in chapters, explained the journey Parcelforce was on, where it was now and the vision for the future, and articulated four priorities – improving service, growing profitable revenue, working smarter and developing skills and capabilities. The storyboard was brought to life through 'comic books', with the key messages supported by real-life stories from the business. A conference for senior managers launched the story and was used to create storytelling evangelists. Delegates were charged with spreading the story and given a storytelling pack to help them do this. Each location was given a story map and four posters, one for each pillar, that were delivered at two weekly intervals using the comic-strip storytelling style. Each location was also encouraged to build their own story.[7]

5.3.3 Aligning actions and words: using the web to help formulate a vision

Yet visions can also be communicated more powerfully through behaviours as well as words, particularly the behaviours of the senior managers and other role models in an organisation. Indeed, behaviours may be a more effective way of

Illustration 5.1

change in action

Creating an internal brand at City & Guilds

City & Guilds is a vocational examinations board delivering qualifications in over 500 subjects. There are 1 million people working towards a City & Guilds qualification on a worldwide basis at any one time. The international vocational qualifications are recognised in 120 countries.

A new Director General was appointed in 2001, placing a renewed focus on the organisation's purpose, mission and direction as part of an effort to reposition the organisation in the marketplace. The vision is of a world in which both individuals and organisations can obtain the skills needed for their economic well-being. The City & Guilds' board chose to develop, communicate and implement this through the development of an internal brand for City & Guilds.

The work started with a workshop for the board and members of the senior executive team at which the brand model was developed, paying particular attention to the vision, mission and values. The term 'modern classic' was developed to highlight the importance of connecting the heritage of the City & Guilds organisation with the need to meet the challenges of the twenty-first century. The four values of integrity, excellence, innovation and engagement were developed. The initial brand proposition was then rolled out across the organisation through brand workshops.

Changes were made as appropriate, based on the staff feedback.

The essence of the brand became 'skills for a brighter future'. A core brand team was established. Fifty brand champions were recruited from across the business, to become the evangelists. They were to help the brand team push information out into the organisation but also help them keep track of progress. Three phases were developed – education, identification and implementation. In the education phase, brand champions were given a toolkit to use throughout the business, including a presentation explaining the brand and examples of how teams and individuals were upholding the values. In the identification phase, the champions had to work with their part of the business to identify where the organisation was on- and off-brand and to identify the areas needing attention. From this, the brand team along with the senior executive team developed an action plan. For example, the competency framework, induction processes, and reward and recognition programme were all changed to support the internal brand. There was also a brand launch to all staff within the organisation, including staff from international offices, at the Café Royal in London, at which employees were encouraged to discuss what they were doing to embed the brand in their area.

Adapted from Causon, J. (2004) 'The internal brand: successful cultural change and employee empowerment', *Journal of Change Management*, 4 (4), pp. 297–307

communicating a vision. If actions and words are not aligned, vision statements, like values statements, are quickly discredited.[8] It is therefore important to understand, as part of the vision process, what new behaviours are required from managers to support the vision, and also what old behaviours, events and actions need to be discarded if employees are not to receive conflicting messages about what is now acceptable behaviour. For this reason, in some companies senior managers

Illustration 5.2   *change in action*

Design Services cultural web

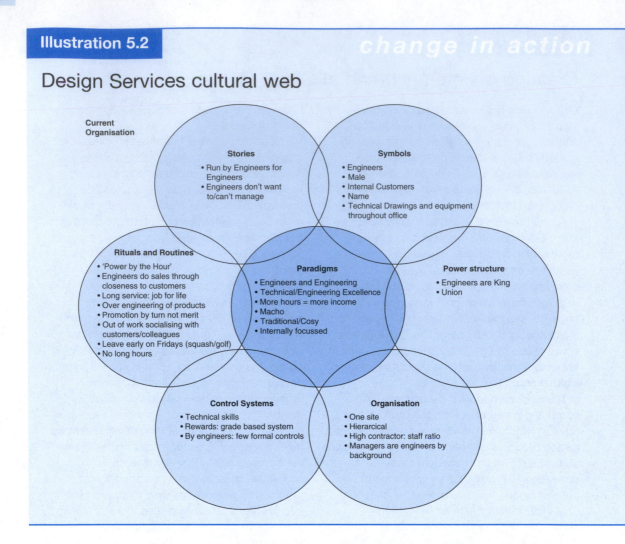

Current Organisation

Stories
- Run by Engineers for Engineers
- Engineers don't want to/can't manage

Symbols
- Engineers
- Male
- Internal Customers
- Name
- Technical Drawings and equipment throughout office

Rituals and Routines
- 'Power by the Hour'
- Engineers do sales through closeness to customers
- Long service: job for life
- Over engineering of products
- Promotion by turn not merit
- Out of work socialising with customers/colleagues
- Leave early on Fridays (squash/golf)
- No long hours

Paradigms
- Engineers and Engineering
- Technical/Engineering Excellence
- More hours = more income
- Macho
- Traditional/Cosy
- Internally focussed

Power structure
- Engineers are King
- Union

Control Systems
- Technical skills
- Rewards: grade based system
- By engineers: few formal controls

Organisation
- One site
- Hierarcical
- High contractor: staff ratio
- Managers are engineers by background

are shadowed by consultants or coaches to ensure they are engaging in agreed behaviours supportive of the vision, rather than old, contradictory behaviours. Other companies use 360-degree appraisal to identify whether or not senior executives are 'walking the talk'.

A picture of the future organisation can be developed by drawing a new cultural web. This is a useful way of building a picture of the future organisation, since the web incorporates not just new structures but also what new symbols, routines and control systems are needed.[9] Illustration 5.2 shows a current and future web for an organisation referred to here as Design Services, an engineering company. As the webs show, since Design Services wants to exploit growth potential in the external market to move from being a traditional engineering company to a more entrepreneurial 'engineering solutions' company, with customers from a wider range of industry sectors, the

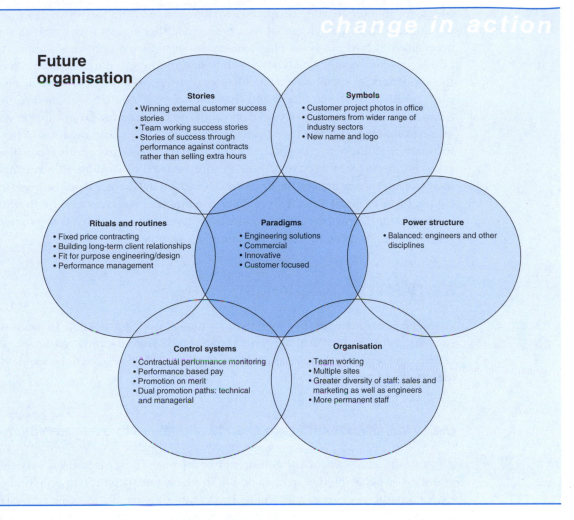

change in action

Future organisation

Stories
- Winning external customer success stories
- Team working success stories
- Stories of success through performance against contracts rather than selling extra hours

Symbols
- Customer project photos in office
- Customers from wider range of industry sectors
- New name and logo

Rituals and routines
- Fixed price contracting
- Building long-term client relationships
- Fit for purpose engineering/design
- Performance management

Paradigms
- Engineering solutions
- Commercial
- Innovative
- Customer focused

Power structure
- Balanced: engineers and other disciplines

Control systems
- Contractual performance monitoring
- Performance based pay
- Promotion on merit
- Dual promotion paths: technical and managerial

Organisation
- Team working
- Multiple sites
- Greater diversity of staff: sales and marketing as well as engineers
- More permanent staff

scope of change envisaged is substantial. Power and organisational structures, routines, rituals, stories, symbols and so on all need to change to support this. Furthermore, as Illustration 5.2 shows, completing the web helps to identify *specifics* about new symbols, symbolic behaviour, routines, and systems that can be acted on to reinforce the espoused vision.

Developing an outline of a new cultural web is an important exercise early on in the design of the change process, even if there is as yet no vision statement. Questions considered in Chapters 3 and 4, such as the scope of the changes to be undertaken by an organisation, cannot be answered unless there is at least an outline of the desired future state. However, as the change design progresses, more detail needs to be added into the web. Consideration must also be given to change levers to do with formal and informal organisation structures and power structures, information systems, management systems, measurement systems and HR systems (discussed in more detail in Chapter 6). Systems extend from the way budgets are developed to how quickly phones are answered. Aligning day-to-day activities to get required behaviours is also about understanding which routines and symbols to change or remove, and which new symbols and routines to put into place. Given the importance of symbolic activity, Chapter 6 also considers this in more detail.

Obviously, not all the *levers* and *interventions* for change identified in the future web can be put in place on day one of the change process to support the vision statement. This is why this chapter is devoted to a consideration of how to phase the different change levers and interventions through the transition state. Furthermore, the cultural web cannot be used to capture all levers and mechanisms by any means. Illustrations 2.6 and 2.8 in Chapter 2 on the Forestry Commission of Great Britain show that in particular, interventions to do with communication and personal development have to be considered separately. Again, these are given more consideration in Chapter 6.

5.4 BARRIERS TO CHANGE

Once the future state for the organisation is understood, it is possible to diagnose the barriers to change. Most barriers to change arise from the old *organisational culture* and *organisational stakeholders*. Barriers to change need to be explicitly identified and removed.

5.4.1 Identifying barriers to change and levers to overcome them

Any *vision* developed of the future will encapsulate new structures, systems, and ways of behaving that have to be put in place, but without consideration of existing barriers it is possible, almost by default, to leave old systems and ways of behaving in place, and these can subsequently prove obstructive. For example, one organisation undergoing change wanted to move to a structure of profit centres in order to devolve responsibility and increase middle manager empowerment. However, old control systems, such as centralised decision making on levels of resourcing and recruitment and authorisation of certain types of expense claims and expenditure, were initially left in place. Old senior manager behaviours, such as countermanding local decisions, also remained, symbolically challenging the espoused move to devolved responsibility. As a result the middle managers perceived little increase in their scope for discretion or autonomy. Interventions needed to be put in place to address these barriers if change was to progress.

Old routines provide a particular barrier to change since they are so engrained in the way an organisation operates and because many of them are to do with the informal and unwritten way of operating. In addition, senior managers in particular may be reluctant to let go of them. This description of the culture at IBM, when

Lou Gerstner became CEO in 1993, illustrates a number of 'routine' ways of behaving, all of which needed to change if IBM was to be turned around and become less bureaucratic and more agile. Decisions 'made by committee' took an exceedingly long time and a 'non-concur' from any one member could overrule general agreement on a course of action. Executives had large staffs and little direct involvement in writing their own reports. They delivered presentations prepared by staff members in numerous 'pre-meetings' in which the staff worked to align positions and eliminate surprises. Armies of staff members attended executive meetings, lingering in hallways or – in the case of very senior staff – seated close behind their executive in the meeting room, armed with volumes of back-up material. Prepared presentations dominated even informal meetings, and most executives had projectors built into their office furniture.[10]

These examples illustrate that existing *organisation cultures* provide some of the strongest barriers to the implementation of change. If the existing organisation culture and the potential barriers to change are not understood from a technique such as cultural web analysis, the way the organisation and its members operate may continue to be driven by the existing culture, rather than by the desired new ways of behaving. In the example of the company referred to as Design Services in Illustration 5.2, the existing organisation, based around engineers and engineering products, presents several barriers to the desired future full-service/consultancy-based organisation. These include the historical power base of the engineers, the notion of the organisation as run by engineers for engineers, and the embedded practice of making money through 'power by the hour'. Traditionally, an hourly rate was agreed with a customer, and Design Services would work however many hours were necessary to deliver the project. There was no total project cost agreed, and no culture of bidding for a job on the basis of cost for total job and then managing the work against this. For change to be successful, the range of levers deployed needed to address these issues. More specifically, the identified barriers, including old behaviours, needed to be removed or destroyed.

However, as emphasised in Chapter 3 when discussing the need for preservation, change does need to avoid throwing out *positive aspects* of an organisation alongside the negative aspects. Therefore, when examining the cultural web, attention should be paid to not just the barriers to change, but also those aspects of the organisation that are either an asset or a facilitator of change and need to be retained.

Powerful stakeholders, such as the engineers at Design Services, can also provide significant barriers to change. The way such stakeholders are likely to react to the proposed changes should have already been built into the design choices made from the consideration of power as one of the contextual features. However, it is also important to understand the way different stakeholders will respond to change as implementation progresses, and then consider how this is to be tackled. Chapter 7 will consider power and stakeholder issues in more detail.

5.5 DESIGNING THE TRANSITION STATE: THE ORGANISATIONAL LEVEL

Once the design of the future state has been completed, and it is known what barriers to change have to be overcome, it is then necessary to design an implementation path to deliver the future state. This involves thinking about which change levers to deploy and in what order. Of course, many levers and interventions will already have been identified. The future cultural web will contain details of new structures, systems, routines and symbols needed. The consideration of barriers to change should have led to some decisions about old structures, systems and ways of behaving that need to be dismantled or discouraged, and the mechanisms that can be deployed to achieve this and facilitate change.

To provide more shape to the way the identified levers and interventions should be sequenced, and what additional interventions may be needed, it is helpful to subdivide the transition state itself into three other phases – mobilise, move and sustain (see Figure 5.2).

This model is based on the one devised by Lewin.[11] The original model referred to 'unfreezing, moving and refreezing':

- *Unfreezing* is about making people within an organisation ready for change by making them aware of the need for change and become dissatisfied with the existing ways of working. It is about creating the *readiness for change* among the workforce at all levels, from senior managers downwards, discussed as part of the change kaleidoscope in Chapters 3 and 4. Change is a painful, difficult experience for both organisations and the individuals within them. To undertake change people need to feel that the problems and the pain change will cause are outweighed by the need to change.

- *Moving* is the implementation of the needed changes through the selected range of levers and mechanisms.

- *Refreezing* involves embedding the changes throughout the organisation to ensure members do not relapse into patterns of old behaviour.

Figure 5.2   Three phases of transition

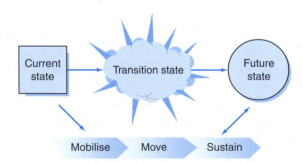

There are many criticisms of this model. One is that it is too linear and simplistic. Whilst such criticisms are true, the principle of *unfreezing* is still widely acknowledged as an important part of any change.[12] Managers introduced to this model will often comment that on reflection, they can see that the change process within their organisation stumbled along rather than acquired momentum, because the staff within the organisation were never 'unfrozen' and made ready for change. Similarly, the concept of refreezing is still recognised as having some merit, as it seems that without efforts to indicate that change is over, change drift can set in. A common comment from managers is that the change processes within their organisations have been left unfinished, since no real attempt has been made to institutionalise the required behavioural and attitudinal changes throughout the organisation. The result is a continual backsliding of staff into old ways of behaving and a confusion over where the change process has got to. As such, the concepts of unfreezing and refreezing are still important.

On the other hand, it is also often commented that unfreezing and refreezing are inappropriate terms to use in modern organisations. Many organisations move from a period of on-going adaptation to a radical change, and then back into adaptation through continuous improvement. This is why it is becoming more common for the unfreeze phase to be referred to as 'mobilisation' and the refreeze phase to be referred to as 'sustain' or 'institutionalise'. Mobilisation is about mobilising people behind the latest change initiative. The term conveys better the sense of redirecting energies and efforts into a new project. Similarly, terms such as sustain and institutionalise embody the need to instil the new behaviours and attitudes throughout the organisation and signal the end to major change, while avoiding the implication that there will be no more change.

5.6 FACILITATING PERSONAL TRANSITIONS: THE INDIVIDUAL LEVEL

Organisations only change if the individuals within that organisation change. To an external customer, the behaviour of the people that the customer encounters summarises what the organisation stands for. If an organisation wants to change the way its customers see it, it has to change the behaviour of its people. Strategic change has to be driven down throughout the organisation. Yet as Chapter 1 explains, all too often, change management is viewed as something that is 'done' to people. Employees of the organisation are treated as passive on-lookers who will comply with the directives and objectives issued from the top.

Therefore, to achieve change, a change agent needs to understand how individuals change, and build this into the mobilise, move and sustain model. Change leaders need to recognise that they have two parallel sets of tasks: (1) leading the organisation through change, and (2) leading the individual organisational members through that change (see Figure 5.3). This is why change capability, as discussed in Chapters 3 and 4, is so important – part of change capability is having the ability to lead staff through change.

Figure 5.3	Dual leadership responsibilities – managing the organisational and individual change paths

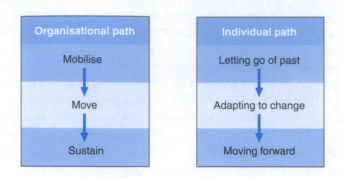

Individual transitions can be likened to the bereavement and mourning process. It is a psychological process that research shows all individuals go through. Individuals will experience feelings of loss, and will have to work through those feelings of loss and come to terms with life afterwards.[13] This takes time, although varying degrees of time for different individuals. This text uses the concept of the *transition curve* to explain how individuals pass through change.

5.6.1 The transition curve

The *transition curve*[14] describes the process individuals go through during change, and is depicted in Figure 5.4. The transition curve suggests individuals undergoing change pass through seven stages:

- In *stage 1,* individuals initially experience *shock* when they encounter the need for change and a dip in their self-confidence, due to the need for them to undertake personal change and to do things differently.

- *Stage 2, denial,* is a stage when individuals may try to rationalise the changes as not really involving a significant change for themselves. Individuals may try to tell themselves that working in a new role will involve nothing different from their current role. As a result their self-confidence goes back up again, but this denial can also prevent them from moving forwards. Trying to fulfil a new job in the same way as they did their old one may mean they do not perform well.

- To move on to *stage 3, awareness,* individuals need to develop a recognition of the need for personal change. However, acquiring this awareness, which may be prompted by discussion with others or a recognition that the old ways of doing things no longer work, also brings with it a *drop in confidence* as individuals become aware of their inadequacy to fulfil their new role.

- Individuals will be able to move forward to *stage 4, acceptance,* when they can accept the need to let go of the past – to let go of old attitudes and behaviours and adopt new ones.

Figure 5.4	The transition curve

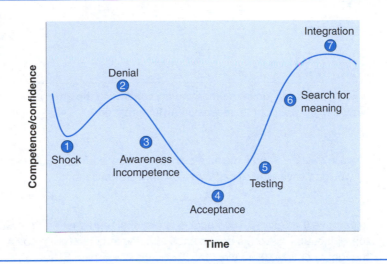

Source: Based on Adams, J., Hayes, J. and Hopson, C. (1976) *Transition: Understanding and Managing Personal Change*, London: Martin Robertson & Company

- *Stage 5, testing*, is to do with identifying and testing out new behaviours, maybe as a result of training. As new behaviours start to enable individuals to perform more adequately in their new role, confidence starts to build again.

- By *stage 6, search*, the individual is assimilating learning from their successes and failures, and starting to understand why some behaviours work and others do not.

- *Stage 7, integration*, is marked by an integration of new behaviours into the everyday way of working by individuals. There ceases to be a gap between an individual's perceived ability to perform and the expectations placed on that individual.

5.6.2 Experiencing the transition curve

Illustrations 5.3 and 5.4 are illustrations of change journeys experienced by individuals. Illustration 5.3 describes the journey undertaken by an individual who quickly adapted to a transition to a new job role, whereas Illustration 5.4 shows an individual who adapted, but found the process far more traumatic than the first individual. Both examples illustrate well the emotional nature of the individual transitions, and the second powerfully shows how an individual can need a lot of help to get through a personal transition. Some individuals never complete the transition. They get stuck halfway through, and never really recover from feelings of loss and that things used to be better in the old days.

The headings 'Shock' and 'Despair' in Illustration 5.4 demonstrate how hard it can be for an individual to let go of the past and come to terms with the need for change. Similarly, the headings 'Disorganisation', 'Realisation', 'Steadying', 'Testing' and 'Acceptance' in Illustrations 5.3 and 5.4 reveal the feelings of loss and inadequacy

Illustration 5.3

change in action

A rapid adaptation

JOURNEY	REACTION
Shock	'I was offered the job in the morning and started in the afternoon. I knew what the job was, but there was an awful lot to learn.'
Acceptance	'It wasn't planned and it meant a significant change of life, but I welcomed it – I wouldn't have liked to have stayed in my previous job.'
Testing	'I learnt very quickly, I asked a lot of questions, read a lot and quickly got on top of the job. I gave the appearance of being in control within days – though, of course, there were many months of learning.'
Moving on	'I'm in control.'

Adapted from Stuart, R. (1995) 'Experiencing organisational change: triggers, processes and outcomes of change journeys', *Personnel Review*, 24, p. 2.

that individuals can experience as they try to understand what is expected of them and what they need to do, but also how there is a gradual acceptance that change is necessary. 'Moving on' in Illustrations 5.3 and 5.4 is about the individuals emerging on the other side of change, feeling competent to perform in their new roles.

Illustrations 5.3 and 5.4 also show that all individuals pass through the transition curve at a different rate and in a different way. The curve depicts a typical pattern or response rather than a prescriptive route that all individuals adhere to. It shows that resistance to change is a natural phenomenon associated, like grieving, with a reluctance to give up possessions, people, status and expectations.[15]

5.7 LINKING INDIVIDUAL AND ORGANISATIONAL TRANSITIONS

The concept of the transition curve can be combined with the mobilise, move and sustain model, as shown in Figure 5.5, to help remind designers of change what interventions in these phases are trying to achieve for the individual recipients:

● The stages of *shock* and *denial,* moving into *awareness,* accompanied by feelings of loss, fits with *mobilisation*. Interventions aimed at helping

Illustration 5.4

change in action

A painful adaptation

JOURNEY	REACTION
Shock	'It was totally contrary to everything that I'd been told.'
Despair	'I felt very criticised, not understood and totally incompetent.'
Disorganisation	'I felt totally confused. I thought that I must be going nuts. Had I the right perception? Paranoid? I'd lost all sense of judgement. I felt out of control. Doubt. Am I dreaming this?'
Yearning	'I had vivid dreams, replaying the events leading up to . . . replaying them in different ways. It was like a dreadful nightmare.'
Despair	'I felt isolated but was unable to talk to other people. I had a real feeling of desperation. At one stage, I didn't think I'd survive. It was a desperate time.'
Realisation	'I realised I had no alternative. I had to get my self-esteem and credibility back into shape sufficiently to carry on. I had to own up and take responsibility for what I'd done; I felt betrayed, cheapened and scapegoated. I was very angry with the organisation for blaming me. I am responsible but look what you made me do.'
Steadying	'I moved (within the organisation). I spent a long time wilfully forgetting. I started to feel better – a sense of more stability. I was defensive – fearful that things could get out of control again.'
Testing	'I was continuously building anew. I attended courses, some things went well; it took a long time to feel better about myself.'
Meaning	'Getting a clear view of what I'm good and not good at. Developing my understanding of the reality and limits of my relationship with the organisation.'
Moving on	'I feel powerful. I've put things into perspective and learned from them. It is okay to be me and to trust my perception – and that it's not the only one.'

Adapted from Stuart, R. (1995) 'Experiencing organisational change: triggers, processes and outcomes of change journeys', *Personnel Review*, 24, p. 2.

| Figure 5.5 | Linking organisational and individual change |

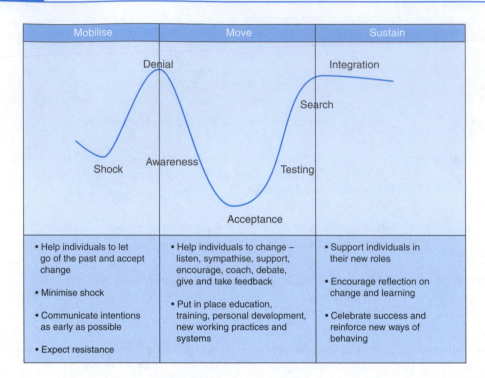

individuals to come to terms with the need for change and to let go of the past should, therefore, be built into the mobilisation phase through the types of mobilisation tactics discussed below. The mobilisation tactic(s) adopted do need to match the context and the selected design choices.

● The experience of individuals as they move through *awareness* to *acceptance, testing* and *search* will underpin the *move* phase. Thus interventions such as education and training, personal development, new work procedures and systems, and new management styles which help individuals through these stages should all be included in the move phase. Coaching and counselling, from either internal or external facilitators, for staff who are having problems adapting may also be necessary here. Again, the range of *levers* deployed in the *move* phase will need to fit the design choices selected. In circumstances where there is little *time* or *money,* it may prove difficult to provide support via counselling or coaching to staff members who are struggling. There may have to be a trade-off between what is ideal and what is possible. If the required change is *transformational* in nature, it will be necessary to drive in value change and not just behavioural change. The levers will need to reflect this, with a greater emphasis on personal development, communication, counselling and coaching rather than just skills-based training.

- The *sustain* phase is about helping the *integration* process. Interventions that can be particularly helpful in this phase when the *change target* is *behaviours* or *values* include reward mechanisms to reinforce and support behavioural change undertaken by staff. Symbolic interventions can also be helpful here to reinforce change. Since both human resource systems and symbolic interventions as levers of change are discussed in more detail in Chapter 6, this point will be revisited there.

The transition process is painful and emotional both for both those doing the managing and the managed. Illustration 5.5 shows the emotional roller coaster experienced by a group of managers having to implement yet also personally experience a major restructuring of their business into three new divisions which would then work together on a contractual basis. The restructuring also

---

Illustration 5.5   *change in action*

Managing change: an emotional roller coaster

Mobilisation: letting go of the past

- Core Division is a small group of people, and the feeling out there is that everybody else is going to be floated off, they are not going to be tied to this company, and this company is my company, I worked 27 years here, and they don't like losing it.
- They have owned the records, and have taken a great deal of pride . . . and suddenly they are not their records . . . and some people find that really tough . . . we created them, we've worked on them, we've looked after them . . . (now) they are owned by Core.
- Maintenance staff now feel like contractors.

Move: adapting to change

- There are still some black holes that we seem to be arguing about, whose job is which. People are reluctant to take on the bits in the middle, the grey areas, and they are saying no that's not mine that's yours.

- On an individual basis we are liaising and working together as much as possible to reduce barriers.
- They need a kick. Some bull-headed managers need to get their heads out of the sand and start working for the business overall.

Sustain: new beginnings and moving forward

- The amount of change we have gone through, actually that is something that I think has gone incredibly well . . . My job description is totally different to what it was . . . and that is not just in our section, you can see it across where ever.
- We have had quite a rude awakening this year, the extent of the change in the way the business has run has been phenomenal. We could never have imagined it . . . there is no parameter, you have got to be so flexible to survive.

Adapted from Balogun, J. and Johnson, G. (2005) 'From intended strategy to unintended outcomes: the impact of change recipient sensemaking', *Organization Studies,* 26 (11), pp. 1573–602 and Balogun, J. (2006) 'Managing change: steering a course between intended strategies and unanticipated outcomes', *Long Range Planning,* 39 (1), pp. 29–49.

involved downsizing and the introduction of many new working practices. The illustration reveals the high level of emotional work required of such managers. Thus both those being asked to undertake change and those managing the change need support during the transition process. This theme is returned to in Chapter 7, which considers issues of transition management in more depth.

An exercise on the transition curve which asks people to consider a change process they have been through and what helped and hindered them at each stage of the personal transition (see Illustration 5.6) reveals that the interventions that most help individuals move through the curve are primarily interpersonal and symbolic. The interventions are to do with communication, coaching, training, support and encouraging appropriate new ways of working through symbolic means such as celebrating successes and achievements. This emphasises the importance of the interpersonal subsystem of change interventions discussed in Chapter 2 as one of the design choices, and reinforces the need to put interventions in place in all four subsystems (technical, political, cultural and interpersonal) for significant change to take root in an organisation. However, whilst it is therefore necessary to spend time considering how the design choices are put together with the knowledge of the current and future states, and an understanding of how individuals go through change, it is first necessary to consider the important phase of mobilisation.

5.8 MOBILISING FOR CHANGE

Mobilising an organisation sounds simple enough in theory, but is far more difficult in practice because it is about making *individuals* ready for change. The use of logic and rational argument will not necessarily be enough to convince individuals – who may stand to lose a lot by change, or who may have to undertake personal change themselves or have to invest considerable effort into the change process – that there is a strong need to change.

Mobilisation may occur because a significant change in the environment has led to a decline in the organisational performance that is tangible to all employees, such as the arrival of new competitors leading to a sharp decline in market share, or a takeover or sell-off. This may lead to a felt need for change, or maybe even a crisis, that can be capitalised on. But this is not always, and is in fact rarely, the case. What creates a crisis for managers may leave the rest of the workforce relatively untouched. After all, that is what managers are paid to do – sort out problems. If no crisis or felt need for change is evident, then mobilisation has to be managed in some other way. The change equation is a useful way of thinking about how to achieve this.

Illustration 5.6

change in action

An exercise on the transition curve

Helps through shock and denial
Finding a coach/mentor to off-load feelings on
Knowing from discussions with others you are not alone
Identifying +ves and −ves
Having friends/trusted people: emotional support
Communications enabling mental preparation – what is to happen, what it will be like
Getting information in advance, and involvement
Understanding the transition process

Hinders
Disinformation
Lack of information
Isolation
Only seeing the negatives
Guilt – others worse off

Helps through awareness phase
Letting go of the past
Identifying new goals
Receiving information: options, facts versus rumour and speculation
Understanding alternatives – receiving options, information
Putting things in perspective
Addressing real fears (new tools, for example)
Creating an enemy
Allowing expression:
    OK to be angry/sad
    Empathy with feelings
    Listening
    Conflict not suppressed
Anticipating falling output and standards

Hinders
Opinions not allowed
Uncertainty
Lack of forums for expression
Blame
Negativity

Helps through acceptance/testing phase
Finding support for yourself
Those who are negative leave
Maintaining focus; first steps; short-term goals
Learning encouraged: new behaviours rewarded (informally), coaching, mistakes allowed, risk taking encouraged
Training
Reinforcing success/celebrating it
Forging new identity/relationships: social activities, peer support groups
Leadership

Hinders
Blame
Punishing failure
Jealousy
Resistance
Keep celebrating the past
Negative attitudes from others

Helps through search for meaning/integration phase
Rewarding/celebrating success
Continuing to emphasise plans/goals
Providing long-term goals – Work starts here
Role models who live the vision
Giving feedback and encouraging reflection/learning
On-going team/network building
Providing on-going development opportunities

Hinders
Moving on to next change initiative and forgetting current
No new goals/targets

5.8.1 The change equation

The change equation, shown in Figure 5.6, states there are three components that need to be present for individuals to be prepared to undertake change. For individuals to feel that the problems and pain of change are outweighed by the advantages of the need for change, it is necessary for people to:

1. be dissatisfied with the status quo;
2. be convinced the proposed changes are a viable way of resolving current problems;
3. believe the proposed changes are achievable.

This equation is particularly helpful when considering mobilisation. It also ties into the discussion in the previous two chapters on readiness for change. Mobilising individuals is about getting individuals to recognise that change is necessary and that they have to let go of the past, but also that the proposed changes are desirable because they will solve the problems the organisation is facing, and that they are achievable.

Consideration of the three components of the change equation gives us insights into how to generate readiness for change. There are a variety of different means that can be used and the following lists only some of them. When considering these different tactics, it should be remembered that a key aspect of any successful mobilisation tactic is likely to be novelly, which means doing things differently from the way they have been done in the past. For instance, previous change attempts may have been initiated the same way, perhaps by the appointment of new managers, the removal of other managers and the announcement in memos and meetings that changes and restructuring are to take place. If, following these past change initiatives, staff have then seen little change, this would not be a good way to launch a new attempt at change. Chapter 6 (Illustration 6.3) describes how senior managers at Kraft Foods UK used employee conferences that were deliberately different in

---

Figure 5.6	**The change equation**

$$C = (A \times B \times D) > X$$

When

C = Change

A = Level of dissatisfaction with the status quo

B = Desirability of proposed change

D = Practicality (risk of disruption) of change

X = Personal cost of changing

Source: Adapted from Beckhard, R. and Harris, R.T. *Organizational Transitions: Managing Complex Change*, 2nd edn. Upper Saddle River, NJ: Prentice Hall. Copyright © 1987 Pearson Education, Inc. Reproduced with permission.

style and had higher energy than previous conferences to engage their workforce with change. At Claridge's (see section 5.3.1 above), as part of the process of developing the vision, managers were taken off-site for a day by the executive team and told to develop five-minute performances (a sketch or a dance, for example) to demonstrate one of the values behind the new vision for the hotel.

5.8.2 Questioning and challenging of the status quo

There are a variety of techniques that can be used to encourage staff to question the appropriateness of the existing way of doing things for the organisation's longer-term survival, creating dissatisfaction with the status quo:

- Encourage debate about the appropriateness of the current way of operating. This was the technique used to mobilise managers at the Forestry Commission of Great Britain. Illustration 2.6 in Chapter 2 explains how consultants designed a three-day leadership event to make managers (and others) more of aware of why change was needed, and to explore the organisation culture and how their own behaviour impacted this and needed to change.

- Hold events at which executives challenge existing ways of thinking and complacency. This was the purpose of events at GSK in 2002 (see Illustration 2.2, Chapter 2). Sporting metaphors were used such as 'on the pitch with GSK' or 'off the pitch and on the terraces'. The tough message given was that if you didn't want to get on the pitch and play, you should leave. When change was required at Compass SA, the contract food services group, one of the initiatives of the Chief Executive to communicate his vision was to convene a meeting of 55 senior executives. The purpose was to allow executives to express freely their thoughts about the strengths and weaknesses of the organisation and their role to help break down hierarchical barriers. The CE then sent personal letters to each delegate, commenting bluntly on their contribution to the meeting to give the message to those who revealed what he considered an inadequate approach to their job that they either needed to change or leave Compass.[16]

- Disseminate information showing how the organisation compares poorly with the organisations with which it competes. This could be done through the use of internal communication media, or it could involve the chief executive of an organisation using the business press to tell his staff that the organisation is performing poorly.[17] The fact that the chief executive is talking openly about the organisation's performance legitimises debate. It could also involve customers sharing their negative experiences or analysts presenting their view of a company's strengths and weaknesses.[18]

- Questioning and challenging may also be achieved by the symbolic means discussed next.

Illustration 5.7 discusses an example of mobilisation for change at Home Depot, the US DIY retailer, led by Robert Nardelli, who has recently moved to Chrysler

Illustration 5.7

change in action

Mobilising through questioning and education at Home Depot

Robert Nardelli arrived at Home Depot in December 2000. The company was well known for its entrepreneurial and laissez-faire culture fostered by co-founders Bernie Marcus and Arthur Blank, who led the company from 1978 to 2000. Home Depot was founded as a large warehouse-like no-frills store providing a complete range of household products at discount prices, for DIY enthusiasts. The culture was an informal one. There were no 'processes' to speak of, and rule-of-thumb was applied to most situations. The organisation was also highly decentralised, and most decisions were made at the local level by autonomous store managers. By 2000 there were approximately 1,100 warehouse-like stores, with a 'pile it high, sell it cheap' philosophy. However, like many successful companies, the formula that had led to success was now leading to underperformance as new competitors with a different customer proposition entered the marketplace.

Nardelli's arrival in itself was a surprise as no one expected Marcus and Blank to leave and no one expected an outsider to succeed them. Nardelli set out to improve the profitability of the existing core business, but also extend the business into related services and to serve new customer segments. This required the centralisation of purchasing to reap the scale advantages an organisation the size of Home Depot should have, the introduction of collaboration between different functions, the re-evaluation of the store environment, and an upskilling of the workforce.

One of Nardelli's early initiatives was to introduce company-wide measurement and performance metrics to replace anecdotal evidence. This challenged embedded ways of thinking about the organisation. For example, data collected on customer satisfaction showed that assumptions about the stores such as low lighting and the warehouse characteristics needed to be changed. A performance management process was also introduced that used primarily quantitative criteria to assess store managers. This enabled the identification of the managers who were and weren't performing and facilitated open conversations with those who weren't performing. A balanced set of metrics also forced managers to base decisions on more than just sales, and to collaborate to solve problems the data highlighted rather than shifting blame between each other. Another of Nardelli's initiatives was the institution of a Monday-morning conference call with the top 15 or so executives, which enabled Nardelli to gradually hold people accountable for their actions. Other structural changes were also put in place, such as the centralisation of the nine purchasing divisions. In addition, a new resource planning system was put in place.

However, significant resistance remained within the organisation, not helped by the on-going poor performance of Home Depot 18 months into the change process. Thus come 2002, the head of HR put in place a series of five-day learning forums for 1,800 district and store managers which included competitive simulation and role-playing exercises. In one of the exercises the managers had to imagine they were Nardelli arriving at Home Depot, and then develop a plan for change. To sustain commitment to change, a number of leadership programmes have subsequently been put in place.

Adapted from Charan, R. (2006) 'Home Depot's blueprint for culture change', *Harvard Business Review,* (April), pp. 60–70. Also 'Home Depot's Cultural Evolution – A Comparison of the Company's Culture under Its Founders and Bob Nardelli'. (2004) IFCAI case No. HROB063.

to lead a turnaround there. Mobilisation was achieved primarily through encouraging questioning and challenging through the use of new measurement systems and data. However, this illustration also shows how one of the mobilisation techniques on its own is unlikely to be enough. Nardelli needed to do more to mobilise his regional and store managers and used education and training to do so. In addition, symbolic changes were occurring to the store environment as traditional store layouts were questioned, and the new performance management systems changed the way managers were assessed.

5.8.3 Symbolic breaks with the past

Questioning and challenging is often supported by symbolic breaks with the past. Making symbolic breaks with the past is about doing things differently to indicate that things actually are changing. This may then also legitimise questioning and challenging of the status quo. There are many different ways of achieving this.

- Senior managers can indicate by their behaviour, the way they dress, or the things they emphasise that things are different. When William Bratton became head of the transit police in New York, he discovered that senior staff never used the subway. To shatter their complacency and bring them closer to the fears of the users of the subway, Bratton required all transit police officials, including himself, to take the subway to work, to meetings and at night, instead of travelling to work and around in cars provided by the city.[19] When Marchionne took over Fiat in 2004 (see Illustration 2.3, Chapter 2), one of the differences people noticed was that he dressed differently and more casually compared to his predecessors and did different things such as playing music in the background at meetings. At Unilever, when Patrick Cescau became CEO, he was neither Dutch nor British as were CEOs of the past; he refused to take his predecessor's prestigious office on the top floor of the London HQ, instead remaining with his team on the floor below; and in general he showed a lack of interest in the status more typically shown by those in his position.[20]

- Changes can be made to the office environment. When the UK Benefits Agency and Employment Service were merged in the early 2000s, one of the major changes to the new joint offices created was that the offices were redesigned to reinforce the sense of the customer as a figure of respect. The offices have been furnished and decorated in a welcoming and professional manner. Users are greeted on arrival and guided to the appropriate location for their needs. All customer-facing staff wear name badges. Staff and customers face each other across desks in open-plan offices. For the Benefits Agency staff in particular, who used to deal with customers through security screens, this change was tangible and had an immediate impact on the way they worked.[21]

● Changes can be made to the way things are done. Older staff due for promotion may be passed over in favour of outsiders with a different skill-set, and other types of staff may even be made redundant. This is a particularly powerful mobilisation mechanism in any organisation where jobs were always for life and promotion was often linked to length of service rather than performance, although there are not many such organisations left these days. One long-established Scottish professional service firm, for example, needed to be repositioned to compete in a tougher marketplace. The new chief executive, who was himself seen as a break from the past with a less gentlemanly, paternalistic management style, put in place redundancies whilst hiring in stars from London firms. He also rebranded the organisation.[22]

● Changes may be subtle. If there is to be more of an emphasis on customer service and less on technical product aspects, then this can be supported by indications of a power shift from production to marketing, maybe by giving marketing a larger budget, or by moving senior marketing people to more prestigious offices closer to the MD and therefore the central seat of power. At Home Depot, Nardelli hired a long-trusted colleague from GE, and made him head of HR, a function that traditionally lacked influence in the company.

● Symbolic breaks with the past can also be achieved by changing things people value. One hospital in the UK, partly in response to the MRSA infection problem and the need to launder more uniforms within the hospital, is moving its nurses out of uniforms and into US-style hospital scrubs. This takes away the symbolism normally associated with British nurse uniforms, such as different colours for different levels of seniority. The intention is to move consultants into scrubs too – another break from the past since consultants don't normally wear any uniform when doing ward rounds.

● Symbolic breaks with the past may be more direct and challenging. The creation of the Police Service of Northern Ireland in 2001 from the more military Royal Ulster Constabulary involved many symbolic changes, not just a name change but a change in recruitment policy to 50–50 Protestants and Catholics, the scrapping of the force's well-known crown-and-harp cap badge and the introduction of a new police oath. All these changes were highly emotional, given the attachment to these emblems in the RUC. (See Chapter 2, section 2.2.3.)

5.8.4 Drastic measures and shock tactics

Some symbolic changes may be quite ruthless, verging on shock tactics. Such symbolic shock moves could involve wholesale closures or sell-offs of parts of the business that used to be core to the identity of the organisation but are no longer. These moves can challenge the very essence of an organisation's beliefs about its identity. Lego's turn-around plan in 2004 (see Illustration 3.1, Chapter 3) involved the layoff of 3,500 of the 8,000 workforce – more importantly, the redundancies affected employment in Lego's hometown of Billund, where 50 per cent of workers faced redundancy. A majority stake in the Legoland theme parks was also sold to a private equity firm. Such shock tactics are common in reconstructions where extreme action has to be taken fast, to both rescue the business and shake staff out of their complacency. See section 5.8.6.

5.8.5 Communication, education and training

The above three approaches are all useful for generating dissatisfaction with the status quo. Whilst symbolic gestures can also be used to illustrate what the new organisation is to be about, it is normally this approach – communication, education and training – that is used to create an understanding of how the proposed changes will help the organisation and to indicate that the proposed changes are achievable. Various communication and training interventions can be used to get across to people why change is needed, what changes are needed, and to provide them with the skills they need to make change happen. Such interventions are becoming increasingly popular, as it is realised that genuine change requires considerable investment in mobilising and supporting the workforce. There are few change programmes that don't involve such events. At Marks and Spencer, the recovery started in 2007 has been supported by investment in training for staff. Staff were given 'Billy Graham-type training'.[23] Over a nine-month period starting in July 2005, the 56,000-strong store workforce was put through motivational training sessions, sometimes 5,000 employees at a time. These sessions covered basics to do with customers and customer service. An additional 8,000 people were trained to take up coaching roles and help others. Illustration 5.7 above talks of the use of learning forums at Home Depot to raise awareness of the need for change and what sort of change, through role-playing, simulations and other exercises that challenged managers to appreciate the competitive threats and the rationale for the new strategy.

However, if training and education is to be the primary means of mobilisation, the investment required is often deeper. Illustration 5.8 describes how education and training was used to mobilise the workforce at Glenbrook Steel Mill, part of the Australian resources company BHP, following the shock of redundancies. There were two aspects to the training. The redundancies and press coverage had already created a level of dissatisfaction – if not despondency – with the status quo. Closure was a definite possibility. The leadership course was aimed at getting the employees to believe they could move forwards together as a team. It was an intensive personal development intervention aimed at altering the employees' attitudes to their situation. The decision-making training was about enabling them to move forwards.

5.8.6 Earlier reconstruction or adaptation

The notion of mobilisation also connects back to the discussion in Chapter 2 on change paths. Sometimes, the mobilisation for an evolutionary change is an earlier change. A common change path is reconstruction, followed by evolution. The initial

Illustration 5.8

change in action

Launching change at Glenbrook Steel Mill

Glenbrook Steel Mill in New Zealand was acquired by BHP, the Australian minerals company, in 1991 when they were expanding their steel division. Although the mill was contributing revenue for BHP, in October 1996 a programme of voluntary redundancies was put in place to reduce the 1,600 workforce by 400 in response to pressure from BHP to cut costs by $50 million (New Zealand dollars). Glenbrook were operating in a competitive market with a small, declining domestic market and a high exchange rate. In addition, the mill's machinery was getting older. Replacement technology was expensive, requiring significant capital investment.

If things didn't improve, the mill faced closure, and negative stories were being reported in the newspapers. There were also a lot of negative stories circulating in the mill, to do with the company closing, and the Australian office not valuing the New Zealand office. The MD, who was close to retirement, was prepared to put his head on the chopping block with Australia and say yes, we can continue to be profitable. He told the workforce he would stay and help them through the difficult period ahead. He put a big commitment into the mill and encouraged everyone else to do the same.

First, it was necessary to make the company more dynamic, to speed up decision making to enable faster reactions to the market and other changes. The redundancies had already flattened the old hierarchical structure. Now it was necessary to make the flatter structure work by pushing decision making down the organisation. Kepner Tregoe decision-making tools were introduced through training to enable staff at all levels to make decisions. The training was started in 1997, but Kepner Tregoe consultants remained on-site for over two years to help individuals put their training into practice.

At the same time, the course 'Leadership for Inventing the Future' was launched. The aim was to destroy a lot of the negative gossip and stories circulating in the organisation, whilst at the same time creating energy and motivation to work for the future – to 'ditch the past' and create a clean slate to move forwards with. The course was designed to encourage employees to acknowledge the reality of the competitive market, but recognise that this didn't have to be the end. If the staff worked as a team, it would be possible to turn things around. Every single employee, and their family, was invited to attend. The course lasted three days, with the entire company going through it in a two-week period. It included sessions on breakthrough technologies, leaving the past behind, looking at what actually happened as opposed to rumours and gossip, and getting rid of personal and work-related emotional baggage that created constraints to doing other things. By the end of the course, everyone was feeling more positive about where Glenbrook was, and people were doing things like writing letters to others who they felt they had tensions with, saying sorry, let's get on with things from now on. The course was an emotional experience for many attendees – some people were reduced to tears.

Adapted from Riordan, D. (4 May 1997) 'Working through trouble at mill', *The Sunday Star-Times* (Auckland), and interview with employee of BHP, 2002.

turnarounds are effected through some hard interventions, which act in part to mobilise the organisations for the more fundamental and transformational changes and the assumptions and beliefs that have to follow, often containing many shock tactics. For example, Illustration 5.9 describes how Ghosn effected a turnaround at Nissan, the car manufacturer. As part of the cost cutting, factories were closed, many thousands lost their jobs, and traditional supplier networks were dismantled. This was shocking not just because it was the first time such a thing had occurred in Nissan, but because it ran counter to taken-for-granted traditional Japanese working practices. However, it must be realised that reconstruction on its own may not be sufficient as a mobilisation mechanism. New investments that grow out of cost savings for a failing business with an out-of-date formula for success will often only produce the expected benefits if accompanied by a change in attitudes about how a business should be run. Thus mobilisation needs to prepare employees for this, showing them what is expected of them in the future. Illustration 5.9 shows how from early on, Ghosn was making many symbolic breaks with the past, from his use of English and allowance of press attendance at shareholder meetings, to his new performance-based reward systems and promotion mechanism, which, again, were not only a break with the past for Nissan, but a break with the traditional way of doing things in Japan. These symbolic changes didn't just show that past assumptions and beliefs, such as a job for life and promotion on seniority rather than ability, were dead, but also gave clear indication as to what would be valued in the future, as did the questions Ghosn asked and the issues he focused on when he was touring plants and meeting with managers. As suggested by the change equation, people need to understand that the past has gone, but also to understand what is expected of them in the future.

Mobilising can also be helped by making demonstrably successful changes early on, which is sometimes referred to as making 'early wins' or 'picking the low-hanging fruit'. However, this step may not just be about identifying projects to put in place early on. This step may also include things such as system changes which remove old ways of doing things that staff have consistently identified as a barrier to change. It involves any interventions that the recipients of change can identify as a positive step on the way to change, and that can be used as an example of progress and success.

5.9 DESIGNING AND SEQUENCING CHANGE LEVERS

This chapter has argued so far that to move an organisation from the current to the future state, it is necessary to mobilise the members of the organisation behind the change, to move the organisation by putting in place a series of interventions that will lead to the desired changes, and finally to sustain the changes to prevent individuals backsliding into old ways of behaving. This chapter has also suggested that many of the change levers should already have been identified, by developing a new web with new systems, structures, routines and symbols, and by considering the barriers to change and how to overcome them. Mobilisation

Illustration 5.9

Turning around Nissan

Renault and Nissan announced their alliance in 1999. At the time, Nissan was not performing well. It had too many plants, car platforms, suppliers and dealers in Japan. In addition, culturally Nissan had rigid functional silos with a bureaucratic blame culture. The company lacked profit orientation, customer focus and a sense of urgency around a shared vision and strategy. It was estimated that Nissan gave away $1,000 for each car sold in the US. Whilst deep cuts seemed the obvious solution, this ran counter to traditional Japanese business practices.

Carlos Ghosn was appointed in June 1999 from Renault to be Chief Operating Officer at Nissan and solve the problems. He was given full control over Nissan and hand-picked a small team of executives from Renault to go with him to Japan. Some immediate and tangible changes resulted. His first board meeting was held in English, and at the first annual shareholders meeting that followed the board meeting, Ghosn broke with tradition by allowing the press to attend. In his first week he announced a stock option incentive plan for executive officers. He introduced a new language policy, English only, and quickly set up a number of cross-functional teams to generate recommendations for change with one goal: to develop the business and reduce costs; one deadline: three months; and one rule: no sacred cows, taboos, or constraints. Meanwhile, Ghosn toured the company to explain the need for change and the severity of Nissan's troubles to the workforce, and talked to workers on the assembly lines as well as managers.

By October Ghosn had a plan together. It included investment in product development and brand development. However, the plan also included cutting 20 per cent from purchasing costs by globalising purchasing and halving the number of suppliers; dismantling the Keiretsu supplier network; maintaining a stake in only a small number of 1,400 companies involved; and closing a number of plants as well as rationalising car platforms. The Keiretsu system is an enduring feature of the Japanese business landscape – dismantling it represented a big break from the past. The plant closures involved 21,000 redundancies over three years – but there was to be a simultaneous increase of staff in R&D by 500, and a new assembly plant in the States to supply the US market. To mark the new start, Nissan launched a new advertising campaign.

Moving forward, Ghosn changed the bonus system from a focus on production levels to operating profit, and made it clear at meetings with managers that there would be no pay increases in purchasing, engineering or administration without a demonstrated contribution to cost cutting. In addition, he instituted a review board for promotions to change the basis for promotion from seniority to performance, and introduced performance-related pay with cash incentives as well as stock options. Like the Keiretsu partnerships, pay and promotion for tenure and age was an embedded Japanese practice. This therefore represented another significant break with the past. Old executives who were considered to be underperforming went, and younger executives were promoted. Ghosn also made himself highly visible at Nissan with tours of factories, at which he would ask managers for explanation of poor performance or limited cost cuts.

As change progressed throughout 2000 and into 2001, many other changes were made to product lines/models and organisation structure. Meanwhile, Ghosn's actions earned him names such as 'samurai' and 'cost killer'. By May 2001 Ghosn was able to announce a turnaround in Nissan's fortunes. However, the changes up until 2001 simply formed a platform for more significant and deeper changes at Nissan.

Adapted from Hughes, K. and Barsoux, J.-L. (2003) 'Nissan's U-Turn: 1999–2001', INSEAD case no. 303–046–1; Ghosn, C. (2002) 'Saving the business without losing the company', *Harvard Business Review,* 80 (1), pp. 37–45; Yoshino, M. Y. and Egawa, M. (2006) 'Implementing the Nissan Renewal Plan', *Harvard Business School Case,* Case no. 9–303–111.

tactics have also been discussed. What now needs to be done is to put the mobilisation, move and sustain phases together with the identified levers and mechanisms to determine when to implement what. However, it must be recognised that there is still additional work to be done on designing change levers and interventions, some of which is discussed in more detail in Chapter 6.

5.9.1 Four subsystems of change

It has already been pointed out above that, particularly if the change is transformational in nature, many communication, education and development interventions may be necessary to help individuals through the transition process. These interventions will be in addition to the levers that can be identified from something such as a web analysis, but they are important for facilitating the process of individual transitions. As shown above, most of the interventions that help people through the transition process are to do with what Chapter 2 identifies as interpersonal change levers. Therefore, the four subsystems identified in Chapter 2 – the technical, the political, the cultural and the interpersonal – can be used in conjunction with the Lewin model to help complete the detailed design. These subsystems map onto the web analysis since the technical subsystem is about structures and systems, the political subsystem is about the power structures and networks, and the cultural subsystem is about symbols, rituals, routines and stories. (See Figure 5.7.)

Exactly how to use the model given in Figure 5.7 is easier to explain with reference to an example. Illustration 5.10 maps out the mobilise, move and sustain process for the creation of GSK Pharma UK (see Illustration 2.2, Chapter 2) from 2000 and the development of the PASSION culture (Pride, Authentic, Stimulating and supportive, Simple, 'I make a difference', Outward looking and Nimble). The range of change interventions used to facilitate this transition was extensive, and illustrates a particular pattern frequently seen in successful evolutionary transformations. Early attention is focused on hard technical (and sometimes political) interventions to build a context that facilitates change. This is often a reconstruction. Subsequently attention shifts to mobilising for

Figure 5.7   Four levels of levers

	MOBILISE $\longrightarrow$ MOVE $\longrightarrow$ SUSTAIN
Technical	Changing all formal and informal structures and systems
Political	Changing all formal and informal networks and power systems
Cultural	Changing all routines, rituals, stories and symbols
Interpersonal	Changing communication, training, management development and education

Illustration 5.10

Building GSK Pharma UK

	Mobilise: 2000 & 2001	Move: 2001 - 2003	Sustain: 2003 ….
Technical	• Selection of staff to fill roles in new merged organisation and exit of those not selected / choosing to go (mid 2000) • Formal merger of GW & SB to form GSK (Dec 2000) • Sales force left alone	• Temperature Check • Objective setting/pay for performance • People Development / 360° appraisal	• New European structure: Implications for UK???
Political	• 60 lunchtime culture web workshops to develop PASSION (end of 2000 - March 2001) • Senior manager support for PASSION	• Reinforcement of PASSION by senior people	
Cultural	• GSK Pharma UK 50/50 GW & SB • New head office layout / design / colours • PASSION awards (April 2001)	• Visible promotion of PASSION everywhere • Adult / adult conversations • (Pay for performance) • Visibility of GSK Brands and vision in office • GM & senior managers as role models (GM informal, approachable, "authentic")	• PASSION stories • UK Performance success
Interpersonal	• Destination workshops & 'wish you were here' postcards (Oct & Nov 2001) • Top Team Workshop: The future of GSK Pharma UK (Nov 2000) • Launch of PASSION & consolidated webs to teams & directorates (March 2001)	• Communications: Quarterly meetings / atrium briefings • "PASSION is not a spectator sport" events • Postcards • PASSION progress report	• On-going PASSION promotion • 'Raising our game': associ-ated activities

Adapted from Illustration 2.1, Chapter 2

and driving in the transformation through the use of extensive cultural and interpersonal interventions with supporting changes in the technical and political subsystems as required.

- *Mobilisation*. Chapter 2, Illustration 2.2 explains the launch of the change process with the creation of the GSK entity, the appointment of people to that entity and the early workshops on the design of the future GSK Pharma UK organisation.

- *Move*. A series of change initiatives were then put in place to measure and support the PASSION culture. Some of these were put in place very early, forming part of the mobilisation (the PASSION awards), and others were developed to support PASSION, but also to fit with global GSK initiatives, such as objective setting and pay for performance. An important initiative was the 'PASSION is not a spectator sport' events since this was effectively part of the mobilisation for the old SB and GW sales forces that had largely been left alone up to this point in time during the merger. Another important aspect of the move phase was the on-going senior management support for PASSION and their role-modelling of the new culture.

- *Sustain*. By 2003–2004 PASSION was well embedded in the organisation but challenges remained in some aspects ('I make a difference', 'Outward looking', and 'Nimble). The 'Raising our Game' initiative was put in place to address this and keep the PASSION culture alive.

5.10 LINKING DESIGN OF THE TRANSITION STATE TO DESIGN CHOICES

Some managers question whether it is really possible to plan out in advance an entire organisational transition as described in this chapter. The answer is no, but key questions should be considered. For example, is the new structure to be put in place to enable changes as part of the mobilisation, or are interrelationships and responsibilities within the new structure to be allowed to evolve and then be institutionalised through formal systems and reporting relationships in the sustain phase? Which new systems are to be used to challenge the status quo, and which to sustain the changes? New measurement systems on, for example, customer service levels may be used as a challenge, and new reward mechanisms may be used to sustain the changes. The degree to which the transition should be planned is also affected by the design choices. For example:

- If the change process is to be more *directive* and *top-down,* it may be both possible and desirable to be more precise about what changes are to occur when, and involve only senior managers in the design of the vision and change process.

- Even in change processes designed to be more *evolutionary* and *emergent* over time, it is useful to give careful thought to how the status quo is to be challenged to achieve mobilisation. Furthermore, some of the early choices that need to be made, such as whether reward and selection systems are to be used to sustain the changes or as part of the move phase, do need to be given consideration. One difference between more *collaborative* and more *directive* change processes may be more to do with who is involved in, or consulted on, the design of the process, rather than the mobilise, move and sustain path selected. Where the change approach and style is to be more *bottom-up* and *collaborative*, then a wider range of employees can be involved in the process of vision and cultural web development, as at GSK (see Illustration 2.2, Chapter 2).

Similarly, the mobilization tactics are affected by context:

- An organisation with *little time* to deliver change and a *low readiness* for change, in which the change agent has the *power* and need to impose change via a type of *reconstruction* or *revolution*, will need to achieve mobilisation quickly. More dramatic and directive means, such as symbolic breaks with the past and shock tactics, may be necessary. See the examples given above.

- An organisation with *more time* to deliver change, whether via *adaptation* or *evolution*, can utilise techniques such as encouraging a questioning and challenging of the status quo, or communication, education and training. Use could also be made of symbolic breaks with the past, particularly if there is a low readiness for change and time could become a factor if change is not initiated.

The strength of a model such as mobilise, move and sustain is not to do with the answers it gives, but the questions it forces change agents to ask. Without such a model, it is all too easy to put in place a series of interventions which have little effect because the members of the organisation are not ready for change and do not understand what the changes are all about. It is also possible to leave the changes unfinished, because steps are not taken to institutionalise the changes. Similarly, without the connection of the organisational change process to the individual change process through the transition curve, particularly when attempting to undertake more fundamental change, it is possible to underestimate the range of interventions needed to achieve the required individual changes. However, it is necessary to remember that different levels of the organisation may be at different stages at different times. Senior managers may have progressed to the move phase whilst interventions aimed at mobilising lower-level staff are still being put in place.

5.11 SUMMARY

This chapter has explained the concept of the transition state as an intermediate state between where an organisation is now and where it wants to be in the future. The transition state requires explicit consideration of how it is to be designed and managed:

- The transition state can be conceived of in terms of three change phases – mobilise, move and sustain. However, it must be recognised that in any organisational transition, these three phases are underpinned by the process of individual change and the transition curve. Organisations can only change what they do if the people within them change.

- To be able to design the change levers and interventions, it is necessary to ensure that there is a vision of the desired future state. The understanding of the desired future state can also be used to diagnose potential barriers to change.

- Some of the levers and interventions to be deployed will be identified when a tool such as the cultural web is used to formulate the picture of the desired future organisation. Others will be identified by a consideration of how to deal with the barriers to change and how to achieve readiness for change. Others may have been identified as part of the original change lever design choices (technical, political, cultural and interpersonal). However, additional interventions, particularly in terms of communication, education, training, personal development, human resource systems and resistance management, also require consideration.

- To help complete the design of the levers and interventions, and decide how to sequence the chosen interventions, it is useful to use the four organisational subsystems that are part of the design choices within the mobilise, move and sustain phases. These four subsystems help to focus attention on the additional levers and interventions needed to help individuals through change and facilitate the development of the appropriate organisational changes.

- An additional design complexity is to ensure that there is a match between the selected change approach and the design of the transition state.

The next two chapters build on this chapter. Chapter 6 looks closely at the design of three critical change interventions: communication, symbolic activity and human resource systems. These interventions must be built into all three change phases in order to support the changes taking place since they have a particular impact on the individual level. Chapter 7 examines how change agents should actually manage the transition once it is underway and considers the role and nature of political activity during change.

REFERENCES

1. The concept of change as three states – the present, the future and the transition – is advanced by Beckhard, R. and Harris, R.T. (1987) *Organizational Transitions: Managing Complex Change*, 2nd edn, Reading, MA: Addison-Wesley.
2. The development of vision statements is discussed by Kotter, J. (1996) *Leading Change*, Boston, MA: Harvard Business School Press; by Nadler, D.A. and Tushman, M.L. (1990) 'Organizational frame bending: principles for managing reorientation', *The Academy of Management Executive*, 3 (3), pp. 194–204; and also by Jick, T. (1989) *The Vision Thing (A)*, Harvard Business School, Case number N9–490–019.
3. See Edwards, C. and Rezac, J. (8 April 2004) 'Five-star strategy', *People Management*, pp. 34–5.
4. See reference 2 above.
5. Chan Kim, W. and Mauborgne, R. (2000) 'Charting your company's future', *Harvard Business Review*, 80 (6), pp. 76–83; Chan Kim, W. and Mauborgne, R. (6 August 2002) 'Pursuing the holy grail of clear vision', *Financial Times*.
6. Speight, R. (2000) 'Changing the way we manage: managing the soft strands of change at British Airways World Cargo', *Journal of Change Management*, 1 (1), pp. 91–9.
7. For the example of change at Parcelforce, see Jackson, S. and Esse, A. (2006) *Making a difference through storytelling at Parcelforce*, Melcrum Publishing, www.the-storytellers.com/wp-content/uploads/2007/04/parcelforce-scm.pdf, July 2007. For more on storytelling see Ibarra, H. and Lineback, K. (2005) 'What's your story?', *Harvard Business Review*,(Jan), pp. 65–71. Also see Mirvis, P.H., Ayas, K. and Roth, G. (2003) *To the Desert and Back: The Story of One of the Most Dramatic Business Transformations on Record*, Jossey Bass Wiley; and Denning, S. (2005) *The Leader's Guide to Storytelling: Mastering the Art and Discipline of Business Narrative*, Jossey-Bass.
8. See Lencioni, P.M. (2002) 'Make your values mean something', *Harvard Business Review*, 80, (7), pp. 113–17.
9. Rewebbing, along with designing new structures, control systems and routines as change levers, is not discussed in detail in this text, as it is covered in *Exploring Corporate Strategy*, 8th edn, Chapter 14. See also Johnson, G. (1997) 'Mapping and re-mapping organisational culture', in *Exploring Techniques of Analysis and Evaluation in Strategic Management*, Ambrosini, V., Johnson, G. and Scholes, K. (eds) Hemel Hempstead: Prentice Hall.
10. See Applegate, L., Austin, R. and Collins, E. (2006) 'IBM's Decade of Transformation (A): The Turnaround', Harvard Business School Case, 9–805–130.
11. The unfreeze, move and refreeze model of change developed by Lewin, K. [(1958) 'Group decision and social change', in *Readings in Social Psychology,* Maccoby, E.E., Newcomb, T.M. and Hartley, E.L. (eds), pp. 197–211, New York: Holt, Reinhart and Winston] remains one of the most widely used change models.
12. For a useful discussion of the unfeeeze, move and refreeze model, see Burnes, B. (2004) 'Kurt Lewin and the planned approach to change: a re-appraisal', *Journal of Management Studies,* 41 (6), pp. 977–1002.
13. For additional information on how individuals experience change, and what helps individuals through the change process, see Bridges, W. (1991) *Managing Transitions: Making the Most of Change*, Reading, MA: Addison-Wesley.
14. The transition curve is based on the ideas presented by Adams, J., Hayes, J. and Hopson, B. (1976) *Transition: Understanding and Managing Personal Change*, London: Martin Robertson and Company. Others identify similar, but compatible, models of stages in individual transitions. See Elrod, P.D. and Tippett, D.D. (2002) 'The "death valley" of change', *Journal of Change Management,* 15 (3), pp. 273–91.
15. This can be seen from texts such as Parkes, C.M. (1986) *Bereavement Studies of Grief in Adult Life*, London: Penguin.
16. See Gordon-Brown, C. and Thomas, A. (2003) 'Compass SA: changing the recipe', *European Case Clearing House,* Case No. 303–218–1.

17. Spector, B. (1989) discusses unfreezing mechanisms in 'From bogged down to fired up: inspiring organizational change', *Sloan Management Review,* 30 (4), pp. 29–34.

18. See, for example, Littlefield, D. (29 July 1999) 'Real change dealer', *People Management,* pp. 44–6, and also Betts, P. (13 September 2007) 'Unilever executives embark on a little soul-searching', *Financial Times,* p. 24.

19. Kim, C. and Mauborgne, R. (2003) 'Tipping point leadership', *Harvard Business Review,* (April), pp. 60–9.

20. Mortishead, C. (3 August 2007) 'Business big shot Patrick Cescau', *The Times,* p. 39.

21. Rosenthal, P. and Peccei, R. (2007) 'The work you want, the help you need: constructing the customer in Jobcentre Plus', *Organization,* 14 (2), pp. 201–23.

22. Beech, N. and Johnson, P. (2005) 'Discourses of disrupted identities in the practice of strategic change: the mayor, the street-fighter and the insider-out', *Journal of Organizational Change Management,* 18 (1), pp. 31–47.

23. Rose, M. (2007) 'Back in fashion: how we're reviving a British icon', *Harvard Business Review,* (May), pp. 51–8.

WORK ASSIGNMENTS

5.1. Develop a vision for an organisation with which you are familiar and which needs to undergo change, drawing on all the different mechanisms suggested in this chapter (action versus words versus pictures versus stories). Where possible, also draw up a present and future culture web for this organisation. Consider the blockages for change that need to be removed if the vision is to be delivered.

5.2. Think about a personal and significant change you have been through. Track your experiences at different phases of this change using the transition curve. In terms of helping you move along through transition, consider what was helpful/unhelpful during each phase, and what you have learned from this process to enhance your future personal change capability.

5.3. Re-examine the Tarmac case in Chapter 4. Using the change equation and the different mobilisation tactics, consider how readiness for change was achieved in the UK versus France. What else could have been done to generate readiness?

5.4. Track a change process either you have experienced or is presented in a case study, against the mobilise, move and sustain model. What interventions were used in the three different stages? How well was each phase managed and what could have been done better?

Designing the transition: change levers and interventions

6.1 INTRODUCTION

The previous chapter explained how to conceive of the actual change implementation, the transition state, as having three phases – mobilise, move and sustain. Chapter 5 also discussed how to diagnose barriers to change, how to mobilise an organisation behind a change initiative, and how to sequence the selected levers and interventions through the transition. This chapter builds on this, by focusing on the design of some additional levers and interventions required to effect change during the transition period. It considers:

- Using communication, both verbal and symbolic, as a lever to facilitate the change process and help individuals through the transition.
- Building new human resource management systems, including the way staff are selected, appraised and rewarded, as levers to support change.
- Using personal development and training to facilitate change.

This chapter also discusses how these interventions can be used to help mobilise and move an organisation, and ultimately sustain the changes put in place.

6.2 COMMUNICATION DURING CHANGE

One of the key things to remember when communicating with other people is that what the speaker thinks they have said, and what the listener hears, may not be the same thing. Communication does not necessarily lead to the transfer of meaning,[1] *since it is the listener who creates the meaning for themselves.* Everyone knows the game of Chinese whispers. Someone whispers a message to their neighbour, who then whispers that message to their neighbour and so on. The message that the last person in the line receives, when recited back, is usually nothing like the message the first person communicated to their neighbour. In reality, even when messages are not communicated by whispers, they still change as they are conveyed from one person to another. This is not just due to an imperfect memory for things that have been heard and read. Listeners absorb more than the words used by a person communicating, because individuals communicate in many different ways. They communicate not just by the words and language they use, but also through their body language, the words and phrases they emphasise, and the degree of emotion used. In addition, listeners make assessments about the validity of what a communicator is saying, based on their knowledge about the communicator's track record of delivering against promises, and the communicator's perceived levels of integrity and credibility.

This is problematic in change situations because the message that counts for change recipients is, of course, the one they have received. And the one they receive may not be the same as the one the communicator intended. The recipients then act on the basis of their interpretations. Communication during change has to be designed to take this into account. One of the advocated techniques for overcoming differences in interpretations is to provide *message repetition*. This is the provision of the same information several times, by repeating the same message in a different way, or by conveying the same message by different means of communication, throughout the change process. Techniques such as verbal and written communication – but also non-verbal and symbolic means of communication such as changing artefacts or using ritual, behaviour, language and stories – can be used to convey certain messages and implications about change. Effective change agents need to understand the many different means by which they are communicating with their staff, so that they can be conscious of what they may be communicating both intentionally and unintentionally, but also so that they can utilise the *different communication mechanisms* to help get their message across.

6.3 VERBAL COMMUNICATION

Verbal communication includes both written and spoken communication. Many change programmes rely on these means of communication. At City & Guilds (see Illustration 5.1, Chapter 5), when they were communicating the brand to staff, they used many verbal communication devices such as the intranet, including an intranet brand toolkit, internal magazine, weekly news and notices, e-mail bulletins and a brand book. However, there are four issues to consider for each key stakeholder group/audience when devising a communications strategy – timing, communication channels, message content, and message presenter.

6.3.1 Stakeholder needs

The stakeholder groups will differ from organisation to organisation. The primary target for communication may always be the employees, but other external stakeholders, such as unions, customers, suppliers and shareholders, must not be forgotten. The mechanisms for reaching them will vary with the organisations' situation. UNISON is the biggest trade union in Britain, with 1.3 million members, a headquarters in London, 12 regional offices, a staff of 1,200 and 1,300 branches. Internal communications with staff take many different forms including workshops and project groups, but also an in-house magazine. In addition, like many other organisations, UNISON utilises e-mail, posters, staff briefings, documents, and meetings, and still more information is on the intranet. However, given the membership base, the branches' and wider stakeholders' external communications are also important for UNISON. The website plays an important role, providing a wide range of information. In addition the work of UNISON involves coordinating campaigns, which requires extensive communication with many different stakeholder groups such as writing to local newspapers and providing leaflets, but also communicating through the media on television and radio stations.[2]

The starting point for any communication strategy should be to identify all internal and external stakeholder groups affected. This should then be supplemented by a consideration of the needs of each stakeholder group. Do they need just to be aware of the changes, or does communication need to lead to their commitment to the changes? (See Figure 6.1.) The differing levels

Figure 6.1   Stakeholder communication requirement

STAKEHOLDER GROUP	LEVEL OF KNOWLEDGE OF CHANGE				
	Awareness	Understanding	Support	Involvement	Commitment
Senior managers					
Middle managers					
Supervisors					
Staff					
Customers					
Suppliers					
Shareholders					

Timi
Char
Cont
Pres

of understanding required affect when people need to be told and which channels to use. Furthermore, whilst a consistent core message may be needed, different stakeholder groups may need to be told different levels of detail or be informed about different aspects of the change process, or may have different needs that have to be addressed. Therefore message content may vary by stakeholder group. Finally, different message presenters may also be necessary.

Even what may seem like a relatively small change within a much larger organisation can need to be communicated sensitively and carefully, with attention to consistency of message and use of multiple channels for the sake of both those directly affected by the changes and the survivors. A British utility took the decision to close one of its three call centres, in-line with business needs to maintain costs and improve service following poor performance against key performance indicators. This meant the redundancy of 20 people. The announcement of the October call centre closure was made in July. Care was taken to develop a number of different briefings for different stakeholder groups (such as staff to be made redundant, staff to be retained, unions, etc.) containing a consistent and carefully scripted message, yet also tailored to the audience. Senior managers were sent a copy of the brief in advance and thought was given to the questions and issues that might be raised during the briefings and suitable answers. A variety of channels were used to communicate the message both verbally and in written form (see Illustration 6.1), including face-to-face meetings between managers and staff, 1–2–1s, and use of intranet and notice boards. Since the changes involved redundancies there were certain legal requirements to be met, such as the presence of a union representative when staff were briefed. The Customer Services Director was selected as the person to communicate the briefings to (1) meet the requirements for a legal right of appeal to a more senior person (in this case, the MD), and (2) because the immediate call centre manager, the Head of Service Delivery, had previously made a commitment to keep the site going, raising credibility issues. Symbolic issues also had to be dealt with. The call centre staff had clubbed together to purchase a call centre goldfish, Oscar, who had achieved company-wide fame in the company newsletter, and had become an object of certain ritualistic behaviour, such as all staff and managers saying hello and goodbye to him as they arrived at/left the call centre. Oscar was to be cared for by remaining non-call centre staff. A closure party was also arranged for those affected.

6.3.2 Timing of communication

When to communicate *what* is a serious issue. *There is no ideal time.* Employees will always want as much information as soon as possible, whereas the designers of the changes may want to give as little information as possible,

Illustration 6.1 *change in action*

Communication during closure of a call centre

STAKEHOLDER GROUP	CHANNEL	PRESENTER	TIMING
Senior managers	Copy of briefing	(Issued by HR)	Prior to briefing
Call centre location: managers	Face-to-face with Q&A session	Quality Manager	Day 1 (9.00)
Call centre location: staff to be retained	Face-to-face with Q&A session	Customer Services Director, HR, Quality Manager	Day 1 (10.15)
Call centre location: call centre staff to be made redundant	Face-to-face with Q&A session	Customer Services Director, HR, Quality Manager	Day 1 (10.30)
	1–2–1s if required	Customer Services Director	Day 1
	1–2–1s if required Individual employee letters Question and Answer Sheet	Team leaders (Issued by HR) (Issued by HR with individual letters)	On-going Following briefing
	Closure Party Handover of Oscar the Goldfish	Staff Staff	Before staff leave Before staff leave
Call centre location: staff to be relocated	Face-to-face with Q&A session	Head of Service Delivery	Day 1 (10.15)
Other call centre locations: call centre staff	Face-to-face with Q&A session	Team Leaders	Day 1 (10.30)
All staff	Intranet/Notice board bulletins Open Door policy for questions	(Issued by HR) Senior Managers	Day 1 (10.30)

Adapted from a report by Sarah Ramsden, James Cheyne and Linus Gregoriadis.

until they are completely clear about what is to be done. The designers may also be concerned about issues of confidentiality; therefore openness may not be possible. As organisations put in place change processes affecting many different country units, this may become more of an issue as legislation to do with, for example, timescales for consultation with employees or work councils, or what can be communicated and when, may vary from country to country, thus affecting what is possible. However, change agents need to be aware that:

- Employees resent hearing of change from sources other than management, such as the press,[3] and there is a need to control potentially harmful rumours.

- The later the communication, the less the time and opportunity for employees to absorb, understand and adjust to what they are being told. Readiness for change helps to reduce resistance.

- Incomplete announcements and honesty are better than cover-ups.[4] If managers are not honest early on, they will lose their credibility. Even if in the early stages of change it is not possible to explain all the details, it may be possible to inform staff of options being considered, or the change scenarios under consideration and the organisational implications of these, and provide timetables of when staff should be informed of which decisions.

- Details will always leak out, even if those leading the change have adopted a policy of silence on the changes under consideration.[5]

For employees who actually have to change as a result of the change process, the types of communication needed during a transition can be mapped against the mobilise, move and sustain model introduced in the previous chapter (see Figure 6.2):

- In the early days of change, communication should be timed to achieve a *readiness* for change, an understanding and a commitment, as part of *mobilisation.*

- As change progresses towards the *move* phase, the communication should start to focus more on giving individuals the *information* and *support* they

Figure 6.2   Communication during change

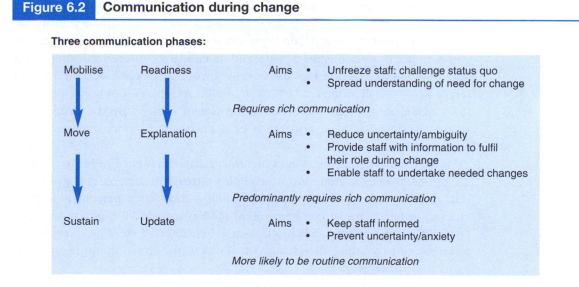

Three communication phases:

Mobilise	Readiness	Aims	• Unfreeze staff: challenge status quo
			• Spread understanding of need for change

Requires rich communication

Move	Explanation	Aims	• Reduce uncertainty/ambiguity
			• Provide staff with information to fulfil their role during change
			• Enable staff to undertake needed changes

Predominantly requires rich communication

Sustain	Update	Aims	• Keep staff informed
			• Prevent uncertainty/anxiety

More likely to be routine communication

need to undertake the changes being asked of them, and also on *reducing* the *uncertainty* and *ambiguity* individuals will be experiencing as they attempt to understand 'what this all means for me'.

● *Update* information on the progress of change and what is to happen next is required throughout the change process, but more so as the momentum of change picks up.

An overall proviso is to remember that the planned communication will *never* be enough. Communication is the responsibility of not just those appointed to run communication seminars and workshops, but also all managers and supervisors throughout the organisation who have teams of people that they need to help through the change process. This also has implications for what should be communicated and to whom.

6.3.3 Communication channels

Figure 6.3 shows the wide variety of communication channels available during change. There are also a variety of informal and *ad-hoc* channels of communication such as conversations over lunch or at the coffee machine. The key to choosing a communication channel is to match it to the audience needs and the communication aims (see Figure 6.1). For example, most organisations these days use company intranets and e-mail to simultaneously communicate important information to staff spread across different sites and companies. However, whilst such mechanisms are a useful means of informing many people simultaneously and providing back-up information, they can only generate *awareness* of change. By comparison, when ICL (now part of Fujitsu) started a knowledge management project called Project Vik (Valuing ICL Knowledge), its first initiative was Café Vik, a global information service as a website on ICL's intranet. To generate more than awareness of the website and actually get people using it, the team invested in some café tables and chairs, and with six PCs established a 'Café Vik' in standard conference rooms at ICL sites. Using different briefings for managers and employees based on their different needs, small groups of staff were briefed and then given the opportunity for a hands-on session in the café environment created by the props.[6] The intranet system has been updated over time, but is now an integral part of organisation life.

Figure 6.4 gives some guidelines on how to match audience needs to channel. As a general rule, in non-routine, complex situations such as change, where staff need to develop a deep understanding of how they personally need to change, richer forms of communication media, such as face-to-face, are best. Less rich forms of communication, such as written and electronic means, are more suited to routine, non-change situations or for updating information and generating awareness.

Figure 6.3 **Communication channels**

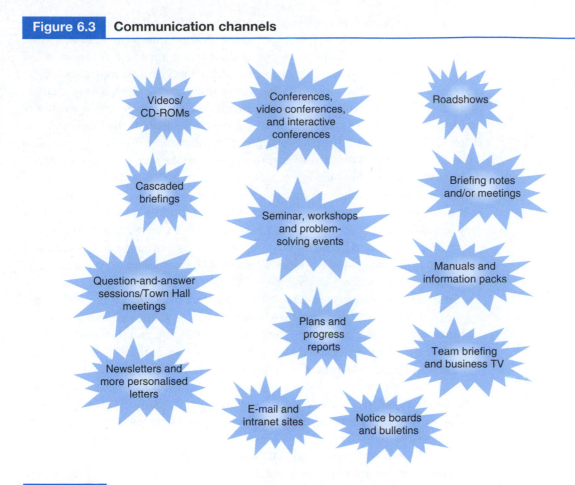

Figure 6.4 **Effective versus non-effective change communication**

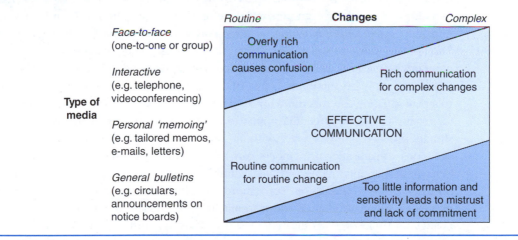

Source: Lengel, R.H. and Daft, R.C. (1988) 'The selection of communication media as an executive skill', *Academy of Management Executive,* 2 (3).

Since rich communication channels are two-way and face-to-face, such as work-shops, they provide an abundance of communication cues. They allow for the expression of concerns, answers to questions, the sharing of interpretations and experiences, and the sharing of problems and solutions. Research consistently suggests that this is the most effective form of communication during change, preferably through small groups, which affords the participants the opportunity to ask questions and air concerns. This approach also enables the message to be targeted to the needs of that particular group of individuals. This is why cascaded communication is popular in many organisations, with the senior managers briefing their managers, and these managers then briefing their staff and so on. However, unless the managers doing the communication are good presenters – well trained in the details of what they are communicating, enthusiastic about the message they are delivering, and sufficiently knowledgeable to answer questions – this mechanism can lead to poorly briefed information about change, and therefore a poorly informed and cynical workforce. A specially trained group of communicators may, therefore, be a better alternative.

Lufthansa recognised the need to utilise two-way face-to-face means of communicat-ing for all groups of staff during the transformation of the airline (see Illustration 2.9). However, they also recognised the different needs of different groups of staff. They ran strategic communication forums for top management, such as the Top 50 Conference and the Top Forum. Then there were more mass communication means for other levels of staff, such as town meetings. Board members and top managers regularly went on-site to talk directly to employees about change initiatives. There were also open-space events and 'learning maps', which involved thousands of employees work-ing in groups of 10 to bring up hot issues in a structured one-day event. In addition, there were trainer conferences and TQM workshops.

If individuals involved in change are to achieve an understanding of the behav-ioural and attitudinal implications of change, rich means of communication may need to be more than just face-to-face question-and-answer sessions. They may include workshops, or even personal development interventions with role-playing, to achieve *experiential learning,* as at the Forestry Commission (see Illustration 2.8 The Forestry Commission of Great Britain). Developing such management develop-ment interventions is discussed later in this chapter. However, something that is now popular in many organisations as part of experiential learning is the use of actors to role-play situations. Actors run workshops at which they act out particular scenarios, for example, halting at certain points to ask the workshop participants how they should proceed. In this way, without directly exposing themselves to real-life situations, organisational members can learn to deal with new required ways of behaving when interacting with, for example, customers. Again, see Illustration 2.8 on the Forestry Commission. For a more complex example of the use of external parties to stimulate change and learning in organisations, see Illustration 6.2, on change at Unilever. This illustration shows how not just actors, but various arts organisations, were used to stimulate and implement change by altering the patterns of communication in the organisation, and also changing patterns of interaction to

Illustration 6.2

Catalysing change at Unilever

A new global strategy, Path to Growth', put in place by Unilever in the late 1990s, included a focus on developing an 'enterprise culture'. Catalyst is a project that draws on arts and creative industries to facilitate this change through the use of, for example, performing arts, poetry, photography, jazz and circus performance to solve business problems and explore critical issues. Project Catalyst started in London in 1999 at Lever Brothers to help encourage creativity and risk taking, and has subsequently been introduced into Ice Cream & Frozen Food and Unilever UK.

One of the first initiatives was to buy an art collection by leading British artists for very little money. Staff contributed to the hanging and captions of the paintings, which were then displayed to generate conversations about design and art. Subsequently, Catalyst developed 'Live + Direct', which brought a team of actors into the company as part of an initiative to help develop straightforward and honest contact between colleagues. These actors observed people at work and then put on performances to enact the issues they observed. In one particular 40-minute performance in front of all staff, the actors performed a number of sketches showing how, for example, success is celebrated, or how aggressive behaviour by some managers dents enthusiasm in others. This helped people to understand the frustrations felt by others within the organisation. This initiative also included workshops based around artistic themes on how to deal with the issues illustrated, such as a hard-driving boss. All participation was voluntary.

Catalyst was also used to aid the merger process between Lever Brothers and Elida Fabergé (now Lever Fabergé), by getting teams to mix. For example, Catalyst staged a debate at a gallery about whether advertising was more potent than art, and focused on skill development such as writing, which appealed to both sides. Another division, to challenge thinking, changed the appearance of the office space, moving from an environment where all departments and meeting rooms looked the same to one in which different departments and meeting rooms were given different themes. This initiative was initially resisted. However, employees subsequently took onboard the 'permission' granted them to individualise their own work spaces and started to do so.

Adapted from Boyle, M. and Ottensmeyer, E. (2005) 'Solving business problems through the creative power of the arts: catalyzing change at Unilever', *Journal of Business Ethics,* 26 (5), pp. 14–21; and Darso, L. (2004) *Artful Creation: Learning-Tales of Arts-in-Business,* Gylling, Denmark: Narayana Press.

enable better communication and behaviour change. This was all done through interventions that created rich means of communication, which is very different from more traditional communication mechanisms and media.

Illustration 6.3 summarises the approach to communication at Kraft Foods UK as part of a culture change embarked on in 2006. The Talk and Soul themes reflected the need to 'get the organisation talking' as opposed to communicating through e-mail and the intranet, and to boost the energy levels and restore some fun to the organisation. The illustration reveals the value of a mix of communication channels. These channels of communication can be supplemented by more symbolic means of

Illustration 6.3

Changing the way we 'talk': changing culture at Kraft Foods UK

At the end of 2005, Kraft Europe embarked on a major transition to change the organisation from a country-centric way of operating into a more integrated European business. The focus of the restructuring was to create an organisation that put consumers first through European marketing teams, yet also put customers (the supermarkets) first through locally aligned sales organisations. This meant significant change for all local country operations. However, in the UK, local market pressures, combined with the broader European changes, convinced the new Vice-President of the UK of the need to embark on a culture change process. He believed that Kraft UK had great people and great brands, and could therefore do more than it was doing.

Having analysed the internal culture of the organisation, he and his management team came to the conclusion that they needed to shift the UK to a higher-performance culture. Drawing on the slogan of moving from *Good to Great,* they developed four 'pillars' capturing the streams of activity required to shift the culture:

- Ideas
- Growth
- Talk
- Soul

A senior manager was put in charge of each theme and a team of volunteers from the senior and middle manager ranks in the organisation were appointed to help. The Talk and Soul themes reflected the need to 'get the organisation talking' as opposed to communicating through e-mail and the intranet, and to boost the energy levels and restore some fun to the organisation. They were intended to create a platform for the Growth and Ideas themes as well as invigorating the organisation.

Employee conference

The employee conference in May 2006 was used as the platform for the launch of Good to Great and the four pillars supporting it. The initiatives to be taken under each pillar were announced. The conference was designed to be uplifting and very different from the previous Kraft UK employee conferences. All employees left with a set of fridge magnets reading: 'Good to Great', 'Soul', 'Talk', 'Growth', 'Ideas'. Many displayed these on their office whiteboards. The conference also launched the logo 'g2G', which is used on all related communications. A similar employee conference was held in 2007 to report progress against 2006 g2G initiatives, and reinforce the continuing focus on g2G through the launch of new growth initiatives and targets for 2007.

Soul

The Sales Director asked the new graduate intake to help with this theme. They were charged with developing ideas to make the organisation have more fun alongside work. Six ideas were developed and put in place between May 2006 and January 2007:

- *Kraft Raise and Give*. The organisation of a number of events for charity. The first was a World Cup football day when the offices were decorated in the World Cup theme and staff could come to work in their favourite football strip. There was a penalty shoot-out in the park at lunchtime with the Directors in goal. Later in the year there was an auction of promises.
- *K-Fest*. The organisation of a family festival for Kraft employees, with activities for children, music and in the evening a band and fireworks.
- *Family & friends to work*. An afternoon was put aside for people to bring their families and friends into the offices to see where they

change in action

worked. Activities were put on throughout the offices for children.

- *Rebranding of meeting rooms*. The meeting rooms were all rebranded, not just in name but in the way they were decorated, to represent particular Kraft chocolate and coffee products. A special opening event was held for the rooms once they were ready for use.
- *Coffee shop*. A free coffee shop with a barista was created to symbolise Kraft as a coffee company. Again, an event was held to celebrate the opening of the coffee shop.
- *Quarterly drinks*. At the end of every quarter, the Directors host drinks for those who want to attend to celebrate the hard work of staff over the last quarter.

At the beginning of 2007, responsibility for Soul was handed to the new graduate intake. K-Fest is becoming an annual event, along with an all-company Christmas party, rather than parties by individual functions. The Soul theme in 2007 was based around a green theme with a bike-to-work week and recycling initiatives, along with on-going charity events.

Talk

The Talk theme worked alongside the Soul theme to change attitudes towards communication. A training programme was put in place that used only six slides (some of them pictures) to get individuals to understand that 'talk' means face-to-face communication. Additional elements:

- *Plasma screens*. Plasma screens were put up in reception and the cafeterias, showing a rolling programme of Kraft news and new product launches.
- *Director's dialogue*. A bi-monthly communication forum was put in place. Every two months, two of the directors host a talk session for all employees at which employees can ask any question they like and can expect an open and honest answer.

- *Newsletter*. A new bi-monthly newsletter was created to give the good and bad news for each category and function.
- *Cartoon characters*. A series of cartoon characters were created for each category, which look happy or sad, depending on the news in the newsletters, on the screens, or for that matter on the intranet.
- *Panorama*. The Kraft UK newspaper was revamped to focus around themes of g2G, with special issues after each employee conference that capture the key aspects of the conferences.
- *Manager's awards*. A new reward scheme was introduced and directed towards those engaging in behaviours supportive of g2G. Those winning the awards are 'celebrated' through pictures placed on the plasma screens. In 2007 a new policy was initiated of inviting employees to vote for award candidates, with the award then given publicly at an employee conference.
- *Ad-hoc awards*. To create a broader ad-hoc award scheme, g2G mugs were designed as an additional, smaller recognition award and given out initially at the 2007 conference for those contributing to one of the Good to Great pillars. These were then given out at the VP's quarterly conversations to create a culture that celebrates success regularly.
- *VP's conversations*. Quarterly informal meetings between the UK VP and staff to share news on quarterly performance were initiated in 2007.
- *Communication employee forum*. This forum is a quarterly venue for the exchange of views with staff representatives from all parts of the business.
- *Talk ambassadors*. Functional ambassadors for 'Talk' were put in place in 2007. These individuals are responsible for ensuring that those who deserve it are rewarded, that rewards are publicised and that appropriate news is shared within and across functions.

Prepared by Sara Stanton, Talk Team, Kraft UK, 2006 and 2007.

communication, such as awards and the rebranding of meeting rooms, discussed in more detail in the next section. It also illustrates the value of doing something different to get individuals energised for change. The employee conferences in 2006 and 2007 were both high-energy events orchestrated to be very different to previous conferences, with much higher participation from a wide range of people and a variety of different events, so that every bit of the conference was different. Similarly, at ICI Paints in 2007, following the merger of the retail and trade divisions, the annual corporate conference was used to communicate the future strategy and reinforce the new 'one company' culture. The leadership team wanted to communicate their determination to succeed in a difficult marketplace. They used a performing arts company to teach everyone – all 850 people – the Haka (a traditional Maori war dance). The senior executives learnt the dance in advance so that they could demonstrate it at the conference alongside the arts company team.[7]

Most communications strategies will utilise many different types of communication, including written communication. To return to Figure 6.2, the richer forms of communication used to achieve mobilisation and explanation may need to be supported by less rich forms of communication. Participants will never remember everything they are told at briefings or workshops. Written documentation can thus provide useful back-up and reference material. Update information, which supplies regular information on change progress, can also be provided by less rich channels of communication. Written communication, in the form of newsletters or notice board bulletins, for example, can be used to provide updates on progress and plans. However, written communication is often used inappropriately. In times of change, people are busy, stressed and concerned. They are unlikely to sit down and read large amounts of written material. The main content of any substantial booklets or manuals may be better covered in some form of seminar, workshop or training, with the manuals issued as reference material.

It is important to remember that temptingly simple channels for direct communication with all employees, such as e-mail and the intranet, are a good means of briefing back-up information and progress, but they do have drawbacks. Employees can't be forced to read the messages, and e-mails may simply become lost among all the other e-mails employees receive. There is heavy competition for employee air space. As a result, organisations are investing in communication management systems, which prioritise and package communications, ensuring that important messages get priority and are not mixed in with trivia. Staff based out of the office can also miss out on such communication mechanisms. Some organisations therefore utilise SMS text messaging to reach field sales employees. New communications technology is constantly being created to make it possible to deliver more sophisticated communication packages in novel ways.

However, the power of simple communication should not be overlooked. Long-serving members of HP were impressed by the new Chief Executive, Mark Hurd, because he arrived at their factory in a Hertz rental car and gave a talk in the canteen using only a flip chart to get across the few simple messages he felt it was important for them to know about the things he would be changing at HP and why.[8]

6.3.4 Message content

Again, the key issue with the message content is to match the detail to the audience needs:

- If the message provides information that is personally relevant, and is couched in language the recipients can relate to and understand, the more likely it is that the message will be understood and retained.[9]

- Employees do not just need an organisational vision, they also need a personal vision. In a change situation, the question everyone wants an answer to is, what is going to happen to me? Until individuals know if they will have a job, or where they will have to relocate to, or how their terms and conditions will change, they are unlikely to take in much else.[10]

- For the change agents and the people who have worked with them on designing the change process, it is too easy to announce just the conclusions and not explain the thinking that has gone into the decision-making process. This can lead to people asking questions about why particular options have not been considered, when they may have been considered, and questioning the feasibility and suitability of the proposals (see Figure 6.5). If there are reasons why more complete information cannot be provided, these should be communicated.

6.3.5 Who should communicate the change?

In situations of dramatic change, the obvious answer to the question of who should communicate the change would appear to be the senior managers, and preferably the MD or CEO. If senior managers do not personally deliver bad news or news of dramatic change, this can be interpreted as a lack of concern for the welfare of staff, or maybe even a reluctance to give bad news personally. The size of the organisation, or the geographic spread, can make it impossible for one or two people to lead all presentations, particularly if there is a need for all staff to hear certain information at a similar time to contain unhelpful rumours, or to avoid the symbolic implication that certain groups of staff are more important to the company than others. Many organisations overcome this by using videos, which are then shown by managers to staff and accompanied by a question-and-answer session. This may work, but like cascaded communication, the communicators need to be well trained and motivated. Resourcing communication is, therefore, a serious issue – particularly since it can be a time-consuming activity.

In some instances the use of the line supervisor may be more appropriate[11] as they are more likely to be able to translate change into language and terminology that is relevant to their staff. It may also be appropriate to involve managers and supervisors in the second wave of communication, when more detail pertinent to particular groups of staff is being communicated. Update and progress information

Figure 6.5	The communication collision

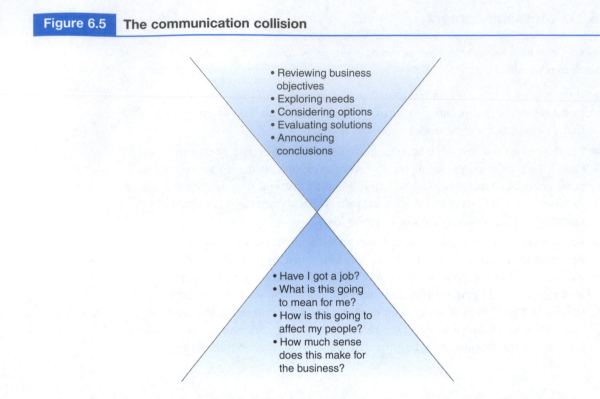

Funnelling information down the hierarchical pyramid means the greatest number of people get the least context, and the lower down the organisation you are, the less sense information makes.

Source: Quirke, B.(1995) *Communicating Change,* McGraw-Hill Publishing Company. Copyright holder: Bill Quirke, Synopsis Communication Consulting, 113 Farringdon Road, London EC1R 3BX.

can also be given by line managers and supervisors. However, if line managers are to be responsible for communication, this should be built into their performance management in some way. All managers are overwhelmed during change, and if communication is not made a priority, it may not happen.

Anyone who has to communicate change to others needs to have as much information as possible. If managers are asked to brief their staff – but cannot answer their questions, and have no means of feeding the questions upwards to obtain answers for their staff – they are unlikely to generate much commitment for change. Furthermore, when change is to be communicated by individuals who have not been involved in the planning, some thought needs to be given to the issues that might arise, and how these issues should be dealt with. This can be enhanced by collating all questions asked and then issuing answers. Organisations may use something like an advisory board or focus group composed of employees from all parts of the organisation to review communications for content and delivery, and to raise questions that may be asked.

Those who are to communicate also need to have the skills to enable them to communicate effectively. When Ericsson took steps to change its approach to communication, the company invested in communication training to improve the skills of those doing the communicating. The three main areas identified for development were facilitation, consulting and message-creating skills. A workshop called the 'Black Belt Program in Internal Communication' was developed to deliver this requirement. In addition, as suggested above, to improve managers' communication abilities, all managers have their communication skills measured as part of Ericsson's annual employee survey. There is even a communication support area on the company intranet, offering hands-on support to managers.[12]

For change to be communicated effectively, it may be necessary to alter the traditional and trusted channels of communication and information flows in an organisation. This was the case for Scienceco (see Chapter 4, Illustration 4.2). The senior managers needed to shift responsibility for communicating with employees from the unions to themselves and the supervisory staff.

6.4 SYMBOLIC ACTIVITY

6.4.1 Symbolism and symbolic activity

Exploring Corporate Strategy, Chapter 14, discusses symbolism and symbolic activity in some depth.[13] The points made include the following:

- Symbolic activity includes a wide variety of message-sending events, activities and behaviours, as well as the manipulation of organisational artefacts such as status symbols, uniforms, language and logos. It can include *rituals* (see below); *physical* organisational aspects; *behaviours and language,* particularly of change agents and of those in positions of authority; *stories;* and *systems* such as reward and measurement systems.

- Symbolic activity is anything that conveys something about an organisation to the individuals within it. For example, organisations that see themselves as being very successful often have impressive head offices located in prime commercial locations, with smart reception areas and polite, uniformed receptionists, and panelled, opulent boardrooms. This symbolism becomes a short-hand representation of what the organisation stands for and attaches importance to. The head office of Bernard Matthews Turkeys, for example, exudes tradition, with ladies serving coffee in china cups on silver trays, clocks ticking loudly in unusually quiet offices, telephones that still 'ring', no computer in the Chairman's office, but many paintings of turkeys, porcelain turkey figures and trophies for turkey breeding. Mr Matthews remains 'Mr Matthews' or 'the chairman'.[14]

- Symbolic activity is powerful because it has an impact on the way individuals interpret things. The prescription commonly encountered in texts on change for senior managers to 'walk the talk' is key, because if all the non-verbal cues about what change means do not support the verbal and espoused messages about change, individuals will interpret the espoused messages as meaningless. If senior managers preach empowerment and greater accountability, but continue to issue orders and countermand decisions made by their staff, then the staff will not believe in the espoused messages of change. It is important to ensure consistency through time of all actions and words.

The intent in this chapter is to move from showing how symbolism helps to preserve the status quo to emphasising how symbolic activity can support verbal messages of change, and help individuals through the mobilise, move and sustain process. Illustration 6.4 describes the change process undertaken at Crummer Graduate School in the US. It describes the range of symbolic interventions used by the Dean to underpin changes occurring and gain the support needed. The illustration reveals how symbolic interventions can be used alongside the more commonly encountered structural and political interventions, particularly in situations which involve the need for a culture change. The Kraft example above (Illustration 6.3) also shows how change needs to be accompanied by changes to the symbolic environment in which employees operate if employees are to believe the rhetoric of change. It describes the transformation of the bland office space at Kraft UK into an environment more representative of a branded consumer goods company that is proud of its brands and its heritage.

Illustration 6.4 also reveals that it is not just behaviour that has impact, but also language. Some organisations do explicitly use language to help foster change. When David Neeleman set up JetBlue, the low-cost US airline, he used different language to foster a functional, family culture of greater equality. Flight attendants are 'crew members', the HR department is 'people', and the uniform group is called the 'appearance standards department'.[15] Disney is famous for its use of language to create the image of theatrics and the stage for its theme parks. Personnel are 'central casting'; employees are players in a live performance and they are cast for a role or are a host or a hostess; employees work on-stage and go back-stage for a rest; they wear costumes, not uniforms; customers are guests and form an audience; and rides are attractions.[16]

There is a warning that needs to be attached to the use of symbolic interventions. Just as verbal messages can be interpreted by the recipients differently from the way they were intended, symbolic communication can similarly be interpreted differently from the way it was intended. Chapter 7 returns to this point when discussing the need for monitoring mechanisms during change to understand how recipients are responding to the change initiatives put in place. Symbolic interventions are less likely to be successful if they are used as one-off interventions, and more likely to be effective if there is a consistent and on-going use of many different symbolic levers throughout the transition. Attention also needs to be paid to the removal of behaviours, events and language that symbolically suggest no change to the way of doing things within the organisation. The key here is consistent communication of the same message through multiple communication vehicles.

Illustration 6.4

change in action

The power of symbolism: changing Crummer Graduate School

In 2000 the new Dean of Crummer Graduate School wanted to ensure execution of the school's strategy. He made extensive use of symbolic action over the next few years to maintain emphasis on existing aspects of the school's strategy but also to encourage new behaviours.

Symbolic actions: At his first meeting the Dean acted to reinforce a key tenet of Crummer's strategy to do with attention to students' needs – he issued rubber doorstops to all faculty members to remind them of the open-door policy to students.

Ritual: To encourage the staff to be competitive about the school's position in MBA rankings, the Dean held a school party the second time the Rollins MBA was ranked in the top 50 of the Forbes ranking. Graduation events give students jointly with faculty the chance to celebrate their achievements. On entering Crummer, the members of each student cohort, along with the Dean and Programme Director, sign a replica of the Crummer Honour Code on a laminated poster board. These boards are displayed to remind students of the ethical commitments they made on entering Crummer. There is an annual faculty retreat at which faculty awards are given out for teaching excellence, publishing and service.

Rewards: In 2003 a leadership component was added to the MBA. To signal the importance of this the Dean created a leadership centre (headed by an executive, not a faculty member) and developed a reward programme for students, including the Sun-Trust Distinguished Leader of Merit award given to the student most demonstrating leadership skills. The faculty reward systems are also aligned to the school's values – 50 per cent teaching, 35 per cent research and 15 per cent service. The Dean has also awarded three endowed chairs to faculty who demonstrate exemplary performance in teaching, research and service.

Stories and myths: When Crummer needed to be more globally oriented, success stories of integrating global issues into the classroom were told by the Dean and members of the faculty to get buy-in from less enthusiastic faculty. The Dean also celebrates faculty successes through stories about those who take leadership roles in their fields, publish in A-level journals and so on.

Language: Many of the school's values concerning the way it teaches and interacts with students are encapsulated in the phrase 'the Crummer Experience', which is similar to the metaphor 'the Crummer Family' that is used to refer to the students, faculty, staff alumni and sponsors.

Adapted from Higgins, J.M., Mcallaster, C., Certo, S.C. and Gilbert, J.P. (2006) 'Using cultural artifacts to change and perpetuate strategy', *Journal of Change Management*, 6 (4), pp. 397–415.

6.4.2 Symbolic activity and transition management

To consider how symbolic activity can help individuals through the transition curve, and therefore to mobilise, move and sustain the change process, it is necessary to consider:

● How symbolic activity can be used to *challenge* the status quo to achieve a realisation of the need for change.

- How symbolic activity can be used to legitimise *questioning*.

- How symbolic activity can be used to indicate what is *expected* of employees in the changed environment.

- How symbolic activity can be used to help employees develop a new and united *identity*.

Chapter 5 has already discussed the use of symbolism during mobilisation. Symbolic breaks with the past, through senior manager behaviours, events, or the removal of status symbols, can be used to indicate that things are to be done differently in the future, and to legitimise questioning and challenging of the status quo. The use of ritual can also be particularly helpful here – see Table 6.1 for a list of the different types of rituals.

Rituals (rites) can be defined as 'a formal action normally repeated in a standardised way' that has become embedded into the way of life in an organisation.[17] It is possible to encourage people to challenge and question, and also to indicate new desired ways of working, by removing or changing the emphasis of old rituals, and putting in place new rituals (see Illustration 6.4). Rites of passage, degradation, enhancement, renewal, conflict reduction, and integration help, to varying degrees, to mobilise, move and sustain organisations.[18] As such, different rituals may have different impacts throughout the mobilise, move and sustain process (see Figure 6.6).

During the *mobilise* phase:

- *Challenge* rituals, such as the publication of declining performance or increasing competition, can be important as they can be used to trigger a recognition of the need for change. They can also be used to create and mandate dissatisfaction with the current way of doing things, be it by new executives doing things in a different way, or competitive benchmarking. One organisation used a wall-smashing ceremony to initiate the start of an open-plan shop floor, followed by the creation of administration rooms on the shop floor to replace the previously separate administration offices to enhance communication flows between blue- and white-collar workers.[19] When Lou Gerstner arrived at IBM back in the early 1990s to lead IBM's transformation, to illustrate his determination to 'put the customer first' he engaged in certain visible actions. First, he started to attend joint IBM/customer sales conferences, which his predecessors and other executives traditionally didn't do, and once at the conference he listened to the customers and *publicly* committed particularly named executives to resolve the problems the customers were reporting. He then visited large numbers of customers to identify, from the customers' perspective, what was wrong with IBM and why it was losing ground to competitors.[20]

- *Degradation* rituals, such as removing and replacing top executives, or discontinuing old practices, can be used to generate questioning about the validity of the old ways of doing things. Clerical Medical, the life insurance provider, have made

Table 6.1	Organisational rituals and culture change

TYPES OF RITUAL (RITE)	ROLE	EXAMPLES
Rites of passage	Consolidate and promote social roles and interaction Confirm transition	Induction programmes Training programmes New offices/logos
Rites of enhancement	Recognise effort benefiting organisation Similarly motivate others	Award ceremonies Promotions Published successes
Rites of renewal	Reassure that something is being done Focus attention on issues	Appointment of consultants Project teams/task forces
Rites of integration	Encourage commitment to shared identity Reassert norms	Christmas parties Uniforms Lunchtime drinks
Rites of conflict reduction	Reduce conflict and aggression	Negotiating committees
Rites of degradation	Publicly acknowledge problems Dissolve/weaken social or political roles	Firing top executives Demotion or 'passing over' Limit scope of previously powerful groups
Rites of sensemaking	Sharing interpretations of, and making sense of, what is happening	Rumours Stories Gossip Surveys to evaluate new practices
Rites of challenge	'Throwing down the gauntlet' Indicate old way no longer the best	New executives' different behaviour/dress Deteriorating company performance Removal of old ways of doing things Redundancies
Rites of counter-challenge	Resistance to new ways of doing things	Grumbling, anti-change graffiti Working to rule, sabotage, absence from change meetings

Source: Adapted from Balogun, J., Johnson, G. and Martin, S. (1995) 'The Use of Rituals within Organisational Change Processes', British Academy of Management Conference, Sheffield, September.

many changes from the mid-1990s, including demutualisation and changing the way they sell their products to independent financial advisers, from product push to customer relationship selling. Senior staff that did not support these changes were openly asked to leave.

● Since challenge and degradation will also create a lot of uncertainty, it is likely that there will be many *sensemaking* rituals – much speculation, gossip, sharing of information and rumours – during the mobilisation phase.

Figure 6.6	Linking change and symbolism

CHANGE PROCESS		SYMBOLIC ACTS	EFFECT
Mobilise:	Shock/denial awareness	*Challenge* *Degradation* *Sensemaking*	Legitimise questioning Show old ways gone
Move:	Acceptance Testing Search	Decreasing: *Challenge* Increasing: *Degradation* *Counter-Challenge* *Conflict-Reduction* Increasing: *Enhancement* *Integration* *Renewal*	Legitimise questioning Provide role models and new identity Tackle resistance
Sustain:	Integration	*Enhancement* *Integration* *Renewal*	Reinforce new identity and new ways of doing things Assess progress

During the *move* phase:

- *Challenge* and *degradation* rituals are likely to continue to be important as individuals are continually encouraged to discontinue old ways of doing things and adopt new ways of behaving.

- The greatest levels of resistance, and therefore rites of *counter-challenge,* may be encountered in this phase as individuals have to actually undertake change. It may, therefore, be necessary to use on-going *degradation* rituals to diminish old social identities, maybe via shock tactics such as redundancies and demotions in crisis-driven change.

- Rites of *conflict reduction,* including consultations and negotiations with unions or staff groups, and dealing with staff grievances may be necessary to overcome resistance.

- Rites of *enhancement*, *passage,* and *integration* are likely to become important as it becomes necessary to establish new role models of how things should be done, and to foster a new organisational identity. This is the time when individuals will be testing out new behaviours and searching for new meanings.

- Rites of *enhancement* could involve the giving of public rewards to individuals performing well according to the terms of new organisational performance criteria, or the public praise of such individuals in newsletters. For example, in GSK UK Pharma, they awarded bronze, silver and gold pins (PASSION awards – see Illustration 2.2, Chapter 2) to staff who exhibited the new desired behaviours for the merged organisation. Similarly Kraft UK (see Illustration 6.3 above) put in place many ad-hoc means of rewarding new behaviours. At City & Guilds (see Illustration 5.1, Chapter 5), the verbal communication about the new internal organisational brand was supported by symbolic communication. A scheme called 'living the values award' was developed to reward individuals demonstrating the brand values through their work and behaviour. The brainwaves scheme was also introduced to encourage people to put forward ideas for improving the business. Ideas are screened and those deemed to have merit are implemented and the individual rewarded.

- Rites of *integration* encourage a common organisational identity, and could include a wide variety of social events or meetings, such as the debates used to facilitate the merger between Lever Bothers and Elida Fabergé (see Illustration 6.2). Siemens utilised many rites of integration when first taking over Westinghouse of the USA. Football matches were organised between blue-collar operatives from plants on both sides of the Atlantic, and there were also ice-hockey tournaments and kart-racing sessions between teams from Germany, the USA and Canada. At the Siemens gas turbine factory in Berlin, staff have had intensive English lessons to enable regular discussions between themselves and workers at the Westinghouse gas turbine factory in Canada, and there have been regular exchanges of staff visits between the two factories.[21]

The *sustain* phase is about reinforcing change. The rituals likely to be of use are those to do with *enhancement, integration* and *renewal*. The rites of integration and enhancement may be a continuation of those introduced during the move phase. These rituals may become part of the new organisational culture, as the PASSION awards have at GSK.

6.5 BUILDING NEW HUMAN RESOURCE MANAGEMENT SYSTEMS

Human resource management (HRM) policies and processes are activities which influence individual and group behaviour within an organisation. Research has shown that for transformational change to be successful and for firms to benefit financially from their change in strategy, there must be 'complementary change' in strategies, structures and systems.[22] In order to reap the performance benefits from strategic changes such as joint ventures or global expansion, for example, firms must correspondingly change their structures by delayering, or introducing horizontal forms of project working, but also change their systems, including HR practices and policies, to support this change. Those firms that only implement partial change – for instance, a shift in strategy with some structural change but no supporting HR system change – will fail to deliver improvements in financial performance. HR policies and systems can, therefore, act as drivers for transformation, and can be redesigned to help mobilise, move and sustain change, whereas if these systems are left untouched, they may become barriers.

This section outlines the different components of an HR system, emphasises the importance of managing HR systems in order to achieve change, and discusses the different contributions made by short-term and long-term HR systems in delivering change strategies.

6.5.1 The human resource system

Figure 6.7 shows that the main components of a human resource system[23] include:

● *Recruitment and selection*: designing jobs, and attracting, selecting and appointing staff into the organisation. *Recruitment* is concerned with looking for people whom the organisation might wish to employ. It is to do with advertising vacancies and attracting people to apply to the organisation. *Selection* is the process by which an individual or individuals are chosen for appointment from the pool of individuals who have either applied through the recruitment process or been recommended for a position. Recruitment is the process that produces candidates. Selection is the sorting of the candidates, maybe through interviewing and profiling questionnaires, to identify the final appointments.

Figure 6.7	Components of a human resource system

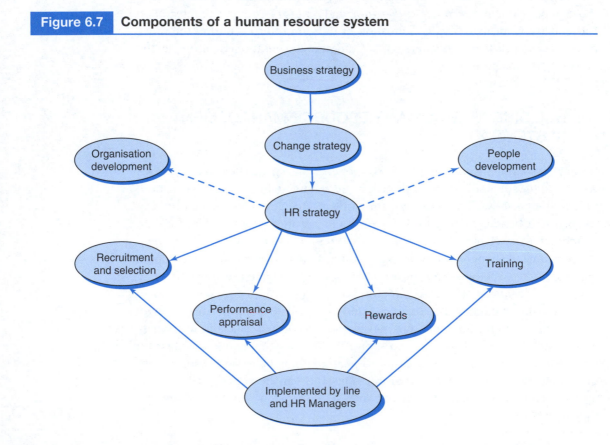

- *Performance evaluation*: measuring, monitoring and assessing staff performance, often against previously set objectives; assessing staff for rewards/bonuses, future training or future development; and defining future performance objectives.

- *Reward*: rewarding individuals or teams for their contribution, and motivating them to stay and/or perform. This includes both monetary and non-monetary forms of reward.

- *Training*: inducting and training staff for either improved performance or as part of general career development.

- *Development*: leadership, workforce and organisational development.

- *HR function and their partnership with line managers*: the role and structure of the HR function can be redesigned so that the function becomes a partner in the change process, delivering changes in policies and systems that fit the needs of the change process. Whilst the HR function redesigns systems and processes, it is line managers who actually implement many of these activities such as performance evaluation.

The rest of this section explains the role of these different components in delivering change as part of the short-term and long-term HR cycles.

6.5.2 Short-term and long-term HR cycles and change

In designing HR interventions to support change, it is helpful to understand the difference between the short-term HR cycle and the long-term HR cycle. Figure 6.8, the People Process Model, separates out these activities.[24] In the *short-term cycle* the model identifies four activities, all of which are concerned with people resourcing and performance management: the recruitment and selection of staff, the setting of performance objectives and appraisal, determining reward and providing short-term skills and technical training. In the *long-term cycle* three main development activities are identified: organisational development, leadership development and workforce development.

The separation of HR activities into these two cycles reinforces the idea that short-term activities such as changing objectives for individuals or teams, or introducing training in new technical areas such as 'lean processing', can help deliver immediate shifts in business performance and/or a change in activities and behaviours on a day-to-day basis,[25] whereas other HR activities are much more concerned with building sustained competitive advantage through longer-term processes such as developing a cadre of executives capable of leading the organisation in the future. The management consultants McKinsey also differentiate these two cycles in terms of delivering change. Short-term immediate change interventions are about delivering significant shifts in financial business performance, whereas change interventions within the longer term are about ensuring 'organisational health'.[26]

Figure 6.8   **The People Process Model**

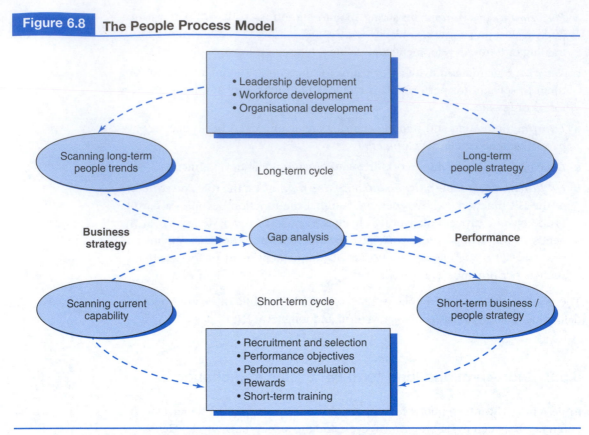

Source: Adapted from Gratton, L. et al. (1999) *Strategic Human Resource Management,* Oxford: Oxford University Press. Reproduced with permission.

Therefore, the way the short- and long-term HR cycles support change differs. The short-term HR cycle is about reconfiguring the resourcing and performance management systems in order to deliver improved business performance. Thus *reconfiguring* these different HR systems can facilitate transition. An organisation's competence to quickly redesign HR systems so that they can facilitate change through rapidly reshaping behaviour or skills is a form of change management capability to do with '*coordination flexibility*'. The HR development activities associated with the longer term should persist in organisations whether or not the organisation is implementing specific change interventions. Leadership development, workforce development and organisational development are on-going activities, always future oriented, and concerned with developing the human resource – both the workforce cadre and the leadership cadre, and the organisation itself – so that all three can respond to change on a continuous basis. An organisation's capability to utilise these three forms of development together in a way that supports on-going change is to do with '*resource flexibility*'.[27] Leading-edge organisations will seek to: (1) nurture senior managers who are responsive to change in attitudes, knowledge and behaviours; (2) equip workforces with a skill base that makes them flexible enough to embrace changes in technology; and (3) use organisation development departments to ensure that the organisation itself is kept as responsive and adaptable as possible in its culture or structures.

If HR systems are reconfigured within the short-term HR cycle, it is essential that they are followed up by complementary changes in the longer-term HR cycle. If a new appraisal system emphasising innovation is put in place, for example, yet succession planning still identifies the more risk-averse members of staff for promotion, then the organisation will retain aspects of its original character.

6.5.3 The short-term HR cycle: recruitment, selection, performance evaluation, reward and training

Recruitment and selection

There are several ways that recruitment and selection can be reconfigured to support change interventions. During the *mobilise* phase of transition, one of the most common mechanisms used to indicate the need for change is announcing redundancies. However, tactics can be more subtle. Organisations could change the *selection criteria* for jobs. Selection criteria may include past experience, personal skills, qualifications, knowledge areas, attitudes, and so on. If an organisation is seeking to achieve a cultural change, for example, these criteria can be altered to reflect the new norms and values that the organisation is hoping to embrace. New selection criteria also enable the use of degradation and challenge rituals. For example, setting new selection criteria for certain positions may mean that alternative people, with different work experience, skills or qualifications, may need to be brought in from outside the organisation to fill vacancies previously filled through internal promotion. This also communicates to existing staff that they no longer have the appropriate skills to respond to the required changes.

Existing staff can also be made to *re-apply* to the organisation for a job, as was the case at the social housing group Prime Focus described in Chapter 3 (see Illustration 3.2). If selection criteria have also been changed, or fewer jobs made available in the new structure, this may mean that some staff are offered redundancy rather than a job. In Prime Focus they managed to avoid mass redundancies but their existing staff still had to go through a prolonged process of selection for the newly designed roles. Organisations can also change the *type* of people recruited. They may decide to start to *recruit* and/or *promote* from a pool of potential candidates previously ignored. Some firms may only have traditionally recruited from a circle of top universities within the world but decide to widen that pool by looking at newer universities with different sorts of graduates.

The disability charity Scope in 2004 launched an external campaign to promote equality in employment within the broad UK workforce. At the same time it had to face the fact that within its own internal workforce, only 3.7 percent were disabled. Scope's HR function responded by setting a target of having 20 per cent of Scope's own staff consist of disabled workers by the end of 2007, taking a number of actions to achieve this goal. One was changing the way it recruited by making sure that advertisements were placed in appropriate places and ensuring that its advertising and recruitment material made it clear that it welcomed applications from disabled people. It also introduced a 'reserved post policy' for certain positions within the organisation, made possible by disability discrimination legislation. At the same time a communications initiative was launched to explain to existing staff why these changes were necessary. Challenging existing perceptions of who fills which jobs can both symbolically and practically aid a change process.[28]

During the *move* phase, the tactics may be similar to those in the mobilise phase. Selection criteria may be altered to allow for an on-going reduction of staff by identification of those staff not able to perform against the competencies now required by the organisation. Job redesign, changing the actual structure of job roles, may also be used. Such changes may in turn affect the number of staff needed and the sort of people required. The changes may also lead to the introduction of more flexible working, or annualised, hours, where staff work more hours at one time of the year than at others to meet the fluctuating level of customer orders.

During the *sustain* phase, the recruitment and selection interventions are likely to be aimed at longer-term change within the make-up of a workforce, rather than short-term change to the staff an organisation already has. Organisations may change the *way* people are recruited or the *selection mechanisms* (interviews, assessment centres, psychometric tests) for both new recruits and for the promotion of existing staff, although some organisations may choose to do this in the move phase. Whenever they are implemented, such moves are symbolic, sending messages about which practices are now valued in comparison to the old ways of doing things.

Performance objectives and evaluation

The most common way of using appraisal systems to help deliver change is to alter either the criteria or the objectives against which staff are assessed. Criteria may be changed by reshaping the appraisal *metrics* – the skills, competencies or behaviours against which staff are assessed – and/or the performance *objectives,* which state what staff have to achieve. For example, to aid a shift in priorities for lecturers at a university from teaching to research, the objectives in the appraisal system leading to promotion, pay rises or bonuses may be altered to include getting research published in academic journals.

However, there are other *symbolic* changes that can be made to an appraisal mechanism to aid *mobilisation* and *movement*. Appraisals that are 360 degrees in scope can be introduced, where a manager is evaluated by their subordinates, their superiors and their peers. For some organisations this can be a shocking development, as managers are subjected to much more scrutiny. Yet sometimes shock tactics such as these can backfire. Illustration 3.8 in Chapter 3 describes how the R&D scientists at Pelican Labs systematically undermined a forced ranking system introduced by their corporate HR centre in California.

Other aspects of appraisal can be changed to aid *move* and *sustain*. The frequency with which managers have to appraise their staff might be changed. It may be specified that managers are expected to *informally* keep in touch with their staff throughout the year to assess how they are coping with change, so that the *formal* annual appraisal is merely a summary of what is already known. Introducing a coaching and counselling style of management may also help to support staff through the awareness, acceptance and testing parts of the transition curve (see Chapter 5) when staff may feel incompetent, anxious and angry about the change they are undertaking.

Reward

Reward covers the whole compensation and benefits area and is a common lever used to obtain changes in staff behaviour and performance. Reward is concerned with both rewarding people for past performance and motivating them for future performance. It also acts as a means of retaining staff. *Reward* is a very broad term and people can be rewarded in many different ways. Reward can encompass being sent on training courses as a bonus for particular performance. It might include extra holidays, payment for college fees, access to childcare, and company cars. Rewards may be symbolic (see section 6.4 above), giving messages to staff about what they have to do to help with the change process – or maybe even just keep their job. Given the links between reward and motivation, it is easy to see how changes to compensation and benefits can be incorporated within a range of interventions to promote change, both through the transition phase and beyond.

To understand how to use a reward system effectively within an organisation, the change agent needs to understand the different motivations of staff groups. For some groups, such as sales representatives or investment bankers, financial rewards are a critical motivator, and immediately changing the bonuses to *mobilise* staff may guarantee a rapid response even in the first stage of transition. For others financial reward is not a primary motivator. Nurses, many academics and people working within the not-for-profit sector may well be motivated more by an appeal to their personal or occupational values in the first instance rather than an immediate change to a reward system. However, even in value-driven organisations, in the *move* and *sustain* stages, commitment to the desired future values will need to be illustrated by changes in the reward systems.

In general, the criteria for which bonuses or other rewards are paid can be altered to either *mobilise* staff to support a change, or to encourage a shift in behaviours as part of the *move*. If, previously, for example, performance-related pay was determined by how many individual sales were achieved over a short period of time, a shift towards relationship marketing might suggest that the reward system should be altered to reflect the ability to sustain longer-term customer relationships. The European Space Agency (see Illustration 6.5) introduced a more democratic way of allocating and paying rewards to support a change programme. Nominations were scrutinised by a staff committee rather than senior managers and the actual bonuses could be used for professional training if people preferred. This appealed to the scientific culture of the whole institution. Bonus criteria can be changed for senior managers as well as for more junior staff. In 2007 the retail group WH Smith introduced a 'co-investment plan' for its senior management as part of the company's turnaround plan. Senior employees, including the CEO, were given the chance to buy shares in the company and keep them for three years. If the company delivers against performance targets at the end of this period, then the firm will issue additional shares to each individual of five times the original amount purchased. The company made it clear that this incentive was intended to immediately motivate the senior team to deliver the recovery plan.[29] More negatively, pay freezes

---

Illustration 6.5

change in action

Operating in a new space? Performance assessment, reward and training in a space agency

The European Space Agency is primarily based in Noordwijk in The Netherlands but also has sites in Germany and Italy. A review carried out by its director-general concluded that there would have to be a 30 per cent increase in ESA's activities by 2007 in order to develop new space infrastructures to support the newly enlarged EU's defence and security policies. In order to deliver this increase in activity, the HR function was asked to ensure that the Agency was getting the best from its talent. Three interventions were introduced to help build the capability of the organisation to deliver increased and improved performance: staff assessment, a merit-award scheme and the creation of an internal university.

Staff assessment was introduced as a top-down exercise where managers review the achievement of objectives for the last year and set new targets for the next year.

Recommendations for short-term training are then fed into training plans. The merit award was brought in to challenge the culture of rewarding employees based on seniority. In 2003 the new scheme introduced cash bonuses worth 3,000–5,000 euros, although these amounts can be doubled in value if the employee chooses to use the funds for professional training. Instead of the bonuses being distributed by management, the awards are decided by a staff committee who look at nominations from across the Agency and make the selection. The creation of an internal university in 2004 meant that there could be a central hub for common areas of training across the different sites. These HR interventions have helped the organisation move the culture towards one that can respond to the increasing demands made upon its services by the enlarged European Community.

Adapted from Kent, S. (9 February 2006) 'One giant leap', People *Management,* pp. 36–7.

or cuts could be introduced to bring home to staff the seriousness of a financial crisis. Alternatively, the non-payment of, as opposed to changes to, the usual annual bonuses can send strong signals that change is really happening.

Staff may be rewarded for simply supporting the changes (see section 6.4.2). Line managers can be given bonuses for spending time counselling their staff through change or implementing change-related initiatives. Similarly, champions of change may be rewarded by other means such as being sponsored to attend high-profile development courses or corporate conferences. Furthermore, if in earlier stages of the transition the recruitment policies have been changed to start attracting different types of staff, such as mothers returning to work or semi-retired people, then a different range of rewards may need to be offered to retain these staff. Such employees may value flexibility over financial reward.

Sustaining change is more to do with maintaining and retaining changed behaviours into the longer term. Changes to reward systems in this phase of change are more likely to be permanent changes to the overall framework of rewards. It is at this point that an organisation may implement, for example, a new cafeteria benefits system, or embed symbolic rewards into the permanent way of working for an organisation.

Training

A key aspect of change programmes is sometimes the ability to rapidly develop skills and competencies within the workforce. This may be crucial in order to keep up with technological changes or cultural changes. Training is the mechanism used to help achieve this. Training seeks a specific outcome in terms of skills or behaviours. There are many mechanisms for delivering training, from off-site courses to *e-learning*. For instance, the pharmaceutical firm Pfizer found that a lack of communication between the global R&D unit in Japan and the rest of the company was hampering the company's early stage drug development. A staff survey at the unit revealed that 96 per cent staff didn't feel satisfied that they were able to present in English, and almost all felt dissatisfied with their ability to participate in teleconferencing. Eighty-nine per cent said cross-cultural training was needed. A training programme was then implemented to deal with these issues. Evaluation of the intervention reported a vast improvement in communications.[30]

Interpersonal interventions are also very powerful during the *mobilise* phase. Chapter 5 has already mentioned this when discussing communication, education and training as a mobilisation mechanism (see Chapter 5, section 5.8.5). Interventions such as these are about challenging the way individuals see their roles, responsibilities, relationships and organisations, to help individuals recognise that change is necessary at a personal level. One website, 'Fierce conversations', recommends three-day workshops that encourage delegates from an organisation to engage in 'productive dialogue' that 'interrogates reality, provokes learning, resolves rough challenges and enriches relationships'.[31] Training interventions, sometimes in the form of workshops such as at the Forestry Commission (see Chapter 2, Illustration 2.6), can also be used to support and encourage behaviour change in the move phase. During the *sustain* phase, interventions will be more to do with sustaining the transfer of the learning within the workplace and adjusting other HR-training practices such as induction.

6.5.4 The long-term HR cycle: leadership, workforce and organisational development

Leadership development

Leadership development is an umbrella term which captures all the various processes and systems that are designed to deliver the future leaders for an organisation. These processes can include coaching, off-site executive programmes, succession planning, career management systems, talent management processes, development and assessment centres, and mentoring, to mention a few traditional forms of development. More unusual activities have emerged recently as part of leadership development, such as developing leaders' ability to be storytellers in order to be able to narrate compelling and accessible visions of the future for the workforce (see Chapter 5, section 5.3.2).

In leading-edge organisations a detailed and systematic competency profile of future leaders will be drawn up based on an organisational assessment of the strategic direction of the organisation. These profiles form the basis of selection and succession planning for those identified as high potentials. Advertising the change in competency profiles, selection criteria and the methods of leadership development sends very powerful messages across the managerial populations about how cultural norms and values are shifting at the top of the organisation.

Ernst and Young UK, a professional services organisation, decided to change the way it developed its future partners in the firm through the introduction of an accelerated leadership scheme (the ALP). See Illustration 6.6. By emphasising the importance of self-managed learning and social networking within the way Ernst and Young UK delivered the leadership development, the firm reinforced the messages about the change in organisational culture that the new Chairman was trying to champion as part of his new strategy to do with People, Quality and Growth. Leadership Development was seen as a critical driver in the delivery of this new strategy. A relationship management ethos at all levels within and outside the business was seen as essential. This required the development of a leadership cadre with strong networks and sophisticated relational skills.

Other important interventions which can support long-term change are focused around formal career development. Any organisation undertaking change

Illustration 6.6

Ernst and Young – cultural change through leadership development

Ernst and Young is one of the world's leading professional service organisations (PSOs), helping companies across the globe to identify and capitalise on business opportunities. It is organised as a Partnership and employs 120,000 people operating in 140 countries. In the wake of the Enron scandal and the Sarbanes Oxley Act of 2002 in the USA, all professional service firms were obliged to review their practices and structurally separate out the auditing from the advisory functions of the business. There then followed a period of restructuring and adjustment amongst the sector as a whole which occupied the firms for some period of time.

Cultural change for the twenty-first century

In Ernst and Young the election of Mark Otty as Chairman for the UK in July 2006 has been particularly significant in terms of articulating a new vision for the business, summed up by the idea of there being three main pillars which will drive the goal of Market Leadership. These pillars are People, Quality and Growth. Changes in the structure consolidated nine business units into three and resulted in concomitant changes in the leadership team.

As part of the structural change the HR function was separated out, with the HR Strategy and Policy Unit being placed within the main People function and the HR operational units being placed into the business units. The intention was to ensure that HR Strategy and Policy had far more interface with the marketing strategy and client interface so that the brand of the company was aligned with the brand of Ernst and Young as an employer. Therefore it logically ensued that as the firm sought to redefine its relationship with its clients, there

was an accompanying need to redefine its employee relationship. At this time there was also a fierce 'war for talent' in the external labour market but particularly within the PSO sector.

The response to all of these changes was to develop a new HR strategy based around the concept of 'employee engagement' (see Chapter 7). The aim was to:

- Rearticulate the Ernst and Young employer brand.
- Enhance employee engagement.
- Develop emotional engagement with employees.
- Transform leaders as a key resource.
- Connect how the Ernst and Young client brand is put out in the marketplace and how people experience employment in the firm internally.

A business director expressed the intention as:

What are going to be the big factors that differentiate us from the competition? One is the extent to which we embed our values in such a way that clients see that when they interact with our people they perceive our people to be somehow different and better than the competition. By linking people and clients we give people the same priority as clients. So we would be looking for our people to have much more engagement with the firm and how they feel about the firm.

Leadership development and the role of the ALP

A critical driver for delivering the business strategy was Leadership Development.

change in action

Nurturing a relationship management ethos at all levels within and outside the business was seen as essential and this required the development of a leadership cadre with strong networks and sophisticated relational skills. All of this would also enhance the HR strategy of 'employee engagement'.

Ernst and Young has had a huge and sophisticated fleet of leadership development interventions, one of which is its new Accelerated Leadership Programme – the ALP. The ALP is essentially a fast-track development programme. If a person is placed onto the programme, it may lead to them, in time, being invited onto the Partner Track programme, which leads to Partnership status, the ultimate goal for many young recruits. Throughout their career in Ernst and Young, people can be invited to join the ALP or be taken off the scheme. In aligning the ALP with the general development of branding, the intended outcomes for the ALP are:

● To develop leaders with a wide range of relationship styles.
● To create leaders who take responsibility for their on-going development.
● To enable leaders to develop their influencing skills, thereby helping them to engage with both clients and employees on a number of different levels.

The ALP emphasises the importance of 'on-the-job-training' and its underpinning philosophy is one of leadership development as a continuous, self-managed process rather than one that sees development as something that happens on off-site development programmes. In the ALP the onus is on the individual to make their own network connections and create learning opportunities for themselves. Whilst 'on-the-job training' has always existed within PSOs, this programme aims to formalise and emphasise its importance.

Each potential cohort for the ALP is initially put forward by their business unit after roundtable discussions with the HR function within that unit, although those individuals interested in joining the scheme can also nominate themselves prior to those discussions. A formal selection process then takes place whereby potential participants present to a business unit panel and that panel evaluates their commitment to engage and learn from the ALP. The National Leadership Development Team then conducts a firm-wide review of the proposed cohort against the ALP selection criteria and the diversity targets within Ernst and Young and confirms the final decisions with the Business Unit heads and HR. The Chairman then writes to the chosen candidates to congratulate them and welcome them to the ALP.

There are four main 'players' within the ALP: Counsellors, Mentors, Action Learning Groups (ALGs) and Partner Sponsors.

Counsellors: Everyone has a counsellor within the firm whether they are on the ALP or not. The counsellor may or may not be the person's line manager. People can meet formally or informally with their counsellor.

Mentors: ALP participants are also given access to a partner mentor as well as a counsellor.

Action Learning Groups (ALG): ALP participants are expected to participate in peer-based cross-functional learning groups.

Partner sponsors: These partners are expected to 'champion' the importance of the ALP within the firm at large.

Participants: These are the people selected to participate and benefit from the ALP.

The interactions with mentors and counsellors are based around the principle of one-to-one personal development through coaching. In contrast, the ALG activity is intended to foster an ability to practice action learning with peers. The learning comes from either sharing their own work experience with each other and then reflecting upon that as a group, or from working on a particular task or project. This could be a project within Ernst and Young or it could involve activities outside Ernst and Young. For instance, one ALG got involved in developing a mentoring scheme for a local school.

Reactions to the ALP

One ALP participant described the changes in Ernst and Young and the introduction as being an investment that enables managers to give more back to the firm. He used the analogy of the J.F. Kennedy speech:

> *Not what can your country do for you but what can you do for your country? That kind of attitude, you know, what can you do for Ernst and Young rather than what can Ernst and Young do for you. That feels like the major difference.*

There is a view amongst some of the managers that being selected for the ALP is seen as a badge of honour:

> *You wear it as a badge and you use it to get onto good client work and make sure you get the most challenging role.*

The ALP participants are seen as crucial in bringing the importance of networking and relationship management alive across the firm. It seems as though there is a hope for a type of 'viral' change process, with the ALP population spreading the word through their enhanced ability to network and spread stories of the ALP's benefits:

> *The ALP people are privileged in the fact that they have access to certain powerful people within the firm. In fact, they are their mentors. So it allows them proven access. But it also allows them to go and spread the news about how Ernst and Young should be operating as well. So it's key, you know, a*

> *lubricant if you like, of how we should be doing things right as well as having to take it forward. So those guys are quite key to that "living stuff", you know, "living the brand". Well they are excellent and good examples of what we should be doing in terms of developing people around this firm and working across sectors. (Partner Sponsor)*

There have been some problems associated with the ALP, namely (1) the contribution of ALGs and (2) the attitude of some of the Partners in the firm.

Reaction to the ALGs has been mixed. The ALP managers on the programme are very well aware of their own visibility and the need to perform well for their own careers. However, some have questioned the added value of participating in peer-based Action Learning groups. One ALP manager said that he felt he had nothing to learn from his peers in the ALGs, as he was constantly experiencing 'on-the-job' learning as part of his day-to-day work. Another participant described that out of a group of seven people in their ALG, a couple of people had no interest in the group nor the action learning process itself. She referred to them as 'badge carriers' who felt they couldn't really refuse to participate in the ALP as a whole once they were selected by their manager because 'you can't really say no to being placed on a programme like that and stay on career track'. However, she went on to explain, 'Once they're on it they're not really contributing as much and are not very interested in what we're doing as a group.'

One crucial barrier is that the activity of the ALGs is not directly connected into any of the reward and recognition structures and systems, and thus the groups are not seen as high priority. In addition, the participants on the ALP are already high performers and are already 'overworked and overcommitted' in terms of long hours spent at work in the short term. Thus the benefits of the learning gained from ALGs may be reaped in the longer term but are

change in action

difficult to reconcile with the short-term pressures and rewards of delivering business performance.

Looking at Partner reactions, unsurprisingly it was the younger but less powerful Partners who were most enthusiastic about the broad general changes instigated by the new Chairman and, more specifically, the ALP itself. There was cynicism about whether the more established Partners were living out the new values. One explanation given was that business needs will always take priority over leadership development activities despite the Partners' endorsement of the ALP:

> *When there are 500 clients calling for our time or staff calling for assistance and support, actually the bit that automatically gets squeezed out, I think, is the ALP.*

Reflections

Ernst and Young is an extremely successful firm and one of the UK's leading employers. Its attitude survey scores at the time of the research were extremely positive: 72 per cent of staff agreed that new ideas were highly valued in the organisation; 83 per cent were proud to tell others that they were part of this organisation; only 4 per cent disagreed that their Partners could be trusted to make sensible decisions about the organisation's future; and 78 per cent agreed that they were aware of what management were trying to achieve.

Whilst there was ambivalence amongst some of the staff about the broad cultural change that the new Chairman was trying to deliver – 'I'll believe it when I see it' or 'I've seen it all before' – others are much more upbeat about what he is trying to achieve:

> *I would say that changing the firm's ethos, if you like, and its public declaration of its values and clear attempts to live up to those values and make them a reality, is the biggest change I've seen in the firm in twenty eight years in terms of its nailing its colours to the mast and the ALP is part of that change.*

Extracted from Hope Hailey, V., Abbotson, S. and Farndale, E. (2007) 'The Change Management Consortium report for Ernst and Young', (January).

needs to make suitable adjustments to its career-planning processes in order to ensure a talent stream of organisational leaders with the experiences required for the future. There is a danger on relying on informal and internal promotion paths planned by existing top managers, since it is unlikely that the behaviours or knowledge that secured the present executive's career progression will be as relevant for the business challenges faced by their successors. Instead, formal succession strategies may be implemented by a series of planned special second-ments, development opportunities, expatriate assignments or job promotions aimed at giving the targeted individuals the range of experiences deemed necessary for future leaders.

When the Marylebone Warwick Balfour hotel group acquired the Hotel du Vin group in January 2005, it announced its intentions to double the number of hotels it owned by the year 2009. At the same time it announced that it also wanted 30 per cent of employees in every new hotel to come from within the group. This required significant changes in the group's career development processes. An online 'talent toolbox' was developed which asks individuals to detail their career aspirations and assists them in the development of personal development plans. Competitions such as 'Ultimate Cook Off', which allows junior chefs within the group to demonstrate their talents to senior managers, were introduced. New forms of training included managers attending top cookery schools and visiting the sites of major suppliers of linen or toiletries to learn about other companies, and the introduction of food, wine and bar schools throughout the hotel group. In addition, in order to secure a talent stream, the group established relations with universities, colleges and schools as a way of identifying and nurturing relationships with students whilst they are still in education.[32]

Workforce development

Workforce development is concerned with the long-term development of the larger pool of human capital within the organisation. It is focused on developing appropriate skills, knowledge and technological know-how at all levels in the organisation. As such it is often done in partnership with external training and education bodies at a local, regional, national or even international level. In such partnerships corporations will seek to influence the provision of education or skills training within the community.

Workforce development involves a number of activities. First is the forecasting of the organisation's skill needs in the future and then the scanning of the external environment to assess how well those needs will be met by the future labour force. This sort of analysis is usually done within HR planning departments, who access information such as labour market demographics or education participation rates on a local, national or international basis. The company also assesses how well its current internal skills development will be able to meet future needs. Putting this information together allows the organisation to make decisions concerning whether they will create their own skill base for the future or partner with other institutions to help build a pool of well-trained labour.

One company that is particularly well known for its prowess in this area is the car manufacturer Nissan. Wherever it has plants in the world it works in partnership with the local communities to ensure that the local labour market is a pool from which it can recruit. An example of this is its activity within Sunderland in the UK. Working with the local Tyne and Wear Learning Council, Nissan has contributed to raising the skill levels within the local community. This expertise is now recognised globally within the company, as the Sunderland plant has been chosen by the parent company in Japan to be one of only two global training centres for manufacturing excellence. Production supervisors from across the world will learn how to become 'master trainers' in Sunderland and then return to their own countries to train up their workforces.[33]

However, this area of workforce development is a contentious issue within Western economies. As more and more organisations choose to develop a core and periphery workforce model – with those employed on the periphery on short-term contracts, or supplied by agencies or consultancies on a contract basis – there are questions over the extent to which this damages or enhances an organisation's change capability in the longer term. In the shorter term, having fewer people employed on permanent contracts makes for a more nimble and adaptable organisation, one which is able to respond immediately to market changes in a more agile manner. Closing down factories or call centres, for instance, in mature economies and opening up new plants in emerging economies is much easier when the organisation does not have direct contractual responsibility for all the people working on its behalf. Yet the organisation may not be able to influence the skills development of those employed on the periphery and as such, will lose an ingredient of long-term sustainable organisational health.[34]

Organisational development

Organisational development (OD) is the process through which an organisation develops the internal capacity to be the most effective it can be in its chosen work and to sustain itself over the long term. Organisational development specialists look at the organisation as a whole entity and assess how the organisation can best grow and change to support the long-term business strategy. Like change management, there are many theories and perspectives on organisational development but few common characteristics.[35] Organisational development:

- Takes a longer-term perspective.
- Takes a holistic perspective.
- Is concerned with people.
- Is concerned with organisational health.
- Sees organisations as a set of interrelated systems and processes.
- Works with the organisation as a whole, not just with individuals and their development.
- Helps the organisation learn from past change and development, thereby increasing its change capability.
- Focuses on culture and structure.

Very often OD specialists sit within the Chief Executive's office, providing a people perspective to the work done by business strategy units. Sometimes they sit within the HR department, and their remit may include responsibility for leadership development and workforce development. They are often extremely influential. The GSK cultural change process in the UK following the merger (see Chapter 2, Illustration 2.2) was led by GSK's organisational development specialists. Similarly, the social housing group Prime Focus (see Chapter 3, Illustration 3.2) labelled their second stage of evolutionary change as a stage of organisational development.

6.6 LINKING DESIGN OF COMMUNICATIONS AND HR INTERVENTIONS TO DESIGN CHOICES

Just as it is important to link the design of the transition state to the design choices (see section 5.10, Chapter 5), it is also important to link choices about interventions such as communication and HR systems to design choices. So, for example, if the change style selected is education and delegation, then the communication strategy needs to be designed to have many seminars and/or training and education interventions upfront that are about creating an awareness of the need for change, an understanding of what needs to change, and providing staff with the skills to undertake change. If, on the other hand, the change style is to be more directive or coercive, particularly since these change styles by their nature are top-down and may be associated with a lack of time, then much of the communication may be more one-way with less of an emphasis on participation. If the change target is outputs, then changes to rewards and performance objectives within the appraisal system are likely to be particularly helpful, whereas if the change target is behaviours, then a range of HRM interventions will be needed, including training and development to help effect the changes to skills and behaviours and new appraisal criteria and rewards to support these new behaviours.

6.7 SUMMARY

The purpose of this chapter has been to describe in some detail the use of particular levers and mechanisms to aid the transition process and help effect the required changes:

- Communication is particularly important during all phases of the transition. During the mobilise phase, communication needs to be designed to create readiness; during the move phase, communication needs to provide explanation; and as change progresses, communication also needs to provide updated information for staff. It is always necessary to focus on matching the communication to the needs of the audience.

- Symbolic activity is important as an alternative form of communication during change. Rituals can be used to help facilitate the mobilise, move and sustain change process by legitimising questioning and challenging in the early stages of change, and promoting new role models and social identities as change progresses.

- Human resource management systems are also key change levers. Short-term change interventions include recruitment and selection, performance evaluation, reward systems, and training. Longer-term change interventions are leadership development, workforce development and organisational development. All of these support change strategies by shaping new skills, behaviours, attitudes or values within employees.

Through the consideration of communication and HR interventions, this chapter completes the design analysis for the transition process, although it also touches on issues to do with how to manage the transition. Chapter 7 picks up this theme to discuss issues of transition management in more detail.

REFERENCES

1. For a discussion of some of the principles of communication, see Axley, S.R. (1984) 'Managerial and organizational communication in terms of the conduit metaphor', *Academy of Management Review*, 9 (3), pp. 428–37.
2. 'UNISON: using effective communication' (4 July 2007) The Times 100 Case Studies, www.thetimes100.co.uk/company.
3. For an examination of some of the factors that contribute to effective communication, see Smeltzer, L.R. (1991) 'An analysis of strategies for announcing organization-wide change', *Group and Organization Studies*, 16 (1), pp. 5–24. Also see Goodman, J. and Truss, C. (2004) 'The medium and the message: communicating effectively during a major change initiative', *Journal of Change Management*, 4 (3), pp. 217–28.
4. See reference 3 above.
5. See Duck, J.D. (1993) 'Managing change: the art of balancing', *Harvard Business Review*, 71 (6), pp. 109–18.
6. Lank, E. (19 February 1998) 'Café society', *People Management*, pp. 40–3. Also see Knight, T. and Souter, J. (4 July 2007) 'Going the distance', *Inside Knowledge, 2004,* 7, (10), www.ikmagazine.com.
7. Hathi, S. (2007) 'Awakening leader's warrior spirit at ICI Paints', *Strategic Communications Management,* 11 (3), p. 12.
8. Burrows, P. (9 October 2006) 'Controlling the damage at HP', *BusinessWeek*.
9. Various authors discuss the need for communication to be relevant to the needs of the audience. See, for example, Klein, S.M. (1993) 'A communication strategy for the implementation of participative work systems', *International Journal of Management,* 10 (3), pp. 392–401; also Bertsch, B. and Williams, R. (1994) 'How multinational CEOs make change programmes stick', *Long Range Planning*, 27 (5), pp. 12–24.
10. For a discussion of the need for personal visions, see Downing, S. and Hunt, J.W. (1990) 'Mergers, acquisitions and human resource management', *International Journal of Human Resource Management*, 1 (2), pp. 195–209.
11. See Klein as in reference 9 above for the role of supervisors in communication.
12. Zetterquist, P. and Quirke, B. (2007) 'Transforming internal communication at Ericsson', *Strategic Communication Management,* 11 (1), pp. 18–21.
13. Also see Higgins, J.M. and Mcallaster, C. (2004) 'If you want strategic change, don't forget to change your cultural artifacts', *Journal of Change Management*, 4 (1), pp. 63–73.
14. Sanghera, S. (11 September 2003) 'It's all turned out bootiful', *Financial Times,* p. 14.

15. Daniel, C. (26 August 2002) 'Inside track: start of a longer haul into the JetBlue yonder', *Financial Times*, p. 8.

16. Peters, T. (1987) 'In search of excellence', video – comments on Disney World, London: Video Arts.

17. For more information on organisational rituals and the use of ritual in change, see Sims, D., Fineman, S. and Gabriel, Y. (1993) *Organizing and Organizations: An Introduction,* London: Sage; Trice, H.M. and Beyer, J. (1984) 'Studying organizational cultures through rites and ceremonies', *Academy of Management Review,* 9 (4), pp. 653–69; Brown, A.D. (1994) 'Transformational leadership in tackling technical change', *Journal of General Management,* 19 (4), pp. 1–12.

18. For more information see the same sources in reference 17 above.

19. Hwee, C.C., Demeester, L. and Pich, M. (2002) 'AlliedSignal Aerospace Repair and Overhaul (Singapore) (C)', INSEAD, ECCH case 602–036–1.

20. See Applegate, L., Austin, R. and Collins, E. (2006) 'IBM's Decade of Transformation (A): The Turnaround', Harvard Business School Case, 9–805–130.

21. Marsh, P. (5 July 2002) 'Siemens generates goodwill in North America', *Financial Times*.

22. See Pettigrew, A. et al. (2003) *Innovating Organisations,* Sage.

23. For a fuller discussion of the different components of a human resource system, see Boxall, P. and Purcell, J. (2007) *Strategy and Human Resource Management,* 2nd edn, Palgrave.

24. This figure is adapted from earlier work done by Lynda Gratton on the People Process Model and presented in Gratton, L., Hope Hailey, V., Stiles, P. and Truss, C. (1999) *Strategic Human Resource Management,* Oxford: Oxford University Press.

25. See Jones, D. and Womack, J. (2005) 'Lean consumption', *Harvard Business Review,* (March).

26. See Isern, J. and Pung, C. (2007) 'Harnessing energy to drive organizational change', *Voices on Transformation 2, McKinsey,* Q1.

27. For a further discussion on these two ideas of coordination and resource flexibility, see Hope Hailey, V. (2004) 'What really matters in HRM and business performance – organizational agility as an alternative perspective', in *Next Generation Business Thinkers,* Chowdhury, S. (ed) John Wiley.

28. See Syedain, H. (3 May 2007) 'Scope for action', *People Management,* pp. 31–3.

29. See 'WH Smith share plan drives profits' (26 January 2006) in News in Brief, *People Management,* p. 11.

30. See Evans, R. (3 May 2007) 'Breaking down boundaries at Pfizer', *People Management,* p. 12.

31. See the website *www.fiercein.com.*

32. See Clarke, E. (5 April 2007) 'Enjoy your stay', *People Management,* pp. 35–7.

33. See 'Training honour for Nissan' (14 June 2007) in TJ online, www.trainingjournal.com.

34. The discussion of long-term skills development and the increasing use of contracted-out labour is a huge debate. For a US perspective see Lepak, D. and Snell, S. (2002) 'Examining the human resource architecture: the relationships among human capital, employment and human resource configurations, *Journal of Management,* 28, pp. 517–43. For a UK perspective see Rubery, J. et al. (2004) *Fragmenting Work: Blurring Organizational Boundaries and Disordering Hierarchies,* Oxford University Press.

35. There is a huge literature on organisation development but for people wanting more information, a good starting point would be the *Leadership and Organisational Development Journal.* Also see Burnes, B. (2004) *Managing Change,* 4th edn, FT/Prentice Hall.

WORK ASSIGNMENTS

6.1   List the different ways that your university/business school or employer communicates with you – particularly at times of change. Why are these means of communication effective or ineffective? How could they be improved?

6.2   Considering somewhere you have worked, what rituals did you observe? What did they communicate about the organisation's paradigm or identity? How could their removal/shift in emphasis be used to aid change? What new rituals could be introduced?

6.3   Examine Illustration 4.1 on Tarmac in Chapter 4. Analyse the different communication mechanisms and channels used with different stakeholder groups, and how these varied through time. What appear to have been the most effective forms of communication and why? How could communication have been improved? To deepen your understanding of different ways of communicating during change, also return to Illustrations 2.2 and 2.6 on GSK and the Forestry Commission in Chapter 2. Again, consider the different communication mechanisms and channels used and why these were effective.

6.4   Using practitioner journals or newspapers, find two examples of the use of HR interventions to deliver change. Evaluate their success.

6.5   Look at the various executive development programmes offered by some of the university business schools in your country. Which programmes are concerned with leadership development? How well do they equip leaders to manage change?

Managing the transition: planning, monitoring and resourcing

7.1 INTRODUCTION

The previous two chapters explained how to design the actual change implementation and the transition state, and also discussed how to sequence the selected change levers and interventions throughout the transition. This chapter builds on this, by focusing on the management of the transition state. It considers:

- The nature of the transition state and the implications of this for the transition management task, including monitoring and assessing progress.
- The competencies required of individuals acting as change agents, with a particular focus on the political aspects of this role, and the need for individuals who can read the political landscape of their organisations.
- The nature of the middle manager and change recipient roles during the transition state and the issues to be considered for the individuals who fill them.

The chapter opens with a consideration of the nature of the transition period. An understanding of what change is like once implementation gets underway is important for a greater appreciation of the skills required by those responsible for managing the transition. The chapter focuses on the competencies required of change agents more than any other characteristic since this links into leadership skills. Chapter 2 discusses the fact that it is necessary to separate out the change role from the individual within it. An individual may be in a role which is nominally a leadership role, such as the change champion role, yet fail to act like a leader. Through the focus on change agency this chapter unpacks some of the qualities required of leaders during change, showing the importance of being able to read and, where necessary, alter the organisation context to enable appropriate action during change.[1]

7.2 MANAGING THE TRANSITION

7.2.1 The nature of the transition state

It would be all too easy to assume from what has been said so far that the key to managing any transition is good up-front planning. It is true that the more planning and forethought given to the transition state, the better the chances of success, which is why the previous chapters devote so much attention to it. However, as Chapter 1 pointed out, it would be wrong to believe that implementation will unfold neatly in a linear fashion in accordance with carefully laid plans. The transition is often characterised by managers as 'frustrating', 'chaotic', and 'difficult': all in all, an emergent process with unpredictable and uncertain outcomes. Yet few challenge the implication often given by books and articles on change that if enough attention is paid to planning, change implementation can be 'managed' or controlled in a top-down fashion, with new practices falling naturally out of senior manager edicts as easily as night follows day.

A good analogy is to think of the old slot machines that used to be found in entertainment arcades for children. A penny dropped in a slot at the top could take many routes. The 'prize' a child would get out of the machine would depend on the route the penny took. Leading change is a similar experience. Managers can drop interventions in at the top of the organisation, but the resulting outcome, in terms of the changes in behaviours or attitudes it produces, can be surprising and disappointing. Change is about managing individual expectations and interpretations, not just structures and systems. As a result, senior management control over outcomes, even in top-down change, is tenuous because of the way change recipients edit senior manager plans through their implementation actions. Therefore, the outcomes achieved are not always as intended. See Figure 7.1.

Figure 7.1   Interrelationships between components of the change process

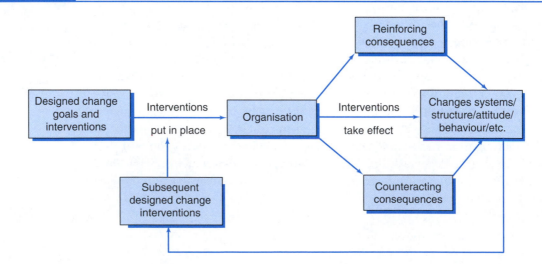

Some of these unexpected outcomes may reinforce and support the direction of change, such as staff showing less resistance than anticipated, or being prepared to work very long hours to make the changes work. Many others are typically negative consequences, counteracting the desired direction of change and slowing the pace of change.

Some researchers have made efforts to categorise different types of unintended consequences. See Figure 7.2. Many of these unintended consequences can be laid at the door of change leaders – although they may not do these things deliberately. Other unexpected outcomes frequently arise because of the way change participants are interpreting the change interventions and communications they receive. For example, a manufacturing organisation introduced a new subsidised staff canteen as part of a change programme which also aimed to improve the work life of the employees. Despite the value for money offered, the workers continued to bring sandwiches and didn't use the canteen. Why? Sandwiches came out of the family housekeeping money, whereas the canteen would have to come out of their 'beer' money (the money retained for personal spending out of their wages).

Figure 7.2   The unintended consequences of culture change

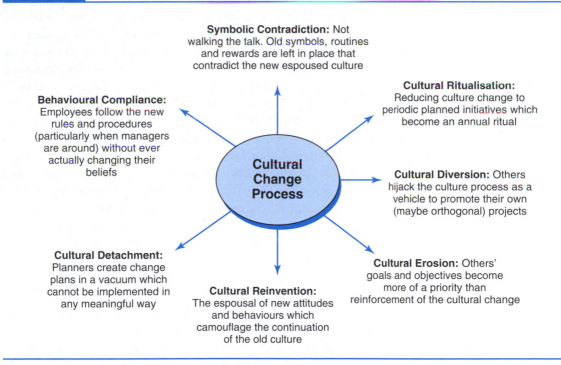

Source: Adapted from Harris, L.C. and Ogbonna, E. (2002) 'The unintended consequences of culture interventions: a study of unexpected outcomes', *British Journal of Management*, 13 (1), pp. 31–49.

7.2.2 Challenging assumptions about implementing planned change

To understand the origins of unexpected change outcomes, it is necessary to understand how people are interpreting things and why. It is necessary to understand which planned (and unplanned) events and activities are having an impact, how these events and activities are being interpreted, and how this is impacting behaviour. Since it is not possible to 'manage' or 'control' the interpretations of others, 'managing' change becomes a more active and on-going process as much to do with facilitating recipient meaning development to create an alignment in understanding between senior managers and others, as it is to do with the deployment and monitoring of actions against plans. Assumptions of senior manager control over change need to be replaced with recognition of the role of change recipients in *creating* change. The emphasis on formal, top-down communications and interventions needs to be balanced with efforts by senior managers to engage more actively with those lower down in organisations, and particularly middle managers, to forge a shared idea of what needs to be achieved. Change leaders also need to be prepared to live the changes they want others to adopt. See Figure 7.3.

Many of the practical implications that fall out of Figure 7.3 are to do with communication – thus the focus in Chapter 6 of this book on not just the use of verbal and written communication, but also the use of symbolic activity, education and development. Whilst it is accepted that change requires extensive communication, in general there are three related assumptions about communication. First, most articles and books on change place emphasis on vertical communication from senior managers to others as a key forum for creating understanding of planned changes. Second, communication is primarily conceived of in terms of formal verbal and written communications. Communication is about the transmission of information. Third, although there is recognition in some texts of the power of symbolic as well as verbal and written communications, this is often coupled with the notion of 'managing meaning'. In other words, senior managers can shape individual's interpretations through the use of a series of stage-managed and interrelated communications, behaviours and events. Again there are assumptions of senior manager control – senior managers can make an organisation dance by pulling the right series of levers, a little like a puppet master pulling the right strings. In fact, change is more about 'aligning interpretations', a two-way process of sharing and negotiating interpretations through many different communication genre. The meaning of the top-down initiatives emerges bottom-up. This is why Kraft UK throughout 2006 and 2007 (see Illustration 6.3, Chapter 6) devoted so much effort to reconceiving the concept of communication, moving from a culture where communication was primarily about e-mail and written memoranda to one that recognised that communication flows through many different channels and that informal, face-to-face communication is often more valuable than formal communication.

Figure 7.3 Challenging assumptions about change management practice

Traditional Assumptions about Design of Top-Down Change	Updated Assumptions about Design of Top-Down Change	Implications for Practice
Change can be controlled top-down by senior managers. Practice falls out of senior manager edict as people adopt well crafted policies and plans. Monitoring of change by ticking activities off project plans.	Senior managers can inititate & influence direction of the change, but not *direct* change. Practice is determined by the way those on receiving end of planned interventions interpret the plans.	Monitoring change is about understanding what interpretations are developing and *why*. Needs to capture recipients developing responses to change interventions on an on-going basis.
Vertical, formal communication from senior managers to others seen as key means for creating understanding of change.	Lateral and informal communication between peers is also a significant vehicle for developing interpretations of what change is about.	As change moves from design to implementation, senior managers need to move away from reliance on formal, vertical communications, and engage with lateral, informal inter-recipient communications – either by taking themselves to the sensemaking, or by bringing the sensemaking to them through events designed to do this.
Communication is equated with formal verbal and written channels. Seen as the transmission of information.	Communication is about conversational and social practices (actions, behaviours, words), and includes formal and informal mechanisms such as rumours, storytelling, gossip, discussions. Communication more to do with generating new knowledge and shared meanings.	Greater investment is required in change conversations, with a recognition of the multiple conversational vehicles that exist. Senior managers/change leaders need to live the changes they want others to adopt. They need to avoid inconsistencies between their actions, words and deeds.
Managing Meaning: Where the need for symbolic communications is recognised, managing meaning is taken to be about a series of one-way top-down interventions.	Aligning interpretations: this is a two way process of sharing and developing interpretations.	Requires a more active involvement by senior managers beyond MBWA. More explicit attention is required to discussion and story telling. Senior managers need to work with the reality of change recipients, responding to their issues and interpretations. In larger organisations, this may need to be achieved through the use of a number of change ambassadors.
Change 'recipients' and change implementers are there to accurately deploy and disseminate senior manager plans	Change recipients actively translate and edit change plans.	Recipients mediate the outcomes of planned changes. For the other recommendations to be adopted, senior managers need to recognise this.

Source: Adapted from Balogun, J. (2006) 'Managing change: steering a course between intended strategies and unanticipated outcomes', *Long Range Planning*, 39 (1), pp. 29–49. Reproduced with permission

In addition, lateral communications between peers are just as important, if not more important, than vertical communications in shaping the interpretations of change that develop and the perceived implications for individuals and their behaviours. Furthermore, much of this lateral communication is informal, occurring through gossip, discussion, negotiations, observed actions, and behaviours as individuals go about their daily work. Senior managers become agents of 'indirect infection',[2] influencing through their appearance as ghosts in stories do, and as gossip exchanged by change recipients about the change process. Only a few people may have direct experience of senior management behaviour, but these experiences are shared through rumour and gossip – whether or not they actually occurred. As such, visible actions – whether planned or not, whether by senior managers or peers – that indicate either that things are different or that things are staying the same despite espoused change, become important influencers of interpretations through the sharing of these behaviours and experiences. This is a type of symbolic activity. (See Chapter 6, section 6.4.)

Paradoxically, senior managers have far less control over processes of change than traditional thinking on the management of change suggests, because they cannot control the lateral interrecipient processes through which recipients 'make sense' of change. However, whilst senior managers may not be able to direct these informal sensemaking processes, if they recognise their existence they may be able to participate in them and shape them. They can participate in the lateral communications between recipients by being out in the organisation, talking to people, sharing stories, listening and generally setting an example through their behaviours and actions. Senior managers can also bring the 'sensemaking' to them by organising events that bring individuals together (with senior managers) to share their thoughts and impressions of the way change is developing. This all implies a much more active and involved role for senior managers during change that goes well beyond 'Managing by Walking About', since senior managers need to be prepared to actively engage others in discussion and dialogue.

7.3 DESIGNING CHANGE OUTCOMES AND MONITORING MECHANISMS

7.3.1 The role of project management and measurement

Change is a complex process. Any change initiative is likely to consist of a number of major projects, such as restructuring, redesigning work processes and procedures, closing offices and factories, relocating staff, designing and installing new equipment and technology, redesigning jobs, and introducing lean processing techniques and/or continuous improvement. It is therefore necessary to create coherence from all these projects, not just in terms of a unifying vision (see Chapter 5), but also to understand dependencies between projects. The more complex the change, the more some form of project management and progress measurement is needed. Thus this chapter on the management of the transition would not be complete without some mention of project management and methods for measuring progress. However, project management, budgeting and measurement setting are well-understood techniques with established mechanisms that can help with developing detailed plans and schedules, monitoring progress against the plans, and developing resource requirements and implications. In addition, as discussed in Chapter 6, results from performance management systems or staff appraisals can be used to assess the achievement of behavioural and attitudinal change outcomes. Other techniques for assessing progress against outcomes include attitude surveys, customer surveys, interviews and questionnaires, as well as data on control measures such as how quickly the phone is answered.

The need for a mutually supportive set of measures that align behaviours with an organisation's strategy, without creating a focus on one area of activity at the expense of another, has led to a technique, the balanced scorecard,[3] that started becoming popular in the 1990s. The balanced scorecard uses four sets of measures:

- Financial measures to assess how the company looks to shareholders.
- Customer performance measures to assess how the company is performing in the eyes of the customer.
- Internal operational measures to assess how well the company is doing on the business processes that impact on customer service.
- Measures of innovation and learning to assess if the company is continuing to improve.

As this chapter has already stressed, much practitioner literature on change gives the impression that knowledge of these management techniques enables change to be controlled by senior managers in a top-down fashion. The key is to develop comprehensive change plans that take best practice into account – lots of communication, clear assignment of responsibility, management of stakeholders to overcome resistance, training in new ways of working, and so on. Monitoring change progress is about ticking the various activities off the project management Gantt charts as they occur, with periodic attitude surveys. Whilst most of this is sound advice, the unfortunate implication is that practice falls easily out of senior manager policy as people adopt these well-crafted and communicated plans. Of course advice to do with detailed planning; a balanced set of measures to assess progress and direct attention, effort and action; early wins; and strong project management is critical to the success of large change projects. However, to gauge change progress in terms of advances in behaviours and practices, it is essential to understand what interpretations are developing and why on an ongoing basis, which in turn requires proximity to those on the receiving end. Furthermore, the senior managers, the ones leading change, may be the last to find out about the things that are not progressing according to plan. Bad news does not travel upwards well. It requires explicit effort to collate information on how change is progressing from the perspective of the recipients.

7.3.2 Monitoring mechanisms

Organisations use a variety of different mechanisms to obtain feedback and evaluate the progress of implementation. See Figure 7.4. Periodic attitude surveys can be very helpful for detecting overall changes. GSK UK, for example (see Illustration 2.2 in Chapter 2), annually conducts a temperature check designed to support measurement of their PASSION culture, and uses the responses to work on areas in which scores change in negative direction. However, attitude surveys cannot be carried out with much greater frequency than every six months, and during major change, monitoring needs to be on-going and frequent. Senior managers need to have their ears to the ground.

| Figure 7.4 | Techniques for monitoring and evaluating change progress |

- **Focus groups and workshops**. Groups of people from across different organisational levels, departments and functions can be drawn together to discuss the change process. Participants can be asked to discuss both what is going well and why, and what is going badly and why. They may also be able to contribute ideas on how problems can be solved, and maybe help each other with problems they are encountering. Workshops can become a way of sharing learning as well as monitoring change.

- **Management by walking about and open-door policies**. Senior managers can make a point of being visible, and available for staff to talk to. They can visit departments and offices and discuss the progress of change with staff.

- **Team briefing**. Many organisations use team briefing to keep staff appraised of progress. These meetings can be made two-way so that comments staff make are collated and passed back upwards.

- **Question-and-answer sessions**. Managers can host question and answer sessions for staff. These may take the form of informal staff/management meetings, such as breakfast or lunchtime meetings, or more formally organised meetings.

- **External consultants to monitor progress**. External consultants can be engaged to run focus groups or workshops, or conduct staff surveys. Staff may be more prepared to be open and honest about what they say in front of an outsider, particularly if guaranteed some level of anonymity.

- **Staff representatives who collate feedback**. Staff representatives can be nominated to collate feedback. They may be the attendees of the focus groups or workshops.

- **Staff suggestion or commentary schemes** can be used to gather feedback, things that need changing or could be done better. This can be done through e-mail or intranet discussion groups, for example.

- **Confidential 'hot lines'** or internal mail mechanisms.

- **Attitude surveys** and other questionnaires.

Monitoring could be achieved through senior manager MBWA, but it is possible that during major strategic change, individuals are nervous about speaking up, in which case it may be necessary to use focus groups or some other means of collecting data in which comments are non-attributable. Similarly, individuals may be nervous about posting comments on a company intranet since these could be tracked. To be open about the way they are feeling, those on the receiving end of the changes may initially need to be afforded some degree of anonymity before they will speak openly. Free exchange of views and opinions can therefore be facilitated by the use of an outsider. The risk of bias in reporting is also reduced if an outsider not involved in advising or designing change is employed to write the feedback reports. In addition it is possible to use a network of individuals who not only pass their own opinions back, but are there for others to pass their concerns onto. A downside of monitoring systems is that they can be abused through attempts to further individual self-interest by what is reported, how things are reported and what is withheld. For people to give feedback there also needs to be visible action on feedback, or staff will feel that their managers are not seriously interested in their opinions, so why bother giving them?

When Kraft UK were undertaking change (see Illustration 6.3), they were able to use the question-and-answer sessions they'd put in place, and the greater efforts of senior managers to be out and about in the offices, to gather feedback. However, they supplemented this with focus groups and interviews conducted on a bi-monthly basis by an independent consultant to track how people were responding to the change initiatives. They were able to use this feedback to design on-going interventions to help them keep the change process on track and respond to employee concerns.

7.4 CHANGE AGENCY

The nature of the transition state and the impact of change on individuals requires special attention to the nature of change agency, and the roles of middle managers and change recipients during change. This section focuses first on change agency.

7.4.1 Change agency and transition management

Chapter 1 has already discussed a number of skills required of change agents. These skills include the ability to *analyse* the change context, to *judge* the key contextual features of the change context and design an appropriate change approach, to take *action* to achieve implementation, to handle *complexity,* to be *sensitive* about the impact of change, and to be *aware* of the potential impact of one's own preferences on the design choices made. Change agents also require good *influencing* skills because of the political nature of their role. However, change implementation is a complicated and difficult task. Transition management involves:

- Ensuring that what is planned happens, but also anticipating, detecting and dealing with the unexpected.
- Providing continuity between formulation and implementation to ensure consistency in the way plans are turned into practice.
- Overseeing the changes, which includes the coordination of the myriad change projects and change-related activities.
- Monitoring change progress against plans.

Whoever is leading the change process may also take responsibility for transition management. However, the more fundamental the transition, the more time consuming transition management is as a task. If change is being led by an individual, such as the MD or CEO, the individual may find that even if all his or her operational responsibilities are delegated, just being visible and championing the change takes up most of the time. Therefore, the bigger and more complex the change, the more likely it is that a transition management team will be needed to support the main change agent(s). Similarly, middle and senior managers with operational responsibilities may also have insufficient time to fully address transition management responsibilities. Therefore, although creating a management team out of the hierarchy, selecting representatives from the main stakeholder groups within the organisation, or even assigning responsibility for transition management to the line managers are all possibilities, in large-scale change it is more likely that the transition management team will be most effective if it is staffed with individuals whose sole responsibility is transition management.

7.4.2 Change agency skills

The individuals within the transition management team, or for that matter, change agents in general, also need specific skills and training. *Process* skills are more important than *technical* skills.[4] Process skills are to do with managerial and interpersonal skills, including communication, consultation, team building, managing politics and being able to motivate others. Technical skills are more to do with control techniques such as planning, budgeting, resourcing and scheduling, or the techniques and technology required by the change project, such as information systems. This does not mean that planning and scheduling tasks are not necessary, but that transition management involves more than traditional project management. Figure 7.5 lists some of the generic competencies typically identified for change agents.

However, the *critical* skill for change agents[5] lies in their political judgement and their ability to not just network, but also to *build* networks or coalitions

Figure 7.5	Change agent competencies

- Goals — clarity, flexibility, creativity
- Roles — team building, networking, tolerating ambiguity, showing courage and perseverance
- Communication awarness — communication/interpersonal skills, enthusiasm, visibility/role modelling, common touch
- Political judgement — influence, persuasiveness and negotiating
- Managing up — political awareness, helicopter perspective

Source: Adapted from Balogun, J. and Hope Hailey, V. (2002) 'Boundary Spanners: Contexts, Personality, Characteristics and Practices', Change Management Consortium, Cranfield School of Management.

around their change agenda. Many individuals charged with implementing change are not the most senior managers in organisations. They often occupy a middle to senior management role. As such, they lack the formal position power to 'persuade' (or coerce) through means such as the granting or withholding of resources, and the capacity to generally hire, fire, reward or punish. Similarly, they often lack the power to affect decision making by setting meeting agenda, or determining who attends what meetings. The extent to which this is the case does vary from organisation to organisation *and* even within the same organisation, dependent on the change agent's own particular role context. Therefore change agents can work in either enabled or constrained contexts. See Figure 7.6.

Organisations vary by (1) the degree to which different divisions are independent and autonomous from the corporate centre, with separate identities and ways of doing things, and (2) the extent to which shared managerial priorities, if they exist across the divisions, such as short-term profitability at the expense of longer-term strategic initiative, focus effort in a way which supports or mitigates against change initiatives. The managerial preferences in turn impact on the financial management and reporting systems, the reward and performance management systems, and the extent to which these systems can be utilised locally to support the change agent's project and incentivise adoption. Within this, the change agent's own role affects the extent to which they can mobilise support for their change initiative, based on their discretionary scope to use a wide range of interventions, their access to higher-level/other decision makers, and their local credibility – are their actions seen as legitimate? These factors, although interrelated, combine to create either an enabling or a constrained context of action.

The more change agents are constrained by their context in terms of their trying to implement initiatives that don't fit with the prevailing norms of the organisation, the more they need to engage in a range of political practices, captured in the centre of Figure 7.6. These practices shift attention from 'networking' to how change agents *build* networks of common interest to mobilise/enrol/draw in others to support their change initiatives. Furthermore, these practices are primarily to do with 'back-stage activity',[6] based on 'symbolic

Figure 7.6 **Constrained and enabled organisation contexts**

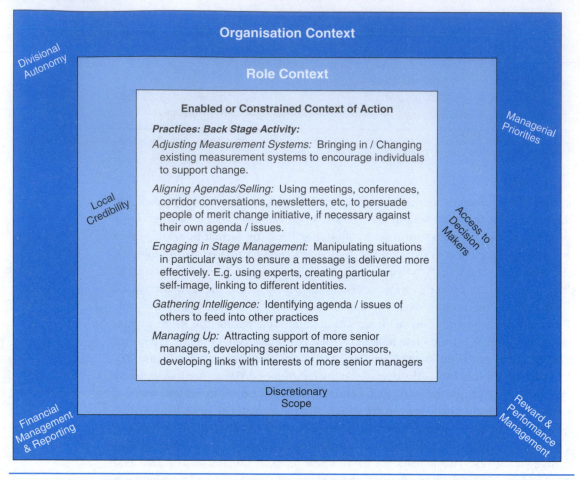

Source: Adapted from Balogun, J., Gleadle, P., Hope Hailey, V. and Willmott, H. (2005) 'Managing change across boundaries: boundary shaking practices', *British Journal of Management,* 16, pp. 261–78.

power':[7] the power to inhibit opposition or get cooperation as opposed to defeating declared opponents, here through the use of language, stage management and aligning agendas with these activities informed by gathered intelligence. See Illustration 7.1 This illustration also shows how a change agent, when blocked by the existing organisational system, is only likely to make progress if he or she can engage more senior individuals who are then willing to exercise their more formal means of power in support. Change agents become more like performers on stage, or spiders spinning a web, consciously trying to manipulate the situation. Most effort goes into back-stage activity preparing for the on-stage performance designed to gain cooperation/allies. The effectiveness of change agents lies in their knowledge of others and the organisation. Local credibility and access to key decision makers greatly affects their ability to influence.

Illustration 7.1

change in action

Delivering change in a constrained context

Corporate, a diversified conglomerate, has a number of diverse divisions that traditionally operated as autonomous silos, with strong, individual identities accountable only to the centre in terms of 'bottom-line' targets. Financial reporting and reward and performance mechanisms therefore focused on divisional financial performance. The power base rested with the divisional general managers, and there were few communication mechanisms reaching across senior managers in the divisions. Implementing centre-led change initiatives was, therefore, difficult, particularly given the tradition of no central mandate for such initiatives, making participation by the divisions effectively voluntary.

Due to the changing shape of the group with expansion outside of Europe, there was an interest in developing more consistent policies and synergies where possible. Projects connected to this were run from the corporate centre. Robert, the group head of remuneration and benefits, was working in areas such as pensions. Dan was running an innovation project.

Despite his seniority, given the nature of Corporate, Robert could only progress his initiatives by working within the system, yet simultaneously changing it. He did this by repositioning the way his initiatives were perceived. In particular, using his boss, a board member, to gain access, he exploited the cost-consciousness amongst all board members to position himself as a partner to senior management, doing work that could have an impact on the bottom line. Through this approach he gained agreement for the inclusion of a broader range of personal objectives in the incentive programme for managers, which in turn he could use himself.

However, Robert engaged in a variety of practices to take his change initiatives forwards.

From early on he saw networks and connections as important:

> I think having done a lot of travelling last year and meeting a lot of people has helped so I don't have to do so much of that anymore. I can now rely on one part of the network and get them to spread it out. I reinforce it a bit but I don't have to go and communicate to every single person in my network now.

He was aware of divergent interests and therefore the need to 'sell' messages. He recognised the different 'personalities' of the different divisions in the group. He estimated that he spent at least half his time gathering intelligence or else 'crafting' his presentations to senior management. In particular, he was quick to link his agenda to the focus on 'margin issues' and 'business reality', given the traditional hard-nosed performance orientation of the business. He had an appreciation of other people's agendas. For example, if a middle manager was resistant to change, Robert explored the reasons behind this:

> I had this issue in the US with one of the guys who was very bright and capable but very resistant and it turned out that it was his boss who was resistant and not him. So then I had to find ways to appeal to his boss.

Robert also had a policy of working with people individually when necessary ('the ones who are probably the most vociferous, resistant or have the most personal power') to get them on his side before calling individuals together to progress things as a team. Robert also consciously set up situations to get his agenda accepted. In one example, he had an outside medical consultant in the audience that he could draw on as part of the discussion on health care

change in action

issues, *'if they can hear it from a different perspective in terms of how they might go about achieving this.'* Additionally, he calls upon others in meetings to help sell his messages, such as senior people, or converts, to tell others how they used to think differently but are now converted to Robert's way of working.

Dan was at a disadvantage in comparison to Robert in terms of building networks of support for the innovation project, as he was further removed from the major decision makers. He had to rely on others to promote the projects:

> We had an 'innovation summit' last year and invited about 100 people who were involved in the process. Our CEO turned up and gave a speech and it spread like wildfire around the place.

Dan worked to establish new networks via giving encouragement to volunteers to do things in connection with the centre-led innovation activity. He arranged meetings for Divisional Coordinators (DCs), including audio conferences as well as physical get-togethers, to create more of a group feel. He also relied on peer pressure. He created a project review website so the DCs could comment online on project ideas submitted. However, comments were available to all DCs, creating peer pressure to perform reviews, and if individual DCs failed to perform a review, the task showed up in red. Dan's senior manager then requested statistics to monitor log-on frequency and comments each quarter.

Dan devoted time to persuading senior people within Corporate that time taken to review ideas submitted was well spent, as these ideas should help the future of their division. He also devoted time to nurturing certain ideas until he could decide how and to whom to sell them to get the ideas taken forward.

Prepared by Julia Balogun, from research from the Change Management Consortium, Cass Business School, on Managing Change Across Boundaries, by Julia Balogun and Veronica Hope Hailey.

7.4.3 Mapping organisational political systems

Acknowledgement of the political reality for change agents suggests two things. First, managers tend to steer clear of anything to do with the political because it has a bad reputation. However, change agents **cannot** afford to avoid the political realities of their world just because 'politics' is considered to be a nasty and dirty business. Second, to work in a political world, change agents need to have high awareness of the different stakeholders affected by a change issue and their perspective on it. Change agents need to be able to 'read' stakeholders' context. Implementation games such as diverting resources, financial or human, away from change projects; using bureaucratic, organisational procedures to slow down acceptance of change proposals; limiting communication of change goals and tasks; damaging the change agent's credibility; or agreeing to change proposals but not doing anything with them are commonplace in organisations. Methods for analysing the political systems within organisations are therefore useful.

Figure 7.7 Stakeholder analysis

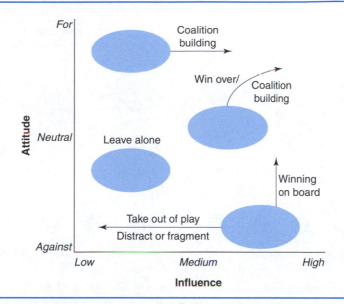

Source: Reprinted from Grundy, T. (1998) 'Strategy implementation and project management', *Journal of Project Management*, 16 (1), pp. 34–50, Copyright © 1998 Elsevier Science. Reproduced with permission.

There are a number of tools that can help with this. Figure 7.7 shows a stakeholder analysis. Stakeholder analysis enables a change agent to identify those key individuals or groups of individuals who have an interest in, or are affected by, a particular change initiative. Stakeholders may include not only employees, managers, shareholders, and unions, but also bankers, customers, suppliers and, potentially, the wider community. The grid as shown in Figure 7.7 can be used to plot the relative power of these different stakeholders to either facilitate or hinder change and whether or not they view the proposed changes favourably. Those that have power and support change need to be encouraged to support and back the changes. Those who have power but do not view change favourably either need to be convinced of the wisdom of the changes or worked round in some way. Such knowledge can then feed into the way a change agent attempts to build networks of support and the diverse influencing tactics required to enlist individuals.

Another technique that allows for an understanding of the formal and informal relationships between people in organisations, and therefore the channels of influence that can be used or need to be developed, is sociogram analysis. See Figure 7.8. Social network analysis,[8] or sociograms, is a useful technique for understanding the political landscape within an organisation because they are diagrams that show patterns of influence and trust, which is likely to be different from the relationships suggested by formal organisation charts since sociograms may be developed in non-work settings. Figure 7.8 shows a sociogram analysis of the old patterns of influence and trust in an organisation, and the way they were

| Figure 7.8 | Sociogram analysis |

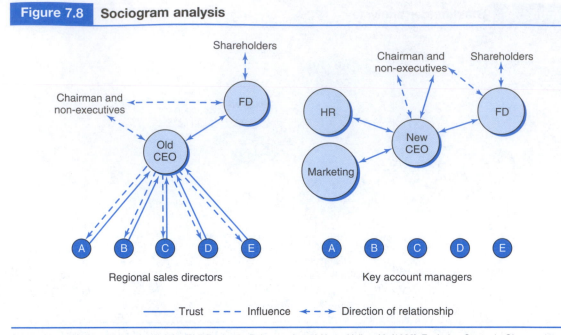

Source: Adapted from Illustration 6.3 by Phil Davies in Balogun, J. and Hope Hailey, V. (1999) *Exploring Strategic Change,* 1st edn, Prentice-Hall. Reproduced with permission.

disrupted by a new key account management structure put in place by a new CEO. The old Regional Sales Managers (now key account managers) felt isolated, as their previous relationship with the old CEO had primarily been a one-to-one relationship forged on the golf course. The new CEO didn't play golf and therefore to get cooperation and bring in the account managers, she had to initiate one-to-one meetings with them.

A third technique that supports stakeholder and sociogram analysis is AID analysis. See Figure 7.9. AID analysis positions change initiatives according to the degree to which they are difficult to implement and how attractive they are in terms of the benefits they deliver. Generally, to get early wins and raise support for change through early success, the high-benefit, low-difficulty projects should be implemented first. Projects that are high in difficulty but low in terms of benefits probably shouldn't be pursued at all! Likely stakeholder response to different initiatives is a key consideration of the implementation difficulty.

The fourth technique is more of a self-development framework. It helps individuals understand how to be politically sensitive. See Figure 7.10. The framework has two dimensions:

● *Reading skills:* how good an individual is at reading the politics of an organisation.

● *Carrying skills:* those skills an individual takes into a situation which predispose them to act with integrity or play psychological games.

Figure 7.9 **AID analysis**

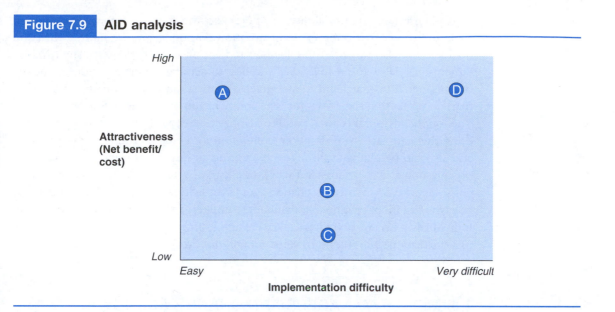

Source: Reprinted from Grundy, T. (1998) 'Strategy implementation and project management', *Journal of Project Management*, 16 (1), pp. 34–50, Copyright © 1998 Elsevier Science. Reproduced with permission.

Figure 7.10 **Understanding political behaviour: are you an owl, fox, donkey or sheep?**

Source: Adapted from Baddeley, S. and James, K. (1987) 'Owl, fox, donkey or sheep: political skills for managers, *Management Education and Development*, 18 (1), pp. 3–19.

Reading relates to the ability to appreciate the hidden, informal, unwritten rules and ways of working in an organisation that underpin the more formal and obvious, and also to gather intelligence and act on it appropriately. The carrying dimension relates to an individual's ability to separate their emotions from the organisational task at hand in any given situation, and focus on the task rather than on protecting their own feelings and behaving in an ego-defensive manner.[9] The four behavioural types (Owl, Fox, Donkey, Sheep) are not meant to be fixed, but rather can vary from situation to situation in which an individual is involved, and also can be changed through augmenting an individual's ability to 'read' the organisation and to understand what they 'carry'. The matrix can also be used to consider who to involve as change agents. Individuals who have a tendency to behave in an inept or innocent manner are unlikely to be successful in such a role. Individuals who are perceived as foxes, unless they can change what they carry into a situation, will not be trusted and will not be able to build support.

7.5 MIDDLE MANAGERS AND CHANGE AGENCY

Middle managers play an important role in change, since they might be nominated change agents to whom responsibility for implementing a particular change initiative is assigned, but also because of the nature of their position in the organisation. They occupy a buffer zone between the senior managers and the rest of the organisation. Furthermore, whilst much has been written about the demise of middle managers in the 1980s and 1990s as many organisations downsized and adopted flatter structures, middle managers are still alive and kicking. Indeed, as many organisations 'globalise', many senior managers used to having strategic decision-making autonomy within their own local country team are dragged into the middle managers ranks, as decision making is moved upwards to a regional level, leaving them as mere implementers of others' strategy and as middle managers of the larger corporation.

7.5.1 Middle managers as change intermediaries

The traditional view of middle managers is that they are a linking pin between the top and bottom of the organisation. They are there to carry out orders unquestioningly, providing little added value. In terms of change they are often characterised as obstructive, resistant, subversive, self-interested footdraggers.[10] In many organisations they have therefore been effectively downsized, silenced and forgotten. However, more recent research shows their role in strategic change and renewal to be a valuable one. They need to 'operationalise' the strategies devised by their senior managers to make them work in practice, and have an impact on the actual change outcomes through the way their actions then edit those senior manager plans.[11]

| Figure 7.11 | Interpretation as the key middle manager task |

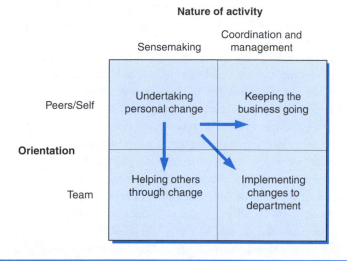

Source: Balogun, J. (2003) 'From blaming the middle to harnessing its potential: creating change intermediaries', *British Journal of Management*, 14 (1), pp. 69–84.

The middle manager change role is in fact complex and demanding (see Figure 7.11). They face certain challenges:

- Communication and interpretation of plans: a translation task.
- Reconciliation of divergent demands and activities from strategic and operational levels: a mediation task.
- Shock absorbers for (emotional/negative) impact on others: a buffering task.
- Are recipients themselves: a negotiation task.

For much of the time, managers are simultaneously change recipients and change implementers, fulfilling a role more accurately described by the term *change intermediaries* since they are responsible for absorbing change and passing it on. Middle manager interpretation becomes critical. Their interpretation of what is needed underpins the changes they undertake personally, the changes they encourage their staff to undertake, and the changes they put in place in their departments. However, many of the activities they need to engage in to further their own understanding of what is required, such as networking and discussions with senior managers and peers, and the activities they need to engage in to help their staff, such as frequent communication, are invisible and an overhead to the business of keeping their departments going. As a result, middle managers can become overloaded. In turn, this leads to a lack of time for important, although less tangible, change-related activities, such as communication with staff, team building, counselling and coaching. Thus designers of change need to recognise the pivotal role middle managers play, and equip them with the necessary skills and support.

7.5.2 Middle managers: a two-headed Janus?

Given that the middle manager role is so critical in organisations at times of change, it is important to appreciate the impact of on-going organisational change on these individuals. Middle managers are often the shock absorbers of the emotional turbulence generated by senior management strategies for the people they manage. They also become buffers, shielding their teams from information and change pressures that are not essential for them to know. Moreover, as discussed above, middle managers are often as much the recipients of detrimental change as the implementers of change. Consequently, in times of adversity this two-headed Janus role of being the implementer of senior management plans, yet also the shock absorber for those they manage, requires middle managers to engage in 'emotional labour', to induce or suppress their own feelings in order to maintain the outward countenance that produces an appropriate state of mind in others.[12] (See Illustration 5.5, Chapter 5.) They become 'toxic handlers',[13] taking on the pain, frustration and bitterness of others.

The continual change in many organisations is leading to intensification of this emotional work for middle managers.[14] Furthermore, this emotional work has certain unique characteristics: it is unscripted, unsupported and unacknowledged. It is unscripted in the sense that managers are not told what to say, or how to look, as those more typically associated with emotional labour such as frontline service workers are (e.g., 'Have a nice day' as part of the McDonald's script). The work is unsupported because middle managers are neither fully in the organisational camp nor fully in the employee camp, a kind of hybrid with little support from those above or below or from peers, who are often competitors for territory.[15] The middle manager's emotional labour is also unacknowledged, simply because recognition of managers and emotional labour is low. Yet the widespread prevalence of emotion work can intensify managers' sense of loneliness and abandonment, which in turn can lead to disaffection and deidentification with the organisation among a group of employees critical to the organisation's capability to deliver on-going change.

7.6 CHANGE RECIPIENTS

Change recipients are those individuals on the receiving end of change, those that must adopt and adapt to change. Chapter 5 discusses the transition curve, and makes it clear that change is traumatic for everyone. As such, this text has already discussed some of the issues about recipients and change, and how managers need to help both their staff and themselves through the transition curve. This chapter has also discussed above (section 7.2.2) the need to change the way managers conceive of change recipients – the word 'recipient' in itself is misleading as it implies passivity and the ability to just 'place' change on those lower down in organisations, whereas recipients in fact create change. However, there are four other issues related to recipients that deserve mention – resistance to change, survivor syndrome, employee engagement and organisational justice.

7.6.1 Resistance to change

Resistance to change can develop at all levels of the organisation. Since change is an emotional process, resistance should be expected and seen as natural. The key is to help people through their resistance so that they can move on to accept the changes. The discussion of stakeholder mapping above (Figure 7.7) is in fact considering who will resist change and who won't. There are a number of different models, lists and categories of reasons why individuals are likely to resist change.[16] Figure 7.12 shows one such categorisation. Considering why people will resist change is a component of stakeholder analysis, since understanding why individuals are not positively disposed towards change is essential to devising strategies to overcome their negative reactions. However, for any change agent, there may be many different types of stakeholder analyses to carry out. An initial stakeholder analysis as described above in section 7.4.3 might focus on senior individuals from whom support is needed to get agreement to change taking place. Analysis of the way different recipient groups are likely to react may come later. In addition, analysis of recipient reactions is more likely to focus on groups of individuals, whereas analysis of senior individuals is more likely to focus on people individually.

Once potential areas of resistance have been identified, it is necessary to consider the appropriate tactics to overcome the resistance anticipated among the different stakeholders. Tactics include education and communication to overcome

| Figure 7.12 | Resistance to change |

Resistance may be due to:

- **Self-interest and politics**: Issues to do with personal loss and cost of undertaking personal change, such as loss of turf, loss of status, loss of promotional prospects, separation from long-standing colleagues, or may be even a less convenient journey to work.

- **Psychological reasons**: Issues such as fear of the unknown, fear of failure, concern about ability to develop needed skills, or a low ability to cope with change.

- **Emotional reasons**: May include lack of energy and motivation, denial of need for change, or demoralisation. Also uncertainty about impact of change on individuals, such as job security and earnings levels.

- **Change approach**: Lack of participation, involvement and communication.

- **Recipient perceptions**: To do with lack of understanding about why change is needed and its implications. May include different assessments about what should be done and the likely outcomes of proposed changes. A lack of trust may result from previous change experiences in which promises were not kept.

- **Cultural bias**: Entrenched ways of thinking, (selective perception), and 'we have always done it this way' attitudes and habits. Conflict between proposed changes and existing values and beliefs.

- **Historical organisational factors**: Traditional relationships between managers and the unions and the workforce, or traditions of rivalry between functions or departments.

negative recipient perceptions and emotional and psychological fears of change; participation and involvement to reduce resistance arising from the change approach and reduce concerns about the impact of change and the ability to cope; facilitation and support for those fearful of the impact of change; negotiation and agreement to help overcome self-interest-based resistance; manipulation and co-option; and implicit and explicit coercion.[17] Many of these tactics are similar to the range of change management styles discussed in Chapter 2 and relate to the tactics for developing readiness discussed in Chapter 5. The difference here is that the approach taken with one or two individuals to overcome their resistance may need to be different from the general approach taken with other employees.

A lack of readiness for change should not be confused with resistance. If people have been prepared for change, and understand what is expected of them, they are less likely to exhibit resistance. For the majority of staff, therefore, most effort in the early days of change should be devoted to strategies designed to create a readiness for change. However, there may be staff that will never be able to cope with the changes whatever assistance they get. Furthermore, much resistance will not be overt. Some staff will hide their resistance, and instead this resistance will manifest itself later in the change process by foot-dragging, or poor performance or productivity from the staff concerned. Therefore, some resistance will have to be tackled as and when it is encountered. Those that continue to resist change well into the move phase may be the staff the organisation should choose to let go. It may even be that the persistent resistors are the ones selected for redundancy, since this also sends symbolic messages.

7.6.2 Survivor syndrome

Another issue affecting change recipients is that of survivor syndrome. Following a change process in which there has been a loss of jobs and a change in working circumstances, those staff left often struggle to cope. Their feelings can lead to lower morale and therefore stress and lower staff performance if this issue is not tackled and managed. Illustration 7.2 discusses survivor syndrome in more detail. The notion of survivor syndrome also leads into issues of justice and fairness. Survivors are less likely to feel guilty about what has happened to their ex-colleagues and friends and less likely to experience fear about the future if they feel that those who have left were treated fairly and justly (see section 7.6.4 below).

7.6.3 Employee engagement

More recently, organisations have become concerned about employee engagement. This term is used to capture the notion that 'engaged' employees will feel more positive about their working life, which will have a positive effect on a variety of outcomes including individual and corporate performance and the organisation's ability to retain

Illustration 7.2   *change in action*

Survivor syndrome

Survivor syndrome describes the individual reactions to changes happening within organisations, often as a consequence of downsizing, reorganisation and restructuring. The emotional responses of survivors are not unlike those experiencing redundancy, and can range from shock, anger, and anxiety to animosity towards management. Survivors are often concerned and guilty about their colleagues who have been made redundant, but also relieved that they still have a job. Survivors can also experience fear about their future security. The reactions and behaviours of survivors after change are not only potentially detrimental to the individual, but may have a detrimental impact on organisational performance and adverse effects on bottom-line results.

Survivor syndrome is also characterised by a variety of behavioural outcomes:

Reaction or emotions	Behaviours
shock	decreased motivation
anger	decreased morale
scepticism	increased stress
guilt	increased work effort
fear	decreased work effort
insecurity	increased loyalty to peers
anxiety	focus on personal goals
excitement	career insecurity

These reactions are often precipitated by increased work pressure. Survivors may be expected to work harder, over longer hours, to fulfil the tasks of departed colleagues. Technological changes and business process re-engineering bring new working practices and different ways of working together. Job security often decreases after layoffs as employees may perceive the threat of additional cuts in the workforce. For many survivors this means a lack of clarity and mission, which feeds insecurity and uncertainty about future prospects within the company. Survivors also face the dismay of losing the peers who have formed the social fabric of their work life and often experience a loss of direction in their own career or future with the company. This can result in decreased confidence and commitment, and a lack of trust and loyalty to the organisation, while for others these circumstances may provide an exciting opportunity to forge a new role.

The extent to which remaining employees exhibit the 'symptoms' of survivor syndrome is mediated by both organisational and individual variables. These include the rationale for redundancy espoused by the company, the individual's position and role in the organisation, their attitudes towards work, their self-esteem and their personal coping mechanisms. The handling of redundancies is also an important factor. Survivors are concerned with the detail of the layoff procedure, for example, how the notice was communicated, what decision rule was used to choose people for redundancy, and whether good services were provided for those leaving – including severance pay, counselling and the continuation of benefits. Such factors influence the perceived fairness of the layoffs, the perceived threat of further redundancies and the ability to cope with change, which in turn determine how survivors react when colleagues leave.

Written by Noeleen Doherty. Extracted from Doherty, N. (1997) 'Downsizing in Tysons Ltd', in *The Practice of Human Resource Management,* Tyson, S. (ed) London: Pitman Publishing.

staff.[18] Employee engagement is concerned with the state of the organisational climate with or without change, but links to change management since a more engaged workforce will be better prepared to implement and experience change in a positive manner. In this sense employee engagement is strongly linked to the concept of 'readiness' (Chapter 3, section 3.9). It suggests that the higher the levels of employee engagement, the higher the levels of readiness for organisational change, since reactions will be more trusting and less negative, whereas in negative organisational climates, with disengaged employees, resistance to change may be related to employees expressing criticism of their experience of employment as a whole – they perhaps hate what has happened to the organisation in recent years, or how their jobs have changed. Their experience of earlier redundancy programmes may have left them with deep feelings of resentment, similar to those outlined in section 7.6.2 on survivor syndrome. If the organisation has not addressed the source of this negative feeling, then employees might find that one way of expressing their disgruntlement is to fight and resist all subsequent change programmes. Negative factors in the general organisational climate spill over and contaminate the change management process.

There are several different definitions of engagement but all agree that engagement operates on three levels: the physical, the cognitive and the emotional:[19]

- *Emotional:* being very involved with one's work.
- *Cognitive:* focusing very hard while at work.
- *Physical:* being willing to 'go the extra mile'.

An engaged employee brings all their energies into the job in a full and positive manner.[20] Disengagement is the withholding of energy, attention, focus or even knowledge – not giving the whole of one's self within the workplace environment. The reaction of the Pelican R&D scientists to corporate changes described in Illustration 3.8 in Chapter 3 was a type of disengagement. In an exhibition of their power, they withheld their knowledge from the company because they were angry with the way they were being treated by the corporate centre.

A further important characteristic of engagement is that it is the product of a reciprocal relationship between employer and employee.[21] Reciprocity captures the idea that employees, in exchange for their giving of their 'full selves' to the corporation, can expect something equivalent back from the employer. However, the old psychological contract of 'a job for life' in return for employees giving fully of themselves to their corporations has broken down, with 20 years of successive rounds of downsizing in large corporations, the decision by many organisations to shift manufacturing sites from the US and Europe into low-cost emerging economies, the continued practice of offshoring jobs and the frequent merger and acquisition activity with associated job losses.[22] Reduced expectations of reciprocity have led to a lessened commitment to the employer and a consequent reduced engagement with all things work related for managerial and non-managerial staff in many organisations.

Different companies use different scales and surveys for *measuring* levels of employee engagement but most incorporate some or all of these themes: pride and satisfaction in the employer; job satisfaction; opportunities to perform well at challenging work; recognition and positive feedback for contribution; support from supervisors; effort beyond and above the minimum; understanding the link between one's job and the organisation's mission; and the prospects for future growth and therefore the intention to stay with one's employer. Certain key drivers of employee engagement have also been isolated. See Figure 7.13. Whilst the outcomes of increased performance and retention of staff may be universal, it is accepted that the five drivers that create engagement – opportunities for upward feedback, feeling informed, managerial commitment, managerial fairness and respectful treatment – are context-specific: the exact weighting of the different drivers may vary by industry, by geographic location or by different demographic groupings.[23] Just as change design needs to meet the needs of the specific context, so too does employee engagement.

What is striking about these five drivers is that many of them would be associated with good change management practice, and reflect issues already discussed in this book. The drivers of 'feeling informed about what is going on' and 'opportunities for upward feedback' are concerned with making sure that effective communication is used throughout the organisation and are explored in Chapter 6. The driver of 'managerial commitment to the organisation' has, in part, been discussed above when considering the role of *middle managers* in change. The two drivers that have not been covered explicitly so far in this

Figure 7.13   **Engagement, performance and retention**

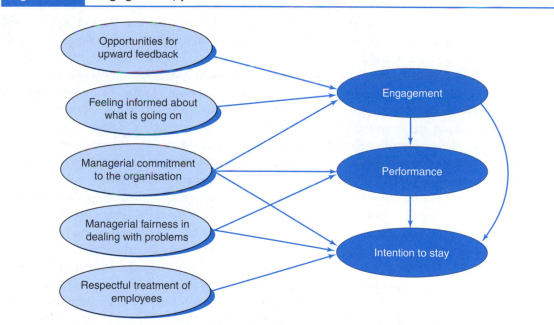

Source: CIPD. (2006) "How engaged are British Employees?", Truss, K., Soame, E. and Edwards, C. Survey Report. The Chartered Institute of Personnel and Development.

book are 'managerial fairness in dealing with problems' and 'respectful treatment of employees'. These are important concepts encapsulated within the ideas of organisational justice and fairness.

7.6.4 Organisational justice

As with the broader concept of engagement, when organisations change, the extent to which employees perceive as 'fair' and 'just' what happens during change in terms of, for example, who stays and who goes, who gets what job, how they are rewarded and appraised affects their emotional reactions to the change process and therefore their levels of commitment to and trust of their organisation.[24] There are three factors that affect employees:

- *Distributive justice:* perceptions of the outcomes arrived at.
- *Procedural justice:* perceptions of the processes used to deliver the outcomes.
- *Interactional justice:* perceptions of the actions of the persons delivering the process.

A good example to illustrate these three aspects of justice and fairness is the process of downsizing and reallocation of work roles and responsibilities that accompany many change processes, such as the redundancies under Ghosn at Nissan (see Chapter 5, Illustration 5.9). In such a downsizing exercise, *procedural* justice would be about the processes used to decide who stays, who goes, and how roles are reallocated. Are the criteria used to determine who goes and who stays transparent and consistently applied? Or is there evidence of bias in the process? Similarly for role reallocation, are the criteria clear, with everyone given equal opportunity to apply for the roles they would like and clear decision processes consistently applied? In addition, do the procedures used recognise and allow the idea of employee voice – the idea that lower levels can air their views and opinions and be heard? Employee voice has been found to be one of the key determinants of fairness and justice in change scenarios.[25] *Distributive* justice would be about the outcomes achieved. Do the employees believe that what has happened to them is fair in comparison to what has happened to their other colleagues, for example? Finally, *interactional* justice is about how employees feel they were treated during the process by their line managers, or whoever was making the decisions. It is about the interpersonal treatment they receive and the extent to which they are treated with dignity and respect.

The experience of the local authority NewCounty described in Illustration 7.3 shows how an organisation going through a substantial change process can maintain perceptions of high levels of justice and fairness amongst its employees through consideration of the factors affecting procedural, distributive and interactional justice. However, it also highlights the important role of line managers in the process.

The overall message from work such as that on survivor syndrome, engagement and justice is that unless the human factor in change is recognised, and managed

Illustration 7.3

Reactions to change at NewCounty

NewCounty came into existence on 1 April 1998, as part of the local government reorganisation in England and Wales. Its formation involved the division of the previous county and district councils into two new and separate groupings, consisting of a unitary authority and a new county council with district councils. Within this structure, NewCounty was the new county council responsible for provision of education, caring services, police, traffic, road building and maintenance, libraries and strategic planning. Its creation involved significant change, altering the geographical area served and introducing new organisational structures based upon five Directorates.

Prior to the creation of NewCounty, formal communication channels had been set up to keep the previous county council's employees informed of progress. This included team briefings and a weekly newsletter along with an online facility to allow employees to seek answers to questions. The timetable for filling posts in NewCounty's structure was published in October 1997, with a target of all posts being filled by Christmas 1997. Posts were filled starting with the top tier of management and working down. An agreement was reached with the Trade Union that salaries of transferred employees would be protected for three years.

Employees who were positive about the changes felt they had been offered the scope to be involved as part of the process, and this was particularly apparent with regard to allocations of individuals to posts and led to a general perception of procedural fairness at the time of NewCounty's creation. Positive employees' perceived involvement in the change process contrasted markedly with employees who felt negative. These employees argued that the procedures, whilst fair, had been reactive rather than proactive and that they were powerless throughout the change process.

Although employees were not necessarily involved in the actual management of the changes themselves, their feelings about the changes were influenced strongly by social aspects of their treatment and the support and respect they received from senior managers. Those who felt positive were more likely to perceive their interactions with senior management as two-way, whereas those who felt negative were less likely to do so. Employees who felt positive about changes were likely to feel they had been listened to and treated with dignity and respect. The newsletter was highlighted by employees as an important source of information, together with explanations about what was happening during the creation of NewCounty. Subsequently, other forms of communication, in particular two-way, increased in importance. Employees who felt negative were likely to be cynical about the use of communication. In particular, they felt that the communication only gave positive messages, spending little time on problems or mistakes.

Interactions between line managers and those they managed appeared to be important in relation to the generation of perceptions of fairness of interpersonal treatment. Employees who felt positive about change when NewCounty was created felt that their line managers had treated them with dignity and sensitivity. In contrast, the majority of those respondents who felt negative regarding changes felt they had been treated with a lack of social sensitivity.

Written by Mark N.K. Saunders from: Saunders M.N.K., Thornhill, A. and Lewis P. (2002) 'Understanding employees' reactions to the management of change: an exploration through an organisational justice framework', *Irish Journal of Management,* 23 (1), pp. 85–108 and Thornhill, A. and Saunders, M.N.K. (2003) 'Exploring employees' reactions to strategic change over time: the utilisation of an organisational justice perspective', *Irish Journal of Management,* 24 (1), pp. 66–86.

appropriately and sympathetically, the reactions of the employees, on whom the organisation ultimately depends for its performance, can nullify the effects of change, leading to poorer organisational results and profits than anticipated following change. Human process interventions – such as team-building activities to facilitate open communication and rebuild trust, morale and commitment; counselling and support to facilitate the personal change required; and stress management to manage work role conflict, feelings of job insecurity, and role and career confusion – can be critical. So can other interventions which facilitate communication and involve employees in the change process to provide more information to survivors about how the change process has been managed and their future role within the company.

7.7 SUMMARY

This chapter completes the discussion of the design and management of the transition state. It highlights the need to pay attention to the human agenda in change, with an emphasis on:

- The nature of the transition state and the particular demands this places on those leading change, which in turn has implications for transition management and monitoring and measuring mechanisms.

- The skills required of change agents, with a particular focus on the need for political judgement, and the importance of being able to understand the power, influence and trust relationships within an organisation.

- The middle manager and recipient roles in change, to highlight the importance and complexity of the middle manager role.

- Issues to do with the general organisational climate and its impact on change, and specifically the concepts of survivor syndrome, employee engagement and organisational justice.

This chapter reinforces the importance of individuals having skills in reading context and the contextual judgement to be effective during change. Change agents need to not only be able to read the political landscape of their organisation, but also be able to consider what they carry into any particular situation, to be able to maximise their ability to influence those around them and build support for their change interventions. This theme is taken up in the final chapter of this book.

REFERENCES

1. See Goffee, R. and Jones, G. (2007) *Why Should Anyone Be Led by You?*, Harvard Business School Press, for an extended discussion of the need for leaders to be able to read their organisation's context and to know how to change it to support their intended change initiatives.
2. For more on the role of middle managers during change implementation, see Balogun, J. and Johnson, G. (2004) 'Organizational restructuring and middle manager sensemaking', *Academy of Management Journal*, 47 (4), pp. 523–49, and Balogun, J. and Johnson, G.

(2005) 'From intended strategy to unintended outcomes: the impact of change recipient sensemaking', *Organization Studies,* 26 (11), pp. 1573–602.

3. For more information on the balanced scorecard see three *Harvard Business Review* articles by Kaplan, R.S. and Norton, D.P.: (1992) 'The balanced scorecard: measures that drive performance', 70 (1), pp. 71–9; (1993) 'Putting the balanced scorecard to work', 71 (5), pp. 134–47; (1996) 'Using the balanced scorecard as a strategic management system', 74 (1), pp. 75–85. For further information on other business performance management techniques, see Neely, A.D. (2002) *Measuring Business Performance: Why, What, How,* 2nd edn, London: Economist Books.

4. See Buchanan, D. and Boddy, D. (1992) *The Expertise of the Change Agent: Public Performance and Backstage Activity,* London: Prentice Hall.

5. See Balogun, J., Gleadle, P., Hope Hailey, V. and Willmott, H. (2005) 'Managing change across boundaries: boundary shaking practices', *British Journal of Management,* 16, pp. 261–78.

6. See references 4 and 5 above.

7. Hardy uses Lukes to develop the concepts of resource power, process power and the power of meaning or symbolic power. See Hardy, C. (1994) *Managing Strategic Action: Mobilizing Change – Concepts, Readings and Cases,* London: Sage, and Hardy, C. (1996) 'Understanding power: bringing about strategic change', *British Journal of Management,* 7, Special Issue: S3–S16.

8. For a discussion of social network analysis and sociograms, see Wasserman, S. and Faust, K. (1994) *Social Network Analysis,* Cambridge: Cambridge University Press.

9. See James, K. and Arroba, T. (2005) 'Reading and carrying', *Management Learning,* 36 (3), pp. 299–316.

10. See, for example, Guth, W.D. and MacMillan, I.C. (1986) 'Strategy implementation versus middle management self-interest', *Strategic Management Journal,* 7 (4), pp. 313–27. Also see Balogun, J. (2006) 'Managing change: steering a course between intended strategies and unanticipated outcomes', *Long Range Planning,* 39 (1), pp. 29–49.

11. The various roles that middle managers can play in change and the implications of this for the middle manager skill set and job roles are discussed briefly in Floyd, S.W. and Wooldridge, B. (1994) 'Dinosaurs or dynamos? recognizing middle management's strategic role', *Academy of Management Executive,* 8 (4), pp. 47–57. For more detail see Floyd, S.W. and Wooldridge, B. (1986) *The Strategic Middle Manager: How to Create and Sustain Competitive Advantage,* San Francisco: Jossey-Bass.

12. For a more detailed explanation of emotional labour, see Hochschild, A.R (1983) *The Managed Heart: Commercialisation of Human Feeling,* London: University of California Press. For more on middle managers and emotion, see Huy, Q.N. (2002) 'Emotional balancing of organizational continuity and radical change: the contribution of middle managers'. *Administrative Science Quarterly,* 47, pp. 31–69.

13. For a more detailed consideration of toxic handlers, see Frost, P. and Robinson, S (1999) 'The toxic handler: organizational hero – and casualty', *Harvard Business Review.*

14. See Moore, C. (2003) 'Individuals and Continuous Change: Developing Change Capability', Change Management Consortium Report on Individuals and Continuous Change, Cranfield Business School. Also Clarke, C., Hope-Hailey, V. and Kelliher, C. (2007) 'Being real or really being someone else? Managers and emotion work', *European Management Journal,* 25 (2), pp. 92–103.

15. Sims, D. (2003). 'Between the millstones: A narrative account of the vulnerability of middle managers storying', *Human Relations,* 56; pp. 1195–1211.

16. For one categorisation of reasons individuals are likely to resist change, and the categorisation of tactics for overcoming resistance used here, see Kotter, J.P. and Schlesinger, L.A. (1979) 'Choosing strategies for change', *Harvard Business Review,* 57 (2), pp. 106–14.

17. A simple technique for helping to clarify what resistance management strategies to deploy for which stakeholders is to use the concept of a commitment chart. See Beckhard, R. and Harris, R.T. (1987) *Organizational Transitions,* 2nd edn, Reading, MA: Addison-Wesley.

18. See Truss, K., Soane, E. and Edwards, C. (2006) 'Working Life: Employee Attitudes and Engagement 2006', Chartered Institute of Personnel and Development, UK. Also Vance, R.J. (2006) 'Employee Engagement and Commitment', Society for Human Resource Management, USA.

19. For various definitions see 'Driving performance and retention through employee engagement'. (2004) Survey Report. Washington DC: Corporate Leadership Council; Konrad, A.M. (2006) 'Engaging employees through high involvement work practices', Ivey Business Journal Online; and Truss, Soane, E. and Edwards, C. (2006) 'Working Life: Employee Attitudes and Engagement 2006', Chartered Institute of Personnel and Development, UK.

20. See Kahn, W.A. (1990) 'Psychological conditions of personal engagement at work', *Academy of Management Review,* 33, pp. 692–724.

21. For a fuller explanation of the idea of reciprocity, see Robinson, D., Perryman, S. and Hayday, S. (2004) 'The drivers of employee engagement'. Research Report: Institute of Employment Studies, UK.

22. See Rousseau, D. (2004) 'Psychological contracts in the workplace – a research brief', *Academy of Management Executive,* 18 (1).

23. See reference 21 above. Also see Farndale, E. and Hope Hailey, V. (22 June 2007) 'Trust during times of turbulent change – the experience of the Change Management Consortium'. Presented at the ESRC Seminar Series on Trust. Oxford Brookes University.

24. For a more extensive discussion on organisational justice and fairness, see Colquitt, J.A. et al. (2001) 'Justice at the millennium: a meta-analysis of 25 years of organizational justice research', *Journal of Applied Psychology*, 86, pp. 425–45.

25. See Farndale, E., Hope Hailey, V. and Kelliher, C. (2006) 'Opening the Black Box in HRM and Firm Performance: Trust as a Mediator of Employee Commitment'. Paper delivered at the Academy of Management Conference, US.

WORK ASSIGNMENTS

7.1 Consider a change process you have been through. What were the unexpected outcomes and why did they occur? How could they have been avoided?

7.2 Using Figure 7.4 consider the pros and cons of the different monitoring mechanisms.

7.3 Using the Bayer case study from Chapter 4, if you were Chris Tobin, what change outcomes would you have identified at the beginning of the change?

7.4 Draw up a job description/personal specification for the recruitment and selection of a change agent for a major change project.

7.5 Use the fox, donkey, sheep, and owl model to consider how effective you are likely to be as a change agent.

7.6 Using a context with which you are familiar, conduct a stakeholder analysis and a sociogram analysis with relation to a change that is needed and consider what it tells you about leading change in this context.

7.7 Consider Illustration 5.9 in Chapter 5. What types of resistance did Ghosn probably encounter and why when making changes at Nissan?

7.8 Consider a situation when you have had to undertake change. Why did you feel the process was fair or unfair? How could it have been managed better?

Concluding comments

8.1 INTRODUCTION

This text argues that successful change is reliant on the development of a context-sensitive approach to change. A diagnostic framework, the change kaleidoscope, is presented, which facilitates context sensitivity in design. The kaleidoscope enables change agents to assess the change context in which they are operating, judge which are the key contextual features of this context, and therefore make appropriate design decisions to create a context-sensitive change approach. This chapter summarises the main arguments put forward for the use of the kaleidoscope by revisiting the change flow chart presented in Chapter 1. It also discusses the future challenges of change, with reference to the need for skilled leaders of change, and change agents in general, to develop capabilities around reading and rewriting their change context using frameworks such as the kaleidoscope to enable the embedding of the changes they wish to implement.

8.2 THE CHANGE FLOW CHART

Chapter 1 presents a change flow chart (see Figure 8.1) to explain the different stages in the development of a context-sensitive approach to change. As Chapter 1 explains, stages 1 and 2, analysing the competitive position to determine the type of change needed and identifying the desired future state, are discussed in detail in this book's sister text, *Exploring Corporate Strategy,* and are not discussed here. However, the design of the future state is revisited in Chapter 5 to reinforce the need for a vision, and the need to identify and remove barriers to change.

Stages 3 and 4, analysing the change context to identify the critical contextual features and identifying the change approach through determining the appropriate design choices, form the first part of this book and use the change kaleidoscope. (See Figure 8.2.) Chapter 2 examines the choices that a change agent must make when designing a change process captured in the centre of the kaleidoscope. The choices include the *change path,* the *change start-point,* the *change style,* the *change target,*

| Figure 8.1 | The change flow chart |

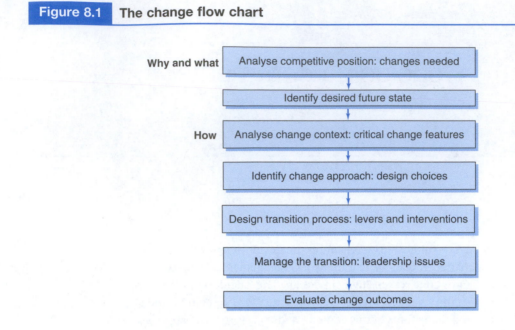

the range of *change levers* and the *change roles*. However, the key argument in Chapter 2 is that it is impossible to choose from this menu of choices without understanding the context of the organisation. The change context and how to assess it is therefore examined in detail in Chapters 3 and 4.

Chapters 3 and 4 examine the change context through the middle ring of the change kaleidoscope, the contextual features. The concept captured within the kaleidoscope is that every organisational change is unique. Therefore, in each change situation the configuration of contextual features will also be unique, like an individual's fingerprints. However, there are questions which remain constant that can be asked about any change context. These questions include the amount of *time* available for change, the *scope* of the change required, the degree of *diversity* within the organisation, the staff's *readiness* for change, the *capability* and *capacity* to undertake change within the organisation, the *power* relations and what needs to be *preserved* within the organisation. Chapter 3 explores each of these contextual features in detail, and examines the implications for the design choices of each feature. Chapter 4 puts the change kaleidoscope into practice and introduces the concept of change judgement. Three case studies of companies undergoing different forms of change are analysed to show how an understanding of context can be used to help a change agent exercise judgement about the critical features of their particular change context and from this develop an appropriate change design. Chapter 4 also illustrates the criticality of *different* contextual features in *different* change situations.

Chapters 5, 6 and 7 consider the design, implementation and management of the transition phase of change – the final stages in the change flow chart. Too often

Figure 8.2 The change kaleidoscope

change management stops after the design choices have been made or, worse still, at the point of strategy development. These three chapters reveal the complexity of change management in action. They illustrate to the reader the different stages of transition, and the relationship between organisational transitions and the personal transitions of individuals. They also describe the different levers and interventions that can be used to support each stage of transition, and consider the issues involved in managing a change process once implementation is underway.

8.3 RESPONDING TO THE COMPLEXITY OF CHANGE: READING AND REWRITING THE CONTEXT

A recurrent theme throughout the writing of this third edition of this book has been the practice of reading but also rewriting organisational contexts in order to make them more receptive to change. Capabilities in reading and rewriting contexts are increasingly recognised as critical leadership competences.[1]

8.3.1 Reading context: there are no universals

As change becomes more complex, leaders need to be able to observe, analyse and diagnose their particular context of action. This art of 'situation sensing' requires leaders to develop behaviours that allow them to adapt to any organisation, workplace and situation in order that they may closely observe what's going on amongst different stakeholder groups, for example, or exactly what is happening in senior management meetings or within different divisions or international operations. In addition, as this book has stressed in Chapter 1, leaders who are truly change competent need to be able to analyse what they see and hear to come up with some form of diagnosis. Change-sensitive leaders also deploy some form of reality check to ensure that they are not losing touch with the organisational experience for customers or employees. Some change leaders use surprise visits to local stores or factories as a way of keeping up to date with the day-to-day operations of their organisation. They want to gauge whether morale is low or, conversely, whether complacency is high. They want to understand whether the different parts of the organisation have unique needs or whether the way that employees are experiencing change is a fairly common and similar experience.[2]

Key to gathering information about what is happening are change agent competencies such as those detailed in Chapter 7, including having the 'common touch': the ability to communicate with people at all levels within the organisation. If a change leader can only converse with a small group of people close to them, then they may gather only a very partial view of their organisation. Close analysis of employee attitude and customer surveys serves a similar purpose for change leaders. Goffee and Jones call all of this activity 'senses working overtime'![3] Other leaders of change invite academics to conduct research on change within their organisations, using the reports produced[4] as an independent and objective reality check for themselves. Many of the models and frameworks presented in this book, including the cultural web, the change kaleidoscope and the transition models, can help managers to do that for themselves.

The models presented in this third edition of *Exploring Strategic Change* therefore seek to provide universally applicable questions, not answers. They ask questions about the features of change contexts that, if ignored by change agents, may become barriers to change in the longer term. Readers may like to see the models as mapping devices which help to hone their judgement in change situations. They are not predictive. They cannot take the place of judgement – but their purpose is to inform that judgement. Furthermore, the models have their limitations. They are not dynamic and organisations may need to use them in an iterative way. In addition, they can only capture the complexity of change if the reader grasps the way the contextual features of any change situation interconnect, and the uniqueness of these interconnections within each new change scenario.

8.3.2 Rewriting context

However, it is not enough to simply analyse change – one must also take action. This book has tried to honour the idea of management as both an intellectual and an analytical pursuit, but simultaneously present it as an activity that is practical and requires action. In particular, it shows how the idea of 'rewriting the context' can be used as part of managing change. There are two ways of rewriting the context. One way is to address strategic change as a phased process just like the change path talked about in Chapter 2. Change leaders may use the first phase of change to reshape the context so that it is more receptive to the ultimate change they are planning. Chapter 4 presents an example of this. Scienceco recognised that they needed to increase the number of supervisors on their shop floor and the capability of those supervisors and the first line managers to implement change. Through recruiting additional supervisors and running training courses for their managers, they rewrote the organisational context such that it was more receptive to the changes they were planning.

A second way of rewriting the context is for change leaders or change agents to use their own leadership behaviour to transform rather than react to a context. Stories of successful change are full of leaders who use their own behaviour to construct a new social reality, a new paradigm and a new mind-set. Their own behaviours become a form of symbolic vision for the organisation. Illustration 6.4 in Chapter 6, which describes how the new Dean of Crummer Graduate School implemented change, is an example of this. The Tarmac case study in Chapter 4 recounts how the CEO's challenge to a haulage contractor in one of their quarries contributed to reshaping the cultural norms and values of that organisation. Similarly, Illustration 5.9 in Chapter 5 describes how the leadership actions of Carlos Ghosn contributed to the turnaround at Nissan. Reshaping organisational contexts needs to be a 'hands-on' management activity for change leaders.

8.4 IN SUMMARY

The ability to manage change is fast becoming a mainstream competence for leaders and managers. It is no longer an optional extra in the managerial toolkit. This is driven by the pace and nature of organisational change, rather than by any fashion pushed by business schools or consultancies. The pace and nature of change is also determining the composition of change competence. Change is so rapid and so constant that it is rendering obsolete universalistic formulae to many management problems. Best questions, rather than best practice, become the key tool. The intent of this book is to arm managers and future managers with some of these best questions and the knowledge of how to answer them.

REFERENCES

1. See Goffee, R. and Jones, G. (2007) *Why Should Anyone Be Led by You?*, Harvard Business School Press.
2. Ibid.
3. Ibid.
4. See the website *www.cass.city.ac.uk/cllc/cmc/index.html for examples of commissioned research reports by the authors of* Exploring Strategic Change.

BCP Aerospace

Julia Balogun, Caroline Clarke and Veronica Hope Hailey

This case describes how BCP Aerospace initiated and implemented change at one of their heritage aerospace sites. It can be used to help students and other readers of the book deepen their understanding of how to implement major organisational transitions. Assignment questions are at the end of the case.

BCP is a focused global engineering organisation, with a turnover of more than £4 billion. Founded in 1759, it employs 38,000 people worldwide and has 30 production facilities across Japan, the Asia-Pacific region, India, South Africa, Europe and the Americas. BCP is involved in the design, development and manufacture of automotive systems and aerospace and defence products, and also provides other industrial services. This case study relates to the aerospace division of BCP, and focuses on the site located at Attcel on an island off the coast of the UK and the changes that occurred there between December 2001 and 2004.

THE AEROSPACE INDUSTRY

The characteristics of the general aerospace industry are quite specific: civil and defence are closely intertwined; the industry has a highly cyclical nature;[1] returns are inherently long term and high risk; and at least 50 per cent of turnover resides within the US. The UK aerospace industry is therefore small compared to that of the USA, although the UK has historically held a good record for quality manufacturing and innovative engineering design (e.g., Rolls-Royce).

The market for civil aircraft began to take an economic downward turn in the year 2001, a trend that was further exacerbated by the events that took place on 11 September of that year. A further blow to the industry was the spread of the SARS

---

[1]The cyclical nature is dependent on investment decisions of airlines and the fluctuating patterns of defence programmes.

virus and the Iraqi war, both of which contributed to a sharp decrease in air travel, and consequently the demand for new civil aircraft. Air traffic in 2001 'eroded significantly and carriers had to reduce capacity by grounding aircraft' (AECMA, 2001:7). Excess aircraft were 'mothballed' and left to sit in the desert unused, and this excess meant that there were no orders for new aircraft. Furthermore, it was predicted that the demand for civilian air travel was unlikely to recover until 2003, and a restored demand for new aircraft was not predicted to filter through until 2004/2005 (AECMA, 2002). The industry's context and general downturn were therefore major factors driving change within the aerospace division. Even prior to the events of 9/11, plans were underway at Attcel for restructuring to handle the reductions in work volume and generally to introduce greater efficiency into the business, but 9/11 brought the need for change forward – and on a more dramatic scale than previously anticipated:

> *The relative demise of the civil aerospace market was predicted before nine eleven but nine eleven certainly hastened the process with the net effect that about half of the activity on the island stopped overnight. Building of regional aircraft just stopped.* (Senior Manager, BCP)

The other factor driving change was the need to make a more 'homogeneous whole' of the aerospace business: to run it more efficiently and to exploit synergies between the various businesses. As a result, in the two years prior to the end of 2001 and the start of the changes at Attcel, the aerospace division was being restructured from a federation of small, autonomous, stand-alone businesses, into an integrated European business managed through a matrix structure. The P&L was now aggregated at a European level and there was a European management team. European functions were being developed and local functional managers were to report into European Directors, with maybe only a dotted-line reporting relationship to a local general manager. So, for example, there was a European sales and marketing director as opposed to a sales and marketing director in each of the businesses. The individual businesses were now, therefore, less autonomous.

THE ATTCEL COMMUNITY

The island traditionally thought of itself as relatively invulnerable:

> *There was always a steady supply of work coming in and they were good at what they did and fairly traditional in the way that they did it with a fairly insular view of the world.* (Senior Manager, BCP)

The previous Chief Executive of Aerospace was born on the island and went on to work there. This had 'huge symbolic value to the rest of the business. As long as he was there in HQ, with his office on the waterfront, everybody felt pretty safe.' However, when the aerospace division head office and decision making moved off the island in 1998 as part of the creation of a European Aerospace division, 'some guy they had never seen before was calling the shots' (Senior Manager, BCP). Thus for those on the island, the relocation was associated with a perceived loss of power and ability to shape their own futures. The viability and long-term security of the site was rocked. Whilst it was not realised in the early stages of the changes by those working on the island, the creation of the European Aerospace division was in fact changing the status of the island. The island was no longer aerospace; they were instead now part of a bigger European Aerospace division:

> *The key for this period is that business moved from being a fairly parochial aerospace business with its headquarters on the island to it becoming an increasingly intercontinental business, with its headquarters actually close to a major airport so that people could travel. Consequently the island moved from having the Managing Director and his entire team to a manufacturing unit within a much larger organisation. So they (the island workforce) may have seen it as a downgrading, but actually we were leaving a manufacturing organisation . . . but the centre of the business moved elsewhere.* (Senior Manager, BCP)

The site is hugely impacted by its island location. The presence of the Aerospace headquarters on the island site had given the workforce an illusion of invulnerability and enabled the island workforce to remain fairly insular. Most managers, for example, had only ever worked at this site. Ninety-five per cent of those who worked there were 'islanders', and the majority had worked there all their working lives ('man and boy'), with a typical service record of 20 years. The surrounding community was tight-knit. Workers were often relatives (fathers, sons and brothers), neighbours or friends. The community was heavily entwined with the organisation, and so therefore was its fate:

> *If BCP sneezes the island catches a cold.* (Site Manager)

The culture could therefore be described as paternalistic, if not nepotistic. The heritage and history associated with working on this site had concerned the cultivation of employees (apprenticeships for sons), the nurturing of family relationships (family firework evenings), intimacy, loyalty, symbolism and status. There had been an implicit message of jobs for life, together with a career path designed for both 'man and boy':

> *it was very much a sort of family firm I thought when I joined, it was everyone knew somebody and everybody knew your dad or your brother or your uncle whatever you know and that was pretty much how it seemed to sort of rumble along for a number of years. . .* (Supervisor)

BCP is a prestigious employer to have on the island, and its retention has implications in terms of finance, heritage and status. Alternative employment opportunities on the island are few, especially at management level. To 'commute' to the mainland is seen as a big step in terms of time and money, but also emotionally. Those who work and live on the island do so because they believe it is a good place to reside, and nationally, prescribed BCP wages together with a lower cost of living affords them a good lifestyle.

This heritage had two implications. First, those working on the island saw the changes personally as opposed to part of a bigger picture affecting the whole Aerospace division:

> So I think whilst in the context of Attcel, maybe because it's a tight knit community, this action may have been perceived as some sort of uniquely occurring event that affected them, but actually wasn't.
>
> (Senior Manager, BCP)

Secondly, the senior managers within BCP generally and the Aerospace division specifically were acutely aware of the social issues their plans for the island site raised and the need to handle planned redundancies in a socially responsible manner to minimise the impact on the local economy:

> what was happening, in my view, was done quite professionally by a group of people who were dedicated to maintaining as much employment as they could for people in the business. They just didn't do it willy-nilly, there was an awful lot of thought put into it.   (HR Director)

As a result there were two aspects to the change plan: the social aspect of how to help those who were to be made redundant; and the business aspect of how to develop the business with those who were left.

RINGING THE CHANGES IN 2001 – PHASE 1, 'DOOM AND GLOOM'

Turnaround for survival: downsizing and cost cutting

As orders and projects associated with the building of new aircraft were cancelled, it became evident that for the island to survive, a turnaround was needed. There was a need to strip out costs and overheads from the business, since the site had suffered heavy losses for some time, and the largest cost to the business was an idle workforce. The workforce was told that the changes were about making sure there was a healthy business for the future, though some interpreted this as meaning that if the site could not return a profit in two to three years, then it would close.

On 13 December 2001 the site manager and the CEO of Aerospace called together the workforce to let them know that for 650 people (nearly half the workforce), their jobs were 'at risk'. The presentation explained the changing aerospace industry context, and the implications for the site in terms of the reduction of work orders. Whilst messages about the future were included – such as details about new work and opportunities, the intention to retain core competencies in areas such as engineering, and the development of new investments to ensure the site was well placed to grow again, once the aerospace industry improved – the presentation's main message was that 50 per cent of the workforce needed to be let go over the next year in order to align the workforce with the new lower level of work and the exit from certain business sectors. In addition, the north manufacturing site was to close and be sold off, with the manufacturing business consolidated onto the remaining south site. However, investment was also to be made in a third, smaller site on the island to develop an engineering centre of excellence for BCP Aerospace. The redundancy process – which included consultation, consideration of early retirement, and redeployment within the BCP group – was described. Support for those made redundant was also discussed, including counselling; access to financial consultants, pension seminars, recruitment consultants and job search agencies; and paid time off for job interviews.

For the senior managers involved in the restructuring, behind these announcements was extensive consultation. They recognised the significant implications for the island, as BCP was a major employer. A lot of time was devoted to talking to bodies such as the Training and Enterprise Council to determine how best to handle the large numbers of people that needed to be made redundant. In addition, there was consultation with other interested stakeholder groups, such as the unions and also local MPs. As a result, for senior managers, the application of best practice approaches had lead to a relatively smooth process:

it has actually been done from an employer relations perspective very professionally and is actually resulted in very little disruption. We have not had strikes and we have not had loads of tribunals and the actual process has actually gone quite well.

The reaction from the workforce was principally one of shock:

well you know we all got taken up to the gym and it was like a mass gassing . . . just shut the door and turn the taps on....and it was economic this and economic that and this works stopped and dar, dar, dar. (Supervisor)

The list comprising those who retained their jobs and those who were 'at risk' was not finalised and released until two months later on 14 February 2002, an event dubbed by some as 'the St Valentine's day massacre':

That was a day and a half, that was St. Valentine's day, it was horrible . . . I was worried sick I'm going to admit it, I just wanted to get into work and get it over and done with. (Supervisor)

I was worried I was going to lose my job . . . it is in the back of your mind that you are making a decision on blokes and you know at the same time that someone is making a decision on you. (Manager)

Shortly after the redundancies were announced, the first employees began to leave the site (at the end of March 2002). The process left little space for the feelings of either those who had been made redundant or those who had to carry out the redundancies. Thus despite a recognition of this issue – *'it was clear that there was not enough work and if there was not enough work there was only one thing you could do'* – managers and employees alike were critical of the way the redundancies were managed:

> *it was 'we've got a problem, we've got a job to do, let's get on and do it'. It was perceived to be far more ruthless than perhaps it needed to be.*
>
> (Manager)

For those (i.e., the managers) who had to make a decision on who was to stay and who was to go, the long-standing and highly intense nature of the relationships made the process extremely onerous. By definition, this organisation was one which was populated with intimate, close and established relationships, the termination of which was particularly difficult:

> *It was a complete emotional rollercoaster.* (Manager)

> *It's an awful task and that's one of the things that does wake me up at night, I have lived and died for these people, I think the world of them.*
>
> (Manager)

However, even if the employees were unaware of it, what was happening was simply a reflection of what was happening elsewhere within BCP and not just within the Aerospace division:

> *if you were to look at a site like XXX it has also gone through some major, major structural change over the last four or five years which includes divesting part of the business and closing parts of the business and downsizing parts of the business and sort of saying that we do not know where the orders are coming from next week but providing we have still got some you have still got jobs boys. For the island to think that it is experiencing this kind of major structural change in isolation would be entirely wrong.* (Senior Manager, BCP)

After shock: building a future

Following the initial tranche of 650 redundancies, the organisation was forced to make a further 100 redundancies some months later in order to meet the projected cost savings. The reaction of the employees to the redundancies, and to the potential threat of further redundancies, showed how the environment had been transformed from one of complacency to one characterised by feelings of uncertainty and insecurity:

> *working in the shop it's like waiting to be hanged, waiting for the execution . . . they know it's coming, no one brings it up at the moment they won't talk about it.* (Manager)

I think now people are still nervous and looking over their shoulder and I think that they do not believe that it has actually finished in terms of those that would have to go.   (Supervisor)

In the immediate aftermath of the downsizing, the organisation's message was consistent and insistent: if the site returned a profit, then it would stay open. The talk of profit was in itself a change. Until very recently the site had operated within a paradigm of turnover, rather than one of profit: 'turnover was king'. Therefore, the route to profitability was not a clear one for everybody. Many people, particularly those below management level, reported a perceived inevitability about the closure of the site, and those who had 'survived' were ambivalent about their own fate. On one hand there was a feeling of relief that they had retained their role, and yet the departure of close colleagues together with the practical consequences of this event had produced a detrimental effect on employees:

There wasn't any [support] for people who were left behind. I know that certainly on some occasions we joked and talked about it but there were a lot of people saying that they would almost have preferred to be booted out than being the people that were left behind. We had to deal with not only the practical side of picking up the pieces but seeing so many friends and colleagues disappear so quickly.   (Supervisor)

There was a sense that the site had changed in a way that would never be reversed, and many employees commented on how 'things would never be the same again'. The unquestioned loyalty and pride in the organisation had been altered for many: the downsizing was seen as an act of betrayal. During this period there were no apprenticeships offered, and succession planning was absent. The remaining workforce consisted of an aging and static population.

However, messages about the future had been communicated. Communication was a priority for the new general manager, Brian, when he was appointed in early December 2001, which is why he worked with the Aerospace Chief Executive to deliver the face-to-face meeting to announce the redundancies on 13 December 2001:

One of the first things I did was produce a presentation and took the site off-site – in two halves because of the size of the population. We did one at Christmas which said unfortunately this is the state of the business so we will have to have redundancies. Then in April I did another which said about growing the business, by then the majority of people had left the business. I do think the one in April had quite a strong effect on the workforce here because first I stood up and talked to them, second I told them what I really wanted. I told them I wanted them to work harder, I asked if they felt embarrassed about the name this place had got as 'Butlins holiday camp', because I did.

Yet there was a concern that the site did not appear to have heard the message or understood the European vision:

What they do not appear to have heard is the message that there is actually a future for them and that independent of the downsizing there is also going to be investment to make what remains a value adding part of the Aerospace Group. (Senior Manager, BCP)

Creating one site, one team

New 'workwear' was introduced by Brian in phase 1, with the aim of breaking down the 'them and us' boundaries between managers and workers. There were polo shirts available in five different colours, sporting the union jack and the slogan 'One Site, One Team'.

In addition, in phase 1 the 'transition' project (announced with the redundancies in December 2001) – to create one consolidated manufacturing site by closing the older north site and moving all employees to the newer south site – was begun, and all employees remaining in the older heritage buildings were moved (although the consolidation and south site development was still on-going in phase 2). This was not popular with all of the workforce. The heritage buildings, located on the seafront, had spectacular views and the biggest union jack in Europe (painted on a hangar for the Queens Silver Jubilee in 1977), but were also old, draughty and difficult to operate in. The new building was clean, and bright, but offered no views or any windows to see them. The engineering department was based at the smaller third site, which was to be developed into a centre of excellence. Brian also tried to reinject a sense of purpose into the business:

We always used to have a barbecue in the Summer, we did not have it last year and this year I said we would have one. People said well if you are making people redundant . . . I said yes but at some point you have to start again and move forward. So we did it differently, instead of it being just a **** up for the employees and all the locals we made it more of a family night, so there were things for kids – bouncy castles.

Continuous improvement

Continuous improvement techniques were utilised in phase 1 and on an on-going basis during the change process to achieve savings in the manufacturing process. The focus was on enhancing quality, cost, delivery and people. The initiative incorporated training in concepts such as lean manufacturing, and was part of the business aspect of the change plans:

I think it's only natural that when you are talking to what remains of the workforce that you're going to focus on the need for continuous improvement and making the business profitable and sustainable. I mean in terms of giving people something to latch on to it is necessary to talk about 'Well we're going to have to do things differently'. It's not sustainable to say we are going to cut a third of the workforce out and go back to doing things exactly as before. . .

(Senior Manager, BCP)

Whilst it was necessary to overcome cynicism about such 'new' techniques ('*As fast as they change something then it is dropped and they are on to another strategy of how they are going to rebuild the company*'), over time, the initiative was seen to be firmly supported by the site manager, helping to create a cultural change. Employees had seen a commitment to the process from the top down, and had also seen some promising results, which had reduced the cynicism:

I think the change that I have seen is the roll out of lean or continuous improvement which is working or starting to work as well as you could expect it to on the shop floor and it's got very good co-operation from the guys on the shops and so on, so I think that's a major business change and it is having an effect on culture as far as the shop floor is concerned.
(Manager)

Overall, continuous improvement was a way of breaking the old mind-set to do with anything new, that 'this is going to threaten my job . . . we've always done it this way, why do we need change' and the expectation of 'negotiation' around the change, 'can we negotiate it, what are we going to get from it?' – whereas the argument had to be, 'Well you have to change because that's the only way we can sustain the business in the longer term.'

Changing leader (ship)

In June 2002, shortly after the redundancies had taken place, it was announced that Brian the site manager was departing for a new role in the USA. Historically, he was the fourth site manager in four years, a situation which fuelled insecurity and instability in the context of the recent redundancies. Although Brian had presided over the dramatic downsizing, he was well respected and well liked. With his departure, some employees expressed concern as to whether the hope for the future was going with him:

Well I think a lot of people have a lot of respect for him . . . through a really tough time and I guess everybody was looking for something to cling to. A lot of the guys in the team saw Brian as the figurehead who was leading us through that time and, of course, they've announced that Brian is going but I think that was a really short sighted thing to do for the company.
(Manager)

For others, the departure of the site manager was an opportunity to express negative feelings, to view the career move as selfish – a sentiment symbolic of the paternalism still residing in the culture – and to see the timing as inappropriate. These concerns were fuelled by the uncertainty surrounding the way the organisation was going to be structured after Brian's departure.

Strategy and structures

Around the time Brian's departure was announced, a number of developmental workshops were put in place for managers, and then supervisors. Brian wanted the workshops to focus on facilitating behavioural change. The purpose of the workshops was to educate attendees on the impact of their behaviour on colleagues and the organisation, to have them recognise the culture in which they worked, and to have them identify the barriers associated with this culture for the future. A secondary purpose was to help managers learn to take on more strategic responsibility for the site.

However, the purpose of the workshops was muddled by the announcement from the European strategy manager that the site manager role would not be directly replaced, as there was going to be a structural reorganisation into a more matrix-style operation. This was consistent with the other changes occurring within the bigger European Aerospace division of which the island was now a part, and the change in status of the island to a manufacturing site rather than a stand-alone Aerospace operation. Functional managers on the island needed to report to their functional European head. However, the reaction of the management team was one of confusion, as they were unsure of both the new structure and their own strategic roles:

> *What they've done is they've said 'we're not going to have a Brian any more, we're going to have a load of functional people at the managerial level now' and they're taking the matrix situation up a level which, in my particular case, confuses the hell out of me because I don't know who to report to any more, they haven't told me.*   (Manager)

It was felt that neither the strategy of BCP nor its organisational structure was ever made visible or accessible to the employees. No documents appeared to contain either of these things, and this lack of visible strategy undermined the employees' perceptions that there was a planned future for the site. Indeed the lack of such information was taken as confirmation that such a future did *not* exist. The new structure also created confusion concerning the way the site was going to operate in the future:

> *We have [had] so many different types of structures in the company in the last eight years I am not sure that we know which one we really want. We have been cellular, matrix, we have been departmentalised.*   (Supervisor)

A new site manager, William, was appointed but up until a week before his arrival, there had been no communication providing any details about him, not even his name. Any information was gleaned through the informal grapevine, reportedly on the 'floating bridge', which was a 'boat' that took cars and people across the stretch of water which separated the west of the town from the east of the town. The 'boat' crossed the water on chains, taking approximately five minutes, and was widely reported to be the place to get the 'real' information on what was happening in the island.

Analysing the present and the future

The developmental workshops were led by external consultants and used the cultural web to help managers identify the present and future of the site. Some of the detail from these webs is shown in Figure 1.

Although the webs all varied in some respects, one universal feature was that the organisation was seen by its managers as autocratic and dictatorial, that the culture was one of blame and fear, and that all groups mentioned 'closure' as a story which was often repeated. There was a feeling that the workplace was not a safe place to work, because of the ever-present threat of unemployment. Many of the symbols mentioned in the webs were status symbols. For example, managers had their own offices, with their names on the doors, and their own parking spaces; thus their true 'grade' was denoted by the type of car they drove. This captured the old-fashioned nature of the site and the need for change and modernisation.

Whilst ideas on the future shape of the organisation varied, the managers recognised that the future organisation needed to be more profitable and customer focused, with greater accountability and an environment that fostered teamwork and two-way communication. Various versions of these themes were captured in the paradigms of the future webs that were drawn up. The future webs showed the current culture to be a long way from the future/ideal culture.

Fear and blame

Come the end of phase 1, there was a lack of clarity. With the departure of Brian, for example, the frequency with which the new workwear (the One Team shirts) was worn decreased, with several departments flatly refusing to wear them. The culture at the site was fearful and insecure. The fear of being 'next on the list' was not the only contributing factor. The saying 'don't stick your head above the parapet' was used as a warning to those who were intending to speak out against certain organisational practices, and in effect it was a deterrent against the use of employee voice. At the root of this fear was insecurity about loss of employment (exacerbated due to the island location), not simply due to cost cutting but also because of the European CEO. There was a perception among employees that the

| Figure 1 | Current cultural webs for Attcel site |

Stories

- *Floating bridge*
- *Butlins Holiday Camp*
- *Site closure*
- *New management*
- *Negatives cloud positives*
- *Nepotism*
- *Doom and gloom*
- *Shortages*

Routines

- Downsize
- Weekly communications
- Meetings
- Turnover
- Checking e-mails and diaries
- Lack of promotion procedures
- Shortages
- Work-in-progress
- Avoid overtime
- Firefighting
- Daily clocking
- Performance monitoring

Control systems

- Procedures – quality controls
- Audits
- Absenteeism
- Health and safety
- Training
- Budgets
- Skill scope
- Quality/Controls processes
- Levels of authority
- Turnover driven
- Job cards
- Customer
- Absence of monitoring

Organisation

- Autocratic (command-and-control)
- Financial controls
- Unproven structures
- Dictatorial
- Constantly changing
- Matrix organisation
- Grading scheme
- Management
- Hierarchy
- Faceless

Symbols

- Union jack
- Colour of coats
- Company car
- Air conditioning
- Aerospace division head office
- Office (name on door)
- Parking
- Grades
- Dress
- Mobile phones and laptops

Power

- Customer compliance
- Aerospace division head office
- Local councils
- Trade unions
- Lack of empowerment
- Local management
- Internal politics
- Captive workforce
- Contractual policies
- Knowledge
- Power shift (from island)

Paradigm

- Expertise
- No change
- Past jobs for life
- Future job for?
- Blame, not reward
- Pass the buck
- Do not consider customer
- Limited internal progression
- Instability
- Quality products
- Insecurity of job
- Lack of communication and interaction
- Accept failure
- Under 50s culture
- Reactive organisation

CEO was determined to close down the site. Yet in the Aerostructures division more generally, his absolute commitment to keeping the island site open was undisputed.

RINGING THE CHANGES IN JUNE 2003 – PHASE 2, 'THE JURY IS OUT'

The future and the aftermath of redundancy

In June 2003 the future of the site remained uncertain, although the outlook was more optimistic than it had been in phase 1. The main aim of this phase for those leading the changes was to consolidate the changes that had previously been made, to make the site secure in its future through winning new work, and to achieve a change in the way the island viewed other sites and divisions of Aerospace. The latter objective was still proving difficult.

Employee views on the fate of the site were mixed, ranging from 'we are still very vulnerable' to 'think it's got a good chance now'. Reports that morale on-site was quite low were widespread, and it was suggested that further instability could have a significant effect on an already vulnerable workforce. Although the redundancies were in the past, their aftereffects continued to distress the employees who remained. The redundancies, and the threat of further redundancies, contributed to the general insecurity and uncertainty around long-term personal job prospects. Furthermore, those who remained now felt considerable pressure from the organisation in terms of workload:

> *Having taken 800 people out of the business that obviously puts an immense amount of pressure on the rest of the people, and there are certain parts of the business that are creaking now.* (Manager)

The new site manager arrived in September 2002. He did not have exactly the same title as Brian but nevertheless appeared to do a very similar role. William was reportedly a more 'people-focused' leader than Brian, and less autocratic in his management style:

> *William's management style has made people realise people are just as important as a key for the success of this business, without the support of the workforce they won't succeed.* (Manager)

Yet the island epitomised a 'revolving door' for site managers. By phase 3 there had been six site managers in six years, all with a different policy, direction and style, which undermined feelings of stability or cohesive strategy.

The organisation structure

When managers were questioned about their site structure, they were still unable to articulate exactly what it looked like, felt like, or even whether they were in fact in a matrix structure:

if you ask me what sort of organisation I work in – a very confused one! Because nobody, I don't know whether they will tell you or not, understands the structure, understands the relationships . . . I think it's confused and de-stabilising.   (Manager)

There is a lot of people that perhaps do not really know what their role is anymore, and the whole sort of middle management level there is a lot of fluidity and people are not quite sure who is responsible for what.
(Supervisor)

Some were starting to make sense of the shift to a European Aerospace division, in which the island was just one of many manufacturing sites:

Yes I think there is a European culture, yes there is, I mean it's not complete by any stretch of the imagination you can't say that's the role model we want, that's the organisation we want, but there is definitely a European organisation now, it's recognised as such.   (Manager)

For others, what a European-focused site felt like or acted like seemed to be a mystery. The relationships with both group and corporate were strained and tense, with island employees believing that they should still be autonomous, a view which made the implementation of, for example, organisational development initiatives difficult and earned the island employees the label of 'introverted' and 'introspective':

The whole issue there is . . . the local HR people on the island, and at each interface you have got none of it is working together, and the whole line and I have not only got issues with Corporate I have got issues with the island, and they have issue with Corporate and it is absolutely crazy . . . it's really embarrassing!   (OD Manager, BCP Group)

RINGING THE CHANGES IN MARCH 2004 – PHASE 3, 'THE SNOWDROPS ARE STARTING TO COME OUT'

The future

By now the site had returned a small profit and the principal aim in this period was to continue to grow the site and build on the profit, to ensure that the site was secure in the medium term. Come March 2004 there was optimism on and about the site, which had not been there in the previous two phases. The order books were starting to look healthier, and for most people there was a belief that the immediate future of the site was secure.

Ironically, in phase 3 the threat to the site had changed from a lack of orders and economic depression to a lack of skilled manpower – a shortage of staff, in terms of both number of heads and relevant skills:

> *I think one of the threats to the site as I understand it is possibly the lack of skilled labour available due to contracts that we have won, and poten- tially hope to win.* (Manager)

Filling the vacancies was not a simple task: there had always been a notion among the workforce that workers had been a 'captive workforce' because of a lack of alternative employment opportunities available on the island.[2] Yet during this phase this myth was challenged:

> *I keep seeing all these people that we made redundant and they're happy as anything. I think ... why not me?* (Manager)

Changing leader (ship) – again

During this final phase of change, there was another new site manager. This change again fuelled instability, and also promoted a feeling of cynicism regarding the longevity of Andrew, the new manager, remaining in the role. On the other hand, Andrew's appointment as site manager also included a seat on the Aerospace board, a privilege which neither Brian nor William had been awarded. Consequently, some employees perceived that the island had more control over its future because their site manager had a strategic voice. This structural change should not be underestimated, as previously the perceived lack of control among managers had been startling:

> *These council meetings and ASEC meetings and so on, unless you are there and involved you can't really have an influence and it's gone past you by then, I mean once they have made up their minds you might as well try and turn one of those tankers in the Solent you know, that's a big turning circle that is, you know they just wouldn't make it.* (Manager)

Regaining 'control' over the destiny of the site, even if it was just a perception, was an important event for its management team, who had felt a lack of sovereignty since the relocation of the headquarters some years before. Effort was also put into organisation development. The 'top' section of the management population was sent on a modular development programme called the

---

2 In previous years smaller redundancies had been made, and then employees had often been rehired at a later date. Those employees had filled in, meanwhile, with taxi driving or a similar activity.

'Step Programme'. This training was differentiated from previous training because it was part of a nationwide development, and therefore took place off the island and with managers from other sites and divisions who were of a similar level. The programme was designed to help managers develop their interpersonal skills, their leadership skills, and their management skills generally. The programme wasn't just for senior managers, though, but spread all the way down through the supervisor level. This development initiative was supported through the introduction of other initiatives such as 360-degree appraisal, so that a change in performance could be measured. Following the success of the Step Programme, an additional programme was developed so that the principles could be taken further down the business. The development initiative was received very positively (and without cynicism) by the managers. It made them feel more valued in their role as managers.

> *Another thing that's been quite interesting is this Step thing that we, this foundation thing we started doing, it's amazing, and you know I'm always cautious when you come away from doing a course or these sorts of things but ... we had our first session on that last week. And we've done, a bit like work-life balance, and being a leader and not a manager, and all this sort of stuff.*
>
> (Manager)

SUMMARY

During the three phases of change on the site, the business had evolved significantly: it was half its former size; it had removed an incredible amount of cost from its processes; and it had begun to receive new orders again. According to one manager it had been a positive journey:

> *We've moved massively away from the current web that we discussed ... massively away from it you know ... it's quite interesting, I took both those cultural webs along with me to the course last week, I keep them, I feel it's very appropriate.*
>
> (Manager)

There was still much to be done in terms of building cohesive leadership, developing clarity over strategy and structure, and addressing shortages of quality manpower. Yet the island site had come a long way since December 2001:

> *The island has gone from being the centre of the universe to being another plant within the growing business and that takes a lot of swallowing if you've sort of sat there thinking as part of the management team, well ... I was here, almost the pinnacle of an organisation, now I find myself down here because they've grown it, wherever I might be, manager, operator, whatever. So it was a significant change.*
>
> (Senior Manager, BCP)

Post script

In July 2004 it was announced that the island would be the site for a world-class Advanced Composites Facility dedicated to the development of the design and manufacturing technologies for large composite aerostructures. The centre was described as *'one of the most advanced facilities of its type in the world'*. This centre of excellence opened in June 2005, and cemented the future of the site for the long term through a strategy of differentiation.

Andrew is still in post as site manager, although he and the staff celebrated his 'supposed' leaving date 14 months after the start of his role. This was the same amount of time that the previous two managers had been in post. Reflecting back on what had been achieved at the site, one senior manager commented:

> *Actually what we did in 2001 is try and right size the business, you know, to actually, sort of, create something that is viable. From that point on, obviously a lot of work was done to consolidate that. I mean new work is being won and the other thing with aerospace is that the programmes tend to be long standing, so they run over a number of years. So there's a lot of work going on to actually deliver programmes. We've grown the capability to do different kinds of work, which has enabled us to go out and win significant new business which comes in to replace business that's going...So what's happened over the period is that the island has gone from being a well thought of but maybe old-fashioned factory to actually doing something now which is actually leading edge technologically.*

ASSIGNMENT QUESTIONS

1 In 2001, at the start of the transformation process, what was the change context at Attcel?

2 What were the design choices taken? Were they appropriate and why?

3 Map out the change process between 2001 and 2004 in terms of the mobilise, move and sustain framework and the different interventions in the four subsystems (technical, political, cultural and interpersonal).

4 What are the strengths and weaknesses of the change approach adopted? What has been achieved?

5 What recommendations would you make to embed and take forward the transformation developing in 2003–2004?

Index